W9-BKY-849

Hierarchy, History, and Human Nature

Hierarchy, History, and Human Nature

The Social Origins of
Historical Consciousness

Donald E. Brown

The University of Arizona Press, Tucson

Wingate College Library

THE UNIVERSITY OF ARIZONA PRESS
Copyright © 1988
The Arizona Board of Regents
All Rights Reserved

Manufactured in the U.S.A.
This book was set in 10/13 Linotron 202 Galliard.
93 92 91 90 89 88   5 4 3 2 1

Library of Congress Cataloging-in-Publication Data

Brown, Donald E.
    Hierarchy, history, and human nature : the social origins of
historical consciousness / Donald E. Brown.
      p. cm.
    Bibliography: p.
    Includes index.
    ISBN 0-8165-1060-1 (alk. paper)
    1. History—Methodology. 2. Culture. 3. Social classes.
4. Social sciences and history. I. Title.
D16.B875 1988
901'.8—dc19   88-15287
                                        CIP

British Library Cataloguing in Publication data are available.

To Donald Symons

Contents

Acknowledgments

I owe thanks to quite a number of people who have read all or portions of the typescript of this book, or who otherwise provided assistance, advice, or inspiration. They include the following: Mikal Aasved, Arjun Appadurai, F. G. Bailey, Alva Bennett, Bernard Bernier, Maurice Bloch, David Brokensha, Barry Brown, Carrie Chu Brown, Susan Brownell, Yuan-ling Chao, Chi-yun Ch'en, Thomas Conelly, Nicholas Dirks, Harold Drake, James Eder, Charles Erasmus, Shelly Errington, Frank J. Frost, Chauncey S. Goodrich, D.G.E. Hall, Elvin Hatch, Thea Howard, William Jankowiak, C. Warren Hollister, Graham Johnson, Roger Joseph, Joi Kawaguchi, Thomas Keefe, Allen Maxwell, Susan Mies, Mattison Mines, Amr Morad, Rose Mucci, Henry Munson, James K. Otte, Triloki Pandey, Doris Phinney, Fitz John Porter Poole, Douglas Raybeck, A. F. Robertson, Sharon Roemer, Raymond Scupin, Elman Service, Betty Siegfried, Joanne Steele, Albert Spaulding, Donald Tuzin, Anita Ward, James L. Watson, Howard Wimberley, and Chia-yun Yu. I believe that the main idea that underlies this book came to me during my research on a project that was funded by the John Haynes and Nora Haynes Foundation, and I am grateful for the financial aid that then gave me the time to think about such matters.

Many scholars have influenced the content and argument of this book in ways that are readily seen in its citations. But two scholars have been of great assistance in ways that may not be so obvious. M. G. Smith's contributions to the analysis of social structure were crucial in a few specific ways. His conceptions of plural societies colored the way I look at caste, his writings on principles of social structure continually drew my attention to the implications of the specifically hereditary nature of caste, and his methods of analyzing the logic that connects institutions and their constituent parts helped me to think through my final chapter. My colleague Donald Symons has had a more subtle but no less important impact on this book. He read one or more drafts of every chapter, and his comments have shaped my arguments and conclusions in ways too numerous to list. His thinking on human nature and the part it plays in channeling human affairs has been especially important. I hope that these two scholars in particular, along with all the persons mentioned above, will share in whatever benefits this book may bring to scholarship, but I absolve all of them from blame for its shortcomings.

Hierarchy, History,
and Human Nature

CHAPTER I

Introduction

Among some literate peoples, historians have flourished; among others, they have not. Why should this be so? That a civilization such as India's long enjoyed literacy yet gave almost no attention to writing its own or any other history presents a substantial puzzle to the sociology of knowledge. Of course, Indians wrote much about things *alleged* to have taken place in the past, but these are accounts of gods and supermen: myths and fables, not "real history." Prior to the Muslim conquests of India, there was only a single work in Sanskrit that is now conventionally described as a history, and it was composed in Kashmir, on the fringe of Hindu civilization. Another apparent exception was presented by the Buddhist chronicles of Sri Lanka (Ceylon), again on the very fringe of Hindu civilization. Many Indians find this so puzzling that some have wondered if the later British conquerors of India might not have stolen all their histories.

India is not alone in this seeming peculiarity. Late dynastic Egyptians, for instance, had been literate for a very long time. In addition, Egypt was highly centralized, and its rulers maintained platoons of scribes who kept the sort of archival materials required for the production of sound historical writings. Yet when their Mesopotamian and Hebrew neighbors began to compose rudimentary histories, the Egyptians did not. The first history of Egypt to merit the name was quite late, and it was written in Greek.

Definitively introduced in the West by the Ionian Greeks, historical writing continued in Rome. But from late antiquity through much of the Middle Ages, historiography slumped in western Europe. When the writing of sound history began to progress again, as in Italy in the fourteenth and fifteenth centuries, it was especially associated with Florence. Venice, which in most respects was a full participant in the Renaissance and which maintained massive and orderly archives, was not at all quick to adopt the new historiographic standards, and it was even slower to apply those standards to Venetian history.

Just as relatively sound histories were composed by the Hebrew and Mesopotamian contemporaries of the ancient Egyptians, so too were they produced by contemporaries of the Hindu Indians, notably the Chinese but also the Kashmiris and Sri Lankans, by contemporaries of medieval western Europeans—the Byzantines and Classical Muslims—and of course by the Florentine contemporaries of early Renaissance Venice. Is there a lesson to be drawn from these contrasts? Should we conclude that writing history is an intellectual frill that a civilization may or may not possess, with little or no consequence for its continuity, its organization, or its productions? Why do peoples differ so markedly in the attention they give to history? Let me retrace the steps whereby I formulated these questions and sought answers to them.

In 1966 I began research on social and political change in Brunei, a small Malay state in northwest Borneo. Although I am an anthropologist, I necessarily undertook historical investigations to complete my project. I began with six months of research in the archives of the Public Record Office in London, for Brunei had been under British influence or control for more than a hundred years. Next I spent fifteen months in Brunei, searching for further archival or locally circulated material, gathering oral history, and getting a grasp of the nature of Brunei's sociopolitical system from firsthand observation and inquiry. I then spent another month at the Public Record Office, followed by several months of library work, before producing a thesis on Brunei.

During that period I conceived of my problem in conventional terms: I wanted to know what actually happened in Brunei's past. In order to achieve this goal, I tried in various ways to take a Brunei point of view. For example, I tried to allow for the prejudice against Bruneis that naturally abounded in accounts so frequently written by persons who found the Bruneis an impediment to their colonizing plans. Also, I tried to understand developments in terms of Brunei institutions. But the reason I undertook these measures was essentially to correct the record, to discover what really happened. I was disappointed in how little historical material the Bruneis themselves could provide. We know, mostly from sources outside of Brunei, that it has existed as a state for about a thousand years and has been literate during much of this time, probably during the entire period. Moreover, the Bruneis—in the sixteenth century, anyway—controlled a vast territory, stretching from Manila in the north to the southern end of Borneo. In the nineteenth century Brunei was still one of the most substantial of the Malay states. Initially I took the scarcity of indigenous historical materials to be unfortunate but not interesting. As time went by, however, I began to shift from thinking about Brunei's past to thinking about Brunei attitudes toward the past. In this way I came to think about *why* Bruneis possessed so little historical writing, why they record or remember some things but not others, and why they allege certain things to have happened that probably did not. In short, I began to think about their principles of historiography. In chapter 3 I present the main outlines of Brunei historiography; here I wish to describe how my analyses proceeded.

I first noted that in Brunei historical writings, as in other Malay historical traditions (Bastin 1964), there was relatively little treatment of concrete individuals, especially in ways that made their individuality stand out. On the contrary, in comparing a Malay and a British account of the same event in Brunei (Brown 1971a), I found in the former only rather stereotyped accounts of people behaving in terms of role, office, and category. The psychological or motivational dimension was attenuated at best. A possible explanation for this was that Malays lacked an interest in the individual, or that at any rate they showed less interest in the individual than Westerners do. This has been shown by Geertz (1966) to be the case among the Balinese, a people in many ways similar to the Bruneis. One of my first speculations was that because the principal actors in Malay history were sultans or other highly placed persons, and because the sultans have been exalted figures in Malay society, candid comments on their behavior would not have been tolerated. Since Malay historians were normally dependent on sultans, their lack of candor and penetration in presenting the sultans' motives, characteristics, and activities seemed understandable. Hence Malay historiography lacked a personality base not because Malays lacked an interest in the individual and his personality but because there were good reasons for Malay historians to avoid close analysis of the personalities of leading Malay figures.

Explanations of this sort, plausible enough in the light of restricted cases, are commonplace in comments on various peoples' historiographies. But a moment's reflection—in the light of wider, comparative data—shows this and many other explanations to be limited indeed. Consider China. Its emperors seem to have been no less exalted than the Malay rulers, yet traditional Chinese historiography was prodigious in its volume and famous for its candor. Consequently, I suggested (1971a) that the ascriptive nature of the Brunei social system—not merely of succession to the throne—made speculation about individual psychological attributes in general not only superfluous but possibly even subversive of societal order. If high status is essentially inherited, discussions of individual variation could well raise the question of whether the heirs to such status were really more fit for it than other people. In the long run this formulation proved useful, but in the short run I was puzzled by the fact that when I consulted an anthropologist who had studied Malay personality, he could attach little significance to the argument that Malays lacked a sense of individual personality.

Having decided to examine the relationship between views of the past and the nature of society, I sought a comparative perspective on the problem. The first cases to come to mind were those of China and India. Anyone working with Southeast Asian historical problems, except perhaps for recent periods, is necessarily aware of Chinese historiography, because very much of what is known from early times comes not from Southeast Asian but from Chinese sources. Similarly, one is equally aware of the dearth of Indian historical materials, for although the connections between India and Southeast Asia are as intimate as they are ancient, very little knowledge of Southeast Asia is to be gleaned from Indian accounts of the past. In chapter 2 I treat India and China at greater length. Now I wish only to say that my next step was to note what Brunei shared with India but not with China that might account for the shortage of Brunei historical materials.

The most striking feature of India is caste; China is no less remarkable for its emphasis on social placement by merit. For long periods, rates of social mobility in traditional Chinese society were among the highest in the world. Ideology, and such state-supported institutions as the Chinese bureaucratic examination system, facilitated meritocracy. The Bruneis have for long been hereditarily stratified; in this and other ways their society is castelike. Thus it seemed possible that some features of caste—with or without any consideration of the sense of individual personality—might in some way be connected with the ahistorical traditions of Brunei and

India. The logic of the argument was not entirely clear to me—I had only a hunch—but it seemed appropriate to widen my comparative framework, test a tentative hypothesis, and see what other ideas could be turned up in the process.

Accordingly, I examined collections of essays on the historiography of various Southeast Asian peoples (Hall 1961; Soedjatmoko et al. 1965). What I sought primarily were the judgments of historians or other qualified scholars on the overall quality of particular historiographic traditions, judgments analogous to the one I had made about Brunei's and which many have made about India's and China's. I found it necessary to look not for absolute statements but for reasonable comparisons: not that particular historiographic traditions were good or poor but that one tradition was better or worse than another. I recorded only comparative evaluations within Southeast Asia, since virtually all of its historical writings were judged unsound compared to modern Western standards. Once I had a set of judgments about the relatively sound versus the unsound, the relatively historical versus the mythical, I turned to analyses of social structure to see if caste was a regular concomitant of unsound historiography. Whereas I relied heavily on the judgment of others for the quality of historiography, I was prepared to make my own assessments of stratification. My hypothesis was that no hereditarily stratified society would have developed sound historiography. I predicted that the historiographies of all hereditarily stratified societies would be judged unsound but that some unsound historiographies might be found in the absence of caste, for there would be, I presumed, other factors besides hereditary stratification that inhibit the development of sound historiography. Only literate societies were considered, since historians rarely evaluate the historiographies of preliterate peoples.

Though my assumptions were questionable, my methods crude, my hypothesis based on an incompletely developed logic, and my sample small, the results were encouraging. I found three cases of caste-organized societies with unsound historiograpies—the societies of Java, Bali, and Malaya (including the Bruneis), and three with open systems of stratification and comparatively sound historiographies—the Burmese, Vietnamese, and Macassarese. One case, involving the long-defunct state of Nanchao, in the long run resisted analysis. Much later I revised my criteria for selecting cases in Southeast Asia and consulted further sources for historians' judgments on the quality of the region's historiographies. The final results are presented in chapter 3.

After my initial analysis of Southeast Asian cases, I decided to widen my sample, searching again for the opinions of historians on the quality of historiography but this time among all the major societies or civilizations that have had an impact on the historiography of Southeast Asia: China and India I have already mentioned, but also to be taken into account were the Near East and Europe. Initially I relied on sources that, whatever their faults, provided broadly comparative studies of historiographic traditions (Barnes 1937; Dentan 1955; Fehl 1964; Fitzsimons et al. 1954; Shotwell 1923; Thompson 1942; Vryonis 1968). Of course I knew in advance that the development of historiography in the West provided partial support for my argument, because historiography is generally considered to have declined in western Europe in the period after the era of classical civilization in the Mediterranean, a period that also saw the rise of castelike estates. But there were unexpected discoveries, too, such as the case of Egypt, which I mentioned earlier. Again I found evidence of a strong correlation. The ancient cases from the Near East and the Mediterranean are presented in chapter 4, the Near East and Europe in the Middle Ages in chapter 5, and the Renaissance in chapter 6.

By this time it was clear that the correlation was very marked, so I shifted my attention to further problems. One was to refine the logic that links patterns of social stratification with patterns of historiography. I assumed, for example, that if one determined the requisites and consequences of the maintenance of caste and the maintenance of a sound historiographic tradition, then one or more requisites or consequences of the former would be found incompatible with one or more requisites or consequences of the latter. Without intelligible linkages of this sort, any correlations would be mere curiosities. The results of the search for logical connections are summarized in chapter 7. The other problem was to trace in more detail—not on the synchronic or timeless plane of cross-cultural comparison and correlation, but on a diachronic axis—fluctuation in the two main variables. Diachronic covariation provides further insight into logical connections and is especially crucial to assessments of causation. Neither Indian nor Chinese materials initially proved very useful in this respect, but a closer look at India did turn up two regional variations— in Kashmir and Sri Lanka—that allowed for useful comparisons. Europe proved to be the best area for diachronic study.

Since European history and historiography have been analyzed intensively, I was particularly concerned that standard histories of Europe and

European historiography made no special point of the link between strat-ification and historiography. Rather, covariation of the two was treated either as a coincidence or as a common result of factors such as economic change. Because of this, I suspected that few if any historians of Europe had seen a close connection between historiography and social stratification or had made much of the connection. And if modern historians said little about the connection, it seemed likely that their Renaissance predecessors may themselves have been unconscious of it. Consequently I constructed a tentative hypothesis that those persons who rediscovered or redeveloped historiography after the Middle Ages would also have opposed the he-reditary principle of social placement, and that those who stood to gain the most from caste would have favored a mythical view of the past or would have fought the rise of Renaissance historical studies. I found that the data only partially supported the latter part of this hypothesis but richly supported the former part. The ideal of open social mobility was a major preoccupation of Renaissance historians, certainly of the Florentines.

But I was also pushed by one problem or another, as well as by sug-gestions from students and colleagues, to an analysis that went backward in time from the Renaissance through the final years of the Roman Empire and on to the origins of history among the Ionian Greeks, and laterally in space from Europe to the medieval Byzantine Empire. This brought my total collection of comparisons outside of Asia to the following: on the one hand were the Hebrews, Assyrians, Babylonians, Ionian Greeks, late republican and early imperial Romans, medieval Byzantines, classical Muslims, and Renaissance Florentines, all of whom possessed relatively sound historical writings and open systems of stratification; on the other hand were the late Egyptians, Homeric Greeks, classical Spartans, late western imperial Romans, Sassanid Persians, medieval Europeans, and Renaissance Venetians, all of whom possessed relatively unsound histo-riographies and relatively closed systems of stratification.

Briefly, my findings at this point concerning Western societies were as follows. During the time represented in the Homeric poems, Greek society was hereditarily stratified. Later, in Ionia, open stratification and historical writing developed. But in Sparta, society became even more castelike, and no historical writings emerged. Open stratification and relatively sound historiography persisted among most Greeks through the Alexandrian period, and in Rome through the early period of the Roman Empire. In the time of the late Roman emperors, culminating with Diocletian and

Constantine, the open character of Roman social stratification both withered and was legislated away. Caste organization became imperial law in the West.

Perhaps merging Germanic notions of nobility with those of the late western empire, medieval Europe's hereditary nobility asserted itself in the West within a few centuries after Constantine. This nobility legitimated itself by claiming hereditary links to prestigious figures of the ancient world and to the saints of Christendom. Turning saints into nobles sanctified nobility. In this and other ways Christianity became the servant of western Europe's hereditary nobles. Fictitious genealogies became a favored genre, and much of the historical literature of the ancient world, at once pagan and anticaste, became an embarrassment.

This state of affairs gradually dissolved in western Europe, with the final blows delivered in Renaissance Italy, especially in Florence. The Florentines broke the stranglehold of nobles (and clergy) on learning and hence on the production and consumption of histories. Historical research and writing was revived with vigor, and it was explicitly linked to the defense of open social stratification.

In Byzantium, events had taken a quite different course, although the starting point was superficially similar. While the legislation of Constantine and other emperors may seem to have applied equally in both the East and West of the late empire, the caste legislation was clearly earmarked more for the West, and it found a more congenial climate there. Moreover, as the centuries wore on in the East, its emperors consistently and in general successfully strove to curb the development of a nobility and to promote or tolerate the sort of social mobility consonant with the Byzantine emperors' strong centralized control. Byzantine historiography was generally maintained at a high level, and on the eve of Byzantium's collapse it was able to transmit its carefully preserved historical treasures and attitudes to those places in the West, such as Florence, that were then receptive.

The more I learned about Florence, in fact, the more impossible it seemed to me that no one would have seen or posited a direct connection between its social mobility and its historiographic developments. In time I found that some historians, especially Marvin Becker (1971), had indeed done so but had not gone on to explore the point in wider perspective.

While pursuing my various readings I tried to gather together alternative hypotheses on the determinants of historiography, to isolate other correlates of open and closed stratification, and, of course, to continue to refine my understanding of the connections between historiography and stratification. European materials were particularly useful, because in many contexts Europeans have been unusually conscious of comparison. Moreover, by the time I approached the European cases I had already assimilated a certain amount of critically useful comparative material that considerably expands the scale for measuring variation in European civilization. Prior to my final write-up, I went back through all the cases, adding Sassanid Persia as well as several more Southeast Asian cases and checking the findings of each case against the others. I refined the main hypotheses and treated a number of apparent concomitants of open and closed stratification as further hypotheses. The results are discussed in chapter 7.

In that chapter I return to the problem of the person or individual, showing that the concept of the individual does seem to be a critical ingredient in a more historical sense of the past. More important, I argue, is a conception of the unity of mankind, the idea that human nature is fundamentally the same everywhere and always. I also argue that an exaggerated concern for predicting the future—by astrology, omenry, and other forms of divination—is also a concomitant of open stratification. So too are a highly developed interest in general education, the development of biography and realistic portraiture, an emphasis on praise and blame or other utilitarian and moral lessons of history, the preparation of works on social and political science, and an expansion of secularism. In fact, these are all facets of a single human problem: the social placement, fate, and effect of the individual in societies where social inequalities are substantial but where birth is not perceived as deciding who will be placed high and who low.

The closed societies exhibit a contrasting syndrome of concomitants: a racialist conception of human nature, reduced individualism, hagiography in place of biography, iconography in place of realistic portraiture, non-uniform education, hypertrophied religious and ritual concerns, little political or social science, less fanatic divination, and perhaps a lesser concern with natural science. These traits are all reflections of the hereditary transmission of social rank.

I also found that various arguments about what determines variation in the quality of historiography can be ranged along a continuum. Some proposed determinants show no cross-culturally consistent relationship with historiography, some are necessary though not sufficient causes, and some lie between these extremes. Chapter 7 weighs the influence of these various determinants.

In chapter 7 I also turn to wider considerations, such as the distinction between knowledge and ideology (which subsumes a distinction between history and myth) and the grand theory developed by Maurice Bloch (1977) that explains their relative development. Bloch argues that social hierarchy generates or is accompanied by ideology, while knowledge is more likely to develop in nonhierarchical settings. In spite of certain flaws in his argument, his thesis (if by hierarchical it is assumed he means *hereditarily* hierarchical, and all his examples are of this sort) seems richly supported by the data I present and analyze. Consequently, both Bloch's thesis and the data I present provide a theoretical and empirical expression of what written history has been about, why it is written, why the composition of history is supported as a human activity, and why it sometimes languishes. Many of the earliest historians believed history to be useful and their reasons, I argue, are still valid. History provides practical knowledge for the conduct of human affairs. History, along with the other human sciences, is part of an endeavor stretching back for two and a half millennia, but it by no means involves all branches of human civilization equally.

A NOTE ON DEFINITIONS

Some of the key terms used in this book are not the ones with which I started. At many points I found it necessary to define my terms more sharply. Since I now use some words in special ways, the following discussion of terms is necessary. I use the terms *account of the past* or *folk history* to refer generically to "real" as well as fictitious or mythical accounts. Occasionally my sources—and perhaps I, when the context is clear—use the term *history* in the generic sense of an account of the past. But in everyday English, *history* is also used in the specific sense of contrasting with *myth* or *legend* to denote a "sound" account of the past, and I generally use *history* in this more specific sense. I use the term *historiography* primarily to denote the general principles—sound or unsound, conscious or unconscious—that underlie any account of the past. Since some historians, and many present-day anthropologists, may object to sorting accounts of the past into the sound and the unsound, the basis for this sorting requires particularly careful discussion.

The distinction between myth and history is an analytic one; actual accounts of the past are often not clearly one or the other but rather a mixture. Myth and history in this sense are two ends of a continuum, with no sharp boundary between them (Lévi-Strauss 1979). Generally I presume that this continuum exists but that it is possible to locate whole accounts of the past, as well as various parts of such accounts, toward one end of the continuum or the other. Historians, and more especially the historians of history, routinely make judgments of this sort (Gilbert 1965). They have definite notions about the success of attempts to reconstruct the past. Using their expert knowledge of historical criticism, it is a proper professional activity for them to judge whether or not a particular historical work is successful, or either more or less successful than other comparable works. More abstractly, historians dissect and analyze specific works of history—or even the collective historical writings of whole peoples over extended periods of time—to discover and judge the general principles upon which those histories were constructed. Although they do not always agree in all particulars, Philip Miller has said, virtually all modern historians "agree in general upon the principles of historical method" (1954:i), and they largely agree upon which historiographic traditions do or do not deserve the historian's professional admiration.

Historians usually make their judgments in terms of the modern scientific standards of objectivity that date from the nineteenth-century works of Leopold von Ranke. In J. H. Hexter's view, historians "are still committed to writing about the past, as Ranke put it, *wie es eigentlich gewesen*, as it actually happened" (1968:384). "The standard of judgment of a historical work," Hexter asserts, "is ultimately extrinsic. Its authenticity, validity, and truth depend on the effectiveness with which it communicates knowledge (not misunderstanding) of the actual past congruent with the surviving record" (1968:382).

Some critics of the idea that an actual past can be recaptured point out that any history is an abstraction, even a distortion, because the real past is too complex to be caught on paper. This is a valid point, and Ranke's dictum must therefore be "understood obversely: history is not to tell what did not happen; that is, it is not to be fictive art" (Kroeber [1935] 1952:64). Others argue that no account of the past can be really objective, since any attempt to recount the past necessarily rests upon subjective judgments concerning the choice of subject matter and the style of presentation (see, e.g., White 1973). This is true, and all accounts of the past are inescapably subjective in at least these senses. What distinguishes a sound history, then, is that in addition to its subjective elements it maximizes its objective content. It is not wholly subjective.

To the extent that historical materials produced by a given people are

not based on the fundamental principles of modern historiography—do
not conform, that is, to what Hexter (1968:384) calls the "reality" rule—
to that extent do those people lack a sense of history. An account of the
past that is too remote from the historians' concept of history is then
classed as legend, myth, folktale, or even as nonsense or deliberate falsehood. Although their practice risks (and sometimes succumbs to) the
danger of ethnocentrism, the historians' judgments in these cases can rest
on the assessment of criteria that are sufficiently objective. For example,
they look for precise orientation in space and time, accurate chronology,
the ability to detect anachronism, access to trustworthy sources, critical
procedures for evaluating sources, an adequate psychology, logical coher-
ence, the exclusion of physical impossibilities, and a minimal resort to the
supernatural. Collectively, all such criteria for assessing the value of an
account of the past, or the potential sources for writing accounts of the
past, are referred to as "historical criticism." Each criterion is a scale along
which any work of history or any historiographic tradition can be scored.
When the scores are very low, the work or tradition is labeled historiographically unsound or even as not being historical at all.

To illustrate, let me compare Bernal Díaz del Castillo's famous eyewitness narrative of the conquest of Mexico with the epics of India. Bernal
Díaz piously reported sightings of Christian saints coming to the aid of
the Spaniards. Most modern readers of the narrative discount the validity
of these sightings, considering them to be assertions of physical impossibilities, products of inadequate psychological theories, or unwarranted
appeals to the supernatural. On one or more scales, Bernal Díaz therefore
earns a less-than-perfect score. But his work is not fatally flawed by his
piety. Supernatural interventions are not the stuff of the narrative and can
be easily ignored; given the historical materials available for the time and
place in question, his narrative is a gem, albeit a slightly flawed one.

By contrast, Wang Gungwu says of the great Indian epics, the *Mahabharata* and the *Ramayana*, that for most of pre-Muslim India "they
were the nearest thing to history and may be said to have performed the
role of history among the peoples who transmitted the stories." But in
spite of their functional similarity to history, he writes, "they did not lead
to the growth of history writing" (1968:421). In short, Wang gives the
epics a low score. His reasoning is clear, for he quotes Ghoshal's description
of the pre-Muslim Indian historical tradition as "marked by obscurity,
exaggeration, paucity of authentic data and neglect of topography and
chronology." (1968:421, quoting Ghoshal 1961:2). Not only the *Maha-*

bharata and *Ramayana* but nearly all pre-Muslim Indian accounts of the past are rightly scored low according to the criteria that Wang (1968:427) describes as the key concepts of modern historiography: "that time and place must be accurate, that knowledge about man's past must be secular and humanistic, and that historical fact and interpretation must always be tested by the best scientific methods."

Thus, even if the criteria for their judgments are not always explicit, the judgments of modern historians on the character of historiographic traditions other than their own are by no means arbitrarily ethnocentric. Consequently, what they find to be acceptable historical writing I will label as sound, or historical; what they find as unacceptable I will label as unsound, ahistorical, or mythical.

Let me emphasize that sound history is not simply modern Western history. An illustration is provided by Butterfield's 1951 criticism of what he calls Whig history. He argues that when modern Western historians attempt to abridge history, they typically employ assumptions of doubtful soundness. But when modern historians do not abridge, their standards may be quite sound. Thus, modern Western historiography is not sound in *all* its genres, even after the inevitably subjective elements are discounted. Yet Butterfield's essay illustrates the relative soundness of modern Western historiography in two ways. First, even if he dwells on its flaws, he finds his standards for judgment *within* that tradition. Second, his very concern for the detection and exposure of flaws reflects the highest standards of historical criticism, standards also found within the modern Western historiographic tradition. Thus the standards of sound history may be used to criticize the modern Western tradition itself, and they find that tradition relatively sound, though not wholly sound. They find some non-European traditions relatively sound too. When I speak of soundness, it must be borne in mind that I speak of relative soundness.

Let me also emphasize that the scale from sound to unsound is not the only scale by which accounts of the past can be judged, nor does it sort them into the good and the bad in a general intellectual or moral sense. To illustrate, Collingwood agrees with the general view that medieval European historiography was deficient as "an accurate and scientific study of the actual facts of history" (1946:55), but he also holds that this is not to say that the period was therefore intellectually inferior. Rather, he contends, if we could but penetrate its thoughts and sympathize with it, the medieval period would look as brilliant as others. Other scholars make a similar observation by distinguishing history as an art from history as a science. Thus the degree of science and art in a given people's historiography may vary independently. An account of the past may be an artistic triumph, an enduring challenge to intellectual and aesthetic analysis, and yet not be remotely sound as history. But for the modern historian, as Huizinga (1963:8) says, "mythical and fictitious representations of the past may have literary value . . . but . . . they are not history." In this book it is primarily science (Hexter's "reality" rule) that is being scaled, not art or other measures of the quality of historiography. Historiographies that in this work are classified as poor or unsound may score very high on scales that are not necessarily relevant to modern historiography.

Turning now to the definitions required to analyze social stratification, a *closed* society is one in which rank is a fundamental feature and in which rank is essentially acquired by birth alone. When rank is fundamental and hereditary, the rank a person holds is decisive in determining the other statuses or roles he may occupy. To give a familiar example, in medieval France and Germany, hereditary rank was fundamental; to know a man's role was to know his birth rank. In modern European societies, this is no longer the case, or is much less the case. As synonyms for *closed* when referring to societies, I use the terms *hereditarily stratified, caste-organized,* or *castelike*.

An *open* society is one in which there is rank, but it is more achieved than ascribed at birth. The greater insistence there is on the priority of merit over birthright, and the more actual vertical mobility there is, the more open is the society. The presence of hereditary kingship will not disqualify a society from being open, nor will the presence of hereditarily subordinate minorities, provided that no two or more of them add up to a majority. The universal or very nearly universal disabilities of women and children, either of whom might in fact constitute a majority, also do not prevent a society from being open in the sense employed here. As synonyms for the open society I use such terms as the *openly stratified society* or *meritocratic society*.

I reserve the term *nobility* for the dominant stratum or strata in a closed society. *Aristocracy* is employed to refer to dominant elements in an open society, with *elite* sometimes used as a synonym but more frequently used to denote dominant strata that have not yet been identified as open or closed. A nobility is thus always hereditary. If the proportion of a hereditarily privileged element in a given society is too large or too small, it is not a nobility. If too large, it ceases to have the sociological consequences of nobility. A nobility is thus always a minority. But if too small a minority, it is normally royalty alone, and royalty is not nobility (unless merely a part of a larger nobility).

Both in arriving at and employing these definitions related to social stratification I ran into serious problems. For one, most authors use terms such as *nobility*, *aristocracy*, or *oligarchy* in a casual way, indicating an entrenched elite, whether hereditary or not. Consequently, accounts of social stratification have to be read with extreme care, searching for unambiguous words such as *hereditary*, and *caste*, or for direct statements about the possibility or rates of social mobility. Finding hard data on rates of social mobility turned out to be a major problem indeed. What one usually finds is the ideology of social stratification, the laws relating to social stratification, or gross estimates of social mobility. The estimates often inspire little confidence. Initially I sought cases where ideology, law, and practice were consonant, preferably over long periods of time; I thought that Hindu India and China met these criteria. But I quickly became uneasy about estimated rates of social mobility. In the long run my identification of open and closed societies reflected ideology and law more than rates of social mobility. Fortunately, it now appears to me that the ideology of social mobility is particularly important in shaping a people's view of the past, perhaps even more so than is their actual rate of social mobility.

None of the above definitions could, of course, be put to use without making various sorts of judgments. I try to explain the basis of my judgments as fully as I can. Where my judgment rests upon the judgments of others—as it often and properly does—I try to make that clear.

THE ORDER OF PRESENTATION, AND HOW AND WHY TO READ THIS BOOK

It is no secret that scholars sometimes read no more than the introduction and conclusion of books of this sort. Accordingly, this introduction gives a very brief summary of the book's contents, and the last chapter contains most of my reasoning about why the book's various conclusions make sense. For the reader interested only in ideas, the first and last chapters may suffice. But if one wishes to sample the evidence that supports the conclusions, chapter 2, on South Asia and China, provides the most succinct and clearly contrastive comparison, and almost all parts of the argument are found there. This is not true of chapter 3, on Southeast Asia, or the sections on the ancient Near East or Persia in chapters 4 and 5. In these cases, reporting on the concomitants is particularly spotty, and reporting on historiography and social stratification is less full than might be wished.

In spite of its shortcomings, however, chapter 3 has distinctive functions. It presents in some detail the evidence that initially led me to think that Brunei historiography was curiously deficient. More important, it is the only chapter to provide an unbiased sample of societies to compare. If there are biases in the selection of cases, they are not ones that I introduced. The evidence afforded by such a sample—that is, by the improbability that it would show the correlations it does by chance—will be particularly compelling for readers who respect the laws of probability.

The ancient Near Eastern cases of chapter 4 could not easily be ignored, since some of them are often cited for having the very earliest examples of historical writing. Sassanid Persia, in chapter 5, must be discussed, however briefly, for a similar reason: it is often said to have provided the initial stimulus for the Islamic world's prodigious outpouring of historical writings. Finally, while chapter 5, on the Middle Ages, and chapter 6, on the Renaissance, both to a large extent stand on their own, their fullest appreciation is achieved in relationship to each other.

This book straddles two disciplines, each of which is sharply divided by an unfortunate and often needless dichotomy between humanistic and scientific goals and methods. I am acutely aware that many of my colleagues in anthropology in particular will be disturbed by my assertion that explanations of such facets of expressive culture as historiography, biography, and portraiture can be reduced even in part to such factors as social stratification and characteristics of a universal human nature. One of the lessons that some historians are currently absorbing from anthropology is that perceptions of the past that seem very remote from our modern Western view may nonetheless merit the attention of the historian and may even lead historians to rethink some of their assumptions (Davis 1981). Let me hasten to say that I agree that historians can profit by absorbing this lesson. But neither they nor anthropologists should make the further leap to the conclusion that there are no cross-cultural standards, that there is no such thing as real history. Not a few anthropologists, and some historians, have made this leap, or stand perilously close to the brink. Given that this is so, I provide the fullest documentation that I can, consistent with a broadly comparative perspective, in the hope that critics will find it as easy to show me wrong by pointing to the facts as by questioning my assumptions. Insofar as the information is reasonably accessible and relevant, I also try to present my case materials in their cultural, social, and historical contexts, since critics are certain to claim that I have ignored those contexts.

With minor exceptions, each of chapters 2 through 6 attempts to summarize information from particular societies or civilizations concerning their historiography, social stratification, and the concomitants thereof, as well as any apparent relationships between all these. In some cases the relationships are easily shown and have already caught the attention of other scholars—for example, the relationship between political science and history in Renaissance Florence. In other cases—in determining, for example, how much interest there was in divination in Renaissance Venice—I must attempt, however awkwardly, to discuss a topic that seems to have received little scholarly attention and that is not explicitly related to the other topics covered. Unfortunately, this leads to a format that is repetitious and sometimes uneven, but it could not be otherwise and still provide adequate tests of my hypotheses.

It must be borne in mind that the purpose of these chapters is to present the evidence that can be used to test a series of hypotheses. The task of showing why a particular historical tradition, for example, is relatively sound or unsound is not an end in itself. It is a task that in this case is imposed by the hypothesis that hereditary stratification somehow stifles historical consciousness, while open stratification allows or promotes its growth among literate peoples. A straightforward cross-cultural test of this hypothesis requires a sorting of historical traditions and patterns of stratification into, respectively, the relatively sound and unsound, and the relatively open and closed (or ambiguous categories in between). Ideally, the cases should be plotted along continua, but this degree of precision, I believe, is not necessary at this point.

It should not be assumed when I speak, for example, of hereditary stratification stifling historical writing that I think these two phenomena are linked in any direct fashion as subject and object. I assume, on the contrary, that in this case people must perceive, believe, or desire hereditary stratification; with this perception, belief, or desire in mind, at varying levels of consciousness, they are then constrained not to write or find much interest in sound history. The constraint may result from their own interests or from the interests of their clients or reading public. The constraint may be negative, or it may result from hereditary stratification promoting literary activities that seem more rewarding or interesting than writing sound history would be.

Although it should not be assumed that I want to determine whether the relative openness or closure of stratification is the *only* important factor related to or determining historiographic quality, neither must it be assumed that in each case I intend to present a well-rounded account of all the factors that determine historiographic quality. I have freely omitted much that is interesting in particular historiographic traditions so long as I did not thereby unduly distort the context of what I do present and so long as what was omitted is not relevant to the hypotheses being tested.

So what rewards await the reader who, bearing all this in mind, will wade through the rest of this book? Although the book is primarily about the relationship between social stratification and historical writing—about the social roots of historical consciousness—it is more of a treatise on the former than the latter. It many ways it owes its inspiration to Louis Dumont's *Homo Hierarchicus* (1970a), but the reader will find that Dumont's explanation for why the Hindu Indians were ahistorical is fundamentally flawed. He (or she) will find that the dichotomy between open and closed stratification had profound consequences for the development of a series of features of modern civilization. He will find that an extreme cultural relativism—one that would convert sound history into just another mythology—is untenable. He will find evidence for the idea that history, however much it can be abused, has practical purposes. He will find that although human nature can be conceived of in sharply divergent ways, yet there is evidence for a common human nature, a common tendency for humans to think alike in widely different places and times. He will also, I hope, find that my reasons for thinking that humanistic and social-scientific studies should not be sharply divided are correct. Finally, my fellow anthropologists may find in this book a further field for comparative study.

CHAPTER 2
South Asia and China

China and Hindu India formed markedly contrasting civilizations. Students of Southeast Asian history are particularly aware of the contrast between Indian and Chinese historiography, for although many of the societies of Southeast Asia have been deeply influenced by Indian culture (Coedès 1968), only rarely can one turn to Indian historical sources for insight into the Indianization of Southeast Asia (van Lohuizen-de Leeuw 1970; Mote 1964; Wheatley 1961). Southeast Asia was not the only lacuna in Indian writings: before the introduction of Islam, historical writing, in the sense in which this genre is usually recognized, was all but absent in India. Because of this "almost complete absence of historical literature in the modern sense," which "stands in striking contrast to [the situation in] China," modern historians of India are unusually reliant on sources from outside India (van Lohuizen-de Leeuw 1970:49), especially for reliable chronology (Nilakanta Sastri 1953).

The situation is reversed with respect to China. Although China's cultural influence in Southeast Asia appears to be much less than India's, Chinese sources are vitally important in reconstructing ancient Southeast Asian history (Philips 1961). The "general problem of Chinese historical sources is their overabundance. Those bearing on the relations between China and . . . Southeast Asia . . . are no exception" (Tjan 1965:194).

The contrast between China and India extends not only to their historiographies and their ideologies of stratification but also to a whole series of connected characteristics. This chapter sets forth these contrasting syndromes of sociocultural development, syndromes that subsequent chapters show to be typical of open and closed societies in the West as well as in the East. It also examines contrasts between Hindu India and two neighboring regional variants of Indian civilization.

SOUTH ASIA

Historiography

The central problem posed by Indian historiography is the absence or meagerness—before the arrival of Islam—of any genre unequivocally identifiable as history, and more particularly the absence of such a genre in the pan-Indian language of learning, Sanskrit. Before addressing this problem I will briefly outline the relevant facts concerning pre-Muslim Indian folk history.

A large corpus of ancient Indian literature—much of which may have been transmitted orally for centuries before being put into writing—survives to the present. Much of it is difficult to date. While this literature is relevant to India's history, little of it is regarded as historical writing because it lacks a critical sense (Thapar 1978). According to ancient tradition, two kinds of specialists, the Suta and the Magadha, were charged with the composition and memorization of genealogies and chronicles. During the period from several centuries B.C. until the fourth century A.D. some of the materials of the Sutas and Magadhas were compiled and ultimately written down. The principal surviving written materials are the Puranas, whose historical or quasi-historical core is genealogical, as is virtually all Indian folk history to the present time (Thapar 1978:278). The Puranas, which are relatively few in number and perhaps all representing differing versions of a common original text, are considered sacred, as are the related epics, the *Mahabharata* and the *Ramayana*. The Puranas are universal in scope; they begin with creation and end with the world's destruction. If the Puranas were not originally composed by Brahmans—rather than the Sutas and Magadhas—they have no doubt been considerably reworked by Brahmans (Thapar 1978; Warder 1972). The materials the Puranas contain that are allegedly historical were written centuries after the events to which they refer (Thapar 1978). However, the genealogical sections are presented in the form of prophecies, because the Puranas attribute their authorship to ancient sages who predated the dynasties they chronicle (Thapar 1978).

Ancient Indian historical writings are generally referred to under the heading *itihasa-purana*. There is considerable controversy over the meanings of the terms *itihasa* and *purana*, but there is substantial agreement that their meanings included factual information about the past. *Itihasa* is generally used nowadays to refer to historical information or concepts in general, whereas *purana* usually refers to the specific genre mentioned above.

After the fourth century A.D. no further additions were made to the Puranas. A few centuries later there developed eulogistic biographies, of which the *Harsa-carita* of Bana and the *Vikramanka deva-carita* of Bilhana are the most frequently mentioned. Although the volume of these is meager (Sircar 1965:17), they mark a new focus, being more delimited in time, space, and topic. From about the same time we also have scattered dynastic chronicle/genealogies (*vamsavalis*) that build from the *itihasa-purana* tradition (Thapar 1978). An outstanding chronicle of Kashmir was written in the twelfth century, and a connected and exceptional series of chronicles of Sri Lanka was produced over a lengthy period. Warder 1972 refers to the entire indigenous tradition as the *pauranika* tradition, because of the central position of the Puranas. Later works, for example, often try to establish a link between their subject matter and the heroes, events, and genealogies of the Puranas.

Let us now turn to an evaluation of these folk-historical materials. MacDonell, in a survey of the history of Sanskrit literature, explains the difficulty of providing a chronology as follows: "History is the one weak spot in Indian literature. It is, in fact, non-existent. The total lack of the historical sense is so characteristic, that the whole course of Sanskrit literature is darkened by the shadow of this defect, suffering as it does from an entire absence of exact chronology" (1929:10; see also Walker 1968). Early in the nineteenth century, when Europeans first attempted to write India's history they assumed or concluded that it lacked history in both senses of the term. The idea that India was unchanging and static, and hence lacked history in the sense of significant events, has long been abandoned. But the idea that India lacked history in the sense of historical writing has been more durable.

This is not to say that India had no interest in the past but rather that Indian conceptions of the past lacked important points of contact with modern historians' conceptions. Cohn (1971:51), who is sympathetic to

Indian views of the past, notes important ways in which they differed from the modern view of history. The Hindu conceptions, he notes, were not concerned with exact chronology, "with establishing accuracy through documentary study," or with "a long-range theory of historical causality based on the accidental juxtaposition of events." Pathak, a defender of ancient Indian conceptions of the past, of *itihasa-purana*, and of the value to historians of understanding these conceptions, nonetheless says that they have "no alignment" with "the modern concept of history" (1966:137–38).

Accordingly, Hindu Indian accounts of the past are generally judged to be either mythical or legendary. India's mythology is too immense to survey here, but it is important to realize that in many respects it necessarily served as history, for "in the culture of India, more than in that of the Greeks and the Chinese, mythology is almost the only sort of history the traditional literature presents" (Brown 1961:325). Georges Dumézil (1970:116), who has extensively researched Indo-European mythology, aptly summarizes the Indian point of view by comparing it with that of the Romans:

> The Romans think *historically*, while the Indians think *fabulously*. In each country every narrative concerns a bit of the past, but to have an audience among the Romans this past must be relatively recent, must be located in time as well as space, must concern men rather than imaginary creatures, and must generally involve as little as possible forces and motives which are alien to everyday life. By contrast, the Indians have a taste for immense stretches of space and time; they are as fond of the magnifying imprecision as of the grandiose monstrosity; and they are partial to miracles.

Concerning the legendary, Basham (1959:44) says, "It is perhaps unjust to maintain that India had no sense of history whatever, but what interest she had in her own past was generally concentrated on the fabulous kings of a legendary golden age, rather than the great empires which had risen and fallen in historical times."

Various lines of reasoning have been employed throughout this century to claim historical—rather than merely mythical or legendary—value for traditional Indian accounts of the past. In some cases this involves the assertion that unless demonstrably false they should be considered accurate, because they were compiled and maintained by specialists (the Sutas and Magadhas), because they agree with each other on many points (and are sometimes corroborated by epigraphy), and because we have no reason to think that specialists would systematically memorize falsehoods. Employing these assumptions, Pargiter early in this century surveyed a mass of puranic genealogies in order to establish the relationships between, and the relative chronologies of, numerous ancient Indian kingdoms—and thereby to vindicate indigenous history. Pargiter's monumental effort ([1922] 1972) has not, however, been entirely convincing. Some dismiss the whole enterprise as speculation (Kosambi 1955); others note that the puranic genealogies "are not apparently factual" and that the reliability of chronology based upon them "has yet to be proven" (Thapar 1978:242).

Another line of reasoning that has been employed to defend the historical value of Indian presentations of the past runs as follows. If an account of the past was written a thousand years ago and it describes conditions from the beginning of time up to fifteen hundred years ago, it may indeed recount myth and legend (i.e., the alleged events up to fifteen hundred years ago). But it also provides very direct and invaluable information about the time in which it was composed: it tells us how people a thousand years ago thought and how they tried to explain the past. Pathak (1966) clearly states this line of reasoning to support his analysis of the value of various eulogistic biographies often cited as high points in pre-Muslim Indian historiography. Since the biographies are more or less contemporary, their value is all the greater, and Pathak shows that a serious and sympathetic attempt to get inside the minds of their authors can be of great importance to the historian trying to glean facts from these accounts. Yet Basham (1961:58), while not denying their value to the modern historian, says that the biographies Pathak discusses "cannot be considered as history in anything like the modern sense." In his foreword to Pathak's book, Basham describes the biographies as "romanticised" and valuable "for want of better material" (1966:[vii]).

A related line of reasoning is that any history of India—at least if it is to be meaningful to Indians—should be informed by Indian conceptions of history, not solely by conceptions imposed from the West. Subject matter, periodization, and organizing framework should be indigenous. Pathak (1966) and Warder (1972) argue this persuasively in recent times. It is a view congenial to anthropologists (e.g., Cohn 1961, 1971), and it is effectively employed by modern historians, as in Dirks 1982 and Inden 1976. However, Dirks is careful to distinguish history written in this manner—which he calls ethnohistory—from ordinary history, and Inden uses his sources in the highly selective and cautious manner.

A fourth line of reasoning is that even legendary materials contain factual information or gross outlines of events that, when separated from the spurious and supplemented by other sources, are essential to piecing together any sort of acceptable history of pre-Muslim India. But the amount of this kind of material utilized from Indian accounts of the past is often small. This can be illustrated by modern histories of the Colas. The Colas flourished from the ninth or tenth century to the thirteenth, controlling the entire southern half of India for a period and even carrying the might of their forces into Southeast Asia. Theirs was the high point of Tamil civilization, when Tamil literature "reached heights of excellence never reached again" (Nilakanta Sastri 1955:vii). The classic on their history is Nilakanta Sastri's *The Colas* (1955). This work is extended in two more recent books: Stein 1980 assesses the degree of centralization of the Cola state, and Hall 1980 examines its trade. Each of these works is overwhelmingly based not on literary or narrative historical sources but upon epigraphy and other archaeological materials. Epigraphic sources are variously described as "rich" (Stein 1980:1-2) and as "incomplete and fragmentary" (Hall 1980:2). Whatever the case may be, epigraphy forms the backbone of modern histories not only of the Colas but of ancient India in general.

The standard work on the subject, Sircar's *Indian Epigraphy* (1965:7), says that "of all . . . sources for the reconstruction of early Indian history, epigraphic records are the most important." This is so because "unlike Greece, Rome or China, ancient India has no history," for "the Indians of antiquity did not care to leave written accounts of all their achievements" (Sircar 1965:7). The most important epigraphical inscriptions are on stone or copper plates and usually commemorate gifts to religious figures or institutions. The donee and the gift are specified in some detail, and a separate section, called a *prasasti*, normally eulogizes the donor or his ruler. The *prasasti* usually contains genealogical information. Thus these inscriptions provide highly pertinent information on social arrangements, religion, and economy, and show that in some contexts Indians valued permanent records. Since much of the information is contemporary, its reliability is relatively high. When inscriptions can be compared to traditions, the details of the latter can be shown to be "mostly wrong" (Sircar 1965:17). Some inscriptions show a relatively sound sense of history in their reconstructions of the past, but many show serious defects (Sircar 1965). Subject matter is quite limited.

A collection of essays on the historical writings of South Asia (Philips 1961) challenges the view that Indians had no sense of history whatever. Majumdar (1961), for example, shows that the *Arthasastra* of Kautalya (Kautilya), a work on statecraft possibly written in the third century B.C., lists historical writings—*itihasa*—as among those high in importance. Majumdar (1961) argues, on the basis of a ninth century Jain work, that this view of the importance of history must have prevailed for a considerable period. He also argues that reasonably accurate king lists were maintained in the Puranas between 500 B.C. and the fourth century A.D., and that after that there almost certainly were royal archives. The latter have perished, however. On the other hand, in certain outlying districts—Nepal, Kashmir, Gujarat, and Assam—the tradition of compiling royal genealogical lists, and even chronicles, survived. Majumdar thought this may have been because these areas were the least ravaged by Muslim invasions. He cites a Jain text from Gujarat as part of his evidence. Majumdar notes the biographies too, but he is reluctant to rank them as historical works, due to their tendency "to eulogize, rather than to give a true and impartial account" (1961:18).

After summarizing all this evidence for ideas of history in Sanskrit literature, Majumdar (1961:20) says only that "it does, to a certain extent, blunt the edge" of the view that only one work in Sanskrit is truly historical, because among all the others there is "no work meriting the title of history."

For the fact remains that except Kalhana's *Rajatarangini*, which is merely a local history of Kashmir, there is no other historical text in the whole range of Sanskrit literature which makes even a near approach to it, or may be regarded as history in the proper sense of the term. This is a very strange phenomenon, for there is hardly any branch of human knowledge or any topic of human interest which is not adequately represented in Sanskrit literature. The absence of real historical literature is therefore naturally regarded as so very unusual that even many distinguished Indians cannot bring themselves to recognize the obvious fact, and seriously entertain the belief that there were many such historical texts, but that they have all perished. (Majumdar 1961:25)

The latter belief has been dashed by the absence of histories among "the fairly large recent finds of ancient Indian manuscripts" stashed away for centuries beyond the hands of Muslim conquerors (Bechert 1978:3). Furthermore, al-Beruni had observed already in the early eleventh century that "the Hindus do not pay much attention to the historical order of things" ([c. 1030] 1910:II, 10).

There is little doubt that Kalhana's *Rajatarangini*, written in about 1150, included a substantial section of relatively sound historical writing. Kalhana showed the critical attitude, skepticism, and freedom from bias that is required of a good historian, and he sought to eliminate error from his account by consulting such original sources as ordinances, inscriptions, and written documents (Majumdar 1961). Kalhana conceived of his work as being useful to kings and of interest to any man of culture (Majumdar

1961). While his work has its defects, Kalhana shows a sound knowledge of geography, of historical detail, and of human character. He provides "vigorous" biographical sketches, and evaluates even his heroes with that "spirit of detachment" that will admit both weaknesses and strengths in the same person (Majumdar 1961:23).

Majumdar (1961) uses the *Rajatarangini* to make two important points. One is that some sort of historiographic tradition preceded Kalhana, because Kalhana refers to works that are now lost, though he did not give them much credit for soundness (Sircar 1965; Thapar 1978). The more important point is that since Kalhana refers to no supraregional or pan-Indian history, it must not have existed. This, Majumdar argues, refutes the belief that such histories once existed but somehow disappeared in more recent times.

Majumdar (1961:26–27) is especially puzzled that pseudohistories could be so popular but not the real things: "It is difficult to conceive of a psychological state of mind in which men revel at the delineation of historical persons and events in a crude form, but shrink from giving it a developed literary form or a truly historical shape." After rejecting several existing explanations for the lack of historical writing in Sanskrit, Majumdar (1961:27–28) is left with only an "accidental" or "great man" theory. Had there been other eminent writers—of the stature of Kalhana—in other parts of India, historical writing would have been established elsewhere.

While I have focused on Majumdar's essay, his view and the views of others in Philips 1961 may be summarized as follows. Although the materials have often or generally disappeared, Indians did at times produce and maintain the materials required to write histories. Although little in the way of historical writings were produced by ancient Indians, this does not prove that they lacked any sense of history; it merely shows that they generally did not bother to write about history even though they could have. The final point—and the proof, as it were, of the second point—is that there are two important exceptions to Indian ahistoricity: the relatively sound medieval chronicles of Kashmir (Majumdar 1961; see also Basham 1961 and Stein 1961) and of Sri Lanka (Perera 1961). Lesser exceptions are also noted, but since only the Sri Lankan chronicles are generally judged as even roughly on a par with the *Rajatarangini*, I will ignore the lesser exceptions.

The two most frequently mentioned historical works from Sri Lanka are the *Mahavamsa*, composed by a Buddhist monk as early as the sixth century A.D., and the *Culavamsa*, which continued the earlier chronicle up to near the end of the twelfth century. The *Mahavamsa* was modeled on an earlier work, the *Dipavamsa* (literally, "history of the island"), that dated from the fifth century. Both the *Dipavamsa* and the *Mahavamsa* were based on historical sections of commentaries on the Buddhist canon. A number of lesser works apparently continued the *Mahavamsa* up to the time of the composition of the *Culavamsa*, but these have perished. A second part of the *Culavamsa* brings it up to at least the fourteenth century, and a third part mentions an updating in the eighteenth century. It was continued until the British occupied Kandy in 1815. The Sri Lankan chronicles cover more than two millennia, the authors are often identified, and they were all Buddhist monks (de Silva 1981; Perera 1961).

The collection of works known as the Pali Canon (the Buddhist canon of Sri Lanka and certain countries of Southeast Asia) itself embodies distinctly historical ideas, and the canon was utilized, as mentioned above, in the composition of the first Sri Lankan history (Warder 1961). The Buddha having been a historical figure, and Buddhism being a missionary religion, time and geography became important to Buddhists (Godakumbura 1961; Perera 1961). The linkage between Sri Lanka, Buddhism, and the Buddhist monastic order is a major theme of the chronicles. While the scope of the Sri Lankan chronicles is impressive, many features are not particularly sound. The authors "had no clear notion of historical accuracy," and the worlds of men and gods are not clearly separated (Perera 1961:37). The authors' conceptions of state and society were elementary at best, and although some sections show "a pronounced interest in politics" and the authors showed a commendable "aloofness from rival political factions and interests," they rarely drew political lessons from history (Perera 1961:35, 37). Perera (1961:29) says that the Sri Lankan chronicles do not constitute "history as we know it today." Nonetheless, they are sound enough to form a clear exception, along with Kalhana's *Rajatarangini*, to the general pattern of ahistoricity that characterized pre-Muslim India (Philips 1961).

If genealogy has always been at the core of Indian folk history and is no less central to Indian mythology (Mandelbaum 1970), we may gain some insight into ancient historiography from a study by Shah and Shroff (1959) of a caste of "genealogists and mythographers" in Gujarat. This caste, the Vahivanca Barots, was one of eighteen such "bardic" castes in the province. Some of them, including the Vahivancas, kept written records, while others memorized their material. The books in which the Vahivancas record their materials are major items of property and sources of income. Consequently, they are jealously guarded, even to the point that older ones are destroyed rather than risk their falling into the wrong hands. Because of the secrecy that surrounds these works, Shah and Shroff could only make a somewhat tentative analysis of their contents.

One of the books dated to 1740, and another, though dated later, gave an apparently accurate genealogical datum independently datable by epigraphy at A.D. 1234. Each book is usually composed of two distinct sections, the first being a continuous narrative, the second consisting mainly of genealogies that are added to as marriages and births occur. Each entry in the second part is normally made in the presence of the members of the lineage concerned and a few respectable nonlineage witnesses. This provides a degree of accuracy, but if the Vahivanca's patrons all agree on a false entry, the genealogist may not be the wiser. It is often alleged that the Vahivancas succumb to bribery too. As the generations pass and a book fills up, the Vahivanca starts a new book, copying the old narrative portion and supplementing it with a summary—also in continuous narrative form—of the old genealogical entries. Much information is lost forever in this process, as the old books are either allowed to perish or are deliberately destroyed.

The Vahivancas are specialized in servicing castes that claim to belong to the Kshatriya *varna*, principally the Rajputs. The Rajput sociopolitical system is based, in theory, on a rigid allocation of status by genealogical criteria. In succession disputes the Vahivancas are regularly called upon to provide the appropriate genealogical records. For performing this valuable service, the Vahivancas are generally accorded an honorable status by the Rajputs.

The earlier, continuous narrative part of the Vahivancas' books is essentially mythical, being derived primarily from the great Hindu epics—the Ramayana and Mahabharata—and other ancient sources. The function of the earlier part is to link the patron's lineage to the heroes of ancient India and to the Kshatriya *varna*. But while historians may consider the epics nonhistorical, the patrons and the Vahivancas apparently do not. Moreover, the Vahivancas have standards for judging each other's knowledge of early "history" and thus maintaining a sort of consensus on the way things really were.

Because of this consensus on the ancient past, and the witnessing of new entries, it is easy to understand why the patrons of the Vahivancas have a certain amount of faith in their books. And if the Vahivancas *casually* changed their books, surely no one would have faith in them. To illustrate this, the authors discuss the case of a large agricultural caste that recently changed its mind about the *varna* to which it believed itself to belong. Since the Vahivancas had already generated—and put into their books— a claim for this caste to Kshatriya status, when the caste decided it wanted to link with the Vaishya *varna* there was nothing to do but to give up patronizing the Vahivancas, who could not change their books so suddenly as to accommodate this new twist. Clearly, the Vahivancas had to maintain a facade of historical objectivity, if not always the substance.

But Shah and Shroff are unequivocal in stating that the earlier parts of the Vahivanca's books are mythical. To meet and maintain the standards of his peers, the Vahivanca "preserves the myths"; to satisfy his patrons, he "creates myths" (1959:51). The creative part consists of linking the genealogies of his patrons with the genealogies of the gods and heroes of the epics, thereby establishing a hereditary claim to the status his patrons seek. Thus, for example, if a Rajput usurps a particular princely office, the genealogist is called upon to "prove" authoritatively the new chief's claim. Even if the chief's real ancestors are known, the Vahivanca would forge a link between the chief and the ancient dynasty of his clan. The Vahivanca provides a "charter" for the new chief (1959:55). In search of larger gifts, genealogists flatter their patrons. If patrons are stingy, the genealogists threaten to record derogatory information. The genealogists also exploit rivalries between descent groups to wring larger recompense for their services.

Shah and Shroff reveal how, over an extended period of time, the Vahivancas created a mythical charter to Kshatriya status for a caste that was upwardly mobile. This took much finesse and depended in large measure on a wider public acceptance of the caste's new status, because the Vahivancas would have lost the patronage of the Rajputs if the upwardly mobile caste had been moved up at an unseemly rate. The Vahivancas were engaged in a delicate balancing act. Its perils were illustrated by the case, already described, of the caste that changed its mind about the *varna* it strove to identify with. The Vahivancas lost the patronage of this influential and wealthy caste. As Shah and Shroff (1959:64) observe, "The Vahivanca is successful in his occupation as long as the myths and facts recorded in his books are consistent with the social life of his patrons." When the Vahivanca does not provide the sort of information his patron wants to know about himself, the patron either seeks a new genealogist or fabricates his own mythical genealogy.

The defects in this system of historical writing are not hard to see. Patronage is a major problem: the genealogist serves not so much a general public as particular interests or persons (so too in the past; see Thapar 1978). The books are not open to inspection and hence are not readily subject to criticism from various quarters. Ancient history is "known" not through the preservation of records and the consultation of all available and more or less objective resources but rather through the consensus of the "historians." True, much sound information must get recorded and maintained to a certain point, but the overall and long-term effect of rivalry between groups that can only validate their status through genealogical links to the prestigious *varna* of a mythical past is clearly the production of much that is unsound. It may be that the genre of genealogy is inherently defective as history: Thapar (1978:326) assumes that "genealogies are rarely faithful records" (Chinese genealogical registers are defective too; see van der Sprenkel 1973).

In a review of the bardic literature of India, von Fürer-Haimendorf says that the literature is of limited value for either political history or chronology. Its defects stem from the bards' paramount interest in the "mythical past" and preoccupation with the sectional interests of particular castes (1961:93).

When the Muslims came to India they produced, in one or another part of the subcontinent, a continuous tradition of historical writing (Hardy 1961; Philips 1961). Under the influence of Muslim ideas introduced in Mughal India, for example, the Rajputs began in the sixteenth century to support the writing of relatively sound chronicles, but by the eighteenth century they had found them to be irksome and returned to the old bardic tradition (Fürer-Haimendorf 1961). In spite of the Muslim example, as late as the turn of this century something in "the cultural background of Indian historians tended to inhibit a critical or analytical study of the sources" of Indian history (Thapar 1978:11). The modern study of history in India has been greatly influenced by Europeans, who were particularly involved in such neglected and basic tasks as the deciphering of ancient inscriptions (Sircar 1965).

Concomitants

In addition to its ahistoricity, another peculiar feature of India is the extent to which individualism is suppressed or ideologically de-emphasized (Dumézil 1970:117; Dumont 1965, 1970b; but cf. Morris 1978 and some of the essays in Moore 1968). Part of the evidence for the reduced sense of the individual is the very paucity of sound historical writings. On the other hand, it is the Western "conception that history and the individual are inseparable" that, combined with the "absence of the individual in traditional India," leads us to conclude by definition that India is "un-historical" (Dumont 1970b:142–43).

When biography did get written in Hindu India, as already noted, it tended to stereotype, eulogize, and romanticize. Individualistic portraiture, as is well known, had almost no place in Hindu India (Coomaraswamy 1931). Realism in general was rare in Indian art, and artists were usually anonymous (Rowland 1953). However, realistic portraits were at times produced. Early Buddhist paintings showed considerable realism in depicting humans (Wilkinson 1949; see, e.g., the frontispiece in Basham 1959) and in Muslim India portraiture reached a very high level of development. When the Mughal Empire flourished in the sixteenth and seventeenth centuries, and under the direct patronage of its rulers, who were Persian-influenced Muslims of Mongol-Turkic origin, a distinctive style of miniature painting developed. Coomaraswamy ([1916] 1975:74) contrasts Mughal painting with a derivative but Hindu style, the Rajput:

Portraiture is the typical mode of Mughal painting. Its predominance there, and comparative subordination in Rajput art, exactly reflect the characteristic bias of the Mughal and the Hindu culture—the one deeply interested in individual character and in passing events, the other in ideal types and symbols. Even human figures . . . stand essentially as symbols of ideas [in Rajput art]. . . . [Mughal portraiture achieved] perhaps the highest level that miniature portraiture has ever reached, [exhibiting] penetrating insight into the character of the individual represented.

Not only do the Mughal paintings delineate individuals, but many are individually signed. Interestingly, the majority of the painters apparently were Hindu, possibly because of the Muslim ban on portraiture. When the Mughals ceased direct patronage of the painters, individualistic realism disappeared (Brown [1924] 1975; Wilkinson 1949). The passing of realistic portraiture may also reflect the fact that, given time, the Muslims, too, developed castelike social stratification in India (Mandelbaum 1970).

Earlier I mentioned Kautalya's *Arthasastra*, which perhaps dates from the third century B.C. This comprehensive work on statecraft is virtually the only one of its kind from India. Moreover, the work was by no means well known there. Only a few copies have been found in modern times, and only after the beginning of this century. Relatively few Indianists, I suspect, have actually read it. The *Arthasastra* gives an altogether different picture of India from the one formed by India's better-known literature.

While Kautalya generally upholds the caste system, he weighs the pros and cons of descent versus merit in the appointment of officials and concludes that both have their advantages. But "from the capacity for doing work is the ability of a person judged. And in accordance with their ability" (1963:18). Kautalya advocates an iron-fisted government, he has a thorough appreciation of the material requirements of statecraft, and his discussions of divination and religion often involve their calculated manipulation for the ends of the state. Although he does not dwell on the topics, Kautalya does make very brief mention of the value of bookkeeping records and of historical tales that might enlighten the king. It is possible, of course, that Kautalya presents a picture of Hindu India widely known to ruling circles. But in its mundane practicality it is not the picture generally presented in Hindu literature (Kosambi 1952). With respect to the far better known literature, Dumézil's (1970:117) summary of the differences between Indians and Romans is pertinent: whereas "the Romans think *politically*, the Indians think *morally*." Whereas "Roman wisdom" is "focused on politics," for the Indians anything treating of the social order can only be a "secondary science, deduced from higher truths." Political history was not central to Indian presentations of the past (Thapar 1978).

Although some of the sciences were well developed in India, there is as yet no work such as Joseph Needham's *Science and Civilization in China* (1954–) to show that overall developments were exceptional (but see the appendixes in Basham 1959). Without history or political science, it is highly unlikely that the social sciences could have gotten far in traditional India (Dumézil 1970:117). Mythology served for psychology and the rest of the study of man in India (Brown 1961:325). Geography was not well developed in Indian thought (Wheatley 1961:177).

Divination is probably a true human universal, and it certainly did occur in India, particularly in the form of astrology (Esnoul 1968). But except for astrology, its scope there is suspiciously limited, considering the flourishing state of most other Indian forms of magic or superstition. While it is difficult to demonstrate directly that divination was relatively underdeveloped in India, it is significant that works such as Basham's *The Wonder That Was India* (1959) make no mention of the subject in the index. Perhaps where gods walk the earth—as was true in Egypt too—part of the rationale for divination disappears. In a 1968 study of body divination, Lessa found little information in Hindu sources—though he did find some from Indian Buddhism. He went on to develop a theory, discussed later in this chapter, that divination is generally linked to high rates of social mobility. In his study of early Chinese pyromantic divination using bone and shell, Keightley (1978) found the practice almost everywhere in Asia except in India and Southeast Asia.

Social Mobility: Hindu India

One of the most fundamental features of Hindu Indian society—past and present—is the pervasive role of hereditary rank. Rank is a fundamental feature of Hindu society, it is essentially transmitted hereditarily, and groups and categories defined by hereditary rank formed the building blocks of society. Silverberg 1968, a collection of essays that mostly attempt to refute the view of Indian society as rigidly stratified by birth, nonetheless has a summary article that states that Hindu India's "socioreligious values and ideologies express what is probably as extreme a disapproval of mobility as is possible, and . . . they have in fact worked to reduce very greatly the amount of mobility in Indian society" (Barber 1968:29). On the other hand, and with no less authority, Marriott and Inden say that "rates of individual rise and fall are not known to differ between class systems and caste systems" (1981:982). Let us examine Indian stratification and then return to the problem of rates of social mobility within it. Most of the information summarized below on Indian social structure derives from recent observation. But some of the information comes from earlier sources, and various fundamental characteristics of Indian society are so widespread and entrenched that their antiquity seems highly likely.

There is no universally accepted definition of Indian caste, in part because the subject is complex and in part because regional and temporal variation is great. But Indian castes are generally conceived of as descent groups or categories whose members tend to marry only among themselves, are associated with a distinctive occupation, and have a distinctive collective rank within a localized system of castes. Although general features of the caste system are widespread, individual castes usually have a limited spatial distribution and are enmeshed in a system of caste interrelationships that is also confined to a more or less distinct region. How these regions may have been bounded in precolonial, or even recent, times is a little-studied matter (Bailey 1963), but evidence from Malabar suggests that the lower castes tended to be specially restricted, while the upper castes were more likely to have supraregional linkages (Miller 1954). This pattern is said to be found "in much of the rest of India" as well (Cohn 1971:129).

The commonest word for caste, apparently, is *jati*, which means kind, species, or genus, often in a broadly biological sense. The term is applied to various levels of classification, so there are *jati* within *jati* (Marriott and Inden 1977; Dumont 1970a). The term is even applied to inanimate objects, but it generally has the connotation of a grouping created by common descent. Etymologically, *jati* derives from a root with the meaning of genesis, origin, or birth. Whatever truth there may be to the claim of common descent, to the extent that members of a caste married only among themselves and bore offspring only from such unions, each caste would be a biologically closed group—a race or racial stock.

As the Indian anthropologist Beteille (1967) observes, the concepts of race and descent in fact overlap to a considerable extent. In north India, he says, *jati* is the best word in various languages for race. In the south of India, the Brahmans and non-Brahmans are considered to belong to separate races. Each caste has its own customs, beliefs, and stereotyped personality (Tyler 1973), and traditionally had its own laws (Kosambi 1952).

In their notion that the members of each caste share a distinctive "substance" that entails a distinctive "code for conduct," Indians think of themselves in a manner very similar to the way we conceive of differences in species or in the way we think of races when we think in terms of racism (Marriott and Inden 1981:983). However, the code for conduct for the members of a particular caste includes certain regulations regarding their behavior—dietary, sexual, and ritual matters are prominent—vis-à-vis themselves and other castes. To the extent that these regulations are honored or violated, the rank of the caste, and even the rank of individuals within the caste, may be raised or lowered (Marriott and Inden 1977, 1981). Outcasting is a correlate of these beliefs, because if a misbehaving member is not outcasted, his pollution may lower the rank of all his fellows. This change of rank is thought to result from the caste or individual actually having changed its or his substance. Thus a caste is potentially more transmutable than a species or than racial character. Nonetheless, Marriott and Inden (1981:985) state that caste rank is not easily changed, partly due to "minds accustomed to a hereditary order."

In Hindu social classification, just below the division between Hindus and non-Hindus, and, among Hindus, between those twice-born and those not twice-born, there are five great categories: the four *varna* (the Brahmans, the Kshatriya, the Vaishya, and the Shudra) and the Untouchables, who lie outside the *varna* scheme. These categories are often likened to the estates of medieval Europe (Dumont 1970a; Morris 1978). Indians generally believe that each caste, except for some of the Untouchables, can be assigned to one or another of the *varna*, or to a certain admixture of them through miscegenation. The substance and code for conduct of each *varna* has its origin in the myth of the first man, Purusa, from whose body the four *varna* were created: from his mouth came the Brahmans, from his arms the Kshatriya, from his thighs the Vaishya, and from his feet the Shudra. The first three, the "twice born," are distinctly superior to the Shudra. There is often disagreement about the assignment of particular castes to the *varna*. As mentioned earlier, each caste has its own origin story, often linking it in some way to the *varna* scheme.

In the sense that *varnas* as well as castes may be called *jatis* in Indian texts, they are part of a common system. However, the discrepancy between the simplicity of the *varna* scheme and the complexity of actual on-the-ground caste organization leads some authorities to describe the former as a purely ritual scheme and to make an analytic distinction between caste and *varna*. *Caste* in this usage refers to more organized groups, *varna* to categories. This leaves any categories in between to be thought of as super *jatis* (see, e.g., Mandelbaum 1970) or small-scale *varna* (Fox 1969). As a further oversimplification of the *varna* scheme, in many areas the Kshatriya and Vaishya are all but absent. Basham (1959) sharply distinguishes castes from *varna* because he rejects the Indian tradition that links them. But he notes the antiquity of the tradition, and clearly the *varna* play a major role in the ideology of caste. They provide a pan-Indian framework for caste that is as familiar to villagers as it is to the Brahmans who cap the system (Mandelbaum 1970). Except where it seems necessary to provide further specification, I use *caste* in this chapter to refer both to groups and named categories.

By virtue of the various roles assigned to the castes, only by their cooperation can society function—at least, this is the ideal. Society is primarily conceived not as a collection of individuals but as a set of castes or *varna*, each performing its role within the larger whole. Dumont (1965, 1970a, 1970b) has written extensively on the holism that characterizes Hinduism, in contrast to the individualism of modern Western society. Each individual is born into his caste as the consequence of the relative merit he achieved in previous lives. He improves his chances of a higher birth in the next life by properly fulfilling the role appropriate to the caste into which he was born in this life. His chances of movement upward during his lifetime are limited. It is often noted that movement at either end of the system (e.g., into Brahman rank or out of Untouchable rank) is particularly difficult.

Much of what I have just outlined can be illustrated by an example drawn from a recent work entitled *Marriage and Rank in Bengali Culture* (Inden 1976). This work is particularly apt, for three reasons. It is presented in terms of indigenous conceptions and is based almost exclusively on indigenous texts, it refers to what Inden calls a "middle period" (c. 1450 to 1800) that is precolonial even if it is not pre-Muslim, and it is particularly concerned with the social mobility that was built into the local caste system. The subjects of the study comprise elements of the two highest-ranked castes or caste categories of the region—Brahmans and Kayasthas (writers).

For middle-period Bengalis, *jati* had the meanings given above. Inden generally translates it as genus. As well as being applied to nonhumans, it was applied to human genera defined, for example, by sex, religion, occupation, or nation. Members of each *jati* possessed in common a distinct substance, *dhatu*, and a distinct code for conduct, *dharma*. *Dharma* and *dhatu* have a common root, *dhr*, meaning "to sustain" (Inden 1976:21). The substance and the code of a living being sustain it. Inden repeatedly stresses the nondualistic way in which substance and code were conceived of, so that they should be thought of as two aspects of a common entity: coded substance. *Dharma* was simultaneously "a sacred, spiritual, and moral element; it was also a secular, material, and natural one" (Inden 1976:19). This is a very important point, for we in the West think dualistically in that we think of a separable natural substance and a moral code for conduct. In this way we think of the separability of body and behavior or body and soul (and hence that character may not be inherited), while Hindus think of these as essentially unitary or combined. If the substance changes, the code changes. Coded substances may combine in some ways with other substances.

Middle-period Bengali conceptions asserted the divinity of the entire Hindu community, defined by the combination of human substance with the substance of the sounds of sacred texts, the Vedas and Tantras. The higher grades were, however, more divine, more combinable with and more combined with the power of sacred words; thus they possessed greater "embodied power [*shakti*] or potential to transform the coded substances of wealth and food into well-being, prosperity, long life, and so on" (Inden 1976:106). Higher grades were deities to the lower grades, and the latter worshipped the former by offering them wealth, food, and daughters. Proper marriage and reproduction were "first and foremost" among the means of preserving coded substance (Inden 1976:61) and comprised a major component in maintaining order and prosperity in the community as a whole. Appropriate acts of worship improved one's substance and rank. Nature, morality, ritual, and divinity were all conceptually linked.

In middle-period conceptions the caste situation of Bengal was periodically confused by episodes of mixed marriages. After one such episode the Kshatriya and Vaishya disappeared from the scene and only somewhat inferior Brahmans and thirty-six castes classified as Shudra remained. In a later period the god Vishnu playfully created five Shudra who possessed some of the attributes of the twice-born *varna*: they could sponsor and benefit from Vedic services and thus were more combinable with the Vedas than was normally the lot of Shudras. These five Shudra men accompanied five exceptionally pure Brahmans who had been summoned to Bengal due to the inadequacy of the local Brahmans.

Descendants of these immigrant Brahmans and Shudras in middle-period Bengal formed a series of subcastes divided into clans and subclans within the Brahman or Kayastha *jati*. The highest-ranked descendants, whether Brahman or Kayastha, were called Kulina. And whether Brahman or Shudra, one could only be born to Kulina rank, which was created by the gods and transmitted in unbroken succession by birth from those who were born to the status and who maintained the code for conduct appropriate to it. A Kulina was considered a "human deity" (Inden 1976:104).

It was possible to lose Kulina status, after which it could never be regained. It was also possible to move up and down within Kulina rank, and this was thought of as a normal, cyclic process in which wealth was traded for rank, or vice versa, depending on the circumstances. It was also thought possible to move up and down within the non-Kulina ranks. In some cases this involved an apparent change of caste. Because of the confusion of castes, Shudras in occupational castes other than Kayastha might be "latent" Kayasthas. If so, they could be "actualized" by offering a daughter to a Kulina, that is, through worship. It is a matter of point of view as to whether this is intercaste mobility. In each case, however, the unit that moves is a family or clan, not a caste. By the same token, improper behavior could lower one's rank. But Shudras did not become Brahmans, no one became Kulina except by birth, and a woman of one *varna* was never a suitable wife for a man of another.

Although Inden correctly points to numerous areas of flexibility and mobility, some of which are at the normative core of this system, one cannot fail to see real rigidity too, particularly in the upward limits of mobility. As one of Inden's sources states, if actions in accord with Kulina code "arose in an ordinary person," it would not make him a Kulina (Inden 1976:109). Thus this caste system was closed at the top.

Some elements of Indian social stratification—the *varna*, for example— can be traced back to about 1000 B.C. In the earliest sources, according to most authorities (Thapar [1978] disagrees), more stress is placed on the function of the castes and less on their hereditary nature. But an increased emphasis on "purity of blood," and "hardened" class divisions long pre- ceded the birth of Christ (Basham 1959), by which time the hereditary character of stratification is clear, as shown by the miscegenation theory of caste origins (Dumont 1970a; Marriott and Inden 1981). Al-Beruni (1910:I) writing early in the eleventh century, describes the *varna* or castes in India and contrasts the hereditary nature of Indian stratification with the essential equality of Muslims. The hereditary aspect of Hindu stratification has therefore prevailed for a very long time. Thapar's extensive discussion of ancient Indian society and of social mobility within it continuously stresses its hereditary nature, particularly with respect to the conception of *varna* but in general too: "In Indian society, the criterion of status was birth" (1978:291).

But most of this, especially concerning the *varna*, is on the ideological level. What of reality? In spite of ideology, mobility has undoubtedly always occurred (Thapar 1978). One source of mobility is the jockeying for rank among castes. Although they agree that they should be ranked, the mem- bers of a caste often think their own caste has been improperly ranked, and they are not at a loss to find a plausible origin story to account both for their "true" rank and for the cause of their "mistaken" rank. In recent times, "through a process of social fantasy the caste alleges that it has been 'incognito' for a period of time well beyond historical verification and that it has now rediscovered its real identity" (Rowe 1968:66). Castes that are near each other in rank are particularly prone to competition over their relative ranks (Mandelbaum 1970). The process of changing the rank of a caste is lengthy, generally extending over generations. Since such move- ments are normally explained away as a resumption of the caste's real rank, this sort of mobility does not prove an embarrassment to hereditary prin- ciples (Bailey 1963). Occasionally a caste or segment of a caste manages to raise its rank by moving to an area where it is unknown (Mandelbaum 1970; Thapar 1978).

Individual mobility is generally stymied by the necessity of marrying someone from one's own caste (Mandelbaum 1970). Thus no matter how affluent, powerful, or prestigious one becomes in his lifetime, this upward mobility cannot generally be validated by an upward marriage (but see cases in Inden 1976). Individuals sometimes succeed in passing in public life for members of a higher caste, but rarely do they achieve this in their private lives, where marriages must be arranged (Mandelbaum 1970). Passing between castes in India is probably less common than passing from colored to white in the United States (Harper 1968).

Stein (1968:80) is among the few who argue that "there was considerable opportunity for individual mobility in most parts of [medieval] India." But the direct evidence he provides is scanty. It consists of the fact that in the context of Bhakti cults, which denied the importance of caste during the early centuries of this millennium, sixteen Shudra households performed priestly functions at a particular temple. Stein effectively shows a kind of mobility that is smaller in scale and perhaps less organized than is characterized by the rise of caste betterment associations of recent times, and of course he has shown that Shudras assumed functions that *varna* theory denies them. In the long run the erstwhile priestly Shudra lost their high position, and Stein (1968:90) describes the episode as ultimately "a failure in mobility." But it is not clear that the sixteen households were unrelated, and so—unless the evidence shows individuals rising to this position, and then others following them up the ladder to replace or join them—it is not at all certain that what occurred was not either an isolated incident or an example of small-scale collective mobility, or both.

Brute facts of political life gave scope to mobility. Usurpations of royal power were common, and Indian thought gave little attention to the stability of dynasties. Again, however, any group achieving royal authority would often claim Kshatriya status (Sircar 1965; Srinivas 1968; Thapar 1978)—as the Colas did, for example (Stein 1980)—and thus bring their usurpation into harmony with caste theory. The ruler also had it in his power to raise or lower the rank of a caste (Dumont 1970a; Mandelbaum 1970).

Analogous to royalty, in most locales or regions there is (and presumably was in the past) a caste that, by virtue of its control of land, wields effective political and economic power. This caste (in the anthropological literature called the "dominant caste") may be of any *varna*, though it is "usually . . . of respectable ritual rank" (Mandelbaum 1970:359). Thus the position of dominant caste, lying outside the ideology of Hinduism, is open to competition (Dumont 1970a). Force clearly has had a role in altering the rank of groups in Hindu India, and it is important to recall that force played a role in maintaining the ranks. Attempts by Untouchables to assume the rights of higher status are particularly likely to be met by force, the boundary between Untouchables and the *varnas* being especially difficult to cross (Mandelbaum 1970; Morris 1978).

In his initial formulation of the concept of the dominant caste, Srinivas (1955:18) noted that its dominance rested on numerical preponderance (among other things). However, Mayer (1958) quickly demonstrated that numerical preponderance was not necessary for dominance. Leach (1960:6), on the other hand, and perhaps misled by his experience in atypical Sri Lanka, went further than Srinivas and said that the dominant caste generally possesses a "numerical majority." If this were true, and if we were to put aside the issue of ritual rank (which need not coincide with dominance), then caste systems in India would not constitute the sort of caste society defined in chapter 1. But this appears not to be true.

The anthology *Village India* (Marriott 1955), in which Srinivas's article appeared, presents studies of seven villages, and only one of them has a dominant caste that forms a numerical majority. Nicholas 1968 charts or discusses the population percentage of dominant castes in twenty-three villages described from various parts of India (and a further village from Sri Lanka). Only nine of the Indian villages were dominated by a caste that formed a majority.

An extensive regional study of caste demography (Schwartzberg 1968) shows that it is very rare for a Hindu caste—dominant or not—to form a numerical majority in a region, and it is not generally the case that a village has a single caste constituting a majority. Schwartzberg drew his data from the 1931 census of India and from a survey he conducted of the whole North Indian Plain, which he notes is the "core and culture-hearth" of the subcontinent and contains a third of its populace (1968:95). He distinguishes five major regions and fifteen subregions. In no region or subregion is a single caste category a numerical majority (Schwartzberg 1968). Exclusive of the heavily Muslim districts in what is now Bangladesh, and in a few adjacent areas in which the Muslim caste category of Sheikh does form a numerical majority, only about 4 percent of the more than one hundred districts has a caste category that forms a majority (Schwartzberg 1968). Schwartzberg shows caste proportions for forty-seven villages in central Uttar Pradesh. They may or may not be representative, but only ten or eleven out of the forty-seven villages possess a caste that is a numerical majority; some of these would be numerically superior but not dominant, since Schwartzberg (1968) points out that numbers are an imperfect indicator of dominance. In the traditional caste region described by Miller (1954:411), there was no majority dominant caste: the highest caste, the Nambudiri Brahmans, constituted about 1 percent of the population; the ruling castes, Samantans and Kshatriyas, were "small"; and the Hindu "middle class," Nayars, comprised about 20 percent. Brahmans, rulers, and upper subcastes of the Nayars were linked by marriage, presumably jointly forming a ruling stratum.

There are grave unresolved problems in this matter of caste dominance, not the least of which are the lack of caste demographic data and knowledge of the boundaries of caste systems (Bailey 1963). How Schwartzberg's regions, subregions, and districts, for example, correlate with the boundaries of caste systems is a moot point. Even more uncertain is the extent to which recent studies present a picture that is representative of pre-Muslim India. But insofar as available materials allow for extrapolation, any dominant caste—whether of village, district, kingdom, or region—that was in a position to patronize writing about the past was quite likely to have been a numerical minority, and hence a sort of hereditary nobility.

In sum, traditional Hindu India possessed an ideology essentially at odds with the notion of social mobility (except between rebirths). But social mobility occurred. Mobility was generally masked in such a way as to maintain or conform with the ideology and was often group mobility rather than individual mobility. Yet the ponderous mobility of a group is surely equivalent to a considerable amount of individual mobility. Finally, it must be kept in mind that the ideology of caste allocates rank on conventional, ritual, or cultural grounds and to some extent ignores, or fails to correlate with, material considerations of rank. On purely material bases—the extent of one's holdings or the number of one's wives or mistresses—individuals may have risen and fallen in rank at rates similar to those of noncaste societies. But because these matters were not of much concern to Hindu India's ideologues, and above all because the relevant historical materials for old Hindu India are either absent or untapped for this purpose, we cannot easily compare rates of social mobility between Hindu India and any other culture area. Suffice it to say that no study has shown that rates of mobility were as high in India as in China or in modern Western societies, and no one has even suggested that they were higher.

Social Mobility: Kashmir

Judgments on the matter of caste in Kashmir are contradictory. For example, Kaul (1967:7) thought that Kalhana, the author of the Kashmir
chronicle, "lived at a time when Hindu religion and culture assumed a
highly conventional form. Classes and castes had long been crystallized."
But Kaul (1967:41) noted that in the same and immediately preceding
periods intercaste marriages were the "order of the day in Kashmir." By
contrast, Saxena (1974:283) reviewed the same data from the same period
in Kashmir and found that "caste regulations were never followed scru-
pulously." Certainly many elements of caste were present in old Kashmir,
and Sudarshan Kumar (1969) points them out in some detail. Like Saxena,
she too noted that the caste system was not rigid in Kalhana's Kashmir,
but she thought it was not rigid elsewhere in India at that time either.
Finally, insofar as there is a connection between Brahmanism and caste,
it is relevant to note that various Kashmiri kings—from the seventh to
the twelfth centuries—took harsh actions against Brahmans and temples
(Kosambi 1955).

There are two good reasons for expecting that caste took an attenuated
form in Kashmir. First, the area is on the periphery of the Hindu world
and is somewhat physically isolated too. Second, until the fifth century
A.D. Kashmir was an important center of Buddhism. Since the Kashmir
chronicle itself appears to be the principal document on old Kashmir, I
turned to it for further light on the matter.

One of the first relevant points to emerge was the impact of Buddhism.
Although to a large degree amalgamated with Hinduism, Buddhist belief,
ritual, and institutions were still important in Kalhana's Kashmir. Kalhana,
though he was a Brahman, had been deeply influenced by Buddhism, was
knowledgeable concerning its doctrines, and was sympathetic to its support
(Stein 1961). Thus it was not out of character for him to state the priority
of merit over descent: "In truth, the character of the great does by no
means conform to the place of their birth" (Kalhana 1961:I, 123). Not only
did Kalhana show a sound knowledge of human nature, he was also
outspoken in his judgments of character, even of the most highly placed.
As Stein (1961:21) noted, these were among features that "show us Kalhana
in a very different light from that of the ordinary Indian Kavi [poet]." On
the other hand, Kalhana could also resort to explaining individuals' fortunes
by their descent. While it cannot thus be said that Kalhana was opposed

to Hindu ideals, his own were complicated in a direction consonant with Buddhism's emphasis on individual merit, a direction favorable to the development of sound historiography.

In addition to the evidence of Kalhana's character, his chronicle provides considerable direct evidence for vertical social mobility in old Kashmir. Miscaste marriages were common, though usually hypergamous and hence not necessarily different from marriage patterns elsewhere in India. But one ruler not only took an Untouchable (of the Domba caste) as a concubine, he ultimately elevated her to be chief queen, and her relatives rose to positions of power (Kalhana 1961:I; Stein 1961). Hypogamy occurred too (Stein 1961). Stein (1961) comments on how common the theme of upward mobility is, but some of the cases merely involved improved fortune for persons born to high caste. He also notes that the position of feudal landlord (Damara), very prominent in Kashmiri politics, appeared to be achievable.

Germane to this pattern of mobility, the period preceding and up to the time in which Kalhana wrote "was for Kashmir one long period of civil war and political dissolution" (Stein 1961:17). Accordingly, conditions were favorable for the meteoric rise of dynasties, families, and individuals mentioned by Kalhana. Not all the mobility was upward, either; Kalhana's father, for example, apparently fell from a high post as a consequence of the fall of one of Kashmir's more spectacular kings (Stein 1961:17).

Interpreting the evidence for social mobility, however, raises a disturbing question: How can the evidence be compared with the rest of Hindu India? Since there is no really comparable work that describes conditions elsewhere in Hindu India in pre-Muslim times, no easy comparison can be made. Moreover, a casual glance at modern histories of other parts of Hindu India in the pre-Muslim period shows the serious difficulty involved in ascertaining the degree of social mobility. Such histories, based largely on sacred texts, epigraphy, archaeology, and foreign sources, lack the necessary detail (for a handy comparison, see Ray 1973, and for a more detailed history, Nilakantra Sastri 1955). Hence it cannot be shown conclusively that rates of social mobility were exceptionally high in Kashmir.

A further consideration is the possible impact of Islam on Kashmir and Kalhana. Although Kashmir was secure in its inaccessible valley, Muslim forces had swept through nearby parts of India by the time Kalhana was writing. Muslim captains were employed by the same king under whom Kalhana's father had enjoyed high office (Stein 1961). There was thus some opportunity for a person as literate and well placed as Kalhana to pick up ideas of historiography from Muslim sources, though there is no direct evidence that this was the case.

In conclusion, de facto social mobility was perhaps as high in Kashmir as anywhere in ancient India. Kalhana, if not other Kashmiris, had been appropriately equipped by Buddhism to see and investigate the relationship between individual character and historical events (Thapar 1978 also asserts that Buddhism may have contributed to Kalhana's historical-mindedness). Furthermore, there may have been Muslim models of historiography to guide Kalhana. Hence the Kashmir chronicle is one of those exceptions that prove a rule, though I readily concede that the absence of sound data on social mobility in Hindu India leaves part of the argument in an uncertain state.

Social Mobility: Sri Lanka

For two millennia Sri Lanka has been a bulwark of Buddhism of the Sinhalese form (named after the island's principal linguistic group). As noted earlier, the chronicles upon which Sri Lanka's historiographic reputation rests were written by Buddhist monks and grew out of historiographic interests focused not only on the island but more narrowly on the Sangha, the Buddhist monastic order.

Ideologically, Buddhism is neutral toward caste, considering it irrelevant (de Silva 1981). The Buddha is credited with belittling the Brahmans on many occasions, saying, for example, "No man is by birth an outcaste and by deeds is one a Brahmin" (Ryan 1953:33; Wagle 1966). Accordingly, the Sangha (whose members formed the highest stratum in Sinhalese society) was not originally the monopoly of any caste and may even have been open to Untouchables (Ryan 1953; Yalman 1967). Monks advanced within their order on the basis of individual merit, as did the officials appointed by the king (Marriott and Inden 1981; Ryan 1953). Many modern Sri Lankans, even villagers, interpret the Buddha's teachings as anticaste: "Caste is not of the Buddha, it is of the Kings" (quoted in Ryan 1953:34; see also Yalman 1967).

In fact, caste exists among the Sinhalese and has various links with Buddhism. But while ideologically defended in various ways, caste was largely a secular matter (Pieris 1956). Very little is known about early Sinhalese social organization, although Sinhalese myth traces caste to hoary antiquity (Pieris 1956; Ryan 1953). Inscriptions mention one or another caste in the twelfth century and earlier. Late in that century a number of inscriptions ridicule the aspirations of the caste that has now long been the superior one (de Silva 1981). A work that dates from perhaps as early as the fifteenth century lists the island's castes (Ryan 1953), but most of the useful information dates from more recent periods. The earliest substantial account dates from the late seventeenth century, and it reports a fact of great importance for understanding Sinhalese caste: the highest caste (excluding, for the moment, royalty), the Goyigama (Cultivators), has comprised half or more of the population since the nineteenth century (de Silva 1981; Ryan 1953; Yalman 1960). Thus caste—depending upon the rate or appropriateness of within-caste mobility in the dominant caste—is reduced in its significance. This, as noted earlier, is a pattern that is not typical of Hindu India.

Yalman 1960 used case material from a Sinhalese community to illustrate the flexibility of caste. The community shows more flexibility than is typical of Hindu Indian communities. In particular, Yalman's comment, made elsewhere (1967:82), that he knows of "many instances" of passing (even if only between strata of Goyigama) strikes me as unusual. He shows a fair amount of mobility based on change of residence, change of name, self-invented titles, status as an outsider, and on ultimately accepted marriages above one's station.

De Silva (1981:148) says that the cultivators were subdivided into strictly endogamous subcastes: "there was considerable social mobility within the lower ranks" of the Goyigama, but the two highest subcastes, the *radala* and *mudali*, "formed the real aristocracy of the Kandyan kingdom, although the rest of the *goyigamas* were also considered honourable." De Silva says further that political power "tended to concentrate" in the upper subcastes and that some families of high subcaste held particular high offices for periods up to 150 years. Pieris (1956) also reports ranked endogamous subgroups within the Goyigama but gives little detail. What these remarks show is that there was a nobility of sorts, consisting of the *radala* and *mudali* subcastes, and perhaps of royalty too, since there was some intermarriage between these nobles and royalty.

Everyone seems to agree that beneath the Goyigama there was little consensus on relative rank, and hence considerable flexibility of stratification. Pieris (1956:176), for example, says that the system of castes "was far from being a clearly defined hierarchy in which the various castes were graded in an immutable order of precedence." Other factors also softened the effects of caste among the Sinhalese. The royal family claimed Kshatriya rank, but only the royal family made this claim (Seneviratne 1978). Sociologically, the royal caste was of no more significance than royalty in, say, modern Norway, unless royalty was somehow seen as part of a nobility. Within castes a family's rank is based more on the achievement of that family than on membership in ranked segments, for there is little development of subcaste segments (Ryan 1953, but cf. Seneviratne 1978). Castes rarely have a council to manage their affairs, and the "caste is seldom a unit of formal organization" (Ryan 1953:16; see also Yalman 1967). The theory of miscegenation to explain the origin of various castes—a theory that implicitly emphasizes hereditary principles—has almost no relevance to the Sinhalese, but this could also reflect a more rigorous insistence on marrying within one's caste (Ryan 1953). Untouchables have been all but absent in Sri Lanka (de Silva 1981).

Despite the Sinhalese notions of Buddhism's neutral or anticaste stance, Sinhalese normally explain their membership in one or another caste as the result of the merit they built up in previous lives: Sinhalese Buddhism embraces reincarnation (Ryan 1953). Also, despite what is believed about original Buddhism, the Sangha in Sri Lanka was at times a monopoly of the Goyigama caste (Ryan 1953). On the other hand, upwardly mobile castes in areas under European control challenged this monopoly early in the nineteenth century (de Silva 1981).

To summarize, Sinhalese Buddhism ideologically gives more attention to meritocracy than does Hinduism. Such caste organization as does exist is significantly different from Hindu caste in that the superior caste, the Goyigama, has long constituted the majority, or nearly so. An apparent nobility within the Goyigama has existed, at least at times, but may have had relatively little ideological basis. Instead of having hereditary Brahmans as allies of the nobles, the Sinhalese had openly recruited monks as the top stratum (assuming that the monks can be seen as part of society, a point discussed in Yalman 1967). The effects of caste were softened in other ways too. Actual rates of social mobility in Sri Lanka are little known—from any period—but the ideological contrast with Hindu India is clear, and there is some suggestion of greater flexibility of caste. The Sri Lankan chronicles therefore also present the sort of exception that supports the rule this work develops. With respect to the concomitants, however, there is no strong pattern of divergence from Hindu India.

CHINA

Historiography and Concomitants

For its combination of depth, comprehensiveness, accuracy, and continuity, Chinese historical writing has no peer (Gardner [1938] 1961; Pulleyblank 1961). The Chinese, Watson notes, are "among the most industrious recorders of change, the most indefatigable readers and writers of history ever known" (1958:vii). The Chinese—"the most historically minded of all peoples" (Pulleyblank 1961:135)—are so historically minded that for them history takes the place of myth (Pulleyblank and Beasley 1961). History was the "queen of the sciences" for the Chinese (Needham 1965). As we shall see, Chinese emphasis on history and de-emphasis of myth have long been accompanied by an egalitarian ideology buttressed with state institutions designed to facilitate meritocratic social placement.

Chinese historical writing apparently had its roots in ritual and divination—topics of perennial and serious concern in China (Gardner [1938] 1961; Keightley 1978; cf. van der Loon 1961; Watson 1958). Creel (1937) dates Chinese historical writings—for the instruction of the ruler—as far back as 1000 B.C. Others find the clear evidence somewhat later. Van der Loon (1961), for example, says that early scribes, with ritual or divinatory functions, provided the idea of chronology as early as 700 B.C. and that by about 400 B.C. a conscious historical tradition had emerged. Historical writing from this early period was concerned with statecraft (van der Loon 1961). Recently discovered sources support the earlier dates for a conscious historical tradition, possibly even before 1050 B.C. (see, e.g., Tsien 1962). Beginning in the eighth century B.C., the Chou dynasty gradually disintegrated and a series of lesser states emerged, each keeping its own archival records. The chronicle of one of these states was edited by Confucius (552–479 B.C.), and has been preserved under the name of the *Spring and Autumn Annals*. Around the end of the fourth century B.C. an unknown compiler prepared another chronicle from the archives of three other states, and portions of this chronicle—commendable for their "objective detachment"—were subsequently appended to the *Spring and Autumn Annals*. Confucius was interested not so much in history as in practical politics: he sought to show the rewards of virtue and the dangers of evil. This "union of political morality with history" had long-term consequences for Chinese historiography (Gardner [1938] 1961:13).

While the *Spring and Autumn Annals* are an important source of information on China's "feudal" period, "the moral significance of the work outweighs its . . . historical aspect" (Gardner [1938] 1961:13; see also Watson 1958). This cannot be said of the *Records of the Historian* (Ssu-ma 1961) by Ssu-ma T'an and Ssu-ma Ch'ien (c. 145–85 B.C.), father and son, court astrologers (Gardner [1938] 1961). This was "the first general history of China," and it marked the beginning of "a systematic historiography capable of transmitting the experience of statecraft" (van der Loon 1961:29). It was also "an act of pure imaginative creation equal to any we know in world literature" (Kierman 1962:1). Ssu-ma Ch'ien gave his father credit for envisioning the project, but subsequent authorities attribute the work largely to the son, who is generally regarded as the founder of Chinese historiography. Burton Watson says that the Western historian Ssu-ma Ch'ien most resembles is Tacitus, a comparison that puts them both in good company indeed (Ssu-ma 1961:I, 8). Watson's comments elsewhere (Ssu-ma 1969:3–4) on the similarity between Ssu-ma Ch'ien and Western historians, and the reasons therefore, deserve full quotation:

The exploits of mankind being basically much the same in any age or clime, the English reader, I expect, will find little in Ssu-ma Ch'ien's account of the Han dynasty that is not already familiar to him from the history of the Classical West. Indeed, Ssu-ma Ch'ien's whole approach to history—his concern with the didactic import of his story, his emphasis upon the life and importance of the individual, his skepticism and relative lack of interest in the supernatural—shows a striking similarity to that of the historians of ancient Greece and Rome.

If human affairs are as uniform as Watson suggests, and if historians so widely spaced as Ssu-ma Ch'ien and his near-contemporaries in the West agree so much on how to record, analyze, or present those affairs, it is all the more curious that people such as the Hindu Indians did not.

The *Records of the Historian* is a prose work of more than 500,000 words divided into 130 chapters, and it covers Chinese history from its beginnings until the first century B.C. Though present-day versions are missing at least one chapter, and several other chapters appear to be incomplete, by any standard this is a remarkable degree of preservation (Ssu-ma 1961:I). The work is divided into five major parts. Two are annalistic in form and consist of imperial annals and the annals of various hereditary local ruling houses. A third part consists of tables—of "The Three Ancient Dynasties," of "The Twelve Feudal States," of "The Six Warring Kingdoms," and of "The Han Princely Houses," for example—that are partly genealogies and partly lists of dated successions to high ministerial offices. Listing officers was an innovation, as was an attempt at synchronization of the chronologies of the various small states. A fourth part, and also a novel element, comprises eight treatises on technical topics, all concerned with the institutional or political economic concerns that were important to imperial administration. Each treatise is chronologically ordered. The final part, which was also largely new, consists primarily of a large number of memoirs or biographies. Included in this part are descriptions of non-Chinese peoples and their environments. The biographies are lively but are full of speeches that surely did not come from documentary sources. It is considered likely that the biographies had some sort of predecessors in novelistic or oral traditions about great men. It is also possible that this section, and Ssu-ma Ch'ien's good prose, stimulated the later development of the novel (Fehl 1964; Hulsewé 1961; van der Loon 1961; Twitchett 1961; Watson 1958; see also de Bary's foreword to Ssu-ma 1961:I).

Although Ssu-ma Ch'ien composed most of his work while a private citizen, he set a standard copied for centuries by official historians. When the first of the "standard histories," the *History of the Former Han Dynasty* (Pan Ku [first c.] 1938), was written, it copied the *Records of the Historian*, dropping only the section on local ruling houses. This section and the tables were rarely employed again. The treatises were also sometimes dropped, but the annals and biographies remained standard for two millennia. However, whereas all the standard histories were written after the fall of a dynasty, Ssu-ma Ch'ien was unique in writing of his dynasty at its peak (Han 1955; Hulsewé 1961; van der Loon 1961; Yang, Lien-sheng 1961).

Ssu-ma Ch'ien's purposes in writing his history were to honor his father and to rescue the worthy from oblivion, but also to record the consequences of degradation and, so far as the record permitted, to write a comprehensive history of the Chinese people. He adhered to a standard of "objective detachment" (Gardner [1938] 1961:17) and was even capable of criticizing his own emperor (Hulsewé 1961). While the moral emphasis of his writing is clear, he was also a "political realist" with an interest in economics (Hulsewé 1961:42). Implicitly, he believed in the educative value of history (Hulsewé 1961). Although both he and his father had been Grand Astrologers for the court, Ssu-ma Ch'ien had a sufficient degree of skepticism to satirize its superstitions (Gardner [1938] 1961).

Before turning to later developments in Chinese historiography, I will note that economics, political science, and social thought had their beginnings in the same period as did historical writing. Thus the collected

works of Han Fei Tzu (d. 233 B.C.) have been published with the subtitle
A Classic of Chinese Political Science (Han 1959), though they and other
works of the time might more properly be called political philosophy. Han
was one of the founders of the Legalist school of Chou times, which
advocated "a strong central government, the suppression of feudalism, and
the regimentation of the people by stern and inflexible laws" (Burton
Watson in Ssu-ma 1961:I, 312; see also Bodde and Morris 1967). Watson
goes on to say that much of China's subsequent political thought pitted
the Legalists against the Confucianists, who advocated "government by
virtue" (Ssu-ma 1961:I, 313). As for economics, Pan Ku et al.'s *Food and
Money in Ancient China: The Earliest Economic History of China to A.D. 25*
([first c.] 1974), translated primarily from a treatise in the official history
of the earlier Han Dynasty but including a chapter from the *Records of the
Historian,* had "no counterpart in Western history, either in content or in
design" (Pan [et al.] 1974:vii). Its contents are described as: "what one
might expect in official reports of a planned society—accounts of 'ever
normal granaries,' changes in agricultural technique, man power shortages,
price-fixing, taxation, changes in coinage, et cetera. These are recounted
as episodes, and their substance and tone are thoroughly modern" (Pan
[et al.] 1974:vii). The treatise covers a period from about the twelfth century
B.C. to A.D. 25. Of the twenty-two subsequent official histories, half of
them included similar treatises to cover their respective periods (Pan [et
al.] 1974).

As for early evidence of social science, Radcliffe-Brown (1952), for example, gave Hsun Tzu (third century B.C.) credit for a sociological analysis
of the functions of religious ritual. From as early as the fifth century B.C.
the Chinese worked with a "highly scientific" version of social history,
including by the first century a grasp of the technological significance of
the stone, bronze, and iron ages (Needham 1965). Chang (1977:1) traces
an "archaeology of sorts" to the works of Han Fei Tzu. The high points
in the development of the human sciences in a historical framework came
much later in the T'ang (618–907) and Sung (960–1126) dynasties, and
will be described below.

As noted earlier, the official history of the Earlier Han, written in the
first century A.D., began a series of official histories the last of which was
written in this century. As time went by, the official histories relied more
heavily on written documentation and often took on more of a scissors-
and-paste form (van der Loon 1961). In spite of the increasingly rigid form
of the standard histories, two mitigating factors were at work: unofficial

history was also written (see, e.g., H. Franke 1961) and the official histories, for all their dryness, were based on a daily or nearly daily set of records of the court—the "Diaries of Activity and Repose." The diaries, which grew out of the records of astrologers, may have been kept from as early as the Chou Dynasty (1050–249 B.C.) but at any rate were consulted as early as the composition of the official history of the Later Han dynasty (A.D. 25–220). In the Later Han the work of the astrologers came to an end, and scholars were appointed as official historians. Later, in T'ang times (seventh century A.D.), the Bureau of Historiography was established, and it lasted until 1911 (W. Franke 1961; Gardner [1938] 1961; Hulsewé 1961; Twitchett 1961). Both modern Chinas, as well as such agencies as the party and the army, have reinstituted bureaus of historiography.

Toward the end of the Later Han dynasty a somewhat unusual "official" history, the *Han-chi*, was composed by Hsün Yüeh (A.D. 148–209). It was official in the sense that it was commissioned by the emperor to review the merit of the Han Dynasty when its opponents were threatening to pull it down (Ch'en 1975), but its format was novel. It is essentially a commentary on Pan Ku's *Han-shu*, the first official history. It is not a mere apologia. Of thirty-nine discourses (*lun*) in the *Han-chi*, thirty-four contain "strictures . . . aimed against the Han throne," and the work as a whole deals with topics so politically sensitive that they were generally tabooed in the official histories (Ch'en 1975:95). The unusually frank discourses were described by Hsün Yüeh as his "own comment which gives a summary evaluation of or provides broad perspective to an important event" (quoted in Ch'en 1975:96). According to Ch'en,

It is Hsün Yüeh who seems to have become the first conscious commentator on historical events themselves by developing the *lun* discourses into a specific genre. After Hsün Yüeh, comment or critique . . . on historical events . . . was much in vogue; authoritative personal comments or evaluation of past events . . . became an important genre in traditional Chinese historiography. (1975:97)

Hsün's comments were made on the Earlier Han, but it was clear that the lessons he drew were applicable to the Later Han as well (Ch'en 1975).

In the longest of his discourses, Hsün set forth his views on the "complex factors determining the outcome of historical events, . . . classified . . . into three broad categories: general conditions, specific situations, and the state of mind" (Ch'en 1980:36). His purpose was to assess the utility of past history for predicting the future and thereby to develop appropriate policies or strategies. He gave many examples of the combinations of the three factors, and since it appeared that all events were unique, he was led to state "the futility of using history to predict the future" (Ch'en 1980:36; Ch'en 1975). However, Hsün did not fall into the trap of all-or-nothing thinking. He thus wrote that "there are those who see something which cannot be changed [by man] and say that man's effort cannot change anything; there are those who see something which can be changed [by man] and say that nothing is destined" (brackets in Ch'en 1980:90). Neither position was Hsün's. "[I]nstead of abjectly describing the overwhelming power of fate, Hsün Yüeh delved into the subtleties of its encounters with man's individual will and abilities" (Ch'en 1980:45). In the end, Hsün advises the "superior man" to "exert his mental power to the utmost and then resign the rest to fate"; he thus "affirmed both the importance and the limitation of human knowledge and action" (Ch'en 1980:37). Hsün's views have very close parallels among his contemporaries in the West and among Renaissance historians. Adding to the parallels is Hsün's use of fictitious dialogue to explore questions of policy or interpretation. One such dialogue explicitly deals with the dangers of hereditary office for the unity of the state (Ch'en 1975).

Ch'en (1975:94) divides Chinese historians into "dogmatists," who looked back to the ancient canonical literature, and "realists," who "reflected upon the changing world in the recent past." Hsün was a realist who saw clearly that the past and the present were different, and he freed historiography from reliance on the classics (Ch'en 1975, 1980). He also advocated an unusually broad view of the scope of history: "all the deeds of men, from the emperor to the masses, for better or worse, should be put on record" (Ch'en 1975:161).

In addition to the *Han-chi*, Hsün later wrote the *Shen-chien* (Extended reflections), at present comprising five chapters of "reflective essays." Two of the chapters, entitled "The Essence of Government" and "Current Affairs," clearly carry over from problems addressed in the *Han-chi* (Ch'en 1975, 1980). Just as his *lun* discourses established a new genre, so his *chien* (mirror) stimulated many similar works. His works received high marks in China until the middle of the T'ang dynasty, after which his qualified advocacy of feudalism became repugnant (Ch'en 1975).

In the four centuries after the collapse of the Han dynasty, China was not unified, but in spite of these conditions, historical writing continued to flourish. There was much nonofficial biography and an emphasis more on individual character than on official career (Twitchett 1961). In the third century, history had been established as a distinct branch of learning, and in the fourth century, schools of history were established in both the northern and southern dynasties (Pulleyblank 1961).

Although historians from Ssu-ma Ch'ien onward commented at least sporadically on their own work, Liu Chih-chi (A.D. 661–721) was the first to write a treatise on historiography, possibly the first such work in any language (Pulleyblank 1961). Liu set forth three standards for rejecting material: internal inconsistency, inconsistency with more reliable sources, and inherent impossibility. He criticized Ssu-ma Ch'ien for employing a supernatural explanation of the fall of a state: "When one discusses the rise and fall of states one ought certainly to take human affairs as the essential; if one must bring fate into one's discourse then reason is outraged" (Pulleyblank 1961:145). He identified "deliberate twisting or concealment" as the principal source of error in historical materials (Pulleyblank 1961:147). Finally, Liu employed a more individualistic psychology than was typical of most Chinese historians and criticized the use of high-flown language in the fictitious speeches of persons not likely to have used such language (Pulleyblank 1961). Joseph Needham (1965:12) ranks Liu with Jean Bodin and L. V. de la Popeliniere, whose sixteenth-century writings were the first in the West "to lay the foundation for a method and critique of history." Liu Chih-chi's son, Liu Chih, and another T'ang historian, Tu Yu, introduced encyclopedic institutional histories, the former's called *Governmental Institutes*, the latter's *Comprehensive Institutes: A Reservoir of Source Material on Political and Social History*.

After Liu Chih-chi, the next major historiographical advance was the work of Ssu-ma Kuang, who lived in the eleventh century during the Northern Sung dynasty. His *Comprehensive Mirror for Aid in Government* chronicled Chinese history from 403 B.C. to A.D. 959 and achieved a stature alongside of Ssu-ma Ch'ien's *Records of the Historian* (Pulleyblank 1961). Ssu-ma Kuang attempted to make his criteria for inclusion and exclusion as objective as possible, he adhered to his criteria, and he then published them so that they might come under public scrutiny (Pulleyblank 1961). For this reason, "Ssu-ma Kuang was certainly a scientific historian, since he first tried to establish the truth on objective grounds. The most impressive thing, of course, is that he insisted on reasons being explicitly given" (Pulleyblank 1961:157–58).

One of the persistent features of Chinese historical writing was the insistence that history teaches lessons. Bodde (1967:224) gives examples of lessons being drawn from history by Li Ssu, the Grand Counselor to China's first emperor, and notes the "extreme frequency" of the practice among the Chinese. Most frequently, perhaps, the lessons were moral, giving rise to what has been called "moral didacticism"—the ideal that history should teach moral lessons, that the praiseworthy should be praised and the evil receive censure. Moral didacticism is generally viewed as something less than scientific. But the idea that lessons should and could be drawn from history had its sounder side too, in what Robert M. Hartwell has called "historical analogism":

Historical analogism was a logical extension of moral didacticism, and elements of both approaches can be found in works of most Chinese historians. . . . [But in the T'ang and Sung dynasties, when historians] substituted environment and continuous and cumulative institutional change for morality and a static and absolute utopian antiquity, they laid the basis for a shift of the focus of didactic historiography from the ethics of the individual to the operation of social institutions. This gave rise to the view that the comparative study of similar historical phenomena could provide an accurate guide in evaluating contemporary policy. . . .

From the eighth through the thirteenth centuries, emperors, statesmen, and historians avowed that history provides the means to understand the success and failure of different forms of governmental organization, the rise and fall of dynasties, the evolution and transformation of laws and institutions, the advantage and injury resulting from specific measures, and the nature of human behavior. (Hartwell 1971:694–95)

For the practical purposes of administration, in short, Chinese history was no less social science—and for a considerable period. Political science or statecraft was its main element (Balazs 1964), but economics was only slightly less important. For example, Ssu-ma Kuang's *Comprehensive Mirror*, after describing a particular set of factions, goes on to provide a short treatise on the "causes and effects of bureaucratic factionalism" (Hartwell 1971:701). In an eleventh-century work on politics, its author employed something close to the experimental method in testing a proposition in political economy. His "test" consisted of setting forth historical episodes in which particular conditions were followed by the consequences he "predicted" (Hartwell 1971:720). Hartwell (1971:721–22) also notes the extensive use of statistics in Chinese historiography and the "close relationship between mathematics and economics from very early times," adding that "controlled observation and even experiment were not lacking in Chinese social analysis."

Hartwell places the development of social science in China in the context of the larger development of science in general. He argues that Chinese science had only one serious shortcoming: the absence of a formal system of logic, such as that which was found early in the West, as in Euclidean geometry. Without formal logic the Chinese could not develop "the habit of framing generalizations in a hypothetical-deductive form" (1971:722; see also Fung 1952; but cf. Needham 1963, 1965). As Needham (1954–) has persuasively shown, considerable technological and scientific advances did take place in China, but Hartwell (1971) argues that inductive procedures alone would have forced them to take millennia to do what the West has done in the last three to four centuries. There are, of course, other reasons given for why Chinese science and technology progressed rapidly for a while and then stagnated (see, e.g., Elvin 1973). But the important point here is that the development of a more scientific historiography in China was to some degree connected with developments in technology and science in general.

During the several centuries when historical analogism pushed moral didacticism into the background, government patronage was an important factor. From the eighth through the thirteenth centuries, historical problems were standard elements in bureaucratic examinations, and historians played an important role in the education of the ruler. A substantial portion of the "policy questions" in the imperial examinations "required the examinee to use historical models in proposing solutions to contemporary problems" (Hartwell 1971:705). The education of the emperor had long been a matter of great concern, but the establishment in 1033 of the "imperial seminar," in which the ruling emperor participated, gave historians direct access to the emperor and influence over policy decisions. In the Sung dynasty (960–1279), an "imperial policy chronicle" "represented the most ambitious attempt to adapt historical writing to the needs of policy makers" (Hartwell 1971:710).

Except perhaps for a brief barren period at the end of the Northern Sung (which ended in 1126), historical writing was generally good during the Sung, a period of rationalistic criticism of received thought (Hartwell 1971; Pulleyblank and Beasley 1961). In the Yuan dynasty (1260–1368), during which Mongols ruled China, the official histories of the preceding dynasties were compiled largely by Chinese, and they maintained a credible standard (H. Franke 1974). The encyclopedic institutional histories pioneered in the T'ang reached their highest development in the Yuan, in Ma Tuan-lin's *Comprehensive Study of the History of Civilization*. In 348 chapters it presents "a general history of institutions, which, together with the social structures and economic situations implied by them, seemed to

Ma a much more important form of history than any chronological catalogue of contingent events" (Needham 1965:12). Needham (1965) considers Ma's work comparable, at least in aim, with the sociological histories of Ibn Khaldun and Montesquieu. Ma was unusual in the extent to which he examined differences of opinion, criticized original sources, and expressed his own opinions (Balazs 1964).

In the Ming period, it has been argued, intellectual activity in general—including historical writing—declined somewhat, giving way to neo-Confucian metaphysical matters; and when the Ming collapsed, historiography reached "new heights" of rigor and objectivity (Hartwell 1971; Pulleyblank and Beasley 1961). De Bary (1959:34, 42) argues that neo-Confucian thought retained an emphasis on historical mindedness (and on humanism and rationalism), though its emphasis was on the earlier, "scriptural" texts and on ethical matters. Wolfgang Franke (1968) says that the Ming, while not strikingly innovative, pushed the general standards of Chinese historiography to new heights both qualitatively and quantitatively. Writing in the subsequent Ching dynasty, Chang Hsüeh-Ch'eng, author of two eighteenth-century works on the theory of history, has been likened to Ibn Khaldun and Vico. According to Demiéville, "the permanent and universal value of his work lies in his profound reflection on the theory of history, its methods, its ideological background" (1961:169; see also Han 1955).

In the course of the development of Chinese historical writing, its genres proliferated. A seventh-century classification found thirteen kinds, and subsequent authorities found from ten to eighteen. Combining all these classifications, Han (1955) finds twenty-seven varieties of historical writing. Gardner ([1938] 1961:100–104) presents the classification from an eighteenth-century work as the "final and most detailed." It included the following types: "standard histories," "annals," "narratives from beginning to end" (each treating a single subject or period), "separate" and "miscellaneous histories" (a residual category), collections of state papers, "biographical memoirs," "contemporaneous records" (accounts of concurrent illegitimate Chinese states and neighboring states), "chronography," "geography" (a major division, comprising all forms of local history), "functions and offices" (on the evolution of official nomenclature and functions), "treatises on government" (an "important series of compilations which set forth comprehensively the fabric of governmental machinery under successive dynasties"), bibliography and epigraphy, and "historical criticism."

In addition to the technical development manifest in this multiplication of genres, other strengths of Chinese historiography should be noted. First among them is the clearly enunciated ideal of objectivity: "an assumption of complete objectivity underlies the whole Chinese conception of historical writing" (Gardner [1938] 1961:17). Closely related was the stern ideal of recording the truth regardless of the consequences (Han 1955). These ideals were rarely openly challenged but were not always maintained (see, e.g., W. Franke 1961). To the permanent horror of the Chinese, the first emperor to unify China ordered, in 213 B.C., the burning of all books that he deemed subversive to his new order. But as quickly as the Ch'in dynasty collapsed in 206 B.C., Chinese scholars embarked on a so-far endless attempt to recover the lost works, one fruit of which was highly developed textual criticism.

Gardner ([1938] 1961) argues that the Chinese were not inferior to Western historians in textual criticism and in fact employed techniques similar to those in West. These included side commentaries, similar to footnotes, employed certainly by the tenth century and probably very much earlier; the establishment of the filiation of texts; the exploitation of textual anachronisms; careful and exhaustive bibliographic compilations stretching over nearly 2,000 years; and "respect for established texts and scrupulous fidelity in their reproduction," which was greatly aided from the tenth century onward by the introduction of block printing (Gardner [1938] 1961:44; Han 1955). In the preparation of those state documents that were to become primary historical sources, the Chinese showed great care (Gardner [1938] 1961).

Two further strengths that have already been alluded to deserve further comment. One is the extraordinary quantity of local historical materials: "China possesses by all odds the finest and most complete series of local records in the world" (Gardner [1938] 1961:15). Geography and history were combined in the composition of local history, which had its own super-visory official historian, and was of vital concern to the economy and defense of the empire (Han 1955). There is at least one local history for "every province, prefecture, and sub-prefecture of the empire, and for almost every district, or even village of importance" (Gardner [1938] 1961:102).

Second is the considerable amount of Chinese biography. About half of each standard history is devoted to biography (Gardner [1938] 1961), "while the collections of specialized biographies of various kinds and entries in Local Gazetteers bring the total to an enormous figure" (Twitchett 1961:95). I emphasize this strength because Chinese biography is often cited as a weakness in Chinese accounts of the past. The weakness is qualitative rather than quantitative. Chinese biography reveals little of the private life of individuals and often omits such matters as date of birth. This weakness should not be overemphasized: from the perspective of the West, Chinese biography may indeed seem shallow and stereotyped, but from the viewpoint of India surely Chinese biography is decidedly rich. From a strictly quantitative viewpoint, I wonder if the Chinese had not, until modern times, rescued as many named individuals from oblivion as had the West.

A related problem is that the Chinese emphasis on objectivity often pushed even the author of a history into the distant background. Many writings lack much in the way of a commentary by the author (H. Franke 1961; Gardner [1938] 1961; Han 1955). At times, of course, Chinese histories did not have an author in the usual sense but rather were the product of bureaucratic efforts extending over decades.

Causation and gradual change were often only weakly grasped, so that many histories were more like compilations of primary sources than synthetic compositions (Balazs 1964; Gardner [1938] 1961; Pulleyblank 1961; cf. Needham 1965). In spite of stern ideals, most treatments of living emperors were highly circumspect, and reports of military setbacks, for example, were not likely to be initially presented in a forthright manner (Gardner [1938] 1961). Historical criticism—in the sense of "the evaluation of individual statements contained in established texts"—was not very highly developed, the Chinese not generally employing, for example, the notion of probability (Gardner [1938] 1961:64; but cf. Pulleyblank 1961, and Balazs 1964 on Ma Tuan-lin). Although no barrier to absolute chronology (Needham 1965), Chinese dating systems were cumbersome (Gardner [1938] 1961). Finally, Chinese historians rarely provided references, or bibliographies of the works they had consulted (Gardner [1938] 1961; but cf. Balazs 1964 on bibliography as a standard monographic subject). Bear in mind that many of these deficiencies are deficiencies only from the viewpoint of quite modern historiographic standards, and many of the deficiencies, as shown by the examples given above, were absent in the better products of Chinese historical thought.

The reduced stature of mythology in China's view of the past is as unique as its intense historical-mindedness. Ancient China had myths, but we have no sound evidence that it possessed a "systematic *mythology*, meaning by this an integrated body of mythological materials" (Bodde 1961:370). Literature prior to the Han dynasty (i.e., before 206 B.C.), says Bodde (1961:376), lacked "any separate genre which might be called myth," and "within any single literary work it is not easy to find a myth recorded in consecutive entirety." The reason for this state of affairs seems to have been a systematic process of euhemerization, which in this case refers to "the transformation of what were once myths and gods into seemingly authentic history and human beings" (Bodde 1961:372). Quoting Henri Maspero, Bodde (1961:372–73) adds that "Chinese scholars have never known more than one way of interpreting legendary accounts, that of euhemerization"; they thus stripped away what they could not believe and thereby transformed "gods and heroes . . . into sage emperors and sage ministers, and monsters into rebellious princes or evil ministers." The result was hardly history, but it conformed to the intense rationalism of Chinese thought.

This process was already recognized, and viewed with skepticism, in the Chou dynasty (c. 1027–221 B.C.), as shown by amusing accounts of how Confucius attempted to explain to his followers the "real" meaning of certain improbable accounts of the past (Bodde 1961). Bodde counts these stories about Confucius as apocryphal but considers it no accident that Confucius is their butt: "For it is precisely the Confucianists who . . . were historically minded and assumed prime responsibility for conserving and editing ancient texts. . . . [T]heir strong humanism tended to make them either indifferent toward supernatural matters, or to seek to explain them in purely rationalistic terms. The results have been disastrous for the preservation of early Chinese myth" (1961:375). Even the Taoists, with "their greater interest in popular beliefs," provide only a somewhat better preservation of myth, because of their preference for natural rather than supernatural explanations (Bodde 1961:375). Such mythology as has persisted into modern times in China is to a large extent the result of borrowing, in part from Buddhism and in part from the many peoples absorbed by the Han Chinese during the spread of their civilization (Bodde 1961). The distinctive and original mythology of the Han Chinese exists today only in fragments.

As for Chinese portraiture, the situation is similar to biography. Chinese portrait art has a long and distinguished history. However, the Chinese artist attached no great importance to achieving a precise physical likeness of his subject, seeking rather to represent the inner spirit or essence of the individual portrayed. Only in the case of ancestral portraits was an attempt made at accurate physical representation, and these works were not considered art; many, in fact, were combinations of stock types of noses, eyes, and other features (Lancman 1966). The antiquity of Chinese attempts at portraiture—or at any rate their sense of individual differences—may readily be seen in the life-size figurines found at the site of the tomb of the

Ch'in emperor, the first to unify China (Hearn 1979). Each figure, and there are thousands of them, appears to have a distinct visage. However, it may be that, like the ancestral portraits, these faces are actually products of the many combinations made possible by combining relatively small numbers of fixed components. Whatever the case, Chinese portraiture is a larger and more realistic art form than its counterpart in India, though it is considerably less realistic than the better examples of Western portraiture.

Individualism has never been strongly developed in China, but it may have been stronger there than in India. The matter is discussed rather theoretically in Moore 1968, where Indian and Chinese philosophers all seem to find ample arguments for individualism in their traditional cultures. I find the Chinese arguments (especially in Hsieh 1968 and Mei 1968) somewhat more convincing, but their evidence does not add much to what has been or will be discussed under such headings as biography and social mobility. I find the Indian arguments less convincing, for various reasons. One is that the Indian defenses of individualism rely heavily on the doctrine of *karma*: that the individual reaps the rewards and punishments of his behavior in previous lives—whether born a Brahman or an Untouchable, he is getting what he has earned. This is supernatural individualism. Another is that the Indians tend to find the evidence for Indian individualism in a poorly documented past or in heterodox religions. Moreover, the Indians specifically state that the caste system was antithetical to individualism (see, e.g., Dasgupta 1968 and Saksena 1968).

I have already mentioned Chinese divination, noting its link to early Chinese historical writing: the title of Ssu-ma T'an and Ssu-ma Ch'ien, for example, is alternately given as Grand Astrologer or Grand Historian. It is curiously fitting that the first true history of the Chinese can be composed from inscriptions they incised on bone and shell for purposes of divination (Keightley 1978). At the time of the infamous book burnings in the first unified China, books on astrology were among the few categories exempted (Bodde 1967). There is scarcely a general work on Chinese culture or history that does not mention divination: it was important to kings and to the lowly too, though intellectuals were often skeptical of its utility. Given the generally rationalistic, secular tendencies of Chinese civilization, this concern for divination is as suspicious as India's relative unconcern. The Chinese passion for divination is very well demonstrated by the Shang period (c. 1520–c. 1030 B.C.). Significantly, divination—or such divination as has left a good record—was particularly associated with kings and the elite (Keightley 1978). This suggests that the early Chinese kings may not have been considered divine. Chapter 4 presents the argument that divination was little developed in ancient Egypt, because the rulers were divinities: the divine do not need to divine. If this argument is correct, and if China's Bronze Age kings did divine, it follows that they were not themselves divine, or were only weakly so. Lack of divinity knocks a major prop from under royalty or nobility. This consideration in turn throws an interesting light on the Chinese notion that their early sage kings were not hereditary, and it strengthens Creel's argument (cited below) that even in the Chou period—which is generally considered to have been one of hereditary closure—the ideal of social mobility was by no means unknown.

In spite of all that has been written on Chinese divination, Keightley (1978) says that its social significance has yet to be studied. An exception to this is a study of Chinese body divination (Lessa 1968) that connects divination directly to social mobility. Lessa's argument is that social mobility generates anxiety and uncertainty—both abundantly generated by the examination system (Miyazaki 1976)—and that these two emotional states in turn generate an interest in divination. As shall be seen, social mobility was a prominent element in Chinese society and history.

Social Mobility

Homo aequalis—to use Dumont's term for the modern Western antithesis of India's *Homo hierarchicus*—was longer and more consistently at home in China than in the West (Munro 1969; cf. Dumont 1970a, 1977). In his study of *The Concept of Man in Early China* Munro (1969:1, 2) says that "what is unique about China is the agreement on all sides that men are naturally equal"; "opposition to hereditary privilege is the single theoretical position common to all the philosophical schools of the Warring States era" (481–211 B.C.). The idea of natural equality, Munro says, "is a central idea to any deep understanding of the Chinese world view" (1969:22).

Munro (1969:4) traces opposition to the hereditary principle to two factors: "a religious idea of the West Chou (1111–771 B.C.) and the changing social conditions of the Spring and Autumn [722–481 B.C.] and Warring States periods." The Chou house, when it overthrew the Shang dynasty (1766–1122 B.C.), espoused the idea that Heaven favored no particular branch of mankind but raised to the ruling position whichever person was virtuous. This was perhaps an expedient to legitimize the usurpation of the Chou, but it was an idea that took hold, and it received a wider interpretation: "Since Heaven was considered impartial, and since merit was the criterion for occupying the top position, one could infer that the same should hold true for all other positions" (Munro 1969:4). The changing social conditions that Munro cites include a progressive weakening of clan ties, the destruction of a great many aristocratic or noble clans through incessant warfare, the attendant opening of positions at the top that were necessarily filled by men from below, a growing recognition of the competitive efficiency gained by promoting men of proved merit, and the rise of a wealthy merchant class. By sometime between the fifth and third centuries B.C. these changes were largely complete, and meritocracy had been established. Closely coinciding with these changes was the Hundred Philosophers period (551–c. 233 B.C.), during which there was a flourishing of teachers such as Confucius and Mo Tzu, "who offered training in statecraft and the associated arts to all comers" (Munro 1969:10; Hsu 1965).

Confucianism was to become and remain the dominant philosophy of China's elite. Munro says that

the doctrine of natural (biological) equality gave the Confucians the strongest possible argument to support the contention that merit should be the sole criterion in awarding political and economic privileges. Since they also believed that a social hierarchy was natural, their demand was for an aristocracy of merit. . . .

As a result of the belief in man's natural equality, Confucianism came to focus on the here and now—on the environmental factors that cause differences in moral excellence among men, and on the training techniques that are available to correct bad habits. Two environmental factors were particularly stressed: economic well-being and education. (Munro 1969:14–15)

Expecting "miracles of moral education," the Confucianists probably overemphasized its efficacy (Munro 1969:16). Whatever the case, the Chinese have had an abiding faith in the importance of education (Munro 1969), and general education has remained an ever-popular subject for Chinese thinkers, Confucianist or otherwise. The Chinese placed an emphasis on learning "hardly paralleled elsewhere" (Bodde 1946:26). A key element in the Confucianist educational program was historical research, through which the Confucians hoped to retrieve moral lessons from the past (Munro 1969).

It is important to grasp the point that Confucius considered society naturally and properly stratified, and that he believed that people differ naturally in "intelligence, ability, and moral character" (Ho 1964:5). What he rejected was the idea that these differences are transmitted hereditarily.

The problem, then, was to discover and train the right people for the various positions. "Confucius' proposal [was] to offer the high and low equal opportunity of education. For only thus can superior men be distinguished and selected from the rest. Hence Confucius' immortal saying: 'In education there should be no class distinctions' " (Ho 1964:6). Confucius believed in "equality of opportunity or equality of possibility" (Hsieh 1968:273; Mei 1968). Confucius attempted to put this into practice with his own students, and his follower Mencius (371–289 B.C.) argued that from ancient times it had been the duty of the state to provide education for the various levels of the populace (Ho 1964). It might be noted in passing that although Confucius described his condition as "low" in his youth (Legge 1960:I, 218), he was a member of the ruling clan of the petty state of Sung (Fung 1952). His admiration for the Chou dynasty, during which hereditary status remained relatively important, may also have lent a degree of ambivalence to his position on hereditary as opposed to meritocratic succession (Bodde 1967; Fung 1952).

Hsün-tzu, the leading Confucianist of the third century B.C., states the meritocratic ideal quite explicitly: "Although a man is a descendant of a king, . . . if he does not observe the rites of proper conduct and justice, he must be relegated to the common ranks; although he is a descendant of a commoner, if he have acquired learning, developed a good character, and is able to observe the rules of good conduct and justice, then elevate him" (quoted in Ho 1964:7). Hsün-tzu also stated succinctly the idea of a uniform human nature:

Everyone has characteristics in common with others. When hungry he desires to eat; when cold he desires to be warm; when toiling he desires to rest; he wants what is beneficial and hates what is injurious—with these attitudes a man is born; he has them without waiting to learn them. . . . A person can become a Yao or a Yü [sage kings]; he can become a Chieh or a Chih [evil kings]; he can become a day laborer or an artisan; he can become a farmer or a merchant; it depends on what training he has accumulated from his ways of looking at things and his habits. (Quoted in Munro 1969:13)

The sage emperor Yao passed over his own son to choose the more deserving Shun as a successor; Shun, too, was not succeeded by his son but by the meritorious Yü. Yao, Shun, and Yü were legendary rulers (reckoned to have lived in the third millennium B.C.), but the example they allegedly set of nonhereditary succession was widely known and often cited as a precedent (Fung 1952).

Confucian writers also stressed the similarity of human emotional responses and the universality of affection for kin. It followed that a basic moral sense was applicable to all (Munro 1969). In sum, "Confucius and his followers . . . heralded the arrival of a new social order, based not on hereditary status but on individual merit" (Ho 1964:6).

The basic Confucian stratificational scheme was *varna*-like in its functional basis and simplicity. At its top were scholars (*shih*), followed, in order, by peasants (*nung*), artisans (*kung*), and merchants (*shang*). At times the order of the latter two was switched. Although legally sanctioned, the scheme was oversimplified. It applied mainly to commoners, that is, those not in government. Above this fourfold scheme were the imperial household and relatives, and the officials; beneath it were small numbers of people in degraded professions. Except for the degraded outcastes, mobility throughout the system was considered possible, and it occurred with measurable regularity (Ho 1964; Mei 1968; Ch'ü 1972 discusses the system in Han China).

In addition to Confucianism, another major politico-ethical school of thought in China was Mohism, named after Mo Tzu, a man of artisan background who probably lived in the latter half of the fifth century B.C. Mo Tzu also cited approvingly the examples of the sage kings promoting the worthy. He said, "When things are going well, gentlemen of worth must be promoted; and when they are not going well, gentlemen of worth must be promoted. . . . [H]onoring the worthy is the foundation of good government" (Mo 1963:21–22). Mo advocated universal love, a doctrine that by implication attacked hierarchy even within the family (Fung 1964; Legge 1960:II).

Taoism, which never had the official recognition accorded Confucianism but which has long had an intellectual (see, e.g., Ch'en 1980), popular, and esthetic impact on the Chinese, was even more radically egalitarian. Whereas the Confucianists believed people to be equal at birth but subsequently to differentiate in merit, the Taoists held that "all people were equally deserving; all should be tolerated, none singled out for favor" (Munro 1969:17). Taoist notions "enabled them to dispense with notions of merit, social ranks, and privilege—in short, to dispense with the trappings of the Confucian aristocracy of merit" (Munro 1969:139). Early Taoism's egalitarianism was so radical that it would seem to have precluded social mobility. In a distinction similar to Maurice Bloch's concepts of ideology and knowledge (discussed in the concluding chapter), the Taoists distinguished the kind of "knowledge" propounded by Confucianists and Legalists—which "knowledge," according to Taoists, was merely a prop for feudal hierarchy—from the true knowledge acquired from the unfettered empirical contemplation of nature's way (the *tao*) that was advocated by the Taoists. Although it eventually became a full-blown religion in competition with Buddhism, Taoism's attitudes toward people and the world may deserve much of the credit for the great contributions of Chinese empirical science (this point and Taoism's egalitarianism are discussed at length in volume II of Needham 1954–). But whatever its effects on the masses or the intellectuals, Taoism was not to be the dominant ideology of China's scholar-bureaucrats.

Of the major schools of Chinese politico-ethical thought, Legalism— referred to earlier in connection with its founder, Han Fei Tzu—was perhaps the least explicitly egalitarian. But it speaks clearly on behalf of merit: "the intelligent sovereign makes the law select men and makes no arbitrary promotion himself. He makes the law measure merits. . . . In consequence, able men cannot be obscured; . . . falsely praised fellows cannot be advanced" (Han 1959:40). Further, "the law does not fawn on the noble. . . . Punishment for faults never skips ministers, reward for good never misses commoners" (Han 1959:45). According to Munro (1969), even Buddhism—which with Confucianism and Taoism formed the trinity of Chinese ethical or quasi-religious thought—had to be made more egalitarian to fit with Chinese notions of human nature. The Buddhist conception of *karma*, which explains inequality as the consequence of behavior in previous existences, "was inherently alien to Chinese thought" (Munro 1969:176). The Chinese instead developed the "doctrine that all men were equal because they equally possessed the Buddha nature," a doctrine found "in T'ien T'ai and Chan Buddhism, both distinctively Chinese sects" (Munro 1969:131).

But enough of philosophy, what of practice? Hsu 1965 presents an extensive analysis of changing rates of social mobility between two early periods, one beginning in 722 B.C. and ending around 464 B.C., the other beginning then and ending in 222 B.C. He finds that in the former period about 25 percent of upper-status men were self-made, while in the latter the majority were self-made. Hsu cited ideological changes and underlying social changes quite parallel to those given by Munro.

In a generalized account of the Chou period (twelfth or eleventh century to third century B.C.) Creel says there was a hereditary aristocracy, and yet movement into and out of it was possible: "individuals were raised to the aristocratic class from the plebeian, and sank to plebeian status although they had been aristocrats" (1937:281). He goes on to cite rulers from the period who ordered advancement of the meritorious and reduction of aristocrats to slavery. One ruler, reflecting on these rises and falls, "concluded that 'really, there is no difference' between the people of various classes" (1937:282).

Ssu-ma Ch'ien's *Records of the Historian* shows ample signs of a preoccupation with mobility in its accounts, for example, of the rise and fall of the brief Ch'in dynasty (221–207 B.C.), the first to unify all of China, and especially of the concomitant "rise and fall of Li Ssu," a man who rose from humble station to become the Grand Councillor of the Ch'in emperor and then fell again (Bodde 1967; Fehl 1964). Ssu-ma Ch'ien begins his biography of Li Ssu with a remarkable statement of the effects of environment over heredity, saying that when Li Ssu was young he noticed that the rats living near a toilet and eating the filth there were weak or timid creatures, while rats living near a granary and living off its grain showed little fear. "Thereupon Li Ssu sighed and said: 'A man's ability or non-ability is similar to (the condition of) these rats. It merely depends upon where he places himself.' He thereupon became a follower of [Hsün-tzu, the Confucianist] in studying the methods of emperors and kings" (quoted in Bodde [1938] 1967:12).

Ssu-ma Ch'ien says that the Ch'in emperor "caused Ch'in to be without a single foot of territory of feudal investiture, and did not establish his sons and younger brothers as Kings; but meritorious ministers were made nobles" (quoted in Bodde [1938] 1967:22). On conquering the other petty states, and thus unifying China for the first time, the Ch'in emperor reduced the ruling class of all the other states to the status of commoners, thus bringing nearly to its conclusion the trend toward the destruction of nobility that began in the Spring and Autumn period (Fung 1952). In spite of his obvious awareness of social mobility, Ssu-Ma Ch'ien claimed ancient nobility for his family and sprang from a long line of court astronomers (Kierman 1962).

The great Han dynasty (206 B.C.–A.D. 220) was founded by a man of peasant origin (Fung 1952). In his account of Han social structure, Ch'ü (1972) provides numerous examples of social mobility as a general pattern. Hulsewé (1961) draws attention to the changes brought about by the establishment of a centralized bureaucracy under the Han. It blurred the lines between nobility and peasantry, and brought about a radical shift in historiography. The emperor's direct appointment of all governing officials, and the introduction of the bureaucratic examination system under Emperor Wu-ti (140–87 B.C.), dealt serious blows to the remnants of the nobility (Fung 1952). The Confucian ideal of meritocracy reached a very high pitch in the Early Han, when Ssu-ma Ch'ien was writing (Ch'en

1980). By the end of the Later Han, when Hsün Yueh was writing, the Confucian ideals that had been so successfully implemented earlier had been greatly shaken (but individualistic Taoism was on the rise). Wang Mang, believed by many to be a sage, had forced the emperor to resign in A.D. 9 and had then set into motion a series of Confucian-inspired idealistic reforms. The reforms were too unrealistic, however, and in addition a series of natural disasters befell the reign. After the debacle, a Han emperor was restored in A.D. 23. But by then the Han dynasty was on the verge of collapse, great landholding clans had achieved regional elite status, and one of the strongmen of the time, who surrounded himself with men of talent, was about to establish himself as the founder of a new dynasty. Although Hsün was a Confucianist and did not question the role of merit in the selection of officials, he was also a spokesman for the new regional elite. He adopted the unorthodox view that the regional elites should have hereditary rights to their lands (but not hereditary rights over people). It was this limited advocacy of feudalism that ultimately made his views unpalatable (Ch'en 1975, 1980). Thus, while it was a period that saw the collapse of Confucianist enthusiasm and the rise of "feudal" regional elites, it was nonetheless a period of considerable de facto social mobility (even if outside the examination system) and one with only a very limited ideological commitment to hereditary principles. In the troubled period after the fall of the Han, society remained essentially open, individualistic Taoism flourished, and Buddhism was introduced (Twitchett 1961).

Not everyone would agree with my assessment of the period of disunity that followed the fall of the Han as essentially open (see especially Eberhard 1962). The period is often called one of feudalism. Some points are certain: with the collapse of the central government the embryonic examination system collapsed too, powerful and durable families in large measure filled the resultant power vacuum, and these families were effective in placing their men in the various government bureaucracies. Thus what Chinese see as the normal or proper mode of social mobility—the bureaucratic examination system—was definitely blocked in this period. But two questions remain: Did social mobility persist in other forms? and, Was the ideology of social mobility attacked or eroded in China's medieval age?

In the *Medieval Chinese Oligarchy* (1977), David Johnson begins with the question of whether the Chinese ruling class was hereditary from the Ch'in dynasty through the T'ang (i.e., from A.D. 265 to 906). He finds that it was not, that office remained the essential mark of high status and that office had to be achieved. But he also shows that in spite of their anxieties about failing to obtain high office, and hence of falling from high status, several hundred great clans developed the means (including effective education of their sons) to prevent that fate for centuries—possibly showing a slower rate of elite circulation than in late medieval Europe. Accompanying this apparent de facto closure of society was a defense of the "familial principle . . . against the traditional claims of the meritocratic principle" (Johnson 1977:20). A system of ranking the populace as a means of sorting out the talented fell under the control of the elite and hence gave them an advantage in seeking office, but once the elite gained that control, the system was under continual attack (Johnson 1977; see also Ebrey 1978). The elite never achieved an ideologically acceptable hereditary claim to high position: unlike the European nobility, "with its semi-mystical quality of the blood which conferred a status that could end only when the family did out, a great Chinese family had always to renew itself or risk social decline" (Johnson 1977:31). While "upward social mobility was difficult," it was "not of course impossible. Military success could bring titles and rank, even to a plebian soldier. And if a man of low birth became a protégé of an emperor, he could rise to great heights" (Johnson 1977:31).

In a related study, Ebrey (1978) traces an aristocratic family over a thousand-year period (which on the face of it is a remarkable sign of de facto immobility). Her definition of aristocracy limits the field to only "a few dozen families and a few thousand individuals" (1978:1). She is more inclined than Johnson to emphasize the hereditary nature of aristocratic standing and shows considerable evidence for a great familial and governmental interest in pedigree, beginning in the second century A.D. Nonetheless, Ebrey notes that the system of recruiting officials that favored the aristocrats "was frequently criticized for selecting officials according to family rank, not virtue or ability as claimed" (1978:3) and that "close studies of the factional politics of the T'ang have failed to produce any evidence that the aristocratic families formed a coherent or self-conscious power group" (1978:6). In short, the meritocratic principle was compromised but not dethroned, and—at least in the later medieval period—great families competed for power and status rather than closing their ranks as a solidary bloc or caste. In some ways China's medieval period is similar to the Renaissance in Italy, which was characterized by an intense competition between hereditary and meritocratic principles, with great families struggling to maintain their positions in *both* frames of reference.

When the T'ang dynasty reestablished centralized authority, the bureaucratic civil service examination system was reinstituted. By the time of the Sung dynasty, the oligarchic or aristocratic families had lost their high status (Johnson 1977). From then on there was no further challenge to the central place of merit. Mei (1968:342) says of the examination system that the competition was keen, the rewards great; with few exceptions it was open to all men who had properly prepared themselves, and Chinese folklore came to be "filled with success stories of self-made men" who, though from poor families, succeeded in passing the examinations by dint of heroic effort. Ho Ping-ti (1964) has shown that rates of social mobility in the Ming and Ch'ing period were as high as or higher than in the modern West.

Clearly it cannot be said that lineage has been meaningless to the Chinese; even the historians at times succeeded one another within a family (Hulsewé 1961). Families certainly tried to maintain their high status by whatever means possible. But in the Ming and Ch'ing dynasties there were no effective institutions for the maintenance of high status within a family (Ho 1964), with the possible exception of the descendants of Confucius. Perhaps most important, the ideology of social mobility—as in the doctrine of the Mandate of Heaven and in the recruitment of bureaucrats—has never been seriously challenged. Hence China has long been remarkable for its idealization of social mobility, and at times for its actual rates of social mobility.

CONCLUDING COMMENTS

Burton Watson's comment that an English-speaking reader will find little that is conceptually unfamiliar in a history that was written more than two millennia ago in China stands in marked contrast to judgments of Indian accounts of the past. Judgments range from saying that the Indian accounts were not historical to saying that they were historical but were also very different from what a Western historian would write.

There were further and equally striking contrasts. For example, the three factors in modern conceptions of history that Cohn said were not found in Indian views of the past—resort to documentary evidence, a concern for exact chronology, and a conception of causation in terms of the accidental juxtaposition of events—were all present in Chinese historiography. Basic research on chronology and the decipherment of ancient epigraphy was begun in India largely by Europeans; nothing of the sort occurred in China, where these activities were indigenous, ancient, and continuous. There is no Indian equivalent of the Chinese emperors' "Diaries of Activities and Repose," or at least none survived in India, while they did survive in China. Students of Chinese society have no serious difficulty in measuring rates of social mobility from very early times. Students of Indian society, in spite of their lively interest in social mobility, have largely confined their research to qualitative studies, almost certainly because the appropriate historical materials are either absent or intractable. It is sometimes asserted, in contrast to the general opinion, that the Indian corpus of historical writings and materials is enormous or even unmatched in richness (Nilakanta Sastri 1953; Warder 1972). If this were even approximately correct it would constitute one point at which China and India were not so different. But the very lack of, say, quantitative studies of rates of social mobility in pre-Muslim India leads me to doubt that the Indian corpus matches China's. If only specific kinds of *generally acceptable* histories and materials—such as biographies, local and state histories, and authentic documents (including epigraphy)—were counted, the difference would be as dramatic as it is frequently asserted to be.

These contrasts in historiographies are even more remarkable when we pause to think that India and the West are far more closely related than the West and China. Indians and Europeans are, after all, both Indo-Europeans, sharing language, culture, and, for whatever it indicates, race. It follows that the similarity of China and the West, in contrast to India, must be explained by something other than cultural relatedness.

The burden of this book is to assess the extent to which the mode of social stratification underlies differences in historiography. Indian stratification is basically closed, but there are exceptions, and considerable attention has been given to the ways in which it is open. China is the reverse: ideally conceived of as open, practice has often fallen short of this ideal. In terms of their actual rates of social mobility, it is difficult to be sure that traditional China and India differed, primarily because we lack comparable studies of rates of social mobility in traditional India. But in terms of their predominant ideological conceptions of social stratification, the contrast between China and India is stark.

Given the centrality of caste in India, it should come as no surprise that at least one Indianist, David F. Pocock, has seen that caste and ahistoricity are linked:

Now it is evident from all we know about the caste system that status is not dependent on achievement. The Brahman is not selected or promoted, he is what he is because he and his ancestors have always been what they are. And the Untouchables likewise. In this scheme of things history can have no place and so long as the people themselves are unconscious of any change, all is well. (1964:18)

But Pocock's insight (found also in Masui 1966, and partially echoed in Walker 1968) has not been pursued.

On the other hand, I know of no one who explains Chinese historical-mindedness in terms of its system of stratification. We will have to wait until the discussion of the Renaissance in chapter 6 before we see an explanation in these terms. For the moment, let us look at other factors present in the Indian and Chinese cases that might form part of the explanation for the relative ahistoricity of India.

The principal ideologues of India were the hereditarily recruited Brahmans; their counterparts in China were the openly recruited scholars. The former thought of themselves as deities and were steeped in supernaturalism. The latter rejected the notion of deities and all forms of superstition. Kosambi (1952:191) describes Brahmanism as "characterized by its extreme, facile adaptability in practice combined with rigid and apparently immutable theory, which leads to a blinking of the facts, to a neglect of reality." If Brahmanical rigidity includes insistence on the inheritance of basic character, and if Brahmanical adaptability includes a willingness to fabricate or accept fabricated genealogies to show that the patrons of the Brahmans have the right pedigrees, we have the makings of my argument.

There appears to have been no shortage of such patrons. It has been argued that there have been no real Kshatriya rulers since the fifth century B.C. (Srinivas 1968), yet countless dynasties were given Kshatriya genealogies. Earlier I cited the tendency for upwardly mobile castes to claim a sort of amnesia about who they really were and then to rediscover their true identity in a past conveniently beyond the range of historical verification. Even the lower castes often account for their position through a mythical fall from onetime higher status (Cohn 1971). Now, if the members of castes at every level of the system have a propensity to claim high descent and a willingness to accept something less than sound history to verify their claims, and if, as Thapar (1978) asserts, genealogy is the core of the Indian historical tradition, we know almost all that we need to know to conclude that the Indian tradition was severely handicapped, even if not mortally wounded. It may well have been artful, as is frequently claimed, but its opportunities for being objective were diminished by the widespread incentive of patrons to want mythmaking rather than history. It was, of course, the benefits of high rank, which should be justified by birth, that provided the incentive. I am quite willing to accept the evidence set forth by Indianists for the occasional signs of historical-mindedness among Indians. There was no real shortcoming in their minds. But the various attempts at sounder forms of history were seeds cast upon an infertile soil.

My argument is that hereditary stratification made the soil infertile, and part of the supporting evidence is provided by the exceptions. Kalhana's history and the Sri Lankan chronicles were produced in times and regions where caste took attenuated forms or had less ideological support. Although I explored only these two exceptions, other heterodox Indian religions that repudiated caste—the Jains and Bhakti cultists—provide similar supporting evidence. In her discussion of ancient Indian historical writing, Thapar (1978) notes an association of exceptional historical-mindedness not only with Buddhism but also with Jain teachers and monks and with the period that witnessed the rise of Bhakti teaching. In her discussion of social mobility in ancient India, she also refers to Buddhists, Jains, and Bhakti cultists: they flourished in primarily urban settings in periods of increased trade, they repudiated caste, and they probably thereby gave themselves opportunities for upward mobility that their original caste statuses may have denied them (Thapar 1978; see also Kosambi 1952).

The evidence presented in this chapter suggests a series of further contrasts: the Chinese wrote more about political science, social science, and economics, and they wrote more biographies, had more realistic portraiture, and showed—perhaps only weakly—a greater recognition of individualism. Not only did science apparently develop more in China, but so too did divination. The Chinese had a sense of a common human nature and hence emphasized general programs of education, while the Indians saw many human natures, each of which had a unique program of education. Myth flourished at the expense of history among the Indians, and ritual was rampant, while the secular humanism of the Chinese pushed myths aside, and ritual was appreciated for its pragmatic benefits.

Subsequent chapters will provide further evidence for a linkage between social stratification and views of the past, and will show that the wider syndrome of correlates is too uniform and too complex to be the result of accident. Although the next chapter is largely limited to historiography and social stratification, and says little about the further concomitants, it is exhaustive in its attempt to pick an unbiased sample of societies to compare and contrast within a delimited cultural region.

CHAPTER 3

Southeast Asia

Southeast Asia provides less-than-ideal conditions for comparing historiographic traditions. Literacy came later to Southeast Asia than to China or India, and no state or civilization in Southeast Asia could boast the continuity and size of its neighbors to the north and west. To further discourage comparison, relatively little historical research has been done on Southeast Asia. This has two unfortunate consequences. First, it means that much of the historical material produced by Southeast Asians has not yet been evaluated. Second, it means that attempts to reconstruct past patterns of social stratification may be of dubious value. Yet my original focus of interest was a Southeast Asian state; two of the first theoretical works that I consulted and that seemed to cast light on the problem of ahistoricity (Bastin 1964 and Geertz 1966) concerned Southeast Asia. Moreover, the comparison between Hindu Indian and Chinese treatments of the past occurred to me precisely because of their strikingly contrasting historical treatments of Southeast Asia.

Consequently, I first attempted to test the hypothesis that hereditary stratification was linked to unsound historiography by examining the existing major works on Southeast Asian historiography (Hall 1961; Soedjatmoko et al. 1965). What I sought in these volumes were explicit judgments on the quality of historiography. Most contributors did not offer such judgments, and when they did they often only noted that historical writing at its best in Southeast Asia fell far short of modern Western standards. But the editor of the earlier work did explicitly raise the question of why one or the other of the Southeast Asian peoples might be more historically minded than the others, and a few of the contributors made the sort of judgments I sought. According to their unequivocal judgments, relatively sound historiographies were possessed by the Burmese, the Vietnamese, and the Makassar/Buginese peoples of Sulawesi. Just as unequivocally, the Javanese and the Malays were judged relatively unsound as historians. By implication, historiography in the long-defunct state of Nanchao was also poorly developed. Unequivocal but quantitative judgments were also made to the effect that the Balinese possessed considerable historical materials and that the Vietnamese possessed more historical materials than the Laotians or the Cambodians. While not denying that quantity of historical materials sometimes reflects qualitative attitudes toward the study of the past, I initially decided to dismiss quantitative judgments. But I elected to look beyond my sample judgments to get further judgments on the quality of Balinese historiography. I knew that Balinese society was caste-organized, and the possibility that Bali might prove an embarrassment to my hypothesis demanded attention. Consultation of other sources (Friederich [1877] 1959; Worsley 1972) led me to classify Bali with the unsound historiographies. The only remaining judgment was an ambiguous one on Cambodian historiography. Because of its ambiguity, I ignored it (for the time being).

Having found judgments by historians (or others equally qualified to judge) on the historiographies of the Balinese, Makassar/Buginese, Burmese, Javanese, Malays, Vietnamese, and the people of old Nanchao, I submitted my reading of these judgments to Professor D.G.E. Hall—the dean of Southeast Asian historians and the editor of one of my main sources. He agreed with my reading (personal communication). I also began to read such works as seemed relevant to assessing patterns of social stratification among the peoples whose historiographies had been judged. As I stated in the introduction, the patterns of social stratification, in my judgment at that time, were successfully predicted by the quality of the historiography; thus encouraged, I moved on to a wider sample of societies.

Later, two further volumes on Southeast Asian historiography were published (Cowan and Wolters 1976; Reid and Marr 1979). In terms of unequivocal evaluations, one or another contributor to these volumes confirmed the soundness of Burmese and Vietnamese historiography and the unsoundness of Malay historiography, and added the Achenese of

Sumatra to the unsound. Among the somewhat ambiguous judgments were that Thai historiography was quantitatively impressive but that in most periods its quality was depressed. Except for the case of Java, no judgments, explicit or implicit, countered those found in the volumes by Hall and Soedjatmoko mentioned above. In setting forth the cases below, I have decided to include *all* societies for which I found judgments, even those I initially excluded from the volumes by Hall and Soedjatmoko. I first present the Brunei case, followed by those for which clear judgments were rendered. I conclude with those cases for which judgments are less clear. I have included all cases, even though some have proved too am-biguous for most of my purposes, because this allows me to exhaust the universe of cases presented in the principal relevant sources. The results therefore approach the standards for scientific sampling and can be seen as indicative of how social stratification and quality of historiography correlate in general.

BRUNEI

Brunei, from which Borneo allegedly derives its name, is now a very small country and therefore would not be expected to produce a great volume of historical writings. But Brunei was a major state in the 1500s, and it was still very large for a Malay state in the middle of the last century. Even during its periods of greatness, however, there is evidence that Bruneis wrote little history and kept few written records from which histories might have been constructed. By surveying Brunei historiography I will try to make the following points: that there are basic deficiencies in Brunei historiography; that the Bruneis have shown relatively little concern for the preservation of the materials required to compose their history; that the Bruneis have written very little history; and that this state of affairs appears to stretch into the ancient past, in spite of the Bruneis' possessing literacy for an equally long period. In addition, I will show that outsiders produce more histories and historical materials on Brunei than do Bruneis and that Bruneis show a debilitating sensitivity to historical studies.

In the nineteenth century when Hugh Low (1880) published a few Brunei histories (*silasilah* or *tarsilah*), he noted that only a single event in Brunei history was dated: the execution of a sultan in A.H.1072 (A.D.1661). This was not completely true, for Low (1880) also published the text of a history engraved on stone in Brunei, the text containing its date, A.H. 1221

(A.D. 1807). Nonetheless, Low's point was well taken: Brunei accounts of the past contain very few dates, almost all of them are later than the eighteenth century, and often they are only the dates on which a text or copy of one was produced. This shows a casual attitude to dating. Such chronology as existed in Brunei accounts of the past was largely genealogical, and there are many points where the genealogical sequence is far from clear. The genealogies are neither continuous nor systematic, so the relations between persons who are mentioned are at times obscure. Thus the genealogical frameworks used in Brunei histories provide less chronological order than they could.

In the sixteenth century, when remnants of the Magellan expedition visited Brunei, there were scribes at the Brunei court. Nonetheless, when a Spanish force captured Brunei some seventy years later, there was little evidence of Brunei archives. The Spaniards only mention finding "a large gourd filled with papers" in the palace (Blair and Robertson 1903:IV, 167). While the Spanish sources do not exclude the possibility of archival materials that may have eluded their search, the evidence suggests that there was little.

Recently a description of traditional government was written by two Bruneis (Yura Halim and M. Jamil Umar 1958). In spite of an extensive listing of officials, with the usual complement of administrative tasks great and small, there is no mention of a court historian. There is an official clerk, Pehin Penyurat, but no indication that he had the duty of maintaining archives.

On the other hand, many sources from the nineteenth and twentieth centuries indicate that each official or man of affairs (and sometimes their wives) kept records individually and probably haphazardly. Some individuals—usually non-noble officials, though at times acting on the instructions of high noble officials (perhaps especially the sultan)—did write histories (Low 1880; Sweeney 1968). But they did so only rarely, often anonymously, with little discussion of method, and with no indication that this was a normal, ongoing official function. In short, the function of historian— court historian or otherwise—was not a regular part of the Brunei administration. It is thus no surprise that official histories of Brunei were rare in the nineteenth and early twentieth centuries.

What other sources for the writing of Brunei history are to be found in Brunei, and hence indicate care in preserving the past? Most are literary items, inscriptions, or oral histories. The still unpublished lengthy poem *Sha'er Awang Semaun* became known to the outside world only very recently. It recounts, among other things, the origins of Brunei, and it is the principal popular history of Brunei. It focuses on the grandiose exploits of Brunei's culture heroes, the fourteen divine or semidivine brothers from among whom was chosen the first Brunei ruler. Nineteenth-century British figures in Brunei possibly ignored it as a work of myth and legend more than of history. Even the official genealogical histories largely neglect it.

Legal texts and Indian romances were also known in manuscript form in Brunei in the nineteenth and twentieth centuries. The only one of the former to be examined by a scholar was pronounced a copy of a peninsular Malay text (Winstedt 1923). Several romances recently unearthed in the Sarawak Museum were examined by Malaysian scholars and judged to be of no historical interest. While I doubt that the judgment is wholly correct, it does remain to be shown that these may be of use.

Finally, a number of documents written by Bruneis have been preserved and are of great importance. The largest collection, I believe, is in the Public Record Office, London. When a British Resident was established by treaty in Brunei in 1906, he set out to gather copies of documents indicating leases of lands (and other things) to Europeans and Chinese from the Bruneis. Interestingly, most of these documents were found in the hands of the wives of the various officials and men of means. Some of the documents were more than fifty years old. Whether they would have survived in Brunei once they had ceased to be effective contracts and had become of primarily historical interest may never be known. My impression is that few did survive.

In the late 1960s the Brunei Museum was made a government archive. Materials began to be collected there on a routine basis, though surely many documents do not end up there, and access is not easy. Anyway, the museum successfully appealed for old letters of an official nature that were in the hands of the families of former high officials and did manage to turn up a number (less than fifty by 1972).

Barring the Indian romances and other more or less purely literary works, whose numbers may be great, the written historical or quasi-historical texts in Brunei, or by Brunei hands in other places, probably do not much exceed two thousand pages (assuming that all related texts are reduced to a single authoritative version and excluding works produced in the last two decades). Surely they do not exceed ten thousand pages of text.

There is one major inscription, reported by Hugh Low in 1880 and republished since (Shariffuddin and Abdul Latif 1974). It is one of the official genealogical histories and is carved on a tombstonelike monument long situated in Brunei's currently used royal cemetery. It is likely that it was commissioned at a time of some dispute or uncertainty over succession to the throne and hence may be seen as an attempt as much to manipulate history as to merely recount it. Nonetheless, its overt intent is historical, and its importance is great. It is very succinct, containing only about four hundred words. In the same cemetery, and elsewhere in Brunei, inscriptions on tombstones provide further useful historical data, mostly concerning dates, genealogy, and, to some extent, the record of officeholding. Vital information on religious history and immigration to Brunei has been found on a few tombstones, but controversy surrounds the correct reading of some of the older ones.

Somewhat similar, though generally much more recent, inscriptions on Brunei bronzes (especially on cannons and household utensils of heirloom quality) may provide a certain amount of historical information. To my knowledge, no one has yet assessed this source. Finally, a very few old coins provide a small amount of insight into Brunei's past (Singh 1980).

I believe that only the tombstones have been put to use in composing traditional Brunei histories, but even this was not done in a thorough manner. On the contrary, false stories about the tombs have developed through time, due partly to the difficulty of reading their inscriptions.

In sum, the literary materials produced by Bruneis and available for writing Brunei history have not been systematically preserved as primary documents and have not been systematically consulted when available. Moreover, writings that may be described as historical in intent are few in number and mostly brief. None contains much in the way of a discussion of sources and method, and none gives any clues suggesting sophisticated methodology. On the other hand, texts now described as "Indian romances" may be, or may have been, considerably more numerous; they may in the past have been seen as real histories rather than mere literary entertainments. Many of their key ingredients—the existence of *sakti*, magical power, for example—are alive in the folk beliefs of present-day Brunei.

Some Bruneis say that oral history is their real source of knowledge of the past. There is some evidence that memorizing accounts of the past was in fact a kind of Brunei specialization, perhaps especially of old women. This was done in part for entertainment, and in part as an adjunct to Brunei's ritual and ceremonial life. Reciting the *Sha'er Awang Semaun* during weddings, for example, was particularly popular. The memorization of old stories may fast be disappearing. There is no need to minimize the tragedy of what may be lost in this way, but very little of Brunei's older history will be lost, for the simple reason that what was remembered—though more or less uniformly reported over a considerable area of old Brunei (cf. Headly 1950 and Lawrence 1911)—was very little, was highly selective and highly packaged, and was sometimes of dubious historical validity. In short, the entertainment and mythic functions of oral history predominated over the purely historical. One of Brunei's present-day historians told me that genealogical materials are frequently in conflict. This is no surprise, since there are ample reasons in a stratified society to tamper with genealogies, and in Brunei there are only imperfect methods of discovering deliberate distortions. In the long run this can lead to serious errors. For example, the royal genealogies do not seem to go back far enough in time to account for the archaeologically demonstrated age of Brunei. Recent tombstone research has turned up at least one sultan who has disappeared from the official genealogies (Abdul Latif and Shariffuddin 1979). Even the nineteenth-century genealogical accounts of succession to the throne disagreed seriously on the number of rulers and showed signs of impending disagreement over successions even within that century. What applies to these official histories, I suspect, applies all the more to oral histories.

While oral history is a very useful tool for recent history in Brunei—if one has access to the persons who were privy to the events in question—and while oral history provides very useful insights into information taken for granted in Brunei and hence unlikely to go into written historical materials, I was astonished to find that in the 1960s many Bruneis did not know that only 120 years earlier, in 1846, the capital of Brunei had been militarily taken by Britain (Mundy 1848). It was an event never adequately packaged for folk history, and so far as I can ascertain, an event recounted in no written Brunei source prior to World War II. Why it was not recounted is a good question; the much earlier Spanish attacks of the late sixteenth century are rather well remembered (see, e.g., Low 1880:9–10). The best that can be said about oral history in Brunei is that while it may not be worse than oral history elsewhere, it is not demonstrably better. With no one specifically charged with memorization, it is hard to imagine how it could be otherwise.

Many of the most important Brunei materials would perhaps not be preserved at all were it not for foreign archives and foreigners' concern for history. The oldest existing writing in Brunei Malay, a letter dated

1599, is in the archives at Seville. Numerous important documents are in London. Even some items of oral history might have disappeared had they not been collected and published by Europeans. Moreover, the great bulk of material on Brunei was not written by Bruneis. It consists of thousands of reports—some published, but most still in archives—all prepared by persons interested in Brunei and routinely committed to maintaining for posterity the fruits of their observation. In London the Colonial and Foreign Office files on Brunei consist of over 240 massive manuscript and typescript volumes. Duplicates of some of these files were at one time maintained by the British in Brunei, but many were lost during or shortly after World War II. The diaries and other eyewitness accounts of Brunei prepared by Europeans recounting their adventures in Brunei run to a dozen or more volumes. Earlier reports have been preserved in the India Office, which is also in London. For the sixteenth to eighteenth centuries, Spanish and Portuguese archives and publications provide extensive materials (some published in Blair and Robertson 1903–9, and Nicholl 1975). A recently published late-sixteenth-century Spanish notebook on Brunei, written in the Philippines, has greatly enlarged our knowledge of old Brunei (Carroll 1982). Earlier periods are covered primarily by Chinese materials. Until recently we knew the name of one Brunei sultan only from Chinese sources. A recent tombstone discovery in Brunei may have confirmed this name (according to my interpretation of inscriptions reported in Abdul Latif and Shariffuddin 1979), and of course it lent weight to the potential accuracy of other names mentioned by the Chinese but not presently included in Brunei histories.

In total, this outside material on Brunei is considerably greater than the internally collected material. There are many things now knowable about Brunei that were unknowable in terms of Brunei's traditional materials. In fact, I believe this material is so rich and detailed, and is maintained in forms so uncongenial to the Brunei packaging of history, that many Bruneis have difficulty making sense of it. Not that it obviously contradicts their views; it just does not fit easily into them.

Of course, many things have changed in the last few decades. Historical materials now accumulate at a good rate in Brunei, and historical writings are produced in numbers (in 1982 a History Center was added to the government's bureaucracy). Nonetheless, it is clear that outsiders, and outside standards, are much involved in this. Bruneis have neither owned nor operated the main newspapers, for example. One Brunei (the head of the new History Center) has been particularly active in historical research and writing, apparently combining Brunei and European standards and methods. But I wonder if all writings by Bruneis on their own history match the quantity of European writings on Brunei over the last few decades.

Perhaps even more significant are the signs that historical research and writing touch specially sensitive issues among Bruneis. As I suggested above, in spite of some legal provision for maintaining government archives, the task seems only irregularly performed. Such archival materials as do exist are notoriously hard to gain access to. Nor do the Bruneis themselves get on with the task of publishing these materials. Plans to publish the *Sha'er Awang Semaun* were afoot in 1967, yet it remains undone as of 1987. I obtained a copy in 1967, but only with the proviso I not publish it. The amateur preparation of textual materials that goes on in local historical societies everywhere in places such as Europe and America has only just begun in Brunei (excluding European authors publishing in Brunei). In another medium, some years ago Radio Brunei started a series on the histories of the various wards of Brunei's old capital. Only the first program was aired, the remainder were canceled when it was discovered that these histories led to sectional squabbles. The scripts for the programs disappeared too. Finally, the publication of some of the tombstone research and other historical research on Brunei has been delayed due to opposition from Brunei authorities.

Some Bruneis are acutely aware that much of the historical writing on Brunei is based on materials that were presented to the world by people with substantial reason to blacken the name of Brunei. In the colonial period it was mostly persons busily engaged in carving up Brunei who sought the public's attention. Bearing this in mind, some Bruneis are quick to discredit European accounts of Brunei. Others add that because Europeans refuse to believe things that Bruneis know to be true (e.g., that some individuals achieve invulnerability), Europeans erroneously question the authenticity of Brunei accounts.

Even Bruneis who are unaware of conflict between domestic and foreign accounts of Brunei tend to show the conflict. I found many Bruneis to be genuinely interested in new information on Brunei's past, but they seemed hard-pressed to say anything about what they then learned. It provoked thoughtful silence rather than conversation. If I could provide copies of published or archival materials on Brunei's past that were not readily available in Brunei, people requested them. So I do not think they considered the materials obviously irrelevant or misleading. I have often wondered how these odd facts have been integrated into their views of the past, or whether they even can be so integrated.

It would be wrong to deny the soundness of Brunei historiography completely. As I mentioned earlier, the Bruneis retained an account of the Spanish attacks on Brunei in the late sixteenth century. While the Spanish archives maintained voluminous eyewitness accounts of the event, and are the indispensable sources at present (Blair and Robertson 1903–9:IV; Nicholl 1975), it is to the credit of Brunei historiography that its account of this event is demonstrably better than accounts published in the Philippines in relatively recent times (Brown 1971b). For a number of important events in Brunei's history, indigenous sources are quite simply the only sources, rendering them invaluable whatever shortcomings they may have. The dated event (mentioned above) that Low drew attention to was the culmination of a disputed succession to the Brunei throne, which dispute gave the sultanate of Sulu (in the southern Philippines) an opportunity to intervene in Brunei affairs. I do not know of any source outside Brunei that throws light on the period (although scholars have not surveyed the relevant archives with this problem in mind). Even those specimens of Brunei historiography that seem most remote from the standards of modern Western historiography, such as the *Sha'er Awang Semaun*, have an important part to play in understanding the beliefs and customs of Bruneis in the past.

Both the strengths and weaknesses of Brunei historiography can be seen by comparing two eyewitness accounts of a coronation that took place in Brunei in 1918 (Brown 1971a). The first British Resident of Brunei, M.S.H. McArthur, returned to Brunei for the coronation to represent colonial authorities in Singapore. McArthur had considerable experience in Malayan countries, and the report he filed after his return from Brunei was brief but reasonably well informed. Also at the coronation was one Haji Abdul Ghaffar bin Abdul Mumin. He was apparently a Sarawak Malay (i.e., from the state of Sarawak, now a part of Malaysia), but until about the middle of the nineteenth century Sarawak was a part of Brunei. In any case, the Haji shows a good grasp of Brunei Malay customs and affairs, and can serve well enough as an example of the best in traditional Brunei historiography.

The Haji's account is longer and more detailed than McArthur's. The treatment of space and time does not vary sharply between the two accounts, except that McArthur follows a strict chronology more closely, while the Haji's account is ordered more in terms of the constituent elements of a coronation. In two respects—the treatment of personnel and material items—the accounts differ sharply and in precisely the ways that now seem to me to go beyond the peculiarities of Brunei and British culture.

With respect to personnel, McArthur mentioned ethnic categories and key personnel. Haji Abdul Ghaffar, by contrast, presented a detailed, almost sociological account of numerous statuses and roles in the Brunei social world. When McArthur mentioned individuals, he mentioned them by name, and he made frequent comments on the psychological states of the participants. The Haji mentioned only a few people by name, referring to all the rest by titles, by their social categories, or in terms of their group affiliations. The Haji offered very little in the way of psychological commentary, contenting himself more with reporting actions and statements.

Concerning material items, the Haji appears superficially to be more materialistic. But the items that he enumerates and describes at comparatively great length are virtually all symbols of social status. The Haji's seeming materialism is largely an extension of his treatment of personnel. The things he mentions—vessels, candles, flags, weapons, and umbrellas, for example—were mnemonics of the personnel and their attributes.

These contrasts seemed to confirm the view that a shallow treatment of individual psychological attributes was a peculiarity of the Malay sense of the past that differed significantly from that of modern Western historians, as Bastin (1964) argues. Geertz's observations on personhood in Bali suggest that the peculiarity was not unique to the Malays (1966). I am particularly struck by the detailed similarity between what I had noted in Haji Abdul Ghaffar's writing and what Ullman (1966a) found to be typical of the Middle Ages in Europe. But it was to be some time before I could reconcile the patterns found in written accounts with the actual day-to-day behavior of Malays. I will return to the problem of individualism in the concluding chapter.

For the present I will only note that while Haji Abdul Ghaffar's account differed in important ways from McArthur's, the former's was in no serious way deficient. But it must also be noted that the Haji wrote in this century and hence may reflect newer standards emanating from Europe and the Near East, that writings such as his are still exceedingly rare, and that although he recorded the coronation of 1918 with commendable precision and breadth, far too few of his predecessors did the same for similar or much more important events.

As mentioned in the introduction, Brunei has a castelike system of social stratification (Brown 1970a, 1970b, 1973). This system can be projected with some certainty back into the nineteenth century, and there is no persuasive reason for thinking that it does not stretch considerably further back in time. For an equally long time the Bruneis have ruled over a congeries of other ethnic groups. Excluding the non-Bruneis within their realm, the ethnic Bruneis may be divided into nobles (*pengiran-pengiran, raja-raja*) and non-nobles. While the nobles were substantial in number (in the 1960s they constituted about 10 percent of the population), they have never been a majority. High office in the Brunei sultanate was open only to nobility. Sometimes by virtue of offices they held and sometimes by virtue of in-heritance, nobles governed, taxed, and exploited substantial portions of the sultanate's territories and peoples. Nobility was a status acquired only by strict patrilineal descent. From these facts alone it follows that Brunei was a hereditarily closed society.

But there were other castelike features too. At the top of the non-nobles were the aristocrats (*awang-awang*). In recent times many Bruneis would say that aristocrats are defined by birth, or ideally so. But aristocratic closure is far from perfect. Whether closure was more perfect in the past is hard to say. The aristocrats also held important offices in the sultanate, but no matter how powerful, theirs were of inferior rank to the nobles' offices. The aristocrats either did not have appanages, or familial rights to rule, or had them on a very limited scale.

The aristocrats tended to be associated with only a few wards in the old capital of Brunei. Each ward, whether aristocratic or not, was much like a caste in India. That is, the residents of each tended to have a particular occupation (often indicated by the ward's name), preferred to marry en-dogamously (allegedly doing so much more strictly in the past), claimed or were assigned a specific rank (there was, however, much dispute over relative rank), and claimed a distinctive ethnic, caste, or descent identity (*bangsa*) buttressed by distinctive customs and speech patterns. In spite of abundant signs of individual mobility—some of it vertical—the notion that the members of each ward had a distinctive character inherited from their respective founding ancestors was vigorous in all sectors of Brunei society.

Like many peoples of Southeast Asia, the Bruneis undoubtedly were participants for centuries in the sphere of Hindu-Buddhist culture. Ac-cordingly, popular accounts of the origin of Brunei, especially its royal line, are couched in Indian terms and symbols (Brown 1980). The royal line is credited with divine or semidivine origin and magical powers. On the other hand, Brunei has long been a Muslim state. Although many

Hindu-Buddhist features persist in Brunei social life, it is possible to find Bruneis who dismiss the origin myths of the Bruneis and some of the practices those myths sanction. In addition, movement across the lower strata in Brunei society, and across the boundary that separates Bruneis from others, has no doubt long occurred in fact. Brunei is not a perfect example of a closed society, but it meets the minimal criteria.

MALAYA

From time immemorial, Malay as a language has been the lingua franca of coastal and seaborne trade in Southeast Asia. The Malays as a people—most frequently associated with the Malay Peninsula and the island of Sumatra but long found in substantial numbers on the islands between those places and in coastal regions of Borneo, Java, and some of the lesser islands—are Malay-speaking Muslims who for centuries predominated in Southeast Asia's far-flung seagoing trade.

Winstedt (1969), who had a broad knowledge of Malay literature, considered Malay historical writing, by virtue of its subject matter, to be the most indigenous of all branches of Malay prose. Yet Winstedt and others have generally pointed out that those Malay historical works that most nearly approach sound standards have non-Malay authors or in other ways reflect foreign influences. Most authorities class Malay historical writings in general, and in particular those that most nearly reflect indigenous Malay culture, as relatively unsound. According to Bottoms (1965:180), "History to the Malay has not until recently been either a science or an art, but an entertainment. Accuracy, completeness, and organized exposition were not the vital principles; what best pleased were legend, fantasy, and a pleasant hotchpotch of court and port gossip." Bottoms (1965) continues with the comment that the sense of history as it is generally understood was not found among the Malays until the nineteenth century, and then only rarely. He quotes A. Teeuw's introduction to the greatest of early Malay histories, the *Sejarah Melayu*, to the effect that the authors of such compositions did not seek any "objective realism in history" (Bottoms 1965:182). The Malays showed "no allegiance to any historical absolute of the kind illustrated by the . . . Chinese" (Bottoms 1965:183). What the Malayan historian did show allegiance to was

reality as it concerns their own prince and as seen through the prince's eyes. . . .
[I]t would be foolish to expect such a historian to observe objectivity in any Western

sense. . . . Episodes which do the royal personage less than justice are skipped or minimized; the royal genealogy is streamlined; the identification of the prince with his distinguished ancestors is zealously guarded. (A. Teeuw, quoted in Bottoms 1965:182–83; see also Johns 1976 and Khoo 1979)

In the same volume with Bottoms's article, Soedjatmoko (1965b:411) notes that the volume's papers on Malay and Javanese historiography indicate "their nonhistorical function," and Djajadiningrat (1965) cites R.A. Kern's view that there is little of historical value in the Malay chronicles.

A.H. Johns has attempted to separate the various cultural strands in Malay-language historical writing. He describes the idea of history as found in Arabo-Islamic writings and then says that "this idea of history is far removed from the products of . . . Malay court culture; . . . indeed virtually nothing of the Islamic sense of chronology or the criticism of reports finds its way into Malay writing belonging to the court until the time of Raja Ali Haji" in the nineteenth century (Johns 1979:59). Asking himself whether the Arabo-Islamic "sense of time, order and particularity occur in later Malay writing about the past, a concern with fact, date, economic concerns and the real world," Johns answers, "Examples are few" (1979:61). The historical writings of the Malay world, produced in the court setting, constitute "a kind of pseudo-historiography"; although these works are "tinged with the dye of literary cultures deriving from Indo-Persian civilization [i.e., Islamic civilization as transmitted to Southeast Asia]. . . , these works are dominated by the archetypal pattern and attitudes to time discernible in the Malay folk tradition" (Johns 1979:64). "[T]he stubborn structure of the ethnic Malay shape of the world impos[es] itself on the material" (Johns 1979:61). In short, it is the specifically Malay cultural component that accounts for those qualities of Malay historical writing that distance it from the historian's normal standards.

According to Khoo (1979:299), for whom "historical works as they are understood today, with emphasis on accurate dates and objective truth, were conspicuously absent [among the Malays] before the eighteenth century," there was no indigenous Malay word for *history*. Prominent among those genres that are generally considered as historical or pseudohistorical are the *sejarah*, *salasilah* (*salsilah*, *silsilah*), *hikayat*, and *sha'er*. *Sejarah* originally meant family tree; *salasilah* is derived from the Arabic for chain and refers to genealogy (Bottoms 1965). Both *sejarah* and *salasilah* are centered around dynastic genealogy, as their names imply. Their authors are often unknown, but most likely they were "court scribes, protocol officers or persons of rank including royalty" (Khoo 1979:300). Like the *sejarah* and *salasilah*, the *hikayat* are prose works that often describe identifiable past persons or situations, but they stand at a further remove from the narrow concept of history. The "consciousness which informs historical writings and that which informed Classical Malay *hikayat* . . . are profoundly alien to one another" (Errington 1979:26). Often translated as "story" or "romance," the genre is "not intrinsically historical," and "time" is not important in the *hikayat* (Errington 1979:36, 39). The genre is, moreover, "intrinsically anonymous, even if we know the author"; that is, the narrator's personality is absent, and irrelevant to the *hikayat's* audience (Errington 1979:35). No effort is made to present realistic or idiosyncratic speech, either (Errington 1979). Although written, *hikayat* were for recitation, perhaps normally in a court context (Errington 1979). According to Errington (1979:37), *hikayat* need to be understood in the context of Malay ideas (with cognates in India) about "power [which] is assumed to emanate from formed sounds," as in magical incantations. Thus the *hikayat*, according to this line of thought, is more like a magical spell than a history (in some cases, however, the term *hikayat* appears to be used in the titles of works with more straightforward historical intent; see, e.g., Winstedt 1969). *Sha'er* are poems, sometimes lengthy and of a heroic or epic nature. As seems to be typical of poetical works, *sha'er* are rarely classed as serious historical works, though in certain circumstances they provide material of serious interest to the historian.

A notable feature of Malay historical writing is the frequency with which its sounder works are attributed to persons marginal in one way or another to Malay culture. The *Sejarah Melayu*, which dates from sometime between the early sixteenth and early seventeenth centuries and which "is the most famous, distinctive and best of all Malay literary works" (Winstedt 1969:158), is a case in point. "[N]ot of direct value for the study of Malay history," it is primarily concerned with "dynastic legitimation," the "preservation of Malay ceremonial tradition," and the "listing of rulers of the Melakan [sultanate's] line" (Johns 1979:46). Yet it presents a lively and lifelike picture of life and government in the most famous of the Malay states (Winstedt 1961, 1969). Winstedt (1969:162) speculated that its anonymous but polyglot author was perhaps a "half-caste Tamil."

In the eighteenth century, and even more so in the nineteenth, sounder historical writings appeared in Malay, but these are quite distinctly linked to authors of Bugis origin (Andaya and Matheson 1979; Bottoms 1965; Johns 1979; the Bugis, their historiography, and their social stratification are described in a later section of this chapter). The most notable illustration is provided by Raja Ali Haji, member of a ruling family on Riau (an island between Malaya and Sumatra). His *Tuhfat al-Nafis* (Precious gift), written in the 1860s and 1870s, "set a new standard in Malay historiography" (Bottoms 1965:188). The *Tuhfat*, covering almost the entire Malay world, was of unprecedented scale. The aim of the *Tuhfat* was to show the "history of Bugis involvement in the Malay world, . . . explaining the reasons behind former conflicts and, by analogy, the lessons these held for the present generations" (Andaya and Matheson 1979:114). These lessons were intended for the common man as well as the ruler (Andaya and Matheson 1979). Raja Ali Haji rarely called upon fate (or God's will, *takdir*), because "an underlying assumption of the *Tuhfat* is that human failings and disavowal of God's law are the basic causes behind the tribulations and conflicts that beset society" (Andaya and Matheson 1979:118). He showed "how human behavior influenced the course of history," and he even examined "the motivations of men" (Andaya and Matheson 1979:115, 121). The *Tuhfat* continued an earlier work by the same author, the *Silsilah Melayu dan Bugis* (History of the Malays and Bugis), and both of them are invaluable historical sources (Andaya and Matheson 1979).

Raja Ali Haji also wrote didactic works on statecraft and the conduct of kings. He noted that kings were "subject to the same temptations as other men," and that if a ruler misbehaved, the "succession should then pass to the most fitting" (Andaya and Matheson 1979:119, 125). But, significantly, Andaya and Matheson (1979) observe that Raja Ali Haji would not himself denounce a sultan, because he knew the *Malay attitude* to such matters (i.e., Raja Ali Haji was aware that his view of sultans as being not so different from ordinary mortals was not the ordinary Malay view).

Others in Raja Ali Haji's line were also historically minded. His father had been a historian, and it was probably he who conceived the idea of the *Tuhfat al-Nafis* (Andaya and Matheson 1979). In spite of a long-standing Malay literary tradition in the sultanate to which Raja Ali Haji and family were attached, it was their family or those closely attached to it—who were "fiercely conscious of their [Bugis] descent and blood relationship"— who produced the bulk of the literature in the period in question (Andaya and Matheson 1979:110).

Raja Ali Haji was clearly under the direct influence of Near Eastern Muslim ideas (Andaya and Matheson 1979; Johns 1979), and he may also have reflected the British presence in his exceptional standards of historical writing (Johns 1979). But it may be just as important to note his Bugis background; his writings reflect the syndrome associated with sound historical writing in the context of an open society. It might perhaps have been just as appropriate to include him not among the Malay historians but among those of Makassar/Bugis.

Another example of the exotic origins of the sounder Malay historiography is provided by the autobiography of one Abdullah. He was from a Mysore Yemeni family that settled in Malacca in the late 1700s and was perhaps one-eighth Malay by ancestry. He was patronized by and wrote for the British. What he wrote would have made little sense to Malays and perhaps even been offensive (for reasons explained below). Abdullah's autobiography probably had an influence on Raja Ali Haji's *Tuhfat* but generally had little impact on the Malay community at the time (Johns 1979; Sweeney 1980). Yet another example is a biographical work translated as the "Memoirs of a Malayan Family," written by one 'La-uddin, a trader and agent for British and Dutch parties in the late 1700s. It was written at the request of a British Resident. It is straightforward and sound, and Johns observes that "it is important to note that [its author] belonged to a family in the service of the British, that he was not beholden to any native ruler, that he was not tied to the soil" (1979:63; see also Sweeney 1980).

A final example is provided by another autobiography, the *Tarikh Datuk Bentara Luar Johor*, described as the first autobiography written both *in* Malay and *by* a Malay (Sweeney 1980). It is actually three autobiographical writings by Mohamed Salleh bin Perang, who had achieved high rank in the sultanate of Johor in the latter part of the nineteenth century. His writings were published well after his death in 1905 and were to have been followed by more. But the volume was suppressed because it contained unfavorable comments on the reigning sultan of Johor, and no further of Salleh's autobiographical writings were published (Sweeney 1980). The translator of Salleh's *Tarikh* suggests that autobiography had no place in Malay literature because among the Malays individualism was not encouraged; he cites evidence that traditionally Malays did not even like to mention their own or their parents' names (Sweeney 1980). According to Sweeney (1980), Abdullah and 'La-uddin had only been able to write autobiographies because they wrote for European audiences. Salleh, by contrast, attempted to write autobiography for a Malay audience (Sweeney 1980). Though he left out some things we might expect in an autobiography, he at times expressed his emotions with freedom, he showed a historical consciousness, and clearly he had been a careful diarist (Sweeney 1980). Appropriately, Salleh's account of his life is specifically concerned with social mobility: "His account is, in effect, a record of achievement—an account of his 'moving up from one rank to another, until I reached my present rank'" (Sweeney 1980:31, quoting Mohamed Salleh). Salleh had been born poor, he rose to high office but was then forced to retire, and he died in humble circumstances again (Sweeney 1980). Just as interesting as his experience of and concern with social mobility is his family background: Salleh was of Bugis ancestry, as were the sultans he and his forebears served. Salleh did not think of himself as an upstart—he claimed descent from aristocracy—but he did try to defend his rise on the basis of merit (Sweeney 1980). Thus although he considers Salleh to have been a Malay, Sweeney (1980) also hints at the significance of Salleh's Bugis ancestry by suggesting that Salleh's diary keeping should be traced to Bugis custom. In addition to his Bugis ancestry, two other features may have contributed to Salleh's impulse to write autobiography. First, he had been a classroom student of Abdullah. While Salleh did not model his autobiography on Abdullah's, he was no doubt familiar with that work (Sweeney 1980). Second, Salleh was unusually familiar with Chinese culture. He learned to read, write, and speak Chinese well enough to lecture in it and to read Chinese literature for pleasure, and he studied Chinese painting and music as well (Sweeney 1980). However much Salleh may have been a Malay, he was far from a typical one.

By way of conclusion it should be noted that there *were* relatively sound Malay historical works, even a contemporary history produced by Malayan royalty (see, e.g., the discussion of the *Misa Melayu* in Winstedt 1969). But sound works, except by persons showing significant influence from outside Malay society, seem clearly to have been the exception.

J.M. Gullick's *Indigenous Political Systems of Western Malaya* (1958) provides a generalized picture of Malay society, though it draws most of its material from certain states on the Malay Peninsula. According to Gullick,

The division of the community into two classes . . . was one of the basic elements of Malay political and social structure. . . .

[L]eadership and control in all aspects of Malay life . . . tended to be concentrated in the ruling class.

The distinction between the two classes was strictly marked. Intermarriage was disapproved—in the upper class. It was almost impossible for a commoner to rise

into the ruling class of the State in which he had been born and where his ante-
cedents were known. Collections of Malay proverbs teem with disapprobation of
the attempted upstart. . . . (1958:65)

Later Gullick adds that "as a general rule membership of the ruling class
was determined strictly by descent" (1958:79). Royalty descended in the
male line. The remainder of the ruling class consisted of "lineages" with
claims to fill certain offices or "chieftainships" of the realm (Gullick 1958:66).

One of the Malay states, composed largely of immigrants from a matrilineal people of Sumatra, had a more permeable boundary between
commoner and chieftain (Gullick 1958). But in general the Malays (including the Bruneis described above and the more distantly related Acehnese
discussed below) conformed to the pattern of the closed society.

ACEH

Aceh (Atjeh, Acheh) was a Muslim sultanate in extreme northwest Sumatra.
Long a powerful state, it was only brought under Dutch control at great
cost early in this century. Acehnese as a language is closely related to Malay,
and in many respects Malays and Acehnese are similar. Siegel (1979) says
that the sultanate was as much Malay as Acehnese and that throughout
most of its history the court language was Malay. Thus Johns (1979:64)
says, "These old Malay courts—Melaka, and more important Acheh—
yield a kind of pseudo-historiography" tinged by Muslim standards but
fundamentally reflecting an indigenous folk tradition. He illustrates his
point with the *Hikayat Aceh*, in which fact and date are not important and
for which the "cultural matrix" is the same as for folk stories that reflect
a "steady state world" and cyclic time (Johns 1979:55). Genealogy and
natural disturbances that portend the future are important in the *hikayat*
(Johns 1979). Neither for Malacca nor for Aceh, in spite of their roles as
trade centers, do we have an archival collection of state or private contracts
(Johns 1976). In a comparison of Dutch and Acehnese accounts of their
mutual past, the Acehnese "were concerned not to preserve the events of
the past, . . . but to lessen their significance" (Siegel 1979:14–15). Elsewhere
Siegel (1976:331) says, on the basis of a text he analyzed and published
(1979), that "the writing of history in traditional Acheh . . . seems to have
been governed more by a fascination with rhetoric than by myth or political
history." As an exception to this pattern Johns (1979) cites the *Bustan al-*

Salatin, a universal history written in Malay in Aceh and partly devoted to a history of Aceh. But this work is clearly inspired by Muslim models and was written by a Gujarati, that is, neither a Malay nor an Acehnese.

The similarity of Malay and Acehnese historiography is matched by their systems of social stratification. Siegel (1969) says that Acehnese society was composed of four parts: the *uleebelang*, whom he cites as similar to the Malayan chieftains as described in Gullick 1958; the *ulama* (religious scholars/officials); the peasants; and the sultan and his group. He also notes that "chieftains, sultans, and peasants were all, in theory, born to their places" (1969:11). The *ulama* accepted the notion of common human nature, and for them social mobility (within their sphere) was possible. But their lifestyle required that they withdraw from village life. In an authoritative and lengthier description of the *uleebelang*, Snouck Hurgronje (1906) stresses that they were the true rulers of the land, that their positions were inherited, that their power was independent of the sultan's, and that they enjoyed very great respect from the populace. They were a hereditary nobility. Therefore, except for the *ulama* (and somewhat parallel examples were to be found in Brunei and possibly other Malay states), Aceh was a closed society.

JAVA

Lying south of the Malay Peninsula and east of Sumatra, Java has long been in many senses the central island of the Indonesian and Malaysian peoples. The rich soils washed down from its volcanic peaks have sustained a very dense population. For close to a thousand years the island was deeply influenced by Hindu-Buddhist culture, but in more recent centuries Islam has prevailed.

It was the contrast between the relatively unsound Javanese historiography and the relatively sound historiographies of Vietnam and Burma that led Hall (1961a:5) to ask, Why do "some communities in South East Asia have ideas of history and not others?" Hall (1961a:4) also noted that Burmese historians "seemed to have had a critical attitude" that Javanese historians lacked. Soedjatmoko (1965a:xix) added that in its various signs of soundness the historiography of the Makassarese/Buginese "differs strikingly from Javanese historiography." Elsewhere Soedjatmoko (1965b:410) describes "the ahistorical view of life, . . . in terms commonly used in the Javanese cultural tradition, where they are stated more explicitly than elsewhere in Indonesia." Early in this century Djajadiningrat concluded his doctoral comparison of medieval European and early Javanese historians by saying that the Javanese "completely lacked the critical faculty. The meaning of historical research was alien to them" (quoted in Mohammad Ali 1965:19).

In pioneering and controversial attempts to interpret and utilize those Javanese works that purport to describe Java's early history, C.C. Berg argues that these works differ sharply from what would normally be called history. "We have to realize that magic did, and love of historical truth did not, play a part in early Javanese social life, and that early Javanese texts are more likely, therefore, to reflect a magician's mind than a historian's interest in the past" (Berg 1961:16). "[T]he Javanese picture of the past reflects . . . the priestly cultivation of verbal magic" (Berg 1965:90). The magic was designed to support a particular state, ruler, or dynasty. Part of the verbal magic consisted of forging inscriptions to support the magical texts, along with the destruction of older texts that were aimed to bring about conditions no longer desired (Berg 1961, 1965). "This means that Javanese documents are generally unreliable and often even fantastic, though individual exceptions are possible" (Berg 1961:22). But elsewhere Berg says that biographical notes in a fourteenth-century work "may have helped to pave the way toward elementary historiography" (1965:108–9) and that a flourishing fifteenth-century interest in stories about the past— "more or less fantastic"—may have stimulated a "historical consciousness and the awareness of chronological order in community life" (1961:21).

But as de Graaf (1965) summarizes Berg, the value of a work for the Javanese generally was in reverse proportion to its value for a historian. In at least partial agreement with Berg, de Graaf (1965:130, 131) said that older Javanese manuscripts seem to have been used as political weapons and that even later works used alleged prophecies to legitimate things that occurred, rarely showed impartiality, and were undoubtedly sacred. But he doubts that manuscripts were systematically destroyed, neglect alone sufficing to eliminate many (de Graaf 1965).

While many authorities agree that many Javanese texts do not easily yield to conventional historical analysis (Soedjatmoko 1965a), Berg has been taken to task by various persons who see more straightforward historical usefulness in Javanese materials. Pigeaud, who translated and edited the *Nagara-Kertagama*, a fourteenth-century Javanese panegyrical poem, says that Berg's reliance on the notion of "literary magic" is an unrealistic oversimplification and that however much Javanese works may yield to mythical analyses, they should not be denied all reliability on questions of historical fact (Pigeaud 1960–63:V, 433). Supomo (1979) says that the *Nagara-Kertagama* has increasingly been shown to be reliable. Kumar (1979) agrees that the *Nagara-Kertagama*, and a slightly later work, the *Pararaton*, can be considered history, but she judges that historical works were rare in the period of Java's Hinduized kingdoms, and she notes that neither of these works was in fact preserved in Java. She thinks that the Javanese produced little in the way of historical writing in the nineteenth and twentieth centuries, as well as in the Hinduized period, but that in between, the quantitative output was considerable (Kumar 1979). Buchari (1965:47) stresses the sheer volume of historical sources preserved in Java compared to elsewhere in Indonesia. This undoubtedly reflects the many monuments left by densely populated kingdoms over a long period of time.

In addition to noting that the quantity of historical writing improved in the later Javanese periods (before the nineteenth century), Kumar (1979:203) also shows that some of the historical materials in these periods approached sound standards, being "secular, political, realistic," complex, and unidirectional in their view of time. Also, they give "a lively commentary on the distinctive physical and mental characteristics of representatives of recognizably different cultures" (1979:203). She is inclined to attribute the florescence of historical writing not to the coming of Islam— because nearby Hindu Bali was historiographically prolific in the same period—but rather to the severe warfare and generally unsettled state of society in the period, for the historical writing came to an end with Dutch pacification (Kumar 1979). De Graaf (1965) and Ricklefs (1976) both defend later, primarily Muslim-period Javanese historical texts on qualitative as well as quantitative grounds. Ricklefs (1976) implies that there are thousands of volumes available and that historical texts without mythological introductions are abundant from the seventeenth to the nineteenth centuries. De Graaf (1965) says that genealogical materials in seventeenth-century sources are often accurate and that the historical value of later texts has been underestimated because the earlier texts or early parts of later texts have given Javanese historiography a bad name. He analyzes a history, the *Babad Dipanagara*, written by a famous rebel of the nineteenth century. It extends from Adam up to the personal memories of its author, and it shows at least some sense of history.

Ricklefs (1976) says that almost all Javanese narratives were poetic and were meant to be read out loud. He does not, nor do any of the others who defend Javanese historiography's quality, say that it is equal to or superior to that of the Burmese, Makassarese/Buginese, or Vietnamese (though it no doubt quantitatively exceeds the output of the Makassarese/ Buginese). On the contrary, Ricklefs (1976) says that severe judgments of Javanese historiography would be widely accepted, even though he disagrees with the least favorable judgments. In sum, the consensus, albeit a severely qualified one, is that for much of its history Java produced relatively little sound historiography.

Old Javanese kingdoms are almost always described as having been Hindu or Hinduized. Even in modern Java the remnants of Indian civilization—in art, literature, language, beliefs, and social practices—are ubiquitous. The extent to which the Indian caste system developed in Java is a point of debate, but it is certain that caste ideology was espoused by at least some old Javanese authors. Schrieke (1957:78) quotes a Javanese seer who explained ancient stability in terms of the four *varna* being "fixed and content" and Schrieke summarizes the point of view as follows: "Everyone should remain within the bounds of the rights and duties laid upon him by the caste into which he was born." However, it is clear that these caste ideals were expressed at least in part because they were not being adequately maintained (Schrieke 1957). Pigeaud (1960–63:IV, 468) notes that although the four *varna* are mentioned in the *Nagara-Kertagama*, it is a mere "scholarly embellishment of Court literature." He finds the most commonly mentioned classes to be "rulers, men of religion, commoners and bondmen" (1960–63:IV, 468). While he gives no supporting cases, he says it "does not seem preposterous" that men of low birth may have risen to high posts as "Royal servants" (Pigeaud 1960–63:IV, 529). He is also inclined to think that, although there is no positive evidence of it, the fourteenth-century Javanese may already have had a rule whereby rank diminished as the number of generations from a ruler increased, nobility being extinguished in a certain number of generations (Pigeaud 1960–63:IV). It also needs to be kept in mind that Buddhist elements were strong in old Java, and the possibility that Buddhist anticaste notions were known there should not be ruled out. One thing that does seem fairly certain is that the ideology of descent was of great importance to rulers. Accordingly, usurpations or other anomalies in kingly succession generated elaborate mythmaking to insure the hereditary legitimacy of new rulers; equally clear is the idea that the rulers were divine, or incarnations of the divine (Schrieke 1957).

In the Muslim Javanese kingdom of Mataram, from the sixteenth to the nineteenth centuries, "neither servant nor master is allowed to transgress the formal dividing lines of the social hierarchy, apparent in birth or rank." One "cannot justify forgetting one's place in society, a place which fate has allotted" (Soemarsaid Moertono 1968:15). Legitimation of kingship by descent remained a strong principle in the Muslim period, but noble or royal status was lost if one was more than seven generations from a monarch (Soemarsaid Moertono 1968). On the other hand, between the king and his relatives was a class of officials, the king's servants, whose very title, *kawulawisuda*, implies mobility, since *kawula* means subject or servant, and *wisuda*, to promote. Soemarsaid Moertono (1968) is explicit in indicating that this allowed commoners to enter the elite. In a discussion of native rulers under the Dutch, Schrieke (1955:279 n. 11) even says that "the history of Java is full of *homines novi*. . . . "The social structure is stable but there is a constant change in the composition of the upper class." This appears to refer to de facto mobility, with little support from ideology except perhaps in the pre-Dutch Muslim period. Barring certain offices, there was, apparently, a tendency in the later centuries of Mataram's existence for offices to become hereditary (Soemarsaid Moertono 1968).

The Dutch preferred to deal with hereditary leaders in Java (Schrieke 1955), and under the Dutch, Javanese society as a whole was rather rigidly stratified by race—as defined by descent, not culture (Skinner 1960). Under the Dutch, the Javanese nobility, the *priyayi*, consisted primarily of the regents and other Javanese officials down to the level of the subdistrict head. The regents were considered descendants of the old Javanese rulers and ultimately of Hindu immigrants. They can be called a "feudal nobility" (Palmier 1960:39). Roughly coordinate with the regents were princes who were left in place and who were less under the direct administration of the Dutch (Palmier 1960). Titles of nobility tended to be inherited both in the principalities and in the regencies (Palmier 1960).

To summarize, ancient Java was sufficiently Hinduized that caste ideology can be detected in its writings. But the correspondence of ideology with reality may have been weak, and a Buddhist ideology may at times have prevailed. In the Muslim period I find no evidence of an ideology of open stratification but strong evidence of social mobility in the ruler's service. By the nineteenth century, under the Dutch, Javanese society was quite clearly closed. This suggests that Javanese historiography should be treated in three phases. In the first, or Hindu phase, the quality of historiography is somewhat controversial. Berg and others judge it unsound, while Pigeaud, Supomo, and Kumar find value in such works as the *Nagara-Kertagama* (a judgment I would confirm). At the same time, the evidence on social stratification in the Hinduized period is not conclusive one way or the other. In the Muslim period a probable improvement in historiography was accompanied by a probable opening of society. Under the Dutch both of these conditions reversed. Except for the uncertainty concerning the Hinduized period, these findings are reasonably consistent with expectations.

BALI

Hooykaas (1961:318) says that "the Balinese have produced a considerable amount of historiography, generally concerning the rise and fall of their petty kingdoms." Kumar (1979:188) notes that at times Balinese historiography was "reasonably prolific." But Hooykaas (1961:318) also says that "one would be completely at a loss for a picture of the past if one had to confine oneself to Indonesian 'historiography.' " It is not certain, therefore, that Hooykaas intended to provide a warm endorsement of Balinese historiography, except quantitatively. Buchari (1965:47) adds a further quantitative judgment, saying that both Bali and Java have been good at preserving "historical sources." As I suggested was the case in Java, so too in Bali: the sheer density of population and long periods of unbroken residence account for much of this quantitative strength. But it is worth pursuing the Balinese case further, because Bali provides probably the best case of caste in Southeast Asia.

As early as the middle of the nineteenth century, Bali's ahistorical nature was noted: "The statements of the Balinese upon historical . . . subjects are extremely inaccurate" (Friederich [1877] 1959:103). Much more recently, Worsley (1972:v–vi) has wondered whether it is really correct to apply the terms "history" and "historiography" to Balinese accounts of the past (i.e., their *babad*). Following Soedjatmoko (1965b), Worsley finds in Bali an ahistorical weltanschauung. Soedjatmoko found this ahistorical attitude characteristic of all Indonesians, though it was best expressed among the Javanese; in many senses the Balinese and the ancient Javanese share a common culture. Balinese and Javanese accounts of the past have "more in common with myth, legend and parable than with history" (Worsley 1972:vi). Worsley makes these comments in the context of his translation of the *Babad Buleleng: A Balinese Dynastic Genealogy*, the chief preoccupation of which is "legitimacy and succession" in Den Bukit, a north Balinese state (1972:vii). In a sense the work is biographical, in that about half of it relates the life of the founder of the clan that ruled the kingdom.

But this sort of work is almost never classified as biography, because, as Worsley notes,

the actors in the *babad*'s narrative have been depicted as types in the form of an ideal image. They are abstract and anonymous men who behave in a way wholly predictable within the logic of the image in which they have been formed. Moreover they are men who do not control their own destiny or the destinies of those about them for . . . they are subject to the vicissitudes of chance and a divine will which is not within their control. (1972:79–80)

Worsley also finds that the *babad* has only a casual sense of chronology. A few dates are mentioned, but they are "clearly not intended to establish a precise date of the developments with which the *babad* is principally preoccupied or to measure their duration." "[C]riteria other than chronological criteria have determined the arrangement of what is ostensibly a chronological narrative" (Worsley 1972:80–82). Thus Worsley finds in the *babad* that "detemporalizing . . . conception of time" (quoting Geertz 1966:44) that Geertz finds characteristic of the Balinese (but cf. Bloch 1977).

Typical of Balinese *babad*, the *Babad Buleleng* is anonymous, even though it was written no sooner than 1872 and perhaps as late as 1928 (Worsley 1972). Related to this are Geertz's views on the relative lack of individualism in Bali. Examining Balinese notions of personal identity, Geertz (1966:43) finds them paradoxically depersonalizing. The depersonalizing and detemporalizing features of Balinese culture are not, according to Geertz, accidentally linked: "The perception of fellow men, the experience of history and the temper of collective life . . . are hooked together by a definable logic," but a logic that is social rather than syllogistic (1966:61). Fortunately, we know rather much about Bali's collective life—and hereditary stratification is central to it.

Bali is among the most thoroughly studied of all the societies in Southeast Asia. The similarity of Bali to India is well known, and it is largely due to borrowing, either directly or by way of Java. Bali was very much in the sphere of Javanese cultural and political influence up to the fall of the great Javanese empire of Majapahit early in the sixteenth century. At that time refugees from Majapahit allegedly made Bali their new home and thereby imposed Hindu-Javanese culture even more firmly on the Balinese.

The Balinese are extraordinarily concerned with rank. "It was surprising to discover the extent to which the question of rank obsesses . . . the

Balinese," Covarrubias observed in 1937. The "Balinese [are] so conscious of caste, the determination of a man's place in society by his birth, that the whole of their social life and etiquette is moulded by this institution" (Covarrubias 1937:46). According to Geertz, in the nineteenth century rank was the "ruling obsession" of Balinese culture, "the axis round which the public life of society revolved" (1980:123).

As in India, the *varna* scheme stratifies society. The three upper *varna*, the Brahman, Kshatriya, and Vaishya, constitute about 10 percent of the populace and are called the *triwangsa* (three races, or three peoples). Members of the lowest *varna*, the Sudra, are called *wang kesaman* (ones of common stock) or *wong jaba* (persons who are outside). The *triwangsa* traditionally dominated supravillage affairs. The constituent elements of the *varna*, the analogues of the castes in India, are generally less concretely organized in Bali. But except for many of the Sudra, Balinese inherit titles. These title-inheriting groups or categories are in theory assignable to one or another of the *varna*. However, just as in India, agreement was not universal as to which titles belonged to which *varna*. In spite of the less-organized nature of Balinese "castes," miscaste marriages were severely punished (Covarrubias 1937; Geertz 1959, 1980; Goris [1929] 1960; Swellengrebel 1969).

Different ranks in Bali result from differing degrees of divinity. The *triwangsa* "are supposed to originate directly from the gods," and as in India, "the Brahmanas sprang out of the mouth of Brahma, the Satria from his arms, and the Wesia from his feet" (Covarrubias 1937:53). The *triwangsa* "consider themselves a superior class of beings" (Swellengrebel 1969:211), and the "common people take for granted the divine superiority of the aristocracy" (Covarrubias 1937:47). Concerning this differential sacredness embodied in social stratification, Geertz (1980:16–17) describes what he calls the "sinking status pattern," which "rests on the notion that mankind has descended from the gods." But mankind "has declined at differing rates in different lines, through various worldly events and social happenings, . . . producing thereby the present . . . system of prestige ranking." This system "gives, at least in theory, an ascribed, unequivocal, and, so far as the individual is concerned, unchangeable status in an honorific hierarchy to every person." Thus each person's rank "is a reflex of the mythical history of that person's paternal line as it has steadily sunk from its divine ancestral origin to its present . . . estate." The various lines have "not all sunk to the same level," with differing ranks resulting from differing rates of decline. Elsewhere, Geertz (1980:102) says that "there is an unbroken inner connection between social rank and religious condition." For the Balinese, "worldly status has a cosmic base, . . . hierarchy is the governing principle of the universe, and . . . the arrangements of human life are but approximations, more close or less, to those of the divine."

On the question of mobility, Geertz claims that "[s]ave for a few unusual exceptions, mobility between levels within the [Balinese] prestige system is in theory impossible and in practice difficult" (1959:996). Both Goris (n.d.) and Swellengrebel (1969) mention instances of vertical mobility, downward as well as upward, but except perhaps for the change of status of a low-caste woman who marries up, the instances seem to be few. In spite of the allegedly hereditary or ascriptive nature of rank, competition between nobles is intense. This competition has its most elaborate expression in rituals, ceremony, pomp, politesse, and courtesy, but in violence too. Thus Geertz (1980:13), having noted that "the ruling obsessions of Balinese culture [were] social inequality and status pride," says that affairs of state took on a theatricality "in which kings and princes were the impresarios, the priests the directors, and the peasants the supporting cast, stage crew, and audience. . . . Court ceremonialism was the driving force of politics." Elsewhere he says that "the ceremonial life of the classical [Balinese state] was as much a form of rhetoric as it was of devotion, a florid, boasting assertion of spiritual power" (Geertz 1980:102). As in Balinese culture, in politics "status was [the] ruling obsession," and ritual and ceremonial "splendor was the stuff of status" (Geertz 1980:123). The "motor" of the state was ceremony (Geertz 1980:129). In addition to competition through ritual and ceremony, a "steady hum of political violence . . . plagued the Balinese state" (Geertz 1980:85).

The exuberant development of religion and ritual on Bali is almost too well known to warrant comment. But the extent to which this development is connected with nobility and the courts deserves stress. Describing the relationships between Balinese courts, Geertz (1980:16) says, "The whole structure was based . . . primarily on ceremony and prestige." The assiduous ritualism of court culture was . . . not merely the drapery of political order, but its substance" (Geertz 1980:32). Later (1980:62) he says that the Balinese state was "a ceremonial order of precedence" and that "there was an elaborate status ethic of honor and politesse, a kind of chivalric code minus horse, homage, and romantic love (but not pride, pomp, and passion) which bound all the great and near-great figures into that sort of baronial community in which etiquette has the force of law and even maleficence must be drenched in courtesy" (Geertz 1980:40).

Finally, Geertz's main argument is that the Balinese state was one of theatricality—its ritual, pomp, and splendor were the very essence of its politics (1980). For Geertz this makes the Balinese sufficiently peculiar that they should not be studied in terms appropriate to Western politics. Yet the resemblance of Bali not only to India but also to medieval Europe (see especially Huizinga [1924] 1950) is too remarkable to have resulted from accident. The resemblance includes not only historiographic quality and mode of social stratification but also a substantial portion of the other concomitants too.

MAKASSAR/BUGIS

The Makassarese and Buginese are related peoples living in the southwest of the island of Sulawesi (Celebes) in Indonesia. Since the seventeenth century they have been Muslims, and they have long been oriented toward the sea as traders and fishermen. At the core of their accounts of the past is a tradition of chronicles, called *pattorioloang* (Mak.) or *attoriolong* (Bug.). The literal meaning of the term is "the things concerning the people of former times" (Noorduyn 1965:140 n. 1). Although the chronicles refer to events dated as early as the sixteenth century, none of them appears to have been written before the seventeenth (Noorduyn 1961, 1965). Noorduyn (1961, 1965) thinks that Makassar/Bugis historical writing was probably an indigenous development, certainly not likely to have been derived from Malay or Javanese historiography.

The chronicles are written in simple prose; they are terse, objective, matter-of-fact, and relatively short (Noorduyn 1961, 1965). Although dates are rare, an overall chronological order is maintained in that each main chapter refers to a single king's reign. Each chapter follows a more or less fixed sequence of topics, including the ruler's names, titles, and appanages; important events in his life; the number of years in his reign; wars; kings and places he subdued; his wives and children; sometimes new techniques or customs introduced; an appreciation of the king's character and capacities; a notice of his death; and his posthumous name (Noorduyn 1965). This format bears considerable resemblance to that of Muslim royal biographies (cf. Rosenthal 1968), in spite of Noorduyn's opinion that Makassar/Buginese historiography developed independently.

The chronicles contain very little in the way of myth and almost none of the backdated prophecies found in Javanese historical writing. Some of the earliest portions of the chronicles are mythical, but the authors seem

clearly to disassociate themselves from the myths (Noorduyn 1965; Soedjatmoko 1965a). Although the chronicles are mostly about kings and
princes, they are generally treated as ordinary human beings "who by birth
and position are the leading forces in history" (Andaya 1979:360; see also
Noorduyn 1961).

The sources of the chronicles appear to have been diaries of kings and
private individuals. Some of these diaries have been preserved, even some
written by Malays living in Makassar. But diaries seem to be peculiar to
South Sulawesi, or to peoples under its cultural influence; none were
known from Malaya or Java (Noorduyn 1961, 1965). Rudimentary archives
were also present, at least in the Makassarese kingdom of Goa, where a
chancellor was officially charged with keeping treaties (Noorduyn 1961).

Noorduyn (1965:154) describes the people of South Sulawesi as possessing "a keen interest in this world and its affairs." And he notes (1961:35)
that the objectivity and concern for facts shown in the chronicles of the
Makassar/Bugis appeared "in other domains as well, as is shown by the
annotations on maps for navigators, the precise data about weapons, houses,
ships, etc., in notebooks, and the inventories drawn up by administrators
of estates." In a minor way, one is reminded both of the secular humanism
and this-worldliness of the Renaissance. Taking a comparative perspective,
Soedjatmoko (1965a:xix) lists the strengths of Makassar/Bugis historiography and observes that it therefore differed "strikingly from Javanese
historiography." Andaya (1979:361), who has himself worked with the
indigenous materials of the Makassar/Bugis world, cites a number of scholars who "expressed great admiration for the historical sense of the Bugis/
Makassar people." At one point Noorduyn (1961) merely ranks the importance of their historiography with that of the Malays and Javanese, but
the general impression he and others give is that Makassar/Bugis historiography is unusually sound for the insular Southeast Asian world.

According to Chabot 1950, the Makassarese divide themselves into aristocrats (*karaeng*) and commoners. Bonds of patron to client link the former
to the latter, but these bonds may be established or broken at will. The
individual ties between *karaeng* and their followers do not give rise to
clearly defined strata; if asked his rank, virtually any Makassarese will claim
that he or his kin group is aristocratic. While rank is considered to be
based largely on descent, it is also based on personal qualities: ancient
sources sanction high status for the wealthy, the learned, the courageous
man. Since all, or virtually all, kin groups consider themselves to be of
high status, all are engaged in a struggle to assert their rank over others.

Marriage is one of the principal arenas of this struggle. Men are expected to try to raise their rank—through wealth, violence, or scholarship, or through simply assuming the behavior of aristocrats—and women are expected not to let their rank fall. If a man shows the appropriate personal qualities, he may properly marry above his station, though it may take a few generations before a kin group previously considered to be of the rank of commoner is thereby fully accepted as nobility (Chabot 1950). At least one of the Bugis states, Wadjo, lacked even a hereditary kingship (Noorduyn 1961).

A very recent study of the Bugis (Millar 1983:478) says that they have "an apparently time-honored cultural preoccupation with 'social location' (knowing one's hierarchical position with respect to all other individuals)," and that this preoccupation is "in terms of a dynamic tension between ascriptive and achieved status." The Bugis are intensely concerned with rank, and it is largely hereditary. Yet they also have highly developed notions of how fate (*takdir*) and the judicious nurturance and balancing of one's *bateng* and *lahiring* (which I will gloss as inner and outer character, though this is a simplification) allow for upward mobility. A commoner man may thereby achieve the highest rank in Bugis society, may properly marry a noble woman, and may see his children accepted as noble. In Millar's view, "the approved incidents of individuals marrying above their level of ascribed rank are at the heart of the dynamic tension in Bugis society" (1983:483). We should note, however, that upward mobility is not itself an ideal; achieving a proper balance between inner and outer character is. But the effect is much the same. "The greater variety of possible resolutions to the effort to achieve a *lahiring/bateng* balance, and the constant ambiguity with regard to the *lahiring/bateng* balances of others, gives to Bugis society the remarkable dynamism for which it is well known throughout Indonesia" (Millar 1983:480–81). While Millar describes Bugis preoccupation with rank as "apparently time-honored," it is of course only speculation that the complex of ideas and behavior she describes was generally characteristic of the Makassar/Buginese peoples of the past.

Noorduyn (1965:147n) quotes Chabot to the effect that the whole of South Sulawesi is characterized by opposition "among individuals or groups, more or less manifestly directed at the enlargement of their prestige and power." This implies social mobility, and Noorduyn—who is concerned more with the area's history than its ethnography—apparently has no reservations about projecting this state of affairs into the past. In sum, social mobility, though perhaps culturally couched in peculiar ways, is a preoccupation of the Makassarese, and the pattern appears to be old, although hereditary claims to rank are acknowledged too. The "tension between ascriptive and achieved status" that Millar (1983:478) speaks of has its counterpart, as will be seen, among various historically minded peoples.

It is instructive to compare Javanese with Makassar/Bugis ideas on matters closely related to the possibility of social mobility. Soedjatmoko describes "the ahistorical view of life, . . . couched in the terms commonly used in the Javanese cultural tradition, where they are stated more explicitly than elsewhere in Indonesia," as follows:

The ahistorical outlook on life . . . perceives life and the flow of human events as a process beyond human control and therefore beyond human responsibility.

. . . [T]he question of man's ability and responsibility to influence the . . . course of events becomes irrelevant and unimportant. The only thing he can do is [fulfill his *dharma*], play out the part assigned to him in accord with that station in the order of things into which he was born. (1965b:409–10)

By contrast, Andaya (1979) analyzes a traditional village tale (based on the hero of an actual event in the seventeenth century) that was still popular in Makassar in the 1970s. Among the "traditional values" expressed in the tale was one called in Makassarese *sare* (in Buginese *were*), which translates as one's fate, or one's destiny (Andaya 1979:369, 378). The uses of this term, in the tale he analyzes, "clearly indicate that one achieves one's *sare* through one's own action in life" (1979:369). It is a folk tale he analyzes, not one of the court chronicles on which the reputation of Makassar/Bugis historiography rests, but by the use of the term traditional, Andaya implies that the concept of *sare* existed in the past, and he nowhere suggests that it is not found in the chronicles. The indicators all point in the direction of an open society.

VIETNAM

For more than a millennium Vietnam was an "integral part of the Chinese empire" (Hall 1964:184). For nearly the next millennium, until the French gained control of Indochina, Chinese remained the official language of Vietnam. Vietnam's historical writings and social order show considerable Chinese influence.

As I remarked earlier, it was the contrast between Vietnamese and

Javanese historiography that led Hall to ask why some of the peoples of Southeast Asia had an idea of history while others did not. Moreover, Malleret 1961 notes various ways in which Vietnamese historiography was superior to that of Laos and Cambodia. And because of the ordered chronology of Vietnamese history, "long periods of time can . . . be surveyed with much more assurance than is possible with the earlier history of other parts of Southeast Asia" (Wolters 1976:204). The author's judgments on Vietnamese historiography in Honey 1961 are uniformly negative, but it is clear that his position for judging was not with respect to other Asian civilizations but from the perspective of modern Western historiography. In fact, he gives considerable evidence that the Vietnamese were very sound historians by Southeast Asian standards. Johns (1976:306) lists some of the conditions that must be met for historical writing to develop and adds that these conditions "almost by definition" did not exist in Southeast Asia—except in Sinicized Indochina. Chandler (1979:208) compares Vietnam with Cambodia and Thailand, and says that historical writing was never "as honoured or as popular" among the latter as among the former. Finally, Marr (1979:313) says that the "Vietnamese take history very seriously, possibly more so than anyone else in Southeast Asia. This is not a new characteristic, nor is it limited to the educated elite." The consensus on the relative soundness of Vietnamese historiography is considerable.

Both official and private histories were written in Vietnam, the former by mandarins of the court at the ruler's request, the latter by private scholars. The earliest extant official history of Vietnam covers the period from the thirteenth to the seventeenth centuries. Relatively few of the private histories have survived, but the earliest, a "Brief History of Annam" by Le Tac, dates from the thirteenth century. The principal official histories order events on a reign-by-reign basis and tend to treat preceding dynasties harshly while inflating the current one. Like the official histories, private histories also follow a chronological order and give little in the way of causes or motives. There is little evaluation of source materials (Honey 1961).

In addition to the official histories, Vietnamese mandarins produced four other kinds of material of historical value: (1) "collections of administrative and legislative documents," (2) imperial family genealogies, (3) "accounts of the doings of an emperor and his forebears," and (4) "biographies of outstanding Vietnamese men and women." In more recent times geographical treatises were produced too (Honey 1961:96). Due to disturbed conditions, the documentation that has survived from before the seventeenth century is minimal (Honey 1961; Malleret 1961). Archives were kept by the Vietnamese, but even in the eighteenth century there were no institutional provisions for maintaining them in an orderly fashion (Honey 1961; Malleret 1961). The use of archives for historical criticism was not common, and the critical spirit in general was weak (Malleret 1961). In spite of these criticisms of Vietnamese preservation of records, Malleret notes that by comparison there was no official care given to the conservation of documents in Cambodia or Laos. Moreover, "there is no evidence in these countries, as there is in Vietnam, of great scholars or compilers who have left precise accounts of the state of early archives" (Malleret 1961:305). This actually speaks very strongly on behalf of Vietnamese historiography and suggests that Vietnam had some of the best archives in Southeast Asia.

According to Wolters (1979:83), Vietnamese cited Chinese historical records because they "were seen to contain valuable practical guidance on matters connected with the welfare of rulers." They "embodied the well-tested" and "practical experience of hallowed antiquity." Historical texts were treated like encyclopedias, to be consulted when apparently relevant to specific situations, such as imperial succession (Wolters 1979). According to Marr (1979:317), history served the Vietnamese primarily to reinforce ethical and religious principles, but also "historians often served the monarch by searching texts and records for precedents on problems of political, economic, or military policy." Because Vietnamese historians believed that the "past contained lessons for the present and the future," historians shaped their accounts of the past in order to teach lessons (Wolters 1976:204). No doubt this did not always have beneficial results, but Wolters (1976) gives an extended analysis of how the historian Le Van Huu, in the thirteenth century, composed history to draw a lesson concerning dynastic structure and orderly succession to the throne. A rudimentary sociopolitical analysis is indicated.

In addition to dynastic national histories, "many local families kept careful genealogical and biographical records" (Marr 1979:313). Biography was very popular in French Vietnam, but collections of biographies date from as early as the fourteenth century (Marr 1979). Marr (1979:316) suggests that divination in China and Vietnam were very similar: "Heaven and humanity were linked together by an abundance of omens."

Having been under intense Chinese influence for nearly two thousand years, many Chinese social and political practices were adopted in Vietnam. Among these adoptions was the bureaucratic examination system, which gave—ideally, at least—institutional backing to meritocracy (McAlister and Mus 1970; Woodside 1971). These examinations were introduced by the eleventh century and were being held regularly by the mid-1200s (Wolters 1979; Woodside 1971). In a comparison of England and Vietnam in the fifteenth and sixteenth centuries, Smith (1976) noted that there had never been a feudal nobility in Vietnam and that in spite of strenuous efforts, each Vietnamese clan that seized the throne tended to lose it fairly quickly to another clan. In at least one period, however, one clan held not only the throne but most high offices (Wolters 1976). Had this situation stabilized, Vietnam would have been more of a closed society.

In the nineteenth century, but "using classical materials, popular scholar poets . . . expounded the idea that men, all men, have the potentiality of changing first themselves, and then external reality" (Marr 1979:318). Borrowing a Chinese proverb, the Vietnamese said, "Nobody stays rich for three generations; nobody stays poor for three generations" (McAlister and Mus 1970:33).

BURMA

D.G.E. Hall, who had a deep familiarity with the Burmese, said that their chroniclers had a critical attitude when compared to the Javanese; he also noted that Burmese chronological treatment was "careful" (Hall 1961a:5). Luce (1976:36) says cautiously that Burmese histories are "not valueless," at least after the fourteenth century. Early Western historians of Burma gave the indigenous sources high marks (Hall 1961b; Tet Htoot 1961; Tin Ohn 1961). One of them, G. E. Harvey, said of Burma: "No other country on the mainland of Indo-China can show so impressive a continuity. The great record of substantially accurate dates goes back no less than nine centuries and even the earlier legends have a stratum of truth" (quoted by Tin Ohn 1961:90). U Tet Htoot (1961:50) thinks that the Burmese chronicles can be compared with Elizabethan chronicles. He also notes that the stated purposes of the Burmese chronicles was "to give moral instruction on the art of government to kings, ministers, generals, envoys, and other government officials" (Tet Htoot 1961:50). These uses are widely associated with sound historiography and show its relationship to political science. Indeed, Sangermano ([1833] 1969:181), who lived in Burma in the late eighteenth and early nineteenth centuries, said of written works "which certain wise men composed for the instruction of the Emperors, and the direction of young men," that they presented "principles of political science, not only sound and reasonable, but nearly of the same nature as those which are known among us as the Machiavelian."

The authors of Burmese chronicles are often known, but there were no official historians (Tet Htoot 1961). A great many inscriptions have been left by the Burmese. Though often religious in reference, they are factual and lack the "Indian flamboyance and exaggeration" (Luce 1976:37). They are good sources but were rarely used by Burmese historians (Luce 1976).

Father Sangermano ([1833] 1969:156) said that "it may . . . be put down among the good qualities of this people, that they consider all men as equal in condition." Officials and monks, when in office or in the order, are treated with great respect, but "when deposed," or "when they throw off the habit, are regarded with no peculiar marks of distinction." A small number of outcaste statuses were, however, of very low and sometimes hereditary rank. Social mobility was sometimes spectacular: "it is a frequent occurrence here for a man to be raised in a moment, by the caprice of the monarch, from the lowest state of poverty and degradation to the rank of minister or general" (Sangermano [1833] 1969:152).

Writing toward the end of the nineteenth century, Scott essentially confirms what Sangermano said (Yoe 1963). The Burmese, Scott said, are very rank conscious and sharply divide their populace into ranked categories. But position in these ranks is determined not by birth but by merit—theoretically, merit achieved in previous lives. The Burmese even have a tradition that their kings were once chosen strictly according to merit earned in previous lives rather than hereditarily. "The Buddhist religion is thoroughly democratic" (Yoe 1963:407). "[A]ll distinction came from office, or from a special patent from the king" (Yoe 1963:409). This is not quite true, however, because lower provincial officials, *thugyi*, enjoyed hereditary succession to their offices (Hall 1950:134). Burmese monastic education was open to all boys, which accounted for a high rate of literacy (Yoe 1963).

In sum, there were hereditary elements in the Burmese social system: the kingship, a relatively small number of outcastes, and district officials. But for most Burmese the system was open, ideologically and actually.

CAMBODIA

Malleret (1961) says of the Cambodians (and the Laotians) that they were not so assiduous as the Vietnamese in maintaining records. The comparison of Cambodia with Vietnam is meaningful, since their sizes and durations are similar. By the time the French established themselves in Cambodia, in the nineteenth century, the Cambodians "had already fallen back upon fiction, to the extent that they attributed the construction of the Angkor monuments to the gods, and allowed the names of [great] kings . . . to be buried in oblivion" (Malleret 1961:305). While not explicit or comparative, this implies considerable unsoundness in Cambodia's historiography. In the colonial period, says Chandler (1979), foreigners showed more interest in Cambodian history than did Cambodians.

Vickery 1979 argues that the Cambodian chronicles were perhaps conceived as part of the royal regalia and hence were written during periods of royal restoration. As late as this century, Vickery reports, the Cambodians saw written history in this sense and thus produced texts more magical than historical. The chroniclers were normally very casual about accuracy, and their writings were just as normally neglected "until a time of stress directed attention to them" again (Vickery 1979:153).

The Cambodian chronicles were always written, but they showed little concern for nuances of language and hence were of little interest as a literary genre. They purport to be true and have a clear context of time and place (Vickery 1979). The chronicles were neither for recitation nor for entertainment. They tended to a flat recital of events and an accurate recording of kingly ceremonial, while suppressing the personality of the author. "Historians outside the palace were not meant to read the chronicles, and neither was the general public" (Chandler 1979:209). Vickery compares various texts from Cambodia and from the nearby Thai kingdom of Ayudhya to show that the historical events presented for Cambodia's fourteenth century are actually sixteenth-century events moved backward to make Cambodia's history as long as Ayudhya's. The first 150 years of Cambodian history "are thus entirely artificial" (Vickery 1979:150). If Vickery's analysis is correct, it indicates a general carelessness about historical preservation in Cambodia, and it is a case of the sort of falsification that earns a historiographic tradition poor marks. However, the only comparative judgment actually made by the historians cited here was that Cambodia's record keeping was not as good as Vietnam's.

For six centuries Cambodia has been a predominantly Buddhist country, its Buddhism being the Hinayana form as found on Sri Lanka and in Burma and Thailand. But before Buddhism achieved dominance in Cambodia, Hinduism had a very strong hold there, and certain aspects of caste, or at any rate of the *varna* system, have shown an unusual tenacity in the country.

The Hinduization of Cambodia during its period of greatness, from the tenth to the fourteenth centuries, is extensively documented in Briggs 1951. This work cites numerous and detailed epigraphical references to the Brahman and Kshatriya *varna*, to clans (*gotra*, usually if not always matrilineal) within the Brahman *varna*, and the various offices, appanages, and privileges of this hereditary elite. References to the lower-ranking *varna* are, however, rare or absent. The inscriptions make it clear that one of the Angkorian kings' principal duties was to insure "domestic peace by imposing on everyone the obligation to respect the social order, that is the division between the various castes" (Coedès 1968:119). Coedès 1966 describes of the Brahmans and the princes (Kshatriya) as forming a class apart. Hall (1964:102) speaks of a "narrow oligarchy" in ancient Cambodia, composed of intermarrying royal and sacerdotal families who "formed a class racially different from the rest of the population" and who embodied the Hindu tradition. Cady (1964:101) also describes the Brahmans and Kshatriya as composing an intermarrying upper class that was "closed to many on racial as well as cultural grounds," and with rigid rules prohibiting relations between it and commoners.

Insofar as these remarks indicate Hinduization, they would not differ greatly from what could be said of many old Southeast Asian kingdoms. But there is evidence that in some ways Cambodia was Hinduized to an unusual degree. The literary quality of the Sanskrit epigraphy in Cambodia is excellent in all periods; the study of the Hindu classics was patronized; full knowledge of the Hindu epics and of the philosophies and mythologies of the various Hindu sects was consistently displayed; and "Cambodia was uniquely productive in examples of original contributions to Sanskrit literature" (Cady 1964:100).

We do not, of course, know the extent to which caste regulations were actually applied (Cady [1964:101] says they "did not strictly apply"), nor do we have any sort of quantitative knowledge of social mobility. But the evidence of caste in an Indian form is strong. It should be recalled that Cambodia's Hinduized age of greatness is known to us only through epigraphy, archaeology, and the study of historical sources from outside Cambodia. The later indigenous chroniclers knew nothing of the period.

Aymonier 1900 describes conditions in Cambodia around 1880, about fifteen years after the French established a protectorate over it. Royalty were called the "Brahman vansa" and consisted of persons who could trace descent to a reigning monarch in less than five generations. More distant descendants of former monarchs (unless of course they could trace royal descent in fewer generations to a subsequent monarch) dropped into the next lower "caste," the Brahman van. The latter were almost identical to royalty but had no right to the throne. The Brahman van transmitted their status patrilineally and had their own officials to regulate their affairs. They ranked next to the ministers of state, and the "chief of the entire hierarchy of mandarins" (a position not then filled) could only be appointed from among the Brahman van (Aymonier 1900:63–64).

In addition to royal descendants there were Brahmans, descended not from royalty but from ancient Brahmans. These were called Bram, Brahmana, or Pago (pronounced "bakou"). These numbered in the hundreds of families. They too now reckoned descent patrilineally. They were particularly associated with the post of guardian of the royal sword (an item of great symbolic significance), and they had numerous privileges. They were exempt from corvée and taxes, and were regulated by their own chiefs, who were selected by the king from among them. Aymonier describes these chiefs as the only priests in the country, mostly involved in court ritual. The Brahman chiefs could marry princesses. It was widely believed that only a Brahman (not a Brahman van) could be chosen as king if the royal line died out, because the Brahmans were truly of the highest caste. In spite of their caste organization, the Brahmans were Hinayana Buddhists (Aymonier 1900).

Beneath the royalty (i.e., the Brahman vansa and Brahman van, roughly coinciding with the Kshatriya of ancient Cambodia) and the Brahmans there were no further hereditary ruling elements. The mandarins, that is, the bureaucrats, held office for life but did not in theory pass on their offices to their sons. But since their sons served as pages in the court, they did in fact tend to follow their fathers in office. The mandarins numbered about one thousand. There were hereditary royal slaves, but apparently they were not numerous (Aymonier 1900).

Aymonier's account of nineteenth-century social stratification in Cambodia is remarkably reminiscent of ancient times. Coedès (1968) equated the Brahmans of the present with those of six centuries earlier in Cambodia—a caste holding out in spite of Buddhism.

Munson et al. (1963) provide a more recent description of social stratification in Cambodia, and it is little changed from the earlier descriptions. Rank is important to Cambodians, and "through the society runs a major distinction between those of royal and those of commoner birth" (Munson et al. 1963:61). Royalty dominates government, and most of its members seek government employment, though some go into the clergy or the military. The distinction between royalty and commoner is officially recognized in the Cambodian civil service. Royalty makes up a considerable portion of the elite. As of the early 1960s, male descendants of King Ang Duong (r. 1847–1859) comprised the category from which monarchs could be chosen; they numbered in the thousands.

Munson et al. (1963:62) note that Buddhism "does not support the ultimate validity of such status differences, and the individual Cambodian is encouraged to believe that through the achievement of merit any man can become a Buddha, [but] the fact of superior and inferior social rank is accepted by most Cambodians as one of the primary reference points for social relationships." The rural population—the great mass of the people—is more interested in betterment in the hereafter, and "competition for status at present involves values foreign to Cambodia's traditional life" (Munson et al. 1963:69–70).

Although education and wealth accounted for some mobility in recent times, the only significant traditional route for social mobility for the commoner of humble origins was in the monastic order (Munson et al. 1963). But, of course, a celibate and ascetic order provides only a limited sort of social mobility. All things considered, then, Cambodia was a closed society for many centuries, and one in which ancient patterns of Hindu-type caste or *varna* have been maintained with surprising continuity.

THAILAND

Older Thai history is marked by what Wyatt calls "an extraordinarily rich chronicle tradition," and the "Buddhist historiography of northern Siam is extraordinarily rich" too (1976:108, 114). It is not clear whether these are strictly quantitative statements or whether a positive qualitative judgment is being rendered too. In either case, the limits in time and place with which Wyatt qualifies his statements make them less-than-clear endorsements of the soundness of Thai historiography. He says that some of the earliest ones are far from easy to work with, due to "disparate points of view . . . [and] severe problems of dating and chronology" (1976:109). Elsewhere he comments on "strong indigenous historical traditions in the form of oral legend and written chronicles, some of very considerable antiquity" in the south of Thailand. But he also says of these chronicles that "their blending of myth, literature, and history demands of those who would use them high critical skills. Their chronology is often confused. Their very words are often obscure and uncertain" (1975:3). Again, the judgment being rendered is not clear.

According to Vickery (1979:150) only the *Luang Prasoet* chronicles of

Ayudhya (a former Thai capital), composed in the late 1600s, showed a concern for factual history, "a concern which does not appear in Siam again until the nineteenth century." Charnvit Kasetsiri 1979 adds that the *Luang Prasoet* chronicle was written by a royal astrologer in Thai; usually the authors are monks who write in Pali, the language of the Buddhist canon. Vickery (1979) suggests that the *Luang Prasoet* chronicle must have been written under foreign influence, either European or Chinese. Vickery's judgment is thus largely negative. Chandler 1979 notes that history was more honored and popular in Thailand than in Cambodia.

In addition to the Buddhist "universal histories" (Wyatt 1976), there were two main types of chronicle in Thailand. *Tamnan* are the earlier forms. Their authors are sometimes, but not normally, known. They are associated with particular localities and principalities of northern Siam. Their contents include miraculous legends, lists of rulers, and Buddhist embellishments (Wyatt 1976). *Phongsawadan* chronicles deal with dynastic history and are secular. "Rather than being written by Buddhist monks, they were written by scribes or officials at the royal court" (Wyatt 1976:118). The date of the first Ayudhyan chronicle is not known, "although it is quite certain that the basic sources for early texts must have been kept from an early time in the form of astrologers' notebooks of extraordinary events" (Wyatt 1976:118–19). *Phongsawadan* chronicles appear to have been produced for the edification of the rulers and may have been part of their regalia. They were primarily concerned with king and court, and more with war than with peace (Wyatt 1976). Reynolds 1979 describes a chronicle written in 1789, apparently *phongsawadan*, that was atypical in some ways. It has a religious theme and was written by a monk. Patterned on the Sri Lankan *Mahavamsa*, it showed that the unity of the state depended on a unified monkhood (*sangha*). It was written as part of a process of legitimating a reign (Reynolds 1979).

Social mobility in Thailand is as difficult to assess as Thai historiography. In the early Bangkok period (1782–1873) Thai society consisted of four major statuses: the descendants of kings, who were very numerous but who lost their status if separated more than five generations from a monarch; an aristocracy of nonroyal officeholders; commoners; and slaves, a small number of whom were hereditary. Royalty and nonroyal officials constituted a ruling class, collectively called *nai* (Akin Rabibhadana 1969). There were also court Brahmans, as in Cambodia, but they appear to have been less significant, less organized, and probably less numerous in Thailand (Wales 1931).

"Although the social system was stratified and ranked," say Hanks and

Hanks (1964:202), "people moved upward and downward over almost the entire range. Commoners were elevated to privilege through official appointment, and nobles automatically became commoners after five generations of decreasing rank." The priesthood also allowed a sort of mobility. But did commoners become officials? According to Akin Rabibhadana, "upward mobility from the lower class [commoners and slaves] to that of the governing class . . . appears to have been extremely difficult" (1969:155). The barrier to such mobility was the ritual of *thawai tua*, wherein potential future officials were introduced to the king, who thereby became their patron. Normally, the laws regulating who could be thus introduced to the king effectively excluded commoners, and "this would seem to make it impossible for a [commoner] to become [an official]" (Akin 1969:155–56). Akin is also of the opinion that the monkhood gave little scope for upward mobility. But downward mobility was common. Upward mobility in unusual times—during or after wars, for example—did occur; and, curiously, Chinese entered the aristocracy of officials with some ease, because of their wealth (not easily acquired by a Thai commoner) and because they were not clearly classed as commoners and could pass themselves off as Chinese nobles (Akin 1969).

It is difficult to arrive at any definitive judgment as to whether Thai social stratification was open or closed. It is even more difficult to say whether the soundness of the *Luang Prasoet* chronicle reflects some period of greater openness in Thai society. But on the basis of the degree to which Brahmans persist in their social systems—and perhaps in a general estimate of their varying rates of or attitudes toward social mobility—Cambodia, Thailand, and Burma seem to form a cline: greater closure in Cambodia and more openness in Burma, with Thailand in between. This cline is consistent with the pattern of judgment on their respective historiographies.

LAOS

Malleret (1961) says that, compared to the Vietnamese, the Laotians (and the Cambodians) gave little or no official or scholarly attention to maintaining and cataloging documents, and few documents have survived in Laos. This comparison indicates an inferior quality of historiography among the Laotians, though in only one aspect. To some extent this could reflect the considerably smaller size and duration of the Laotian kingdom compared to the Vietnamese.

In the old Laotian kingdom of Lan Xang in the fourteenth and fifteenth centuries, the Tai populace was divided into commoner and noble, but the degree of permeability of the boundary between them is not noted. In the later Laotian kingdom of Luang Prabang, at the time the French established a protectorate over it in the late eighteenth century, there was a definite royalty-nobility of birth. But the writings of modern authorities on Laotian society suggest that the "concept of nobility, except within royal lineages, has probably never been too strictly defined among the Laotian Tai" (LeBar, Hickey, and Musgrave 1964:218). Given the weak or uncertain character of the judgment passed on Laotian historiography, it is probably not necessary to push further the attempt to judge Laotian social stratification as either open or closed.

NANCHAO

Nanchao was a state in what is now the south of China. In a discussion of the extent to which China's historiographic tradition may have spread beyond its borders, Hall noted that in Nanchao, "Chinese traditions of historical writing had apparently failed to make any impression" (1961:5). Hall's comments imply that at least in some respects Nanchao's historiography was inferior to that of Burma and even more so to that of China. Hall implies that either very little in the way of historical writing was produced in Nanchao or that it has all disappeared, and this is confirmed by Backus 1981.

Until recently the prevailing view of Western writers was that Nanchao had been a Tai kingdom. If it had been Tai, the widespread hereditary ranking systems among Tai speakers (LeBar, Hickey, and Musgrave 1964) would provide an important clue in reconstructing Nanchao stratification. Various lines of research, however, have shown that there probably never were large numbers of Tai speakers in the Nanchao area and hence that "at most, Nanchao appears to have been ruled by a thin stratum of Tai aristocracy" (LeBar, Hickey, and Musgrave 1964:187). If there indeed had been a Tai aristocracy in Nanchao, there may also have been a closed stratification system. But more recent research argues that the Tai never had an important role to play in Nanchao (Ma 1962; for a general review of the literature, see Mote 1964 and Backus 1981).

Linguistic and ethnological research now leads to two important conclusions. One is that Nanchao was greatly influenced by Chinese culture (see, e.g., Stott 1963 and Wiens 1954). Nanchao may thus have borrowed ideas about advancement on the basis of merit, and some instances of such advancement are reported. But the various Tai aristocracies of Southeast Asia were also highly sinicized, while limiting advancement to within their stratum. Such data as are available on Nanchao do not show whether advancement was thus limited.

The second important conclusion is that the dominant peoples of Nanchao were the Pai and Yi (Mote 1964), also known as the Lolo and Minchia. These are apparently linguistically related peoples, but they are not Tai speakers. The Minchia live in the area of ancient Nanchao and are considerably sinicized. Stratification among them is largely a matter of wealth, especially as reflected in landownership (LeBar, Hickey, and Musgrave 1964). If the Minchia were the rulers of Nanchao, their present-day institutions do not suggest that they were once hereditarily stratified.

The Lolo are quite different: "Here was a blood-proud caste of nobility . . . who fought, rode, herded horses, and ruled a stratum of underlings and slaves" (Wiens 1954:94). The "stratification of classic Lolo society [was] into two endogamous castes—an aristocratic landowning elite, the Black Bones, and their serfs, the White Bones" (LeBar, Hickey, and Musgrave 1964:19). Three genealogies collected from Lolo chieftains in the nineteenth century trace their lines back to the rulers of Nanchao. Two of the genealogies give a sequence of two rulers whose names are surprisingly similar to the names independently recorded by the Chinese during Nanchao's period of greatness (Blackmore 1960). In sum, a case could be made for a system of hereditary ranking in Nanchao, but the data are few and sometimes confused.

Given the inadequacy of the materials and the apparently contradictory indications of Minchia and Lolo stratification, no firm conclusion can be drawn for the Nanchao case.

CONCLUSION

The cases just discussed fall into four categories. First, the Bruneis, Malays, Acehnese, and Balinese all had relatively unsound historiographies and closed societies. Second, the Makassarese/Bugis, Vietnamese, and Burmese had relatively sound historiographies and more open societies. Third is a category of ambiguous cases. Of these, the Cambodians could perhaps be safely moved to the first category, but the Thai, Laotians, and people of old Nanchao are genuinely difficult to assess. Fourth is the complex case of Java, which in its Hindu phase belongs to the third category, but in its Muslim and European periods appear to fall, respectively, into the second and first categories. Since the cases in the third category proved unrewarding—and have been included only to provide an analysis sufficiently exhaustive to eliminate bias in selecting cases—they will not be discussed further. Excluding them has no bearing upon acceptance or rejection of the main hypothesis.

Although in this chapter I analyzed every case from a universe of cases that I have no reason to think was biased in favor of confirmation of the hypothesis that the quality of historiography varies directly with the openness of social stratification, the inferences drawn from the results just presented must be made with some care. Various considerations prevent, for example, the direct applicability of a chi-square test. One is that the individual cases are not necessarily independent of each other. It could well be argued that the Brunei case should be subsumed under the Malay case. Even the Acehnese case is not entirely independent of Malay influence. Alternatively, it could be argued, less reasonably, that each Malay state should be an independent case. Another consideration is that one case, the Javanese, ended up as three cases, a treatment not accorded to other cases (because it did not seem warranted elsewhere). However, *if* we set considerations such as these aside, the odds against the cases falling into the confirmatory pattern in which I have found them are greater than one hundred to one, even if the Javanese case is excluded. With the Muslim and European phases of Java included as separate confirmatory cases, the odds rise sharply. Certainly it can be said that the Southeast Asian cases tend rather strongly to support rather than disconfirm the hypothesis. No other chapter attempts, as this one has, to assess all relevant cases in the regions and periods they cover, but I see no reason to think that if all relevant cases were assessed, the results—in terms of the proportions of confirmatory, disconfirmatory, and ambiguous cases—would be much different from those in this chapter.

Generally speaking, the Southeast Asian cases throw little light on the other concomitants of variation in the pattern of social stratification. Nowhere in Southeast Asia was there realistic portraiture or much in the way of natural or social science. Insofar as traces of political science were found—among the Burmese and Vietnamese, and in the writings of the Bugis-Malay Raja Ali Haji—they were found in the expected settings. So too with biography, which was found as a distinct traditional genre only among the Vietnamese and which was introduced to the Malays by relatively late authors of foreign extraction writing in Malay. In this context it is of interest to note that "the first prominent Indonesian to write something like an autobiography" was a Javanese whose father under the Dutch "rose to the rank of *wedana*, then the highest bureaucratic rank normally open to Javanese not born to aristocratic *bupati* families" (Anderson 1979:223). Individualism was muted among the Bruneis, Malays, and Balinese. But a developed individualism is nowhere well documented among literate peoples in Southeast Asia, though the diaries of the Makassarese/Bugis suggest a greater individualism among them. The Bruneis, the Balinese, and probably the Malays did not possess a uniform conception of human nature; the Burmese most certainly did. So, too, the Burmese system of monastic education was probably the best case of a uniform system of education. The humanistic-secular attitude was to some extent apparent among the Makassarese/Bugis, and the writings of Raja Ali Haji, the Bugis-Malay, also showed a degree of humanism. However spotty, all these findings are in the right direction.

The one apparent exception concerns divination. Snouck Hurgronje (1906) reports at length on Acehnese divination, but he provides no comparative perspective. Pigeaud ([1928] 1977:65) says that "many Javanese let their lives be governed entirely or partially by the results of divination, even in the present day." It is not clear what this implies for the past, but Pigeaud ([1928] 1977) does imply a limited variety of divinatory techniques (mostly numerological) among the pre-Muslim Javanese. A fair selection of divinatory techniques are reported for Malays (Skeat [1900] 1967; Winstedt 1951), but little is said about the context or frequency of Malay divination. My own impression is that the Bruneis, while concerned to determine lucky and unlucky days, put relatively little time and effort into divination when compared to their neighbors the Overseas Chinese, but it may be that Chinese techniques are simply more publicly visible. Both this concomitant and the others deserve more careful, comparative study in Southeast Asia. To a lesser extent the same can be said for the region's systems of social stratification and traditions of historiography. A pressing problem is to separate analytically the influence of borrowing—which has obvious attractions as an explanatory framework in explaining Southeast Asian historiographic traditions—from the conditions that motivate authors to use what they can borrow. The findings of this chapter provide good evidence that social stratification deserves to be taken into account in assessing such motives.

CHAPTER 4

The Ancient Near East, Greece, and Rome

To widen my sample beyond Asian historiographies, I examined the two remaining historiographic traditions that have at times influenced the historiography of Southeast Asia—the European and Near Eastern. General summaries of historiographical development (Barnes 1937; Dentan 1955; Fehl 1964; Shotwell 1923; and Thompson 1942) produced a number of contrasts in antiquity. While there is considerable disagreement over the relative soundness of Hebrew, Assyrian, and Babylonian historiography, there is substantial agreement that the Egyptians, and more certainly the later Egyptians, were not historically minded. Some authorities argue that they contrasted in this respect with the Assyro-Babylonians and the Hebrews.

Greek historiography developed somewhat later—possibly independently, possibly stimulated by the earlier historical writings of the Near East. Despite considerable agreement on the quality of Greek historical writing, its development was far from uniform, as the Spartans were not historians. Nor, for that matter had the early Greeks—as opposed to the classical Greeks—been historically minded. The Romans, too, produced sound historians, but in the later years of the western empire, the quality of Roman historiography declined, setting the stage for the historiography of the Middle Ages.

ANCIENT EGYPT

Historiography

Egypt constantly changed, but the changes were ignored (Wilson 1951). The ancient Egyptians "had very little sense of history"; they saw the world as "essentially static and unchanging"; historical events were "superficial disturbances of the established order" (Frankfort 1951:20–21; see also Frankfort [1948] 1961, and Bull 1955). "There is something medieval in the attitude of later Egypt toward its own past, a sense of dimness, a failure to grasp reality" (Shotwell 1923:53). "The Egyptians were never much of a history-writing people," contrasting in this regard with the Babylonians and Assyrians (Thompson 1942:I, 7). If any substantial Egyptian history was written at any time during the dynastic period (c. 3100–663 B.C.), it has not survived (Barnes 1937; Bull 1955). The ahistorical attitude of the Egyptians "is all the more striking when one considers that . . . an Egyptian historian—if there had been one—had available their enormous mass of archive material" (Thompson 1942:I, 8). The Egyptians maintained their enormous corpus of records over a very long period, for a variety of purposes and in a variety of places. In the third century B.C. when Manetho, under Greek influence, did write an Egyptian history, he drew on the archives rather than on inscriptions (Thompson 1942:I).

According to Bull (1955:3), "There is no ancient Egyptian word . . . which closely corresponds to the English word history, . . . nor is there any Egyptian text . . . which can be said to express 'an idea of history' held by an ancient Egyptian author." Moreover, the Egyptians did not have an "idea of history," "in any sense resembling what the phrase means to thinkers of the present age or perhaps of the last 2,400 years" (Bull 1955:32). On the other hand, the Egyptians did possess a word, often translated as *annals*, which apparently referred to "historical records as physical documents" (Bull 1955:3). Thus the Egyptians possessed some of the materials required for writing history but did not write histories. Among these materials were king lists that stretched over enormous periods of time (Bull 1955). After the First Dynasty of the Old Kingdom (c. 2700–c. 2200 B.C.) king lists were supplemented with events of importance for each year of a king's reign (Bull 1955; Frankfort 1951; Wilson 1951). The Egyptians were also keen on genealogies, some of which "cover many generations and involve periods ranging from 300 to 750 years" (Bull 1955:9). Portions of the genealogies are demonstrably inaccurate, but some portions are "probably fairly accurate" (Bull 1955:10). The most outstanding genealogy is an inscription listing Memphite priests over no less than 1,350 years. Bull (1955:10) says that the "general correctness" of the genealogy is supported by other dated sources.

Egyptian kings erected monuments or notices of their victories, assuring a kind of historical record of their achievements and showing that they were at least "conscious that they were making history, and [that] they wished the story to last forever" (Bull 1955:16). Thompson (1942:I) considered these notices considerably less useful historically than their Assyrian and Babylonian counterparts. Frankfort ([1948] 1961:46) agrees with Thompson, saying that the "Egyptian monuments and texts . . . consistently hide the individuality of the kings under generalities." Things, such as portrait heads, that were once thought to show individuality, have been found to be conventional for the period. Frankfort observed that "even in the accounts of royal achievements which we should classify as historical texts, we find, to our exasperation, that everything that is singular and historical is treated as of little account" ([1948] 1961:48). He gives examples, stretching over a very long period of time, of inscriptions that claim for one ruler the actions of a predecessor, even when the deeds of the ruler being memorialized would have been illustrious enough.

Although personalities emerge only to a small extent in these dry records, there was an attempt to perpetuate in Egyptian tombs "the name, titles, and deeds of the deceased, whether he were king or commoner. In these inscriptions we have autobiographical data which showed the appreciation of the people for private as well as public history" (Bull 1955:18). Thus the Egyptians "knew their history" in the sense that they "remembered the great figures of the past" (Bull 1955:19), and it was not merely kings who were remembered, but other great personages too (Bull 1955). Bull (1955) also cites as further evidence of their love of the past the Egyptian tendency to copy ancient architectural and artistic styles.

Of course the Egyptians had a considerable mythology, which they came to consider part of their history (Bull 1955). "Egyptians may have done little with history," says Shotwell (1923:54), "but they treasured myth and legend." Frankfort ([1948] 1961:50) noted that creation stories were more important in Egyptian thought than in that of their neighbors, for in a "static world, creation is the only event that really matters supremely, since it alone can be said to have made a change."

One final point is that in his generalized account of the origins of civilization in the Near East, Frankfort (1951) noted that written documents were rarer from Egypt than from Mesopotamia. This may indicate less historical-mindedness in Egypt, but it may also reflect differing rates of preservation of texts in the two areas (to be discussed further below).

Social Stratification

Since it stretches from approximately 3100 B.C. up to the Persian conquest in 525 B.C., few generalizations about Egyptian dynastic history seem safe. We do know that from the very earliest times social mobility occurred, though hereditary transmission of status was normal too. These seemingly contradictory generalizations are partially reconciled by the apparent predominance of openness in the earlier periods and of closure in the later.

Frankfort concluded that "there were no castes, and men of simple origin might rise to the highest posts. . . . The talented and industrious were not frustrated by a rigid class distinction or by a colour bar" (1951:90). He goes on to give examples of upward mobility, one from the Sixth Dynasty (c. 2350–2200 B.C.), one involving a Nubian, and one involving a dwarf who ultimately married a woman of the class of "royal kinsmen" (1951:92; Frankfort 1961; see also Maspero [1894] 1968). Frankfort ([1948] 1961) also says that cases of social mobility may be found in all periods of Egyptian history. This does not, however, deny that it may have been more common in one period than another.

Theoretically, the key to social mobility was the authority of the pharaoh to appoint or demote whomever he wished. In practice, the pharaoh often lacked the desire or power to prevent hereditary succession to priestly and other offices, but his theoretical right was apparently never publically denied (Frankfort 1951). Correspondingly, we find such things as individuals expressing satisfaction at having risen in rank "through personal merit" (Frankfort 1951:89); a king during the first period of dynastic breakdown (c. 2200–2050 B.C.) urging his son to promote the worthy regardless of their condition (Wilson 1951); a territorial ruler (nomarch), also during the first period of dynastic breakdown, saying that he took men and serfs from other districts (nomes) and made them "rank as notables" (Frankfort 1951:94); and a father advising his son "to get ahead in the world" (Wilson 1951:92).

But there were contrary tendencies too. In early times the kings appointed their sons and other close relatives to high positions and more distant kinsmen to lower offices; when the first vizier was created, in the Fourth Dynasty, he was a "prince of the royal blood" (Frankfort 1951:84).

By the end of the Old Kingdom (i.e., by 2200 B.C.) the nomarchs normally transmitted their positions to their sons and thus became a sort of "landed gentry" (Frankfort 1951:86). In spite of theory, it was already the practice in the Old Kingdom for sons usually to follow their fathers in office (Frankfort 1951).

The first period of dynastic breakdown, which marks the transition between the Old and Middle kingdoms, was apparently the period in which egalitarianism reached its zenith in Egypt. Wilson (1951:121, 142) calls it a period of "social equality," a "democratic age," and a time when commoners bragged of their repute. Wilson cites a text from the period in which the creator god says that he made all men equal in opportunity. He also cites a very popular story in which the king is amused by the eloquence of a common peasant demanding his rights. But egalitarianism was swept away in the second period of dynastic breakdown (c. 1800–1550 B.C.) (Wilson 1951).

By the early Eighteenth Dynasty (c. 1550–1375 B.C.), according to Wilson (1951:186), "class cleavage" had become marked, and it was rare "to move upward in the social scale." The power of the priesthood of Amon was especially notable, but during the reign of Akh-en-Aton (1369–1353 B.C.) it was sharply curbed. The final element in Akh-en-Aton's name signified his allegiance to the god Aton rather than Amon and hence his patronage of a new priesthood. In Akh-en-Aton's entourage came a "swarm of parvenus," and the old "hereditary aristocracy" of bureaucracy and priesthood were eclipsed (Wilson 1951:207). But the setback of hereditary stratification was brief; under Tut-ankh-Aton (1352–1344 B.C.) the old priesthood of Amon and the hereditary bureaucrats pushed out the parvenus, and the king changed his name to Tut-ankh-Amon (Wilson 1951). On the whole, the tendency to inherit rank was strong throughout the empire period (c. 1465–1165 B.C.). Before the end of the period the pharaoh became a virtual prisoner of the high priests of Amon, the high priest then being depicted in art on the same scale as the pharaoh (Wilson 1951). As Wilson (1951:308) puts it, after about 1100 B.C. Egypt began to "petrify." "The formation of society into rigid classes, with priests and warriors constituting castes of special privilege, . . . unknown in Egypt before the late Empire . . . [became] more and more important from that time on" (Wilson 1951:306–07).

Maspero's lengthy summary of the ancient Egyptian "political constitution" ([1894] 1968:245–344), provides further insights into Egyptian social stratification. At the top were the pharaohs, descendants of the sun god. Their "souls as well as bodies" were of "supernatural origin" (Maspero [1894] 1968:259). An extraordinary emphasis was placed on depicting and defining the supernatural character of the pharaohs, but very little was said about "the individual disposition of any king in particular, or of their everyday life" (Maspero [1894] 1968:267).

In the Old Kingdom only the pharaoh had a *ba*, a soul, which "was an expression of continued function after death" (Wilson 1951:86). But as early as the later part of the Old Kingdom, the pharaoh shared some of his divinity with the priesthood (Wilson 1951). Later other high-ranking persons "assumed the formerly exclusive [mortuary] prerogatives of the king and became . . . god[s] after death" (Wilson 1951:86). Whether this fundamental, and at least partially hereditary, distinction was ever extended to include the masses is not clear.

Beneath the pharaoh were high officials and "the great feudal lords" (Maspero [1894] 1968:270). Maspero ([1894] 1968) describes the case of a man who rose to territorial lordship—but he was not allowed to pass his status on to his heirs. Maspero thought that such cases were not uncommon but that the ultimate solidification of achieved high status required marriage into the hereditary nobility, which was composed primarily of children of the pharaohs and of the feudal lords. The feudal lords, who had extensive administrative and military authority in their territorial domains, normally inherited their status (Maspero [1894] 1968). Maspero's "great feudal lords," I presume, are equivalent to, or at any rate include, the nomarchs mentioned earlier.

At lower levels in the bureaucracy were a host of scribes of varying rank. They, too, usually inherited their status: "in most of the government administrations, we find whole dynasties of scribes on a small scale, whose members inherited the same post for several centuries" (Maspero [1894] 1968:289). Thus not only were the high priests hereditary but so too were the positions of many lesser priestly functionaries, who collectively formed "a sort of sacerdotal nobility" (Maspero [1894] 1968:305).

A genealogy of Memphite priests, preserved on a limestone slab, gives the names of sixty men, "each of whom is said to be the son of his predecessor in the list" (Bull 1955:10). The early Greek traveler and historian Hecataeus reported an even more astonishing father-to-son transmission of priestly office in Thebes—345 generations (Bury 1909). Herodotus in *The Persian Wars* reports the same. The genealogy of Memphite priests, with a time span of c. 2100 to 750 B.C., cannot be taken at face value. The claim made to Hecataeus and Herodotus has even less credibility. But that later Egyptian priests believed in or even claimed such rigidly hereditary transmission of status is important in itself. The priests and their subordinates formed a society "distinct from . . . the civil population, and freed from most of the burdens which weighed so heavily on the latter" (Maspero [1894] 1968:305).

The army, about which details are obscure, appears to have been somewhat less privileged than the priesthood and was not ordinarily a hereditary occupation, though at times it tended to develop into a sort of nobility. Herodotus described the Egyptian warriors in his time as hereditary, and Wilson (1951) seems to agree. Together with the priesthood, the army formed the source of power with which the pharaoh and the feudal lords ruled the bulk of the population (Maspero [1894] 1968).

The lot of the artisan and the peasant was a hard one, and the requirement that everyone must have a master who would represent him in law and who would be the principal beneficiary of any extra effort expended, robbed the people of an incentive to improve their condition. Although the artisans were more organized than the peasants, and perhaps less subject to corvée labor, neither possessed much scope for vertical mobility (Maspero [1894] 1968). Slaves counted for little and after a few generations probably merged with the general population into a serflike condition (Maspero [1894] 1968; see also Frankfort 1951).

Concomitants and Discussion

Quite certainly the line of pharaohs was seen as a race apart, but whether a nobility was thus distinguished from the masses is unclear. Some light may be shed on the matter by Egyptian art, famous for its preoccupation with animals and man-animal hybrids (Frankfort 1961; Wilson 1951). The Egyptians believed that the gods were manifest in animals (Frankfort 1961), which makes hybrid forms an expectable mode of expressing the interpenetration of divinity and humanity. Frankfort (1961:13–14) speculates that the Egyptian interest in animals, whose species they depicted with considerable accuracy, stemmed from the immutability of species (unlike humanity, in which "individual characteristics seem to outbalance generic resemblances"). Animals appealed to the Egyptians, according to this reasoning, because they more clearly manifested the static nature of the universe. If I may extend Frankfort's speculation, it is possible that the Egyptian preoccupation with animal and hybrid forms was an attempt to link the immutability of species differences with the nature of stratification, to equate social divisions with speciation. Analogues of this notion, which connects art with caste or castelike social orders, are, I suspect, found in India and medieval Europe, and will be discussed later.

As noted in the discussion of Egyptian historiography, Frankfort (1961) asserts that individualism was not characteristic of the Egyptians. Wilson (1951) disagrees in that he finds considerable individualism in earlier periods, though little in later times. Wilson (1951) says that conformity to the local group was actually more pronounced among Babylonians and Hebrews than among Egyptians, and that there was considerable individualism as late as the Middle Kingdom (c. 2050–1800 B.C.). But after the period of Hyksos rule (c. 1730–1570 B.C.), individualism was repressed (Wilson 1951). This, Wilson says, was accompanied by an increasing separation between the high and the low, and an emphasis on resignation: "Theology then advised . . . [the masses] that this was their predestined fate and that they must submit to it with quietude, in the hope of a reward in paradise" (1951:298). The Empire (c. 1465–1165 B.C.), and especially the Late Empire and Post Empire (c. 1150–663 B.C.), "could not tolerate . . . individualism" (Wilson 1951:302). If Wilson's assessments are correct, individualism and social stratification co-vary in the expected pattern.

While biography as a literary genre may have been absent, Egyptian funerary practice did give outlet, apparently throughout the entire dynastic period, to a species of biography or autobiography, as mentioned earlier (see also Misch 1950). In addition, portraits labeled with the name of their subject were found in all periods of Egyptian history. However, these portraits were rarely if ever true portraits.

In his comparative and historical study of ancient portraiture, Breckenridge (1968) discusses Egyptian portraits at considerable length. He says that probably no Egyptian portrait, before the conquest by Alexander in 332 B.C., is an actual likeness of the person it allegedly portrays. On the other hand, Egyptian sculptors were technically capable of producing actual likenesses, and at various times produced heads of markedly natural or realistic appearance. These apparently realistic portrait heads are at all times rare, and two characteristics cast doubt on their authenticity as portraits: either the various portraits of the same subject do not resemble each other, or the same physiognomy is imposed on more subjects than are likely to have shared a family likeness. In the former case each portrait may be unique, but it is not demonstrably a likeness of the alleged subject; in the latter case the portrait is not unique and is just a natural-looking icon. In some cases, highly realistic masks were used as the armature upon which an idealized portrait was built up; where these masks have survived, they give, according to Breckenridge, a false impression of realistic portraiture.

Breckenridge (1968:44) says that "taken as a group, the portraits of the Old Kingdom are the most individualized and naturalistic of any major period of Egyptian history," which fits nicely with the apparent tendency of Egyptian social stratification to start out open and end up closed. A resurgence of naturalism in the Amarna period, ushered in by Akh-en-Aton and his entourage of parvenus, is also consistent (Breckenridge 1968; Wilson 1951). Wilson (1951) found naturalism up to the end of the Empire, that is, up to the point where he began to see Egypt petrify. After the Greek conquest of Egypt, true portraits were produced there, but they remained rare (Breckenridge 1968).

Wilson (1951:9) says that "Egyptian literature of all periods contained books of instruction, characteristically addressed by a father to his son," which hints at hereditary transmission of status. But in the Empire period, instruction in the scribal school became more common (Wilson 1951). No firm conclusion about patterns of education can be drawn from these observations.

Wilson also asserts that "there was no written and detailed statecraft for Egypt" (1951:72), nor do I see any signs of social science. For a short time in the earliest dynasties a "scientific spirit" prevailed in Egypt, especially in medicine (Wilson 1951:55). But after this good start, science and technology ceased to develop, and no later period came up to the early standard (Wilson 1951).

Wilson mentions an oracular function of the pharaoh, as well as scribes "who could foretell what was to come" (1951:262). Herodotus also mentions Egyptian oracles. But Speiser (1955:62) says of the pharaoh that "a god incarnate does not take his cue from the liver of a sheep." Egyptian priests showed little interest in any form of divination, which Leclant (1968) attributes to their religious notion that the future could only repeat the past. But Leclant's explanation is almost certainly wrong, since the possibility that the future may repeat the past is precisely the reason often given for the utility of divination.

One thing certain is that a lesser development of divination in Egypt cannot be attributed to a lesser religiosity or superstitiousness. Herodotus depicted the Egyptians as "religious to excess, far beyond any other race of men" ([5th c. B.C.] 1942:II, 37). He described some of their ritual practices, noting that the priests observed "thousands" more (but not at the cost of enjoying material advantages). Wilson (1951:306–07) agrees and makes the additional comment that the stress on ceremony and magic was greater in the later periods of Egyptian history.

From the foregoing it seems safe to say that Egypt ended up as a castelike society, though it did not begin that way. Many of the concomitants conform to that generalization. But if early Egyptian society was open, why did good historiography not develop then? Perhaps the correct answer is that Egyptian historiography actually was better in the earlier periods. Recall that Shotwell (1923:53) said that "there is something medieval in the attitude of *later* Egypt toward its own past" (my italics). When we also recall that annals (however rudimentary) and rather detailed biographical information survive from the third millennium B.C., perhaps we can say that that was not, after all, such a bad start on the development of historiography. In this context we might note that the three texts that Barnes 1937 gives as examples of minor exceptions to the rule that Egyptians did not produce histories all date from before the period in which Wilson sees caste developing in Egypt; the latest, the Turin papyrus, dates from the thirteenth century B.C. or earlier (Dentan 1955). We might further note that Frankfort (1951:50) describes the earliest art of Mesopotamia as mostly religious, while the earliest works of Eygptian art "celebrate royal achievements and consist of historical subjects," a sign of comparatively great historical-mindedness in the earliest times. If Egyptian stratification had remained open, we would perhaps expect improvements in historiography. Because it did not remain open, either the maintenance of archaic standards or the actual decline of standards suggested by Shotwell are predictable historiographic responses.

BABYLONIA, ASSYRIA, AND ANCIENT ISRAEL

Historiography

Sayce (1900:58) is among those who lump the Hebrews, Babylonians, and Assyrians together in contrast with the Egyptians: "Like the Hebrews," he wrote, "the Assyrians were distinguished by a keen historical sense which stands in curious contrast to the want of it which characterized the Egyptian. The Babylonians also were distinguished by the same quality, though perhaps to a less extent than their Assyrian neighbors." Dannenfeldt 1954a, Speiser 1955, and Thompson 1942:I essentially agree. Since if the Babylonians and Assyrians did write history, they may have written it earlier than the Hebrews, I will examine the former two first.

Thompson (1942:I, 11) credits the Assyrians with being "the first people who created a genuine historical literature." He traces this development from dedicatory inscriptions on buildings, which in time gave way to annals of a king's reign. Misch (1950) argues that Assyrian historiography had roots in kingly biography, which in time became political autobiography, sometimes sensitively personalistic. Developments in Assyria may have been based on prior developments in Babylonia, which in most respects is treated as roughly parallel to Assyria in basic cultural features. Thus Thompson (1942:I, 10) quotes Olmstead (1916) as follows: "The historical writings of the Assyrians form one of the most important branches of their literature. Indeed, it may be claimed with much truth that it is the most characteristically Assyrian of them all. The Assyrians derived their historical writing, as they did so many other cultural elements, from the Babylonians." For many purposes the two may be treated together under the heading of Mesopotamian society (Speiser 1955). Oppenheim (1964), who attempts to portray Mesopotamian civilization in its own terms, demurs to some extent in the evaluation of its historiography. He points out that those texts that were intended to be histories are proportionately few and generally late.

While many aspects of Mesopotamian historical writings were less than sound—the destruction of predecessors' annals, claiming predecessors' deeds for oneself, and grossly exaggerating one's own feats, for example—some portions of the literature are largely free of such distortions (Oppenheim 1964; Thompson 1942:I). According to Thompson, a highpoint was reached in the Babylonian Chronicle, of the New Babylonian Empire, which provides contemporary history for almost a century, ending in the seventh century B.C. (1942:I; see also Contenau 1954). Speiser (1955:67) seems to agree and quotes Olmstead's (1916:62) commendation of the chronicle's "sobriety of presentation and . . . coldly impartial statement of fact."

The ancient Mesopotamians, like the Egyptians, also lacked a word that corresponds to our word *history*, yet they had some idea of history, for they were very much aware of the past, were "forever busy recording its details," and were "intent on drawing from the past certain practical lessons" (Speiser 1955:38). Oppenheim (1964:233) also sees practical reasons behind the earliest annals and lists. It is this attempt to draw lessons from the past that gives Mesopotamian historical writing a peculiar stamp, differentiates it from the Egyptian interest in the past, and aligns the Mesopotamians with the truly historically minded peoples.

Finkelstein (1963) incisively addresses the peculiarity of Mesopotamian historiography and the question of whether it produced history. He concedes that many common conceptions of history, shaped by Western experience, could not easily accommodate the Mesopotamian treatment of the past. But if we accept Huizinga's concept of history as "the intellectual form in which a civilization renders account to itself of its past" (1963:9), then the Mesopotamians did have history (Finkelstein 1963). Finkelstein, I might add, understands the terms "intellectual form" and "account . . . of its past" in such a way as to preclude myth (1963:469–70 and n. 35).

The Mesopotamian genre that Finkelstein (1963) sees as most closely fitting Huizinga's concept is composed of "omen texts," which have long been considered as somehow closely connected to Mesopotamian historiography. The omen texts were key elements in Mesopotamian divination, which in turn "was rooted in, and is most characteristic of, the fundamental cognitive mode of the Mesopotamian intellect" (Finkelstein 1963:463; see also Oppenheim 1964 and Speiser 1955). In Mesopotamian thought, man was not the center of the universe; an autonomous study of man would have made little sense. "To the Mesopotamian the crucial and urgent subject of study was the entire objective universe. . . . There probably has never been another civilization so singlemindedly bent on the accumulation of information, and on eschewing any generalization or enunciation of principles. . . . [N]o phenomenon was too trivial to record" (Finkelstein 1963: 463). It was not merely things that the Mesopotamians were interested in but, more important, occurrences: "A moment of time was apprehended and defined as the sum total of the occurrences and events known to be in temporal conjunction" (Finkelstein 1963:463). Just as things repeat themselves in space, the Mesopotamians held that events co-occur and recur in time. Hence, in order to ensure their well-being, the Mesopotamians collected information on conjoined occurrences so that these could be used to predict human events. If a particular human event, such as a victory in war, had been conjoined with certain natural events and/or with particular results of artificial divinatory procedures, then those natural events and/ or divinatory results were omens of victory in war. The objective and consistent collection of tables of co-occurring events—even though its purpose be omenry—is much like the keeping of ordinary historical records. The omen materials collected by the Mesopotamians "lie at the very root of all Mesopotamian historiography"; moreover, "as a historical genre they take precedence both in time and in reliability over any other genre of Mesopotamian writing that purports to treat of the events of the past" (Finkelstein 1963:463). Texts concerning divination are the commonest element in Mesopotamian literature, and references to divination in other kinds of texts are numerous (Oppenheim 1964).

The Mesopotamians were fundamentally empirical scientists, agreeing that "the best insurance for coping with the future is the most reliable and accurate knowledge of the experience of the past" (Finkelstein 1963:463). Oppenheim (1964) seems to agree, often referring to Mesopotamian divination as a "science" (see also Contenau 1954). The one failure of the Mesopotamians—and of course it was a fundamental one—was vastly to exaggerate the interconnectedness of phenomena and hence to fail to distinguish accidental co-occurrences from those that are causally connected. Omenry was an official function as early as 2500 B.C. in Sumer, but the period in which omen history was most developed was that of the Akkad dynasty (c. 2350–2200 B.C.). The co-occurrences collected for this period became the standard for divination and unfortunately were not much supplemented in later periods (Finkelstein 1963; Oppenheim 1964). Much later, when the Mesopotamian chronicles developed, they relied on the omen literature for information on the Akkadian period.

Finkelstein (1963:469) does not consider any sorts of Mesopotamian information about the past—other than the omens and chronicles—to be real history, primarily because they were not motivated by "the desire to know what really happened" as Mesopotamians understood this problem. Speiser (1955) gives a concise summary of the other forms of Mesopotamian historical materials which, if they were not written to be history, are nonetheless useful to present-day historians. His concluding evaluation of the Mesopotamian contribution is that it marked "a significant early milestone; a milestone in the progress of the idea of history as well as of the history of ideas" (1955:73).

Finkelstein (1963) correctly draws attention to the analogy with China, whose historiography also grew out of omenry; equally appropriately he quotes Thucydides on the applicability of past events to predicting the future. It may be noted in passing that most of what we know of Mesopotamian omenry was almost exclusively connected with the affairs of kings, whose fate represented the fate of society (Finkelstein 1963). But omenry was used by commoners too (Contenau 1954:286; Oppenheim 1964).

As for the Hebrews, Thompson (1942:I) notes a similarity between the Babylonian and Assyrian historical records and Kings and Chronicles in the Old Testament. Thompson considers the Old Testament to be primarily historical, with seventeen of its books manifestly so. In their present forms they were written very much later than the Mesopotamian chronicles. Oral traditions, however, no doubt go back to the time of David, (c. 1000 B.C.). The quality varies considerably (Thompson 1942:1). Although the Hebrew texts are less detailed than those of Babylonia, Dannenfeldt (1954a) thinks the former were more unified, presented more personalities, and gave a larger role to the individual. Oppenheim (1964:153) considers the "realism" of the account of David in the books of Samuel to be greater than in any Mesopotamian text. For Barnes (1937:19, 22), who is not willing to concede that "truly historical narrative of considerable scope and high relative veracity" was found among Mesopotamians, the Hebrew narrative "marks the earliest appearance of true historical narrative of which any record has anywhere been preserved."

One of the outstanding peculiarities of Hebrew history is its lack of inscriptions; the literary texts are all we have (Burrows 1955). They combine a variety of possible sources, and many portions have probably been re-written through time. As with other ancient histories, authorship is obscure, although various portions can be linked to specific unknown authors. When exploring the various primarily religious ideas of the past that inform the Old Testament, Burrows (1955) finds much that would not pass muster as history. But he does not wish to discount it entirely:

A disinterested curiosity as to what actually happened and a desire to preserve an accurate record of events for posterity may have been at work in some of the records consulted and quoted in the historical books, but for the most part these have been preserved only in fragments. . . . There is one outstanding exception to this rule. The full, frank, objective account of David's reign in II Sam. 9–20, which gives the impression of having been written by an eyewitness, or at least a contemporary, has been widely recognized as one of the finest examples of historical narrative in any ancient literature. (Burrows 1955:110)

Shotwell (1923) is the least charitable toward the ancients. For lack of the idea of criticism, he says, neither the Egyptians nor the Babylonians wrote history. He implies that the Hebrews did little better, but he refers specifically only to Genesis. The ability to evaluate material about the past *critically*, and thus to compose sound history, first developed, according to Shotwell (1923), among the Greeks. Many historians apparently agree, but that is the topic of a later section in this chapter.

Social Stratification and Concomitants

According to an older view, some sort of feudal landed nobility existed at an early time in both Babylonia and Assyria, but in Babylonia the nobility was early displaced or absorbed by priestly and mercantile classes, leaving behind little trace of itself. By the time of Nebuchadnezzar (seventh to sixth centuries B.C.) high status was based on wealth from trade or on high office (Sayce 1900). In Assyria the traces of the old feudal nobility were stronger, but the nobility was steadily replaced by royal appointees. Under Tiglath-pileser III (eighth century B.C.) the tendency became policy and the nobility disappeared (Sayce 1900).

The current view, based on Jacobsen's 1943 study of Mesopotamian myths and epics, is that the earliest Mesopotamian (Sumerian) communities were egalitarian "primitive democracies." Since there was no writing in the period to which his analysis refers, Jacobsen's views cannot be proved, but they are now generally accepted (Frankfort 1951; Oppenheim 1964; Saggs 1962).

The earliest community or city-state officials were not hereditary (Saggs 1962), and there seems to be a consensus that in principle Babylonian kingship was never hereditary. In Assyria the hereditary principle of kingship probably did develop, but it did not drive out the ideal of the "self-made" king. Most authorities reject the notion that the Mesopotamian kings were gods, but Oppenheim says that they were to some extent seen as divine, at least while in office (Contenau 1954; Oppenheim 1964; Saggs 1962; Sayce 1900).

In the Code of Hammurabi (c. 2100 B.C.), which presents a very early picture of Mesopotamian society, only three classes are mentioned: free men, slaves, and a middle class about which almost nothing is known (Contenau 1954). Oppenheim (1964:74) says it was a "primary characteristic" of Mesopotamia that, except for kings and slaves, the only form of social stratification was economic. Thus the distinction between free and slave seems to have been the major division in social stratification.

The Babylonian and Assyrian conceptions of slavery demonstrate clearly that their societies were open. A slave "could become a free citizen and rise to the highest offices of state. Slavery was no bar to his promotion, nor did it imprint any stigma upon him. . . . Between his habits and level of culture and those of his owners was no marked distinction, no prejudices to be overcome on account of his color, no conviction of his inferiority of race" (Sayce 1900:67).

Slaves in both Babylonia and Assyria were of various origins, including previously free men enslaved for debt. In both places, slaves had extensive property rights. They could own businesses and cattle; they could save money and could bank; they could own other slaves and could purchase their own freedom; they could become craftsmen; they could trade with each other and with free men; they had few disabilities in court; they could be adopted and unadopted. Intermarriage between slave and free was not uncommon. Slaves were never a majority and were never decisive in the economy (Contenau 1954; Oppenheim 1964; Saggs 1962; Sayce 1900).

There may have been temple serfs in early Babylonia, recruited from prisoners of war. The use of the term *serf* suggests lesser mobility for this class (Oppenheim 1964; Sayce 1900). Peasants and artisans were held in considerable esteem. Legend held that one of the very early Mesopotamian kings of great prestige, Sargon, had been a gardener and that in his day the sons of kings willingly took jobs as secretaries and librarians (Contenau 1954; Sayce 1900).

Finally, we may note some of the concomitants. The Babylonian legal code was based on individual responsibility, and people of all classes, from high to low, could be moneylenders (Sayce 1900). Although nowhere explicitly stated in the works I have consulted, a conception of uniform human nature is implicit in Assyrian and Babylonian notions of slavery and of individual legal responsibility. Oppenheim (1964:112) notes that ethnicity did not "articulate" the structure of Mesopotamian cities, which also suggests a uniform conception of human nature and its correlated individualism. But none of my sources explicitly describes the Mesopotamians as individualistic, or even discusses their views on human nature. Moreover, little mention is made of biography in Mesopotamia (but see Misch 1950), and its portraiture showed less individualism or naturalism than Egypt's (Breckenridge 1968).

Not enough is known about education in Babylonia and Assyria to draw any firm conclusions concerning its relationship to social stratification (see, e.g., Saggs 1962). There is some, but not much, reason to think of the Mesopotamians as humanistic-secular in thought. In Sumerian literature (cherished in Babylonia and Assyria) there was a term, *nam-lu-lu*, which was "exactly the equivalent of the Latin *humanitas* . . . in both of its meanings: (1) 'the collectivity of mankind' and (2) 'the complete blossoming forth of human values, humanism' " (Gordon 1960:123). Oppenheim (1964:181) says that "religion's claims on the private individual were extremely limited in Mesopotamia." And specifically human affairs were a concern in divination. On the other hand, Contenau (1954:302) notes that the Mesopotamians showed little interest in the human form in art and says that they were "enslaved" by ritual. It is also difficult to see a substantial beginning of political or social science in Mesopotamia, except that its history was generally of political affairs and its divination was concerned with cause and effect in political affairs, and perhaps social affairs too. Furthermore, Gordon (1960:123) says that among the subjects treated in Sumerian and Akkadian "wisdom literature" (known to us primarily from copies made in Babylonia or Assyria) were "such everyday practical matters as the economy and social behavior" (for Babylonian examples, including rudimentary political science, see Lambert 1960). But to count these as beginnings of political and social science may stretch the meaning of those terms. In the natural sciences Mesopotamia fares better. Mesopotamian mathematical methods were better than, or comparable to, any others up to the early Renaissance. They grew out of administrative and practical needs but toward the middle of the first millennium B.C. were linked to astronomy, where they became "a vehicle for scientific creativity" (Oppenheim 1964:306–7; Saggs 1962). Astronomy, possibly even preceding astrology, was highly developed (Saggs 1962). Botanical gardens were created late in the eighth century B.C. (Contenau 1954; Saggs 1962). The Babylonians put considerable effort of a protolinguistic character into etymological studies of Sumerian (Sayce 1900).

The importance of divination in Mesopotamia has already been shown. It remains only to note that virtually any phenomenon could be taken as an omen (Saggs 1962) and to suggest that for the Mesopotamians, divination was the queen of the sciences. That it was considered to be a science, and is still often so described, was mentioned above. Its linkage to historical studies was also shown. Given the connection of divination to kingship, it is not unreasonable to suggest that such political science as the Mesopotamians may have developed was no less under the umbrella of divination.

A note of caution must be sounded, however, in connection with our knowledge of Mesopotamia. The much greater durability of Mesopotamian portable writing material—clay, as opposed to the leather and paper of Egypt—has given us unequal access to information about the two regions. Oppenheim (1964:220) suggests, therefore, that Egypt "probably" developed as many techniques of divination as did the Mesopotamians, but the Egyptian techniques have not been preserved. In a similar vein, he says that the assiduous maintenance of old texts in Mesopotamia was merely, or largely, a consequence of the Mesopotamian technique of training scribes to copy accurately, in conjunction, of course, with the remarkable durability of the texts once they were produced. By implication, the Mesopotamians were not intrinsically interested in history; for accidental reasons they just happened to preserve more of the past than others did. In keeping with this point of view, Oppenheim tends to belittle the historical-mindedness of the Mesopotamians. As mentioned earlier, for example, he notes the lateness and infrequency of historical texts. He also notes, quite correctly, that the Mesopotamians' interest in the past was more antiquarian than historical. But at the same time he draws attention to signs of historical-mindedness difficult to document for Egypt. He mentions "astronomical diaries" that record on a day-to-day basis various sorts of human events. He notes the annals that cover many of the years from c. 744 to 264 B.C. He says that the "historical preamble" of a treaty between Assyria and Babylonia, covering a period from the fifteenth to the eighth centuries B.C., "bespeaks a serious interest in history dictated by political exigencies" (1964:146). Finally, he notes that there must have been an oral tradition of history too, in which the "deeds, crimes, and victories of famous rulers" were remembered, becoming the source of the later literary stories of early kings (1964:151). Thus, although the evidence may be skewed by the better preservation of texts in Mesopotamia than in Egypt, the available evidence does suggest a sounder sense of history in the former area.

For my purposes, the Babylonian and Assyrian cases turn out to be virtually indistinguishable, except that historiography and biography developed further in the latter. Both cases meet expectations with regard to historiography and divination, somewhat less so with regard to natural science and individualism. The remaining concomitants are either neutral or contrary to expectation. By themselves the Assyrians and Babylonians did not display the full syndrome connected with open societies. But they did have more of the open-society syndrome than did late Egypt, which was closed. Unlike Egypt, the Mesopotamian societies appear to have been open throughout all, or nearly all, the period they are known to us.

The ancient Hebrews do not provide such a clear picture of openness, though their society was considerably more open than that of later Egypt. The descendants of the royal house of David had prestige but no special privileges. Neither the king nor his person was sacred. The kings could appoint whomever they would to high office, which provided considerable scope for social mobility and a counterweight to aristocratic factions (Baron 1952:I). Part of Jewish tradition stressed that the Davidian dynasts were not exalted figures. As Weber notes, "the ancient Israelite leader had been an ass-riding, charismatic prince of the people, without a train of war chariots, treasure, harem, forced labor, taxes, and airs of world leadership"

(1952:184). Kingship and high office, therefore, did little to encourage caste among the Hebrews.

The matter was to be, at times, quite different in the priesthood. There is a goodly amount of debate about the origins, boundaries, and divisions of the priestly caste or castes—the Kohen or Levi—but there is little doubt that hereditary priesthood existed among the more ancient Hebrews and was of high status (Baron 1952:I). Weber (1952) asserted that originally they were oracle takers (by casting lots), and possessed no monopoly. The Levi eventually achieved, or nearly achieved, a monopoly in ritual affairs that was ratified by the kings, though they maintained the right to appoint high priests from among those qualified by birth (Baron 1952:I; Weber 1952). For a brief period after the return from Babylon, a more complex set of "genealogical classes" existed—almost a caste system. It broke down in a few generations, but the Kohen and Levi still remained genealogically separate (Baron 1952:I, 275).

On the other hand, the Hebrews as a whole resented the priestly monopoly, and the proportion the priests represented—about 1 to 3 percent of the populace—was "too insignificant to keep the masses in check" (Baron 1952:I, 272). The priestly class was seriously divided, there was a memory of a time when there was no priestly caste, and this caste was often the target of prophetic denunciation (Baron 1952:I; Weber 1952). Whereas at times genealogies were carefully maintained, at other times they were revised to suit the needs of one or another priestly faction (Baron 1952:I; Weber 1952). In short, the existence of a priestly caste did not give rise to a system of castes, and although the priests may have shared dominance with the rulers, the priests were not the dominant class. Thus Baron (1952:I, 75–76) places considerable stress on the legal equality of all Israelites: "In legal theory there were no class distinctions in Israel. . . . Israelitic laws, starting with the Book of the Covenant, recognized no separate estates, no special privileges. All Israelites, with the exception of the *gerim* (strangers) and perhaps the landless proletarians were supposed to enjoy perfect equality before the law." Elsewhere Baron says that the claims to priestly descent "did not, according to Jewish law, carry with them any special rights. . . . Before the law every born Jew was an 'Israelite,' in some respects inferior in rank to a 'Kohen' or 'Levi,' but absolutely equal to any other Jewish layman" (Baron 1952:I, 274).

This is not clear evidence that the ancient Israelites had a conception of a uniform human nature. The doctrine of the "chosen people," in fact, suggests otherwise (Baron 1952:I). This point will be taken up again in the final chapter, where a distinction is drawn between endo-racism (which is like caste) and exo-racism (which characterizes such conceptions as that of the chosen people). But for the time being it may be noted that mass education began in Israel under Ezra in the fourth or fifth century B.C. (Baron 1952:II; *Encyclopaedia Judaica* 1971:VI), which is consistent with a uniform conception of human nature within Hebrew society.

Concerning other concomitants, Hebrew history contains a fair amount of biographical information, but biography was not a separate genre. The Book of Nehemiah is autobiographical, or substantially so (*Encyclopaedia Judaica* 1971:IV; Misch 1950). Many individuals, from many stations in life, stand out in Hebrew history, but many other features of individualism are clearly absent. Hebrew history contains substantial secular and political history—Nehemiah again provides examples (Misch 1950)—but secular humanism, as well as political, social, and natural science was inconspicuous among the ancient Hebrews. Divination, by a variety of methods, certainly occurred among the Hebrews, but most forms were condemned by the prophets (Baron 1952:I; *Encyclopaedia Judaica* 1971:IV; Hastings 1928:IV). It does not seem as ubiquitous as in Mesopotamia. Realistic portraiture did not develop (*Encyclopaedia Judaica* 1971:III, XIII).

The ancient Hebrews showed less of the open-society syndrome than did the Mesopotamians. This may reflect some concession to the hereditary principle, as in the case of the priesthood, but it may also reflect the considerably smaller scale of Israeli society—both in population and time span—compared to Assyria or Babylonia.

To summarize social stratification in our societies from the ancient Near East, ancient Israel showed elements of caste but not nearly as much as Egypt, and the Babylonians and Assyrians were even less caste-minded than the Hebrews. Compared to Egypt, and certainly later Egypt, society among the Mesopotamians and Hebrews was open. These findings are basically consistent with the respective historiographies.

GREECE

Historiography

Within the antique Greek tradition, two contrasts are of special interest. One is the marked contrast between the early or ancient period of the great epic poems of Homer and Hesiod, and the later period of such prose historians as Herodotus and Thucydides (Starr 1968). The second contrast is found within the classical period, between the Athenians and the Spartans. J. B. Bury's views provide an introduction to the first contrast:

Long before history, in the proper sense of the word, came to be written, the early Greeks possessed a literature which was equivalent to history for them and was accepted with unreserved credence—their epic poems. The Homeric lays not only entertained the imagination, but also satisfied what we may call the historical interest. . . . [T]he story of the past made a direct appeal to their pride . . . [and] was associated with their religious piety towards their ancestors. Every self-respecting city sought to connect itself, through its ancient clans, with the Homeric heroes, and this constituted the highest title to prestige in the Greek world. The poems which could confer such a title were looked up to as authoritative historical documents. (1909:2)

Hesiod belonged to a school of "genealogical poets" whose . . . aim was to work into a consistent system the relationships of the gods and heroes, deriving them from the primeval beings who generated the world, and tracing thereby to the origins of things the pedigrees of the royal families which ruled in the states of Hellas. (1909:5)

Up to the middle or end of the sixth century, then, their epic poetry satisfied the historical interest of the Greeks. For us it is mythical, for them it was historical. (1909:7)

In *The Awakening of the Greek Historical Spirit* (1968), Starr sees many features of Greek historical writing foreshadowed in the epic poems. Though not physically described in much detail, the heroes are individualized, their characters emerging to some degree. And although the gods figure in the epics, men, with their human passions, are the center of interest. While elements of human nature were presented in the epics, according to Starr, "one does not sense that deliberate analysis of human nature was a tool anywhere available" (1968:18). It was a long step from the epic poems to the historical world, for Homer's "mental attitude," says Starr (1968:12), was far from that of the historian, and Hesiod was little more historical than Homer. In neither "can we detect a consciously historical attitude" (Starr 1968:34). While an occasional writer, even in antiquity, may have counted Homer as the father of history (Pearson 1939), the vast majority agree in assigning that role to a later figure.

Collingwood concurs, describing Homer's works as "legend" and Hesiod's as "myth" (1946:18). He identifies the first major step toward scientific history in the fifth century B.C., giving Herodotus (c. 484–c. 425 B.C.) the principal credit. Momigliano's authoritative essays on Greek historiography give Herodotus the position of the father of history (1966; 1978b). Starr (1968) agrees, but Bury (1909:12) gave credit to a lesser-known figure: "Hecataeus . . . initiated the composition of 'modern' history."

Hecataeus (c. 550–478 B.C.) was born in a time and among a people (the Ionian Greeks) characterized by broad contacts beyond the Greek world, and by a growth of religious skepticism and scientific rationalism (Momigliano 1966; Starr 1968). Hecataeus wrote, among other things, a prose work entitled *Genealogies*. He began the work with a statement of considerable skepticism toward Greek stories, for which reason, according to Bury, he undertook the task of critically editing them. "What I write here is the account which I considered to be true. For the stories of the Greeks are numerous, and in my opinion ridiculous" (quoted in Bury 1909:13). Bury concluded that in "aim and effort he was a pioneer" (1909:16; see also Momigliano 1977).

In an extended discussion of the various Ionian historians, Pearson (1939) gives a quite different interpretation of the opening lines of Hecataeus's *Genealogies*. He says they express his "aristocratic pride," presumably by belittling the genealogies of others. It is therefore a mistake, he says, to interpret the opening lines as the preface to an "impartial" and "rationalistic" analysis. Starr (1968:115) also doubts that Hecataeus "can in any serious sense be called a historian," even if he did have an important influence on Herodotus's methods. On the other hand, even though he would reduce the contribution of Hecataeus, Pearson argues for the development of historical writing on a rather broad front. Xanthus the Lydian, Charon of Lampsacus, and Hellanicus of Lesbos wrote in a manner similar in content and style to Herodotus. While they appear to have been his near contemporaries, it is not always clear who may have been copying whom (Pearson 1939). Thus, although Herodotus may widely enjoy the position of the father of history, he was not entirely without competitors immediately before, during, or very shortly after his time (see also Starr 1968).

Although born in a Dorian city, from which he was subsequently exiled, Herodotus "was educated in Ionian rationalism" and wrote his great history of the Persian Wars while living in Athens (Starr 1968:120). Herodotus conducted two basic types of research: inquiries into events that had occurred a generation earlier and travels to ask questions about past and present conditions. "Sightseeing and oral tradition" provided his materials (Momigliano 1966:129). Geography and ethnography were no less a part of his work than was narrative history. He showed much curiosity and considerable objectivity in treating non-Greek peoples, especially the Persians. He seems to have grasped the notions of cultural relativity and ethnocentrism, and he has often been described as a "barbarophile" (Momigliano 1966; Starr 1968). His ethnographic reports were widely disbelieved, and he was not to shake his reputation as a liar until the sixteenth-century, when travelers provided accounts of customs that made the ones he had described seem believable and when travel and oral tradition were again shown to be effective research methods (Momigliano 1966).

Herodotus wrote to preserve the glory of Greek and barbarian deeds, and the causes of their quarrel. He was concerned more to collect and perpetuate than to criticize existing information. This preservationist attitude was widespread in the early fifth century B.C. Fortunately, his extraordinary curiosity was matched by a no less extraordinary memory, and his contributions to international chronology were important (Momigliano 1966, 1978b; Starr 1968).

Perhaps because his style was admired and copied until well into the Byzantine period, Herodotus's work has survived more than well enough to show that he grasped the essentials of historical writing. He saw the present as resulting from complex chains of events brought about by human action in diverse parts of the world. He made a remarkably successful attempt to ascertain, analyze, and present these events to explain the conditions of his time, and with relatively little political or religious bias. In spite of his lively interest in mythology, he moved the Greek sense of the past "from the zone of myth to that of the recent past" (Momigliano 1966:212; see also 1977 and 1978b, and Starr 1968). It should also be remembered that Herodotean historiography established a precedent for an intimate connection between history, on the one hand, and ethnography, sociology and political science, on the other (Momigliano 1978b).

Many authorities would agree that if he was not the first "real" historian among the Greeks, Thucydides (c. 460–c. 400 B.C.) was nonetheless the best of them, the most scientific. Cochrane (1929) undertook an extensive attempt to show the roots of Thucydides' scientific approach and to argue that the degree to which he maintained scientific standards was unsurpassed for a long time. According to Cochrane (1929), the atomistic philosophy of Democritus (c. 460–c. 370 B.C.) provided conditions appropriate to the scientific study of human behavior. The study of "human nature" was, in fact, one of the principal headings in Democritus's division of scientific endeavor. Closely related to this was the distinct humanism—in the sense of an orientation toward human affairs—of fifth century Greek science.

Protagorus (c. 481–c. 411 B.C.) said, "Man is the measure of all things," and according to Cochrane (1929:94), Greek humanism was the "first fruit of the Democritean method." Political science, modestly labeled history, was Thucydides' contribution to humanistic science (Cochrane 1929).

The immediate model for Thucydides was not physics and mathematics but the biology and medical science incorporated by Hippocrates (c. 460–357 B.C.) in his *Ancient Medicine*. According to Cochrane, "The *Histories* of Thucydides represent an attempt to apply to the study of social life the methods which Hippocrates employed in the art of healing, and constitute an exact parallel to the attempts of modern scientific historians to apply evolutionary canons of interpretation derived from Darwinian science" (1929:3). Hippocrates' *Ancient Medicine* "stands out for all time as the first clear statement of the principles of rational empiricism" (Cochrane 1929:7). Thucydides applied these principles to the study of society and history and attempted "to bring *all human action* within the realm of natural causes" (Cochrane 1929:17). But whereas in medical science there were three stages—diagnosis, prognosis, and therapy—Thucydides confined himself to the first two, considering therapeutics to be the province of philosophy. It was Thucydides' objectivity and detachment that made him a good historian (Cochrane 1929). He accepted the view "that life itself is the real teacher of mankind," and that it is necessary to know "how men do in fact behave, before considering how they should" (Cochrane 1929:32).

Thucydides was explicit in seeing historical writing as a utilitarian activity (Cochrane 1929; Momigliano 1977): "The accurate knowledge of what has happened will be useful, because according to human probability, similar things will happen again" (quoted in Bury 1909:243). Respect for the facts and an attempt to interpret them as a physician interprets symptoms yield prognoses or predictions that turn history into political science (Cochrane 1929). Thucydides chose his historical topic—the Peloponnesian War—in keeping with his utilitarian views, and then fastened upon those personalities and events that were of demonstrable relevance to the topic (Cochrane 1929).

Thucydides considered personality to be a factor that had to be taken into account to understand history, and he set the standard for the psychological interpretation of history that long prevailed. But he was not as extreme in this as was Thomas Carlyle in his Great Man theory of history. Moreover, Thucydides always related genius to the circumstances that gave it scope (Cochrane 1929). Thucydides, like Hippocrates, considered human nature to be more or less uniform and stable, though conditioned by the environment and circumstances (Cochrane 1929).

As already mentioned in passing, Thucydides was no less a sociologist and political scientist than a historian. He was a sociologist because he applied scientific standards to an attempt to outline the development of Greek society and to offer a prognosis on the disease of war that had the Greeks in its grip in his time (Cochrane 1929). Furthermore, Thucydides did not envision society as an organism but considered "the problem of society and of history from the view of the relationship of individuals to the group" (Cochrane 1929:23). Cochrane credits Thucydides with offering "the first suggestion of a classification of states along the lines of rational empiricism" and says that the scientific view of Thucydides "visualized the relations of men as determined by considerations of power and interest" (1929:47, 94).

According to Cochrane, no one surpassed the high standard set by Thucydides until modern times. Only the Old Oligarch, the unidentified author of *The Constitution of the Athenians*, came close in ancient times. Polybius (c. 205–c. 123 B.C.) maintained a high standard in the narrative portions of his history of Rome but stumbled badly, according to Cochrane, in his cyclical analysis of constitutions (cf. Walbank 1966). St. Augustine also came close, but only with Machiavelli does the possibility of real improvement come, and it was not to be fully realized until the nineteenth-century work of Barthold Niebuhr (Cochrane 1929).

Starr (1968) agrees with the relationship between Greek historical writing and science—especially medicine (and anthropology), as embodied in Hippocrates' *On Airs, Waters, Places*—but argues that this relationship was already implicit in Herodotus. Thucydides thus differs from Herodotus only in making historical science more conscious of its method and then adhering more rigorously to that method.

The essentials of Thucydides' more rigorous method also greatly narrowed the scope of history. Whereas Thucydides agreed with Herodotus in relying almost exclusively on oral information, Thucydides believed that Herodotus had been led to error by not restricting his research to what he himself had witnessed or to other eyewitness or participant accounts. Thus Thucydides decreased the time span of history, making it essentially contemporary. Moreover, he narrowed the topics of history to politics and war, because of their potency as factors of change. In the Western world before the nineteenth century, only contemporary or very recent politico-military history was considered "real" history. When more remote periods were studied, only materials prepared under Thucydidean standards were utilized. Archival sources (assuming they existed) and other written sources were largely ignored. Thus what Thucydides gained in rigor was not without its costs (Momigliano 1966, 1977, 1978b; Starr 1968).

In an important sense, the classical Greek historians began a tradition that continued with only relatively minor interruptions until the fall of Byzantium. But for the purposes of this chapter, Polybius serves well as a final example. He was writing after Rome had conquered Greece and had brought much of the known world under its sway. Indeed, Polybius was conscious of initiating and writing a *universal* history, which he began while he was being held in Rome as a high-ranking hostage. Writing some two and a half centuries after Thucydides, Polybius was an innovator in certain ways, and yet he was also among those who "consolidate[d] the Thucydidean approach" (Momigliano 1966:215). Given his subject matter, he marks the transition to the development of Roman historiography (Bury 1909, Walbank 1966).

Most of the Greek historians had undertaken institutional analyses, but book 6 of Polybius's *Histories* provided the most sustained discussion of this topic by a prominent historian. He argued that constitutions tended to go through a typical cycle of transformations but that both Sparta and Rome had broken the cycle and had achieved stability by combining the best features of different constitutions. According to Walbank (1966), Polybius's analysis of the Roman constitution was one of two essential parts of his comprehensive attempt to explain Rome's rapid rise to dominance. However, subsequent events sharply altered Polybius's views on Roman constitutional stability (Bury 1909). As I have already noted, Cochrane (1929) considered book 6 an unforgivable lapse from scientific standards. Momigliano (1977, 1978b), on the other hand, credits the Greek (and Roman) historians with insights into the causes of revolutions that were considerably better than their understandings of the causes of war— precisely because the historians could utilize the results of philosophers' extensive studies of constitutions (see also Bury 1909).

Polybius also provided a more extensive discussion of historical standards and methods. Largely in agreement with Thucydides, Polybius set forth three requisites of historical research: "study and criticism of the sources," "personal knowledge of lands and places," and "political experience" (Bury 1909:197). He commented critically and in detail on the historiographical flaws in his predecessors' works and set forth his own principles so clearly that he provided virtually a "handbook of historical method" (Bury 1909:212; see also McDonald 1954 and Walbank 1966).

Although he was not alone in emphasizing the instructional value of history, Polybius put exceptional stress on its practical utility. He was writing for statesmen, who must understand causes and the interrelations between events. Polybius therefore adopted a sober, didactic style and avoided rhetorical excess. He wrote to instruct, not to entertain (Bury 1909; Momigliano 1966, 1978a, 1978b, Walbank 1966).

Polybius gave considerable attention to Fortune (*Tyche*), which, according to Walbank (1966), was the second essential part of Polybius's explanation of Roman dominance. According to Bury (1909), this emphasis on Fortune was especially true of Polybius's earlier writing, but as his experience deepened and his writings progressed, he eventually abandoned recourse to Fortune as an important factor in historical explanation. He "came to entertain the view that nothing happens without a natural cause, and the operation of Tyche or chance is, in general, an invalid assumption" (Bury 1909:203). The supernatural was even less a part of his causal explanations. Polybius considered religion "the keystone of the Roman state," but only because the masses needed it; "wise men" had no need for religion (Bury 1909:215).

"Like Thucydides and the ancients in general, Polybius believed in the eminent significance of the individual in history" (Bury 1909:212). He dissected character but criticized the inclusion of needless biographical detail. He thought deeply about individual and mass psychology, and about national character and its relationship to the physical and institutional environment (Bury 1909). Polybius was remarkably impartial in his allocation of both praise and blame, for he found the character of individuals to be inconsistent, changing according to circumstances and over time (Bury 1909, Walbank 1966).

Because of his impartial and intelligent devotion to the truth, Polybius stands out among the ancients. For the period his writings cover, he remains an indispensable source (Bury 1909, Walbank 1966). This is not to say, however, that Polybius avoided the shortcomings of the writings of most or all the ancient Greek (and Roman) historians. In addition to a narrow emphasis on politics and war, these included a difficulty in accounting for gradual social change and little concern for economic factors. Methodologically, Polybius continued the reliance more on oral sources and observation than on documents (Bury 1909; Momigliano 1977; Walbank 1966).

But historians were not the only Greek students of the past. Alongside Thucydidean history grew the various antiquarian studies. These included local histories, descriptions of monuments, lists of secular and sacred officials, collections of constitutions, linguistic studies, and the like. Unlike the historians proper, antiquarians often did draw on archival and other written sources. It was only in the eighteenth century that the ancient distinction between history and antiquarian studies began to dissolve (Momigliano 1966, 1978b). For whatever reasons, then, by the fifth century a broad interest in the objective study of the past had developed among various Greek peoples—certainly the Athenians. Both the historians and the antiquarians of that period were to have many successors over the next several centuries (Starr 1968). Developments in related nonhistorical areas, such as ethnology, sociology, and political science, should also be kept in mind (Momigliano 1978b; Starr 1968). Also, it is generally assumed that archives and other forms of record keeping developed along with the Greek sense of history, but even for Athens too little is known about this aspect of the sense of the past to allow for detailed comment (see, e.g., Starr 1968).

Biography as a distinct genre grew alongside of history as one of the antiquarian studies. But history, too, had a personality base. While most authorities consider Greek historiography in general to have been an independent development (see, e.g., Starr 1968), Momigliano (1977) does not preclude the possibility that Greek biography owed something to Persian or other Eastern models (many of the Ionian cities were in Persian territory). To some extent, the Greek concern with the individual and biography may have reflected the marked individualism that developed in Athens. Biography became much more important in Alexandrian and Roman Greece than it was in the fifth century (Momigliano 1966, 1977, 1978b; Starr 1968).

Somewhat related was the concern for understanding human nature. According to Momigliano (1966:214–15), Thucydides concentrated on politics because "it was here that he found the meaning of human effort. By understanding the political life of the present . . . he believed that he had understood the nature of man in its perennial elements." "He was at pains to understand the Peloponnesian War as the sum of human nature." (Greek ideas on human nature are discussed further below.)

The Greek interest in biography, personality, and human nature was apparent in the arts too. Statues of named individuals became increasingly common, as did the practice of signing works of art. Poetry and drama were no less oriented to concrete individuals. On the other hand, although the Greeks grew ever more competent at depicting the human figure and spirit, the classical sculptors were more concerned with depicting ideal figures than with capturing the unique features of particular individuals. It was not until the fourth century B.C. that literary characterization and true portraiture reached their fullest development (Ashmole 1964; Breckenridge 1968; Starr 1968).

Breckenridge (1968) sees a nexus between individualism, realistic portraiture, literary characterization, science, and a materialistic philosophy in ancient Greece. He sees a portrait of Aristotle, probably made during his lifetime, as "the first portrait of an individual in the strongly realistic sense of the word" (1968:120). For Aristotle, mind and soul could only be apprehended through the physical appearance and action of the individual, thus establishing "the fundamental premise of the scientific method" (Breckenridge 1968:123). "Only when such an attitude toward physical reality is accepted," Breckenridge (1968:123) suggests, "is portraiture in its most fully developed sense a possibility." This materialistic attitude corresponds with the secularism typical of open societies. Theophrastus's book *Characters* (319 B.C.), which was organized around personality types rather than occupations and thus marked a new level of literary naturalism, coincided closely with the pinnacle of realistic portraiture in ancient Greece (Breckenridge 1968).

The classical Greek contributions to natural science have already been alluded to. The Greek contribution to education and to a secular view of society are too well known to require discussion here. It might be noted that history played only a small role in the educational curriculum of the classical Greeks (Momigliano 1977, 1978b; Starr 1968).

The other contrast presented by the Greeks is that between Athens and Sparta. Many of the generalizations made about the Greeks are more properly generalizations about Athenian society or, more broadly, the Ionian branch of the Greek-speaking peoples. Although they were not all Ionian in origin, all or very nearly all the Greek historians wrote in the Ionian dialect (Pearson 1939). It was well known even in antiquity that the Spartans were strikingly anomalous in many ways (Cochrane 1929; Michell 1952). In some respects, perhaps, the whole branch to which the Spartans belonged—the Dorian—differed from the Ionian. The difference of greatest importance here is that the "Spartans had short memories" (Jones 1967:1). In the period when historical writing developed and floresced in Athens—and when Sparta was scarcely less a power in the Greek world—no Spartans wrote history. No Spartan wrote anything resembling history before the third century B.C., and what was produced then was a work of antiquarianism rather than political history (Forrest 1968). It is not certain that *any* contemporary literary source on Sparta before the Roman period was actually written by a Spartan (Chrimes 1942). Michell (1952) is not certain that the Spartans were even taught to read and write!

Not only did the Spartans not write their own history, they were downright secretive about their affairs, making it difficult for anyone else to compose a political history of Sparta (Forrest 1968; Huxley 1962; Michell 1952). It may have been the deliberate policy of the Spartans not only to be secretive but also deliberately to mislead outsiders (Chrimes 1942). In addition, there is no evidence of state archives in Sparta (Huxley 1962). Except for the Roman period, epigraphical materials are meager: there were no inscribed lists of magistrates, decrees, or laws (Chrimes 1942).

An apparent or partial exception was the support Xenophon received in Sparta. Xenophon (c. 434–c. 355 B.C.) was an Athenian citizen by birth, but during a lengthy exile he lived in Spartan territory. In this period he wrote some of his historical works (Bury [1937] n.d.; Momigliano 1977), but only one was specifically about Sparta, *The Constitution of the Spartans*. A translation of this work is prefaced by the statement: "This work furnishes us with what amounts to the official Spartan view . . . though it can scarcely be considered as genuine history" (Godolphin 1942:II, 658). Another of Xenophon's works, the *Hellenica*, treats Sparta in various parts, and yet it is these very parts that draw sharp criticisms of bias and unfortunate recourse to divine interference as a cause of events (Godolphin 1942:I, xxxi–xxxii). In short, whatever strengths Xenophon may have had as a historian, they do not unambiguously make him a historian of Sparta, even though he did live and write within Spartan lands.

There was some sort of oral tradition in Sparta, and the Spartans were said to have been especially fond of tales about the past (Momigliano 1978b; Starr 1968). Huxley 1962 mentions genealogical poetry based on king lists, and an elaborate mythology of royal houses.

Sparta ultimately acquired a reputation for considerable stability, as illustrated in Polybius's comparison of the constitutions of Sparta and Rome. Forrest (1968:18) argues that the Spartans took pride in this, and that "change was therefore unthinkable." When in the third century, Forrest continues, change was obviously required, the Spartans generated a new myth of the past so that the required changes could pass for a restoration of ancient conditions.

Although their fellow Greeks were enormously curious about the Spartans, the foregoing makes it clear that attempts to reconstruct the nature of Spartan society will not be without their difficulties. These difficulties are compounded by the fact that much of what was written about classical Sparta was written by men associated with Athens, which for long was Sparta's principal rival (Chrimes 1942). However, let us face that problem later, turning first to the nature of society in ancient Greece.

Social Stratification and Concomitants

The epic poetry of the ancient Greeks indicates that they originally possessed hereditary kings and nobles, both descended from the gods. M. I. Finley provides an authoritative and concise description of social stratification in Homeric Greece (c. eighth to seventh centuries B.C.):

A deep horizontal cleavage marked the world of the Homeric poems. Above the line were the *aristoi*, literally the "best people," the hereditary nobles who held most of the wealth and all the power, in peace as in war. Below were all the others. . . . The gap between the two was rarely crossed, except by the inevitable accidents of wars and raids. The economy was such that the creation of new fortunes, and thereby of new nobles, was out of the question. Marriage was strictly class-bound, so that the other door to social advancement was also securely locked. (1962:61)

Baldry (1965:15) adds further detail: "Homer regularly assumes that there is a hereditary physical difference between nobles and the multitude, a *natural* division separating them in bodily physique as well as spirit and way of life." Before turning to the classical Greeks, we may note that divination, which was to become a significant element in Greek culture, was not very important in Homer (Hastings 1928:IV).

The development of cities, trade, and industry ushered in more open societies among the Greeks. New classes arose, and by the seventh century B.C. most conditions were ready for stratification based on wealth. In the sixth century B.C., coinage was introduced and stratification by wealth was legally established. Democratic tendencies were strengthened by the reforms of Cleisthenes late in the century (Baldry 1965; Bury [1937] n.d.; Finley 1962; Starr 1968).

Let us look more closely at the sixth and fifth centuries. An important issue to examine is slavery. It is sometimes argued that since Athens was a slave state, it does not really count as the sort of open and democratic society found in various parts of the modern world, and that the difference between democratic Athens and the oligarchic Greek societies, of which

Sparta was the paragon, was relatively insignificant—a mere difference in the size and structure of oligarchies (Cochrane 1929; Forrest 1968). Without at the same time providing evidence, Finley (1973:15), for example, states that "the Athenian *demos* was a minority elite from which a large slave population was totally excluded." If females and children are not counted in the *demos*, Finley's statement may well be correct. But elsewhere (1959) he takes a more cautious line. He provides considerable evidence for substantial numbers of slaves in Athens but stops short of saying that they outnumbered the free populace. In part this reflects the obscurity of the data; in part it reflects his view that the precise number or proportion of slaves is not the most important fact in assessing the economic importance of slavery (Finley 1959). Cochrane (1929) had earlier noted that the data were poor on this subject, and no doubt we should keep an open mind on the proportion of slave to free in Athens. But recent students of the subject place the proportion of slaves in Athens and its vicinity (i.e., Attica) at no more than one-third of the populace, probably as little as one-fourth (Hopkins 1978; Starr 1958; Westermann 1955).

Even more important than the proportion of slaves was the permeability of the boundary that separated the various strata of ancient Athens. All authorities agree that the boundaries were open and that movement occurred in both directions. "Slave status might fortuitously be the lot of any person," and from the time of the Persian Wars to the time of Alexander, "the transition of status of individuals from freedom to slave condition and conversely from slavery through manumission to free status occurred with greater frequency and ease" (Westermann 1955:5). Finley (1959) also notes that anyone, regardless of status, could become a slave. On the other hand, manumission, which Finley (1959:160) says was an important incentive for the slaves, was a normal procedure: "we are baffled by the absence of numbers, but it was a common phenomenon in most of the Greek world."

Baldry 1965 provides an excellent account of the ideological accompaniments of the change in Greek society from hereditary to open stratification. As time went by, "in the eyes of a minority at any rate, wisdom took the place of birth or wealth as the mark of the 'good' members of society" (1965:5). In Aristophanes' plays, written at the close of the fifth century, Baldry notes evidence of "the breakdown of the traditional respect for the aristocracy and the rejection of the division of society, which we first saw in Homer, into a well-born upper class and a humble mass of common folk" (1965: 33–34). The rise of a moneyed class, says Baldry, was largely responsible. This process was sharply accelerated in the last part of the fifth century, and the ideal of nobility was "finally crushed" (1965:34).

For a considerable period the old and the new ideals clashed. Ion of Chios (d. 442 B.C.), for example, was an important earlier autobiographer, and yet he said that one could usually tell a noble by his appearance (Baldry 1965). Baldry cites many contrary views as time passes. For example, a speaker in a lost play by Euripides (c. 480–c. 407 B.C.) "debunks 'nobility' as merely a matter of hard cash: 'That man is noble, in whose house wealth stays the longest' " (1965:36). Menander (c. 342–291 B.C.) spoke on behalf of merit over blood: "If nature's given a man good character by birth, then he's well-born, even though he comes from Ethiopia" (Baldry 1965:138). Baldry says that the dominant theme about humanity in Menander "is the thought that character . . . matters above all else, and can transcend all the divisions of race and class." "Menander sets up merit as a universal standard" (Baldry 1965:139–40).

Thucydides himself, in the *Peloponnesian War* (ii, 37), put a defense of meritocracy in the mouth of Pericles, who says that "while the law secures equal justice for all alike, . . . the claim of excellence is also recognized; and when a citizen is in any way distinguished, he is preferred to the public service, not as a matter of privilege, but as the reward of merit. Neither is poverty a bar, but a man may benefit his country whatever be the obscurity of his condition" (Godolphin 1942:I, 648). In the time of Pericles (c. 490–429 B.C.), full Athenian citizenship—the most coveted status— was by no means easy to achieve (Cochrane 1929; Michell 1952), but it was not impossible. Frost (1987) describes social mobility among Greek slaves and recounts the life of a slave who ultimately achieved full citizenship and was reputedly the wealthiest man in Athens when he died.

The relatively lenient treatment of slaves in Athens, and the difficulty of distinguishing them from free men in dress, appearance, and even occupation is noted by many authorities (Cochrane 1929; Westermann 1955). In his attempt to explain the rise of science and of scientific history in Periclean Athens, Cochrane (1929) dwells at length on the problem of whether Athens really did differ from its neighbors. He says that even if Athens failed in some ways to live up to its high principles, it was more than a democracy in principle. Although the aristocrats might grumble, a substantial middle class shared power with the commercial class and the large proletariat. In spite of the existence of slavery, "the spirit and atmosphere of the state was that of liberty and equality" (1929:98).

It may be recalled that two of the most famous Athenians—Plato and

Aristotle—spoke of slavery as natural, Plato being the more unequivocal on the point. (Plato was a member of the old aristocracy.) Rifkin (1953) argues effectively that the very fact that the two philosophers defend slavery at such length reveals that the ideal of natural equality must have been powerful at that time. Thus, Aristotle quoted Alcidamas as saying, "God has left all men free; nature has made no man a slave" (Baldry 1965:205 n. 7). We should also note that to say slavery is natural is not to say that it is hereditary. Both Aristotle and Plato were fully aware of the biological unity of the human race (Baldry 1965). And if the Old Oligarch could claim "that the upper class was the wisest, Socrates' followers could maintain that the wisest should be the upper class" (Baldry 1965:56). Whatever the general thrust of Aristotle's and Plato's views, therefore, they were by no means unequivocally hereditarian or representative of the full spectrum of Greek opinion. Cochrane (1929) adds that whereas philosophers saw men as composed of gold and baser metals, Greek science knew nothing of such distinctions. In the entire corpus of Hippocratic treatises, in which the phrase the "nature of man" is common, it is nowhere "stated or implied that man's basic nature differs according to whether he is noble or humble, rich or poor, Greek or Barbarian, free or slave" (Baldry 1965:49). On the contrary, Hippocrates' On Airs, Waters, Places, traces human differences to the effects of the environment acting on an essentially uniform human material (Baldry 1965; Cochrane 1929). The Hippocratic Oath demanded similar treatment for all (Baldry 1965). The main argument of Baldry's book is that the idea of the unity of mankind was fully developed in Greek society.

Cochrane (1929:23, 24) draws attention to individualism in Athens: "Thucydides was a child of Periclean Athens," which was characterized by "intense individualism" (see also Baldry 1965 on the individualism of the cynics, and Bury [1937] n.d. on the individualism fostered by Socrates). Perhaps of no less interest, Solon (638?–559 B.C.)—whose reforms put the stamp of approval on social mobility—was the first Athenian "political figure to stand out as a real personality in Greek history" (Starr 1968:67).

In spite of its rapidly developing connection with Athens as Athens became the spiritual and political center of Ionia, Greek history had its beginnings not in Athens but in those portions of the Persian Empire where Greeks were numerous. Even there, however, a connection between social mobility and historiography is discernible. According to Momigliano, "The atmosphere of vigorous personal initiative which Persia aroused and partly encouraged was probably responsible for the attention paid by

Herodotus—and presumably by . . . Hecataeus—to their own and other people's personal experience" (1977:30). Pearson (1939:14) adds that the Ionian cities in Persia were democratic.

In sum, we may note three points. First, individual social mobility was ideologically and legally a fact of life in Ionia generally and in Athens in particular. Second, rates of mobility seem substantial, and certainly expectable if we consider the rapid growth of Athenian hegemony. Third, historians of Greek historiography have actually noted some connection between these social conditions and the rise of Greek historiography.

What of Sparta? Conditions were wholly different there from the sixth through the fourth centuries B.C. In an extensive analysis of slavery in Greek society, Westermann (1955) virtually ignores Sparta, because its system of serfdom—helotry—more or less precluded the need for slavery as he understood the term. However, most authorities do refer to the Spartan helots as slaves, the difference being that they were tied to the soil of the state: no individual could either manumit or sell them overseas. Hence their status was hereditary; only rarely could they achieve freedom (Cochrane 1929; Forrest 1968; Chrimes 1942; Jones 1967; Michell 1952). The term *caste* is regularly used in describing Spartan social structure, as in Michell's description of the dominant caste, the Spartiates, as "the most exclusive economical and political caste in all Greece" (1952:29).

There were three principal strata in the Spartan social structure during the period of Spartan greatness: at the top were the Spartiates, a military caste raised under strict conditions and ruled by two kings, a council, and an assembly but considering all save the kings to be equals before the law. A Spartiate could lose his status by failing to meet certain conditions, but this does not seem to have been a very common occurrence (Chrimes 1942; Jones 1967; Michell 1952).

Ranking beneath the Spartiates were the *perioikoi* (dwellers around), inhabitants of areas conquered by the Spartans. Though clearly subordinate to the Spartiates, the *perioikoi* were in some senses like allies. They lived in autonomous cities, paid rent to the Spartiates, and served in the army. They outnumbered the Spartiates and could not easily enter their stratum, if at all (Chrimes 1942; Jones 1967; Michell 1952).

Beneath the *perioikoi* in status were the helots. The standard estimate of their proportions, based on a reference to 479 B.C., is that they outnumbered the Spartiates by seven to one (Huxley 1962; Jones 1967; cf. Chrimes 1942). This proportion may be suspect, but all the authorities agree that the helots substantially outnumbered the Spartiates. Finley, who inclines to the high side in estimating the proportion of slaves in Athens, does not narrow the gap between it and Sparta by reducing the proportion of helots: they "outnumbered the free population on a scale without parallel in other Greek communities" (1959:158). He sees the contrast as no less sharp on the matter of social mobility. After his comments on the commonness of manumission in Athens, he adds: "This is an important difference between the Greek slave on the one hand, and the helot . . . on the other" (1959:160).

There is some evidence that both the *perioikoi* and the helots were considered "aborigines," and the Spartiates a conquering, invading race. Some have argued, however, that the helots were in fact Dorians who had been reduced to their humble status (Huxley 1962; Michell 1952). (This is a familiar debate about the origins of long-standing caste systems.)

In very early times—up to the seventh through early fifth centuries— the helots may not have been so numerous in Sparta, but in those times Sparta was less anomalous in other respects, too—showing, for example, a greater interest in the arts and in nature (Huxley 1962; Jones 1967; Michell 1952). By the third century the helots may have receded to insignificance again (Chrimes 1942). But in between, the helots, a hereditarily repressed majority, were a prominent feature of the Spartan social structure, no less important than the secretive, highly disciplined military caste that ruled them. At the same time, no Spartans wrote history; only in the third century was a weak beginning made on writing Spartan history and keeping the materials needed to compile its history in later times.

It was apparent to contemporaries that helotry was a highly significant aspect of Spartan society. Thucydides noted that most Spartan institutions were designed to guard against the danger presented by the helots (Michell 1952). For example, it was alleged in antiquity that the Spartiates annually declared war on the helots so they could be killed without the religious implications normal to murder (Jones 1967; Michell 1952). Aristotle thought Sparta's political system was worthy but that social system was fatally flawed by "Sparta's failure to see the need for social mobility" (Forrest 1968).

Modern writers are no less inclined to attribute the generally depressed state of art and science in Sparta to the attention the Spartiates were forced to give to their subject populace; "holding down a sullen and resentful peasantry" was like living "on top of a volcano" (Michell 1952:3, 28). It entailed eternal preparation for war, which in turn was the root of Sparta's deliberate policy of secrecy (Chrimes 1942). Secrecy was particularly associated with the helots; Huxley noted that "the Spartans veiled their treatment of them in secrecy" (1962:95).

Spartan education has long been famous, for peculiar reasons. As noted above, Spartan education may not have included reading and writing. It was rigidly designed to foster the esprit de corps of a small, militaristic caste. It bred a respect for the collective good that left little room for the development of individualism. Bury notes the paradox in Plato's and Xenophon's admiration of Sparta, for each had been students of Socrates, whose lifework had been to foster individualism. In "Sparta . . . their beloved master would not have been suffered so much as to open his mouth" (Bury 1937:566).

Sparta was almost perversely the opposite of Athens. In Sparta neither natural science, nor political science, nor any other social science flourished. Although Breckenridge 1968 notes that the Spartans commissioned portrait sculptures at Delphi in 404 B.C. at the end of their war with Athens, none of the artists appears to have been Spartan, and others state that the once-flourishing arts of Sparta languished after the sixth century B.C. (Jones 1967; Michell 1952). Literary portraiture in Sparta did not develop either. The individual was molded to his role in a simplified organic state. A myth of unchanging stability was fostered, concern for genealogy was strong. The Spartans were fond of stories of the past, probably part of an oral tradition, but there is little evidence that these stories were substantially accurate. The Spartans did not write history when their neighbors did; the Spartans had a system of caste when most of their neighbors did not.

In summary, the contrasts examined in the Greek setting—ancient Greeks versus classical Greeks, and Athenian or Ionian Greeks versus Spartans— provide strong evidence for the relationship between social stratification and historiography and tend to support the concomitants too.

ROME

Historiography

Divided into three major periods, Roman history stretches from the legendary founding of Rome in the eighth century B.C. to nearly the sixth century A.D. (excluding the Byzantine period). In the earliest period, Rome was allegedly ruled by kings, the last of whom was expelled in about 500 B.C. In the next period, which lasted almost five centuries, Rome possessed a republican form of government. In the several decades surrounding the birth of Christ, the republic collapsed, giving way to a period of government under emperors. The republican and imperial periods in turn have conventional subdivisions. For the present purposes, the most important is the period of Rome's decline, stretching through the third to fifth centuries A.D. This is the late imperial period, in which it is often necessary to distinguish the western and eastern halves of the empire, a division ultimately recognized by a system of co-emperors: one in Rome, one in Constantinople.

Most authorities do not consider the Romans to have begun writing history until some time late in the third century B.C. (Martin 1981). This observation needs two qualifications. First, the Romans did maintain historical materials earlier, and if they did not possess forms of history that would pass muster as literature, they did nonetheless possess rudimentary forms of historical writing well before the second century B.C. They maintained treaties, laws, family records, and the yearly records of the *pontifices* (the principal ritual officials). The pontifical annals recorded famines, eclipses, lists of consuls (the chief magistrates), and triumphs (Badian 1966; Martin 1981; Walsh 1966). Second, it was not merely histories that the Romans lacked before the second century B.C., but almost all forms of literature (Badian 1966).

Late in the third century, Rome produced her first historian whose name is known, Quintus Fabius Pictor. He wrote Rome's history from early times up to the first of the wars with the Phoenicians of Carthage—the Punic Wars. His writings were morally and politically committed, somewhat autobiographical, annalistic, and written in Greek. The time was ripe for borrowing Greek ideas, and he was quickly imitated (Badian 1966). Thompson (1942:I) lists four commendable annalists from about the middle of the second century B.C. Another figure, Gnaeus Gellius, wrote in the same century on cultural anthropology. He also wrote annals, drawing on the material in the pontifical annals, and was notable for the attention he gave to portents, which became a staple of Roman annalistic writings (Badian 1966).

Probably the first Roman to write Roman history in Latin was Cato the Elder (234–149 B.C.). He wrote in the Greek tradition, showing a lively interest in geography and natural science "but particularly in human life, customs, and character" (Badian 1966:8). He was interested in political theory and had political and didactic aims. He wrote political autobiography and contemporary history. Cato established Latin historical writing and was much imitated (save in one respect: so that the common soldiers would be credited with Rome's victories, he omitted personal names). Many fragments of his work survive (Badian 1966; Thompson 1942:I).

Gaius Fannius (consul in 122 B.C.) improved on Cato, but at almost the same time another important historiographic milestone was passed when in 133 B.C. the Pontifex Maximus published the pontifical annals, the *Annales Maximi*, in eighty books (Martin 1981). They had always been available to the senators, even if not often consulted. When available to the public, they established a basic framework for Rome's history. Their publication also made it possible for nonsenators to write history. Senators thereafter concentrated mostly on contemporary history, and annalistic writing fell to men who, working in their studies, had little experience with public affairs. The later annalists did not maintain high historiographic standards, but they were popular (Badian 1966).

Licinius Macer (d. 66 B.C.) found an alleged alternative set of ancient documents that differed in some ways from the pontifical annals. He is credited with consulting various unpublished sources, with being conscientious, and with maintaining a careful chronology (Badian 1966; Martin 1981; Thompson 1942:I). The monograph was introduced by Lucius Coelius Antipater, who wrote a history of the Hannibalic (Second Punic) War after 121 B.C. He chose his sources carefully; where they conflicted, he consulted documents and other sources, including a Carthaginian history. He was a "serious" historian who strove for accuracy. In the long run his influence was very great (Badian 1966; Hammond and Scullard 1970; Martin 1981; Thompson 1942:I). Sempronius Asellio (born c. 160 B.C.) compiled a notable set of memoirs. Judging from the fragments that survive, he consciously aimed not merely to relate facts but to give causal analyses. Possibly influenced by Polybius, Asellio distinguished "pragmatic" history from annals. This was a new conception of history in Rome (Hammond and Scullard 1970; McDonald 1954; Thompson 1942:I).

Before the end of the second century, contemporary history began to add an autobiographical dimension. Marcus Aemilius Scaurus, for a quarter of a century the chief senator, and probably the most powerful man of his time, was the first to write a straightforward autobiography, probably in the nineties B.C. A more important autobiography followed shortly, written by P. Rutilius Rufus (born c. 150 B.C.), an important Stoic philosopher who also wrote a history (Badian 1966). Politicians' memoirs became a prominent genre.

Lucius Cornelius Sisenna (died c. 67 B.C.) wrote a history of Rome's Social and Civil Wars, rejecting excessive concern for chronology in favor of "grouping by subject matter" (Badian 1966:26).

The age of Cicero (106–43 B.C.)—centered on the final decades of the Republic—saw significant antiquarian research by Atticus and Varro (among others) and the writings of Julius Caesar (d. 44 B.C.). Atticus produced a chronology of world, but mostly Roman, history; Varro wrote some six to seven hundred volumes (Shotwell 1923). Caesar's *Commentaries*—the most notable of the political memoirs—were historiographically distinguished (Badian 1966). In his *Gallic War* Caesar maintained the standards of Thucydides and Polybius, placing accuracy above style (Dorey, "Caesar," 1966).

Cicero was not a historian in the usual sense of the word, but his writings bordered on contemporary history and provide us with our most detailed understanding of any Roman period. Moreover, his comments on the theory of history have been very influential. Cicero thought that he should write a history of Rome (McKeon 1950). One of his contemporaries, Cornelius Nepos, agreed, lamenting on Cicero's death that it was uncertain "whether history or the Republic lost more" (quoted in McKeon 1950:16). Fortunately, according to Nepos, Cicero's letters were themselves a near substitute for history:

Whoever reads them does not have much need of a sequential history of those times. For there, all the details concerning the rivalries of great men, the faults of leaders, the revolutions of the Republic are so set forth that nothing in them is left in doubt, and it can easily be said that prudence becomes in a manner divination. For Cicero not only predicted future events which did indeed occur in his own lifetime, but also rendered oracles worthy of a prophet concerning events which are now coming to pass. (Quoted in McKeon 1950:16)

Cicero's speeches, as was typical of the time, were centered on concrete individuals, their policies and practices. Praise and blame were normal parts of political oratory, as was detailed reasoning on the consequences of one or another proposed policy (Rawson 1975). A careful microhistorical analysis of cause and effect in public policy was essential in effective public oratory. Cicero stressed the practical value of history, particularly in matters of public morals and politics (McKeon 1950), and he developed notions of probability and causality (McKeon 1950). In the *De Officiis* (On duties) he says that men, "blessed with the power of ratiocination, by means of which they can foresee consequences, understand the reasons for events and even anticipate them, and apprehend causality, are able to compare like with like and, by interweaving and reconciling present and future, easily to evaluate the whole of life and adequately to prepare to live it" (Cicero 1950:470). Interestingly, Cicero noted that the "truth of history" was "much corrupted" by accounts of their ancestors that "families of note" produced (quoted by Shotwell 1923:225).

It was in Cicero's time that the Roman state began to maintain state archives (Thompson 1942:I). By the time of Cicero's death, Roman historiography had reached its full development, by then including the traditional annals, contemporary history, antiquarian studies, and political autobiography (Badian 1966). In Cicero's view, however, no Roman had yet managed to pull it all together in a work that would rival the best of the Greeks' because the Romans were still deficient in "rhetorical embellishment" (Martin 1981:19). Livy was to remedy this deficiency.

In the meantime, C. Sallustius Crispus (c. 86–34 B.C.), the "first great Roman historian," (Thompson 1942:I, 70) wrote history from an antiestablishment viewpoint, trying to analyze the sources of decay in the state. He considered his analysis to be of practical use in statecraft. Sallust was particularly good in his depiction of character, and he borrowed from Thucydides a special attention to the sharp contrast between what people said and what they did (though he failed to note this trait in himself). Sallust "laid down the model and categories of Roman historiography for ever after" (Syme [1939] 1979:249) and was probably a successful historian in his own time (Paul 1966; Martin 1981).

Among the major Roman historians only Livy (59 or 64 B.C.–c. A.D. 17) had no practical experience in political affairs, though he was directly patronized by the emperor Augustus. His style was good and he wrote prodigiously. His *Ad urbe condita* (From the founding of the city) would run to about nine thousand pages in a modern book. He was judged to have met the Ciceronian ideal, although modern critics often give him more credit for style than for scientific history or sharp political analysis. For some purposes, however, he is excellent. Livy provided more information on social and economic conditions than did any other Roman historian, and he gave much information on religious feeling and Roman cults. He relied primarily on secondary sources, but if he found no single reliable source, he examined conflicting accounts with care and then reported the variations. Less concerned than most Roman historians with institutional analysis, he focused on the words and actions of people, providing much information on psychology, emotions, morals, motives, and character. It was his concern for motives, in fact, that led to an excess of moralizing (Dorey, ed., 1966; Martin 1981; McDonald 1954; Shotwell 1923; Walsh 1966).

Brief mention should be made of a contemporary of Livy, Trogus Pompeius, who wrote a *Historiae Philippicae*, the first known effort at universal history. Though written in Latin, its author was a Gaul by birth (Thompson 1942:I).

Contemporary political history suffered greatly with the advent of the imperial period, but various kinds of historical works were still written. Augustus (r. 27 B.C.–A.D. 14) suppressed political history but encouraged antiquarian studies (McDonald 1954; Syme [1939] 1979; Thompson 1942:I). The Emperor Claudius (r. A.D. 41–54) wrote an autobiography and was himself a prolific writer on antiquarian topics (Thompson 1942:I).

Rome was yet to produce her greatest historian, Tacitus (A.D. 56 or 57– c. 120). Tacitus's intellectual heritage was primarily from Cato and Sallust. He wrote a biography of his father-in-law, *De vita Iulii Agricolae*, and an ethnography, the *Germania*. The latter included cultural and physical geography as well. The comparative perspective acquired in writing the *Germania* made Tacitus a better historian (Martin 1981; see also McDonald 1954). In his *Histories* Tacitus examined the causes of the rise and fall of the Julio-Claudian dynasty. According to Ronald Martin, it "contains some of the most brilliant descriptive writing of any age or language" (Martin 1981:68). Martin also notes that in his *Annals* Tacitus used the "traditional framework of year-by-year narrative," and yet he was the "most original of Roman historians" (1981:104).

We know that Tacitus presented some speeches with accuracy, and his fictitious speeches showed more individuality than was usual. Tacitus was quite aware of the difference between peoples' motives and their statements, and between their statements and their actions. He was very good at seeing the complexity of things and was impartial in praise and blame (Martin 1981; cf. Shotwell 1923).

Among the sources Tacitus consulted were memoirs, earlier historians, probably the *acta senatus* (a daily gazette that had been instituted by Julius Caesar), biographies, autobiographies, occasional inscriptions, and some oral sources. He was critical of his sources, though he sometimes relied on only a few sources when more were available, and rarely can he be caught in a falsehood. While he did not depart too far from the methods of his time, he achieved a "penetration" to the heart of matters that rivaled Thucydides and a pungency that was not matched in the Greco-Roman world (Martin 1981). Tacitus even achieved a sense of comparative historiography, noting that "the subject matter of history varies according as the constitution about which the historian writes is democracy, oligarchy, or monarchy" (Martin 1981:137). In spite of these strengths, Tacitus was not much read in Rome, because pragmatic or serious history "became unfashionable," "giving way to imperial biography and panegyric" (Martin 1981:236). (A decline in Roman historiography after Tacitus is noted by virtually all authorities. Two important exceptions will be noted shortly.)

The new importance of biography is well illustrated in the *Lives of the Twelve Caesars*, by Suetonius (c. A.D. 75–160). He had been private secretary to the emperor Hadrian, but there is little reason to think that he used his position to consult original source material. Although all but the *Lives* are lost, Suetonius wrote voluminously on history, antiquities, and especially on science. He was indifferent to political and military matters. His biographical method of writing history persisted into the Middle Ages (Thompson 1942:I).

The last of the sounder Latin historians in the classical genres was the pagan Ammianus Marcellinus (born c. 330). He showed a great interest in nobles and their origins (Alföldi 1952), but he was born a Greek at Antioch. He wrote a history so filled with accurate and vivid material that we understand the political, diplomatic, and military situation of the period he covered (353–378) better than any period after those described by Tacitus (McDonald 1954; see also Momigliano 1977).

The two important exceptions to the general pattern of decline in historiography in the late empire resulted from the efforts of Greek writers in the eastern empire and from the initiation of church history. A series of authors writing in Greek wrote distinguished histories throughout the period that Romans ruled their lands. Dio Cassius (c. 155–235), for example, wrote an eighty-volume history of Rome from 1000 B.C. to A.D. 235. Although a conventional work, it and other Greek histories "to some extent made up for the deficiency" in Latin historical writing at the time (Shotwell 1923:275; McDonald 1954; Thompson 1942:I) Ammianus, though he wrote in Latin, can also be seen as part of this Greek tradition within the empire.

Such creativity as occurred in historiography in the late empire was associated with the Church: comparative chronology, ecclesiastical history, and hagiography were important new genres, while citations of sources, footnotes, and appendices were introduced too (Momigliano 1977; Thompson 1942:I). Eusebius of Caesarea (c. 260–340), the "father of ecclesiastical history" and author of the "greatest of all church chronicles" (Thompson 1942:I, 128–29), illustrates these developments. His *Chronographia* was a vast exercise in comparative chronology in two books: one established each people's own chronology; the other comprised a concordance of these disparate chronologies, with important events noted in the margins. Although its core was the Old Testament, the *Chronographia* was the first attempt to grasp the whole of history as a single entity (Thompson 1942:I). Eusebius's *Historia Ecclesiastica* presents a "co-ordinated, sustained, critical and interpretive history of the Church" (Thompson 1942:I, 130). On the other hand, Eusebius's *Life of Constantine*—more hagiography than biography—"is without value as history" (Thompson 1942:I, 130). Eusebius was prolific and much imitated.

Although Eusebius was not the only sound church historian—St. Augustine's *City of God* and his autobiographical *Confessions*, for example, were soon to be written—there is substantial agreement that much Christian historiography was not sound. This will be discussed further in the next chapter.

Social Stratification

Little is known about Rome's regal period, but at the dawn of the republican period the body of free Roman citizens consisted of patricians and plebs, the former monopolizing office. The dominant theme of early republican history is the "struggle of the orders," in which the plebs achieved effective equality and the right to intermarry with the patricians. The two-century struggle of the plebs culminated in 287 B.C. when decisions of plebiscites were recognized as binding Roman law. Patricians retained a certain social prestige into the imperial period, though they steadily dwindled in number. They also retained control of some offices—mostly ritual offices—until Caesar and the Triumvirs in a decade beginning in 43 B.C. opened virtually every high office and status to their henchmen (Wiseman 1971). Patricians could renounce their status, and in the early imperial period emperors gained the power to appoint people to patrician status (Gelzer [1912] 1969). In the third century A.D. patricians disappeared as a status group. The term *plebian* had come to serve as a generic label for the lower orders of society (Hammond and Scullard 1970).

In the middle of the republican period the dominant historical events were the three Punic Wars fought against the Phoenicians of Carthage in 264–241, 218–201, and 149–146 B.C. After each of these wars Rome gained control of larger portions of the lands and trade surrounding the Mediterranean. As Rome's power grew, so did its wealth and the opportunities for upward mobility (Hill 1952; Wiseman 1971). Under these conditions, a whole new "middle class" formed, eventually crystallizing around the equestrian order (to be described below). The new class was counterposed against the senators (Hill 1952).

Wealth, education, family, and officeholding became key elements in determining rank in the republican period. From very early times, Roman citizens had been divided into legal classes based on wealth (Hammond and Scullard 1970; Gelzer [1912] 1969). Generally speaking, only persons in the wealthiest class could hold office, and the weight of an individual's vote was effectively lessened to the degree that he fell in lower wealth classes (Hammond and Scullard 1970; Taylor 1966). Once the patricians had lost their position of superiority, Rome's aristocracy was shaped by officeholding. Those who held the higher offices became eligible for, or were automatically inducted into, the Senate. There was an expectation of the sons of senators becoming senators too—provided, of course, that the wealth qualification continued to be met and that the son could win an office in a popular election. From the fourth century B.C. until the early empire no one became a senator without a decent education (Gelzer 1969) and without winning office, presumably thereby demonstrating his merit (Hammond and Scullard 1970; Hopkins 1974; Wiseman 1971). The highest office was that of consul. The consuls—there were normally two—were the successors to the early Roman kings. Consuls held office for one year but could be reelected. The descendants of consuls were looked upon as nobility (*nobilis*), though the status was not codified in law and "never became a closed caste" (Hammond and Scullard 1970:736; Hill 1969).

The *nobiles* tried to prevent the admission of "new men" (*novi homines*), i.e., persons who were the first in their family line to hold consular office. So, too, the families of senators attempted to win high offices and senatorial seats for their members and to keep new men out. The elite were aided in their attempt at exclusiveness by an ancient right of the holders of high office to erect wax death masks. This made their personalities and families more widely known, and even more awesome when a whole series of death masks of ancestral officeholders could be arranged in the order of a family tree. The familiarity of a family, by virtue of its public images, conferred advantage in public elections (Hammond and Scullard 1970; Wiseman 1971). Insofar as *nobiles* and senators prevented the admission of newcomers to their status, the system was closed; insofar as new men got in, it was open. Historians differ in their assessment of this, some stressing closure, others openness (see, e.g., Hammond and Scullard 1970; Rawson 1975;

Stockton 1971). Time and place, as we shall see, were important determinants of openness and closure.

A factor that may have promoted openness at the top was the often-noted tendency of Rome's highest families not to reproduce themselves, a tendency manifest over a considerable period (Frank 1916; Gelzer [1912] 1969; Hopkins 1974; Weaver 1974). It is also important to note that senators could be demoted because of bankruptcy, or even relative impoverishment (Wiseman 1971).

Another important factor in openness at the top of Roman society was the rise of the equestrian order (Henderson 1963; Hill 1952), which as the name suggests, developed out of the ancient Roman cavalry. Entry into the cavalry required a set standard of wealth. Of those who qualified, a relatively small number were chosen for the honor of receiving a horse at the state's expense. In the latter half of the second century B.C., in the course of an attempt to reassert the power of popular assemblies over the senate, senators were banned from entry into the equestrian order (Wiseman 1971). This effectively pitted *equites* against senators (Gelzer 1969; Hill 1952). In the widest sense, the equestrian order consisted not only of the equestrians proper (i.e., those with public horse) but also all retired equestrians and all persons legally qualified by wealth and citizenship status to be equestrians (Garnsey 1970). The equestrians in this broad sense must have been conscious of their distinction from the mass of Romans, as well as from the senators, well before the middle of the second century B.C. (Hill 1952).

Since senators were in theory banned from commerce and finance, which would have demeaned their status, the equestrians predominated in these fields, made so lucrative as a result of the Punic Wars. Having the profits of office and great landholdings, senators were of course far from impoverished, but the *equites* were in a good position to become wealthy, and they did (Gelzer 1969; Hill 1952). With their wealth the *equites* were in turn in good position to assail senatorial status. Wiseman (1971) and Syme ([1939] 1979) both show that the *equites* did so with considerable success.

Insofar as there was a middle class apart from or beneath the equestrians, it was "too heterogeneous" to be conscious of itself as a class (MacMullen 1974:94). Little is known about the common man in Rome, but mobility was possible for him, more so in urban settings and in the east of the empire (MacMullen 1974).

At the bottom of the Roman social pyramid were the slaves. As in most of Greece, in Rome slavery was undeniably an important institution. Yet slaves never constituted a majority (Hopkins 1978). "Public opinion in Rome," Treggiari notes, "accepted the freeing of slaves as normal and even desirable" (1969:12). This was not because the Romans questioned the concept of slavery but because they recognized individual merit (Treggiari 1969). All authorities attest to very high rates of manumission, at least of urban slaves (Frank 1916; Hammond and Scullard 1970; Hopkins 1978; Symes [1939] 1979). Freed slaves had better opportunities "to rise in the world than the freeborn poor" (MacMullen 1974:124). If manumitted by a Roman citizen, a freedman almost invariably thereby acquired Roman citizenship (Hopkins 1978; Treggiari 1969). Slaves and freedmen were prominent in trade, the professions, and in small industry (Hill 1952; Treggiari 1969), generally serving in all occupations in which ordinary Roman citizens were to be found (Hammond and Scullard 1970; Treggiari 1969). Slaves lost the ethnic, kinship, and religious ties that they possessed prior to enslavement and were identified with the household and society of their masters (Hammond and Scullard 1970). Freedmen suffered a variety of legal disabilities, but a freedman's son was essentially free from the bonds that held his father (Garnsey 1970; Gelzer 1969; Hopkins 1978; Treggiari 1969).

Some freedmen became very wealthy, and in the early imperial period some of the imperial freedmen, who formed the embryonic imperial bureaucracy, became not only extremely wealthy but no less powerful (Hammond and Scullard 1970; Hopkins 1974, 1978; Weaver 1974). The pattern of entrusting to freedmen some of the most powerful and lucrative posts in the empire persisted into the second century A.D.

It was rare for freedmen to become equestrians and even rarer for former slaves to become senators, but both occurred (Weaver 1974; Wiseman 1971). As early as 312 B.C. the censor Appius Claudius attempted to have the sons of freedmen admitted to the Senate (Treggiari 1969; Wiseman 1971), but it was long resisted. Eventually the precedent was set, yet the entry of sons and grandsons of freedmen, let alone the freedmen themselves, always raised eyebrows (Hammond and Scullard 1970). Treggiari (1969) argues that in the republic there was neither a legal barrier to admitting the sons of freedmen to the Senate nor even conclusive evidence that freedmen were ineligible to enter the Senate; however, custom was against both. Freedmen were legally barred from the equestrian order, but their sons were not, and sons of freedmen achieved equestrian rank in considerable numbers (Wiseman 1971).

Roman citizenship was progressively expanded, not only to include specially honored individuals (Wiseman 1971) and manumitted slaves (Hopkins 1978; Treggiari 1969), but also the various inhabitants of particular communities or regions in Italy and the empire. From 91 to 88 B.C. the so-called Social War was fought between Rome and her Italian allies (*socii*), at the conclusion of which many of the *socii* were granted citizenship. The fact that 900,000 citizens were registered in 70 B.C. and 4,000,000 in 28 B.C. well illustrates the rapidity with which citizenship was expanded (Wiseman 1971). The grandsons of the newly enfranchised not uncommonly achieved senatorial rank (Wiseman 1971). By A.D. 212 all Roman subjects had been granted citizenship. The conditions of slavery and of citizenship led to an astonishing feat of acculturation, spreading the Latin language, Roman institutions, and the sense of being a Roman far beyond the Roman homeland and also drawing hordes of once-foreign peoples laterally into and vertically up through the ranks of Roman society (Frank 1916; Gordon 1924; Hammond and Scullard 1970; Hopkins 1974; Treggiari 1969).

While all the statuses described above—patrician, plebian, consul, senator, equestrian, freeborn citizen, freedman, and slave—formally persisted from the republican into the imperial period, some of their most important interrelationships were transformed in the process. Two thorough investigations of the subject are Ronald Syme's qualitative analysis of *The Roman Revolution* ([1939] 1979) and T. P. Wiseman's quantitative study of the *New Men in the Roman Senate, 139 B.C.–A.D. 14* (1971). Both show that it was a period of unprecedented and explosive social mobility.

In the course of the Roman revolution the *nobiles* were decimated by the Civil Wars and by proscriptions in which their property was redistributed. Trustworthy men, notably military figures, rose to high office regardless of their background, though they might quickly fall when their patrons toppled one another. Senatorial rank became heritable, within limits, but the Senate was degraded by alternately packing it with newcomers and purging it. Patrician status was conferred by fiat, and citizenship was greatly expanded. Rome became a true plutocracy, and wealthy non-Roman Italians or provincials increasingly entered the highest Roman strata. Imperial freedmen grew rich and powerful. Provincial soldiers would soon rise through the ranks to become emperors (Syme [1939] 1979).

Wiseman (1971) identified 563 *novi* senators and 52 *novi* consuls between 139 B.C. and A.D. 14, with the sharpest increases occurring during and immediately after the period of the Triumvirs, who succeeded Julius Caesar in 44 B.C. By contrast, only ten *novi* held thirteen consulships in the 227 years before 139 B.C. (Gelzer [1912] 1969).

Treggiari thought that the transitional period between the republic and the empire "provided more opportunities than ever before for ability, or unscrupulousness, to assert itself against mere right of birth" and that there was an "explosive rise to power of . . . moneyed classes outside the Senate in the late Republic" (1969:162, 244). Central to this mobility was the rise and fall of competing dictators and ultimately the emperors: they sought talented and powerful supporters where they could find them, and ambitious men could further their own goals by supporting the competitors at the top. Once the emperors were established, they sought policies that would curb the senatorial and consular authority they had overthrown. To this end the emperors constructed a bureaucracy composed of equestrians, on the one hand, and freedmen and slaves, on the other (Arnheim 1972; Weaver 1974). From the beginning of the empire, the emperors strove to appoint fewer and fewer senators to high office, culminating in the reign of Diocletian (A.D. 284–305), who turned the set of offices open to senators into a cul-de-sac (Arnheim 1972). At the same time as senatorial access to office was restricted, it became easier to enter the Senate, which further degraded it (Arnheim 1972). By the end of the first century A.D. 23 percent of the senators were of provincial origin and hence presumably not of old senatorial family. By the middle of the second century the figure had risen to 42 percent, and by the third century it was 56 (Hopkins 1974).

Social mobility in the republican and early imperial periods was not without ideological support. The mobility and its ideology can often be found in the lives and writings of the Roman historians. Cato, born of peasant stock, was unequivocally a new man, and an eloquent spokesman for the claims of merit over birth (Hammond and Scullard 1970; Syme 1958; but cf. Gelzer [1912] 1969, who considered Cato to have been born to equestrian status). Cato rhetorically idealized a plebian war hero who served as consul four times and was credited with "humble birth, incorruptibility, and frugality" (Hammond and Scullard 1970:332). Lucius Coelius Antipater was not a senator (Martin 1981). Licinius Macer as a politician defended the people's rights against "self-seeking nobles" by reasserting the authority of tribunes (plebian offices) and advising the people to refuse military service until their demands were met (Martin 1981:18; Thompson 1942:I). Marcus Aemilius Scaurus, the first to write an autobiography, was of modest beginnings (Badian 1966). Sallust was a *novus homo*, though he must have come from a locally prominent family. He was critical of the *nobiles* and their exclusiveness but also of the plebs. He espoused popularism, and a number of the speeches in his histories were vehicles for attack on the *nobiles* (Martin 1981; McDonald 1954; Paul 1966; Syme [1939] 1979).

Cicero, though not formally a historian, deserves to be considered along with them for the reasons given above. Born a provincial but of equestrian status, he strove from early life to excel. Through good education, military service, patronage of the powerful, a marriage above his station, and above all his forensic eloquence, he achieved the consulate (Boissier n.d.; McKeon 1950; Rawson 1975; Stockton 1971). Cicero is undoubtedly the most famous of the *novi homines* and is our main source for the ideology of the new man (Wiseman 1971). His barbs at noble privilege are famous, perhaps the best known being his remark "about those fortunate people who do not need to have any merit, who do not require to take trouble, and to whom the highest places in the republic come while they are sleeping" (Boissier n.d.:29). Like Cato, Cicero idealized a plebian war hero, one who was twice consul and whose "poverty, austerity, and incorruptibility" were legendary (Hammond and Scullard 1970:428). While he was no democrat and made little effort to actually help new men (Boissier n.d.; Stockton 1971; Syme [1939] 1979), Cicero has had considerable influence into modern times as a spokesman for men of talent in their opposition to the privileges of birth (Rawson 1975).

The theme of social mobility is consistently detectable in the lives or writings of the Roman historians, whether new men or not. Thus Julius Caesar was a patrician and "proud of it," but he earned his position by merit, had a keen eye for it, and his dictatorship "meant . . . promotion for merit" (Syme [1939] 1979:94). Livy was not a senator and may have been a stoic (Walsh 1966). Moreover, one of the two major themes of his work was "the domestic struggles out of which the plebs won an honourable role in government" (Walsh 1966:126). The antiquarian Claudius made a speech in A.D. 48 in which he spoke on behalf of granting to certain Roman citizens the right to seek senatorial office and outlined a history of the advancement of the meritorious that stretched all the way back to the period of the Roman kings (Martin 1981; Wiseman 1971). He was a bitter enemy of the *nobiles* (Syme [1939] 1979). Valerius Maximus, one of the lesser antiquarians of the early imperial period, gathered materials under the heading of "men of obscure birth who became famous" (Thompson 1942:I, 81).

Tacitus's origins are obscure, but he "was neither aristocrat nor Roman born" (Martin 1981: 24–25; Syme 1958:II). Martin (1981) thought that the period in which Tacitus lived provided considerable scope for mobility.

Martin (1981:41–42) also argued that by emulating Cato, through Sallust, Tacitus indicates "an allegiance in thought to Cato, who had sought to champion the view that political advancement should be won by personal merit, . . . not by birth and privilege." In a speech to his troops by the emperor Otho (r. A.D. 69), Tacitus succinctly sets forth a view of Roman mobility: "For as senators come from your ranks, so do emperors come from the ranks of senators" (quoted in Martin 1981:77). The care with which Tacitus reported the speech by Claudius recommending meritocratic appointment suggests more than casual interest in the matter (Martin 1981).

Atticus and Suetonius were sons of equestrians (Hammond and Scullard 1970). As noted earlier, Trogus Pompeius was a Gaul, Ammianus Marcellinus a Greek. Eusebius was from Palestine. St. Augustine was from a "poor family," and like many of the other church fathers he had made his way to eminence from the "obscure towns" of the empire (Brown 1971:30, 33). He advocated faith and conduct above birth (Murray 1978).

With some exceptions, then, the Roman historians show a significant tendency to be new men and to be members of a class defined more by wealth than by birth (Syme 1958:II; Syme 1979).

There are other indictions of a meritocratic ideology. Stoicism—with its belief that all mankind are essentially similar (Hopkins 1978) and "that slaves could be the moral equals of their masters" (Treggiari 1969:12)— was influential for a period in Rome, though mostly at the upper levels of society. A populist ideology stressing merit over birth was espoused in the latter half of the second century B.C. when the Gracchi brothers led an attempt to reassert the authority of popular assemblies. (McDonald [1954] thought that this period, which saw the publication of the pontifical annals, reminded people of the Struggle of the Orders and stimulated an interest in history.) However, populism was a force in politics for only a half century; no democratic or egalitarian ethos ever took root in Rome (Hammond and Scullard 1970; Syme [1939] 1979). At all times the consciousness of rank was as salient as occupation is in the modern West, and the climb up the social pyramid was very steep (Hopkins 1974; MacMullen 1974). But with the opportunity to change one's rank, this consciousness was an incentive to action (Syme 1958). The theoretical openness of the Roman system—even the office of emperor was not in principle hereditary—may have been an important part of the popular conception of Rome, a conception perhaps deliberately fostered to maintain popular consensus.

On the other hand, there were hereditarian strains too, one example being the lingering prestige and ritual offices of the patricians. The consistent ease with which persons of distinguished lineage won office in the republic lends weight to arguments that the people preferred the rule of the highborn, that is, that there was some sort of popular ideology of inherent nobility. The evidence for this, however, is only circumstantial (Gelzer [1912] 1969). Arnheim (1972:75) says that in the imperial period the hereditary ideal of the succession of emperors was "always dear to the troops." Julius Caesar claimed divine descent, but he was the first to do so (Hopkins 1978). Hopkins (1974) notes the strength of a hereditarian ideology in Rome by A.D. 300 and yet also notes an "undercurrent of an ideology that ability should be rewarded" (1974:111).

Martin (1981) makes the intriguing observation that the Romans considered character to be immutable. His example is Tacitus's showing how the emperor Tiberius slowly unmasked his true personality as the restraints on it fell in the course of his life. This notion seems to fit the tendency in Rome for social mobility not to be accepted in one person's lifetime but to be normal across the generations. Perhaps Romans thought character was formed at birth, hence their great interest in astrology (Hopkins 1978); or early in life, hence their interest in education, generally in a familial setting (Gwynn 1926; Rawson 1975).

I have so far concentrated on stratification in the republic and early empire; what was the situation in the late empire? First we should note that certain traditional forms of mobility disappeared in the late empire. Mobility provided by admission to citizenship status necessarily came to an end in A.D. 212 when all subjects became citizens. About a century later, mobility out of slave and into free status came to an end, after a long period of slow decline, when the condition of servitude in the classical sense fell into disuse. At about the same time, the middle class, either in the sense of the equestrian order or in the sense of a bourgeoisie, also ceased to exist (MacMullen 1964).

Some historians judge the Late Roman Empire to have actually been caste-organized. An example is Ferdinand Lot in his *The End of the Ancient World and the Beginnings of the Middle Ages* ([1937] 1961). During the reigns of Diocletian (r. 284–305), Constantine (r. 306–337), and their immediate successors, and in the face of severe economic difficulties, "the State saw only one way of salvation; to bind every man by force to his occupation, to chain him and his descendants to the same post, and it established a real caste system" (Lot [1937] 1961:84).

Lot ([1937] 1961) describes the development of caste legislation in the late empire as follows. At first, certain military posts were made hereditary.

As a result of a shortage of specie, work in some mines became first compulsory, then hereditary. Similarly, workers in the mints pursued their craft for life, and it was made hereditary; moreover, their children could not marry out of their hereditary craft group. Imperial armorers, smiths, muleteers, grooms, cartwrights, veterinary surgeons, postmen, weavers, and others, were similarly organized. Major aspects of maritime commerce were made hereditary occupations. Even gladiators, mimes, musicians, charioteers, actors, and actresses were "hereditarily chained to their professions." Eventually, large segments of the military could only be entered by persons meeting certain hereditary qualifications, and once in these occupations their status was inherited.

According to Lot, who quotes E. Garsonnet, Constantine issued the laws that bound agricultural workers, *coloni*, to their estates: "The colonus . . . is a perpetual and hereditary but non-voluntary farmer for life, for whom attachment to the soil is both a right and an obligation; he cannot be given public duties which will take him away from it, nor ordained as a cleric, unless it be on the land he cultivates and on condition that he remain on it" (Garsonnet, quoted in Lot [1937] 1961:108; see also Jones 1974). At first it was only long-term *coloni* who were to be affected by these laws, but Valentinian I (r. 364–375) made the law apply to all: "We do not deem that *coloni* have liberty to leave the land to which their condition and birth attach them. If they go away from it . . . let them be brought back, put into chains and punished" (quoted in Lot [1937] 1961:111). Ultimately, even the free man who worked for another for thirty years was reduced to the status of *colonus*, a position inherited by his children. *Coloni* could only marry *coloni*. Lot (1961:112) describes the law as more and more "inflexibly severe."

Lot argued that the colonate outlived the Roman Empire by "a considerable number of centuries." Moreover, those free peasants not regarded as *coloni* but grouped in independent villages were also bound to the soil, becoming "the serfs of their village" ([1937] 1961:113–14). At the same time, agricultural slaves were converted to serfs by legislation that forbade their sale except with the land they worked (Jones 1956, 1974). Further, not only the lower strata of society were converted into castes. The *curiales*, the upper- and middle-class elements of Roman municipalities, were also bound to their position hereditarily. They were forbidden to pass into the provincial senatorial order, and in A.D. 320 the *curiales* even lost the ability to become clerics (Lot [1937] 1961; see also Hammond and Scullard 1970). The result of these changes was "the arrangement of society into 'orders' or closed classes [that] brought almost to a complete standstill the upward movement from class to class which quickens modern socities" (Lot [1937] 1961:124–25). Coincident with these developments, Lot noted that "historical writing declined" ([1937] 1961:152; see also Hollister 1966).

Although it is not clear from Lot's account who could have entered it, the senatorial order remained theoretically open. A recent work (Arnheim 1972) throws light on the extent to which it was open. Arnheim argues that the emperors pursued a policy, culminating in Diocletian's reign, of curbing the power of the Senate as a body and senators as individuals. Constantine reversed this policy and appointed substantial numbers of senators to high office (Arnheim 1972). To be sure, the Senate remained a hollow institution, but the senatorial order was reinvigorated by Constantine's policy, a policy continued by all his successors in the West (Arnheim 1972). Arnheim is less concerned with senators per se—for some achieved that office anew, especially in the eastern empire—than he is with them as a landed nobility in the hereditary sense (1972). Arnheim speculates that since the landed nobility had remained cohesive and powerful, at least in the western empire, Constantine and his successors decided it would be more convenient to woo the nobility than to continue to fight it (1972). Peter Brown (1971:332) calls Constantine the "restorer of the Senate" and says that his policy contributed to the development of a nobility in the western empire.

The nobles flourished under these conditions, so that within 150 years the hereditary nobility had important claims to high governmental and ecclesiastical office in spite of the emperor's theoretical right to appoint whomever he would (Arnheim 1972). The estates of the nobles tended to become economically and socially self-contained. They also tended to be fortified, the larger ones resembling towns. Owners spent more and more time on their estates. The master's power over his *coloni* was great, and by 365 the distinction between *colonus* and slave had largely dissolved (Arnheim 1972).

Arnheim shows that there was mobility to high places: both Diocletian and Valentinian (r. 364–375), for example, were of humble origin. But, as noted earlier, Arnheim also saw a pervasive ideology of descent in the late empire. Pride of lineage was strong, and the lower orders respected the nobles in the fourth century (Arnheim 1972). Nobles continued to be held in esteem under the Germanic invaders of the western empire (Arnheim 1972; see also Jones 1964:II). Like Lot, Arnheim sees an essential continuity between the conditions of the late empire and medieval Europe: The

German invasions of Rome "strengthened the underlying amalgam of economic, social, and political forces in society, centrifugal in tendency and aristocratic in tone, which had been prominent since the reign of Constantine and which were to continue to dominate Western Europe for close on a thousand years" (1972:171). It should be observed that Arnheim stresses the lesser role of nobility in the eastern empire, and hence the greater scope for social mobility there.

Among the recent historians who still talk of caste in late Roman history is MacMullen (1974). He notes a five-century trend of increasing concentration of landholding in the Empire and its effect on social mobility: "Class hardened almost to the point of caste, at least in the late Empire" (1974:126).

But some historians have challenged the view that the social structure of late antiquity was castelike. Examining the writings of Ausonius, a professor at Bordeaux in the middle of the fourth century, Hopkins (1961), for example, provides convincing evidence that the professors or teachers of Bordeaux were not in fact a hereditarily defined group. In a later paper Hopkins (1974; see also Jones 1964:II) argues that social mobility may actually have reached its peak in Rome in the fourth century, the many laws prohibiting social mobility actually being evidence that it was perceived as a persistent problem. This is a radical reassessment of what the caste legislation was all about and what its effects may have been. Unfortunately, as Hopkins (1974) concedes, quantitative data on mobility are scanty, and the evidence on entry into the Senate by provincials that Hopkins provides indicates that the highest rate was in the second century. What Hopkins does show is a fairly clear picture of a hereditarian ideology. After saying that admission of provincials was a slow process of the climb of families over generations, he adds that "this gradual mobility existed unsupported by any major ideology of advancement." "There are occasional statements that praise ability rather than birth, but the dominant ideology praised aristocratic birth, blood and nature above all else" (Hopkins 1974:117). Thus, although Hopkins has shown that late imperial Roman society was not wholly closed, his argument that social mobility may have peaked in the fourth century A.D. is not demonstrated. What he says about the ideology of social mobility suggests that it was more hereditarian in the fourth century than it had been in the days of Cicero, Sallust, and Tacitus.

Alföldi (1952) says that in the time of Valentinian I (321?–375) new appointees to senatorial rank, largely from the military, outnumbered those who acquired the status by birth. This suggests much mobility, but the relative proportions at Rome, as opposed to Constantinople, are not stated, and this may be crucial.

The resolution of these disparate views of social stratification in the late empire lies at least in part in the differing conditions of eastern and western empires. Consider Peter Brown's *The World of Late Antiquity, AD 150–750* (1971). Brown repeatedly stresses the social mobility and creativity of the late empire, speaking of "exceptionally open" stratification and a galaxy of self-made men who either became emperors or who produced a vigorous Latin literature that was largely associated with the Church (1971:36, 38). But Brown just as often notes that these developments are more associated with the *eastern* empire; the western empire was closing down. "By the fifth century," he notes, "the wealth of the West had snowballed into the hands of a few great families. . . . In the East [there was] . . . a more balanced, even a more egalitarian society" and that "the peasants of [Roman] Asia Minor, Syria and Egypt were very different from the dragooned and excluded serfs of the western provinces" (Brown 1971:43, 44). Trade was more vibrant in the East, and Constantinople—the "goal of gifted provincials"—was more centralized yet a "whirlpool of change" (P. Brown 1971:28, 141). Brown is not alone in this view; MacMullen contends that in the imperial period "the preponderance of the empire's wealth in the Roman homeland . . . concentrated into the hands of a narrowing nobility," and social mobility "becomes far more the rule than the exception as one moves eastward" in the empire (1974:91, 101).

The Church, "professedly egalitarian," was, Brown says, "the most flexible and open group," "made most headway in just those areas where Roman society was most fluid," and thus flourished more in the East (1971:65, 66, 88). In the fifth-century West, by contrast, "a double oligarchy of senators and clergymen—now closely interrelated—maintained the splendid isolation of the city [of Rome]" (P. Brown 1971:131). By the sixth century, the western Church was "a closed elite" whose "senator-bishops towered above an increasingly passive and uncultivated laity" (P. Brown 1971:148). The monastic order in the West was also "captured by a . . . narrow . . . section of the aristocracy" (P. Brown 1971:109).

Finally, there is reason to think that from the time Constantinople was made the co-capital (A.D. 330) there was a legally more open society there than in Rome. For example, in the Theodosian Code, which was issued in 438 but which covers Roman legislation back to A.D. 312, it is readily apparent that much of the caste legislation was specifically designated to apply to the guilds of the city of Rome (Pharr 1952). Although the legislation was published in the names of both eastern and western co-rulers, the laws did not necessarily apply to all parts of the empire. By the end of the fourth century, urban craftsmen were tied to their trades in the West, but they were never, or only rarely, so tied in the East (Charanis 1944–45; Jones 1964; Ostrogorsky 1957).

Concomitants

In chapter 2, I quoted Dumézil (1970) on the contrast between India and Rome, crediting the Romans for thinking historically, practically, empirically, politically, and juridically. Cicero illustrates one of the high points, marking an advance even on Greek political science (McKeon 1950:53). McKeon notes that in his *Republic* Cicero

employs three great strands of political theory which have continued to be influential: . . . (1) a dynamic evolutionary conception of the state; (2) a treatment of political doctrines and actions in terms of conflicts of interests of groups and individuals and in terms of their duties; and (3) an analysis of the application and enforcement of law conceived as the source of virtue and happiness. (1950:54)

Cicero also contributed to the functional analysis of political myths (McKeon 1950). In his *De Divinatione* he defends state augury for its contribution to religion and hence to the stability of the state, even though he exposes state augury as a sham (1950:426–27). This, too, is functional analysis. The working of the republic as a system emerged with considerable clarity in Cicero's voluminous writings (the rediscovery of which was to be of great import in the Renaissance (Rawson 1975).

Cicero was not alone in his basically secular, humanistic mode of thinking. Dumézil points out that "the Romans very early isolated the idea of *persona*, and it is on this idea, on the autonomy, the stability, and the dignity of persons, that they constructed their ideal of human relations—*ius*—with the gods intervening only as witnesses and guarantors. India on the other hand persuaded itself more and more that individuals are only deceptive appearances." (1970:117). The idea of the *persona* is a key element in modern comparative social science (Krader 1968).

The surest signs of the individualism that Dumézil sees in Rome, as compared to India, are to be found in Roman biography, autobiography, and realistic portraiture. Biography and autobiography were discussed earlier. Roman portraiture probably had its roots in the wax death masks of high-ranking Romans. Originally they were not realistic, but in the second century B.C., and under the influence of Greek patterns, they became so (Breckenridge 1968). Eventually they became extremely realistic, "as far removed as possible from the generalized and the typical" (Breckenridge 1968:143).

As in Greece, Breckenridge (1968) sees in Rome, too, a connection between the individualism fostered by materialistic philosophies and re-alistic art—which in Rome, and only slightly less so in Greece, became the predominant form of sculpture, produced for common citizens as well as heroes. In the second century B.C., Epicureanism, which Breckenridge (1968:182) describes as "the farthest extreme of Greek Humanism," was brought to Rome, where Lucretius became "its most eloquent spokesman." Epicurus's doctrines were "uncompromisingly individualistic" (Brecken-ridge 1968:181). Stoicism was also strongly individualistic, and like Epi-cureanism it held that "all we can know is to be found in the world of the senses" (Breckenridge 1968:184). After discussing Lucretius's materialistic views—he aimed "to rid the world of superstition" (Shotwell 1923:220)— Breckenridge (1968:185) says that "a naturalistic art would seem almost an inevitable concomitant." Biography developed along with portraiture, so that "toward the end of Cicero's life," Rawson observes, when "portrait sculpture in Rome reached a new level of vividness and psychological penetration, we know the faces as well as the minds of some of the prom-inent men of the time" (1975:xiii).

Cicero also illustrates a conception of mankind that fits the picture of Rome as an open society with a sound sense of history. In his survey of Greek philosophy he noted that all schools agreed on the common nature of mankind (McKeon 1950), a view with which he seemed to agree, having "written . . . that all nations are only one and the same family" (quoted in Boissier n.d.:55). Tacitus explicitly rejected the idea that senators (or equestrians) differed by nature from other men (Garnsey 1970). Stoicism, espoused by a number of leading Romans, held that human nature is essentially the same everywhere. We might also note the connection be-tween Stoic ideas and the development of the idea of natural law in Rome's *ius gentium*, the law of nations, which rests upon notions of right and wrong common to the human mind.

The Stoics were also greatly concerned with divination (McKeon 1950). While Cicero attempted to debunk divination, the attention he gave it illustrates its importance in Rome. Hopkins concludes that "among the Roman elite astrology was a major intellectual pursuit, a preoccupation which, like economics nowadays, coloured serious political behaviour" (1978:233–34). "The credit of omens and astrology grew steadily" in the revolutionary period, and when in the early empire, astrologers were expelled from Rome, it was so the rulers might "monopolize the control of prophecy" (Syme [1939] 1979:256; McKeon 1950). Interpreting auguries was a topic of antiquarian studies that flourished in the late republic (Shotwell 1923:236). Divination was popular with the common man too; he consulted astrologers in hope of finding an inheritance in his future, much as nowadays he would pin his hopes on a lottery ticket (MacMullen 1974).

On the legitimate side of science, Roman achievements were less spectacular than those of the Greeks but were substantial nonetheless (Edelstein 1963). One of the high points is surely Lucretius's *The Nature of the Universe*, written in about 55 B.C. It presents a secular view of the universe, its origins, and evolution. Lucretius's discussion in book 5 of the evolution of human society and culture not only expresses an important philosophy of history but was also remarkably prescient (Shotwell 1923).

Rawson (1975) says that the Greeks and Romans were very concerned with education, but at present I find it difficult to show that the Romans were peculiar in this regard. In other respects, however, the Romans of the late republican through the early imperial periods show quite unmistakably the full syndrome of concomitants of the open society.

In the late empire some of the concomitants shifted, especially in the West. Thus while the Platonic tradition in the East maintained the interest in politics, in the West it went "otherworldly and mystical" (P. Brown 1971:139), this in spite of the fact that Christianity took root quicker in the East. Peter Brown (1971) thinks that the bishop-scholars in the West by the sixth century had gotten "too busy" to maintain classical civilization, though they were not too busy, he notes, to engage in considerable forgery or show more interest in relics than in men.

Portraiture, however, seems to have shifted to iconography more or less at the same time in both East and West: "from Constantine onwards, there is no longer anything which has any worth: there are only lifeless images in the Oriental frontal style" (Lot 1961:138; see also P. Brown 1971; Hoxie 1966; Ullmann 1966b). Berenson, who traces the decline of realistic portraiture during the lifetime of Constantine, wonders if the artists had not suddenly deserted Rome, "leaving mere artisans" to do their work (1954:34).

Summary

To summarize, we may note two comparisons. First, in comparing the Romans with the Greeks, Roman historiography, excellent though it was, is sometimes considered to have been inferior to Greek historiography (Barnes 1937; Shotwell 1923; Thompson 1942:I). Correlatively, there is a somewhat lesser commitment to openness in Roman society in many periods. More important, however, and more convincing, are comparisons within the Roman tradition. As I understand the original distinction between patricians and plebs, early republican Rome was closed. By the time the plebs achieved the last of their political goals, in 287 B.C., Roman society was open. Before the third century was over, Rome's successes in the Punic Wars were to provide vast scope for upward mobility, and Fabius Pictor began the Roman historiographic tradition shortly thereafter. Even more striking is the relationship between the flowering of Roman historiography—between the times of Sallust and Tacitus—and the dramatic increase in social mobility during the period of republican collapse and the emergence of the empire. Thompson (1942:I) thought this flowering was anomalous, but as noted above, at least two historians (McDonald 1954; Syme [1939] 1979) saw a connection. Syme puts it most explicitly in his discussion of the decade that saw the most explosive mobility at the top: "In Rome of the triumvirs men became intensely conscious of history" ([1939] 1979:250). Assessments differ on social mobility in late imperial Rome, but there is substantial agreement that the East and the Church were relatively more open and that the quality of their historiography was superior too. Nearly all the concomitants conform to expectations in the late republican and early imperial periods, but some anomalies appear in the late empire.

THE ANCIENT NEAR EAST,
GREECE, AND ROME: DISCUSSION

While the Greek and Roman cases presented above provide rather strong evidence to support my arguments, the earlier Near Eastern cases are more equivocal. Factors in addition to social stratification seem to have been significantly at play. Some of these factors, especially primitiveness and scale, should be noted. It would be wrong to equate the open society with civilization and the closed with primitiveness, but many of the features of the open society can only really flourish under civilized conditions. Primitiveness may account for some of the findings in this chapter. Thus, whereas Assyria, Babylonia, and ancient Israel came closer to manifesting the open society syndrome than did late Egypt, they did not manifest it as much as did classical Greece and classical Rome. Presumably it took time to develop the social sciences, for example. The Greeks and Romans reached that level, but the Mesopotamians and Hebrews did not. The "wisdom literature" of the Mesopotamians suggests, however faintly, that they had an interest in the secular, objective analysis of social affairs, but such humble beginnings may have been no less apparent among the Egyptians.

Conditions in ancient Israel may also partly reflect primitiveness, but three other factors are relevant too. One is scale: compared to Babylonia and Assyria, ancient Israel was a small-scale society. This could hinder some developments, but there is no strong reason to think it was decisive—classical Greeks lived in relatively small societies too. Second, Israel was an independent kingdom for only a brief period, its people usually existing as minorities in other political entities. This is a difficult factor to assess. Third is the equivocal nature of stratification in Israel. The society was basically open, but for a time it had a hereditary priesthood, and its doctrine of the "chosen people" is partly hereditarian. For reasons to be discussed in the last chapter, I do not think a racial or semiracial doctrine that separates the members of a society from the rest of humanity is a decisive breach of the concept of human nature as uniform, which appears to be a correlate of openness. But my reasons for thinking this apply with more force to large-scale societies, such as China, than to small-scale ones embedded in larger civilizations, such as was the case with ancient Israel. For whatever reason, ancient Israel, and perhaps Egypt before 1100 B.C., least conform to expectations. But all cases summarized in this chapter show contrasts in the appropriate direction, and almost all show more of the expected syndromes than not.

CHAPTER 5

The Medieval World

This chapter examines the relationship between social stratification, historiography, and other concomitants among four approximately coeval civilizations in Europe and the Near East. Two, medieval Europe and Byzantium, developed from common seed in the Roman Empire; the other two, Sassanid Persia and the classical Islamic world, stood approximately as predecessor and successor in the same region.

MEDIEVAL EUROPE

Historiography

The Renaissance view of the Middle Ages as a period of abysmal decline, a Dark Age, has long been challenged. Nonetheless, there are those who see in the period, particularly in earlier centuries, a general decline in historiographic quality; others see a leveling off, a plateau, in the otherwise progressive trend of historiographic development in the West. No one says the Middle Ages in Europe were historiographically superior to earlier and later traditions. For example, Thompson (1942:I), himself a medievalist, in his several chapters on medieval historiography makes no overall judgment. Yet when he turns to Byzantine historians, he states flatly that "in the early centuries of the Middle Ages [they] were better observers and recorders of events than those of the West" (1942:I, 295). Vryonis (1968:1), who compares medieval historiography in the West, Byzantium, and the Islamic world, says that historiography in the West deteriorated after the second century A.D. and "remained inferior until the Renaissance." Shotwell (1923:286) considered the revolution in thought that marked the beginning of the medieval period to be a "calamity for historiography." Hollister (1966:179) describes the fifth to the ninth centuries in the West as a "twilight" in which the historical record is "unquestionably dim." Russell (1954a:49) called the historiographic tradition of the twelfth century "jejune," even though some individuals rose above it. Sanford (1944) argues that medieval standards did not seriously decline from the high standards of antiquity but did not improve, either. In his study of the Renaissance sense of history, Burke (1969:1) says that the sense of history "was lacking in the Middle Ages."

Setting forth the differences between Renaissance and medieval historiography, Cochrane (1981:xv) says that the scope of medieval histories tended to be limited only by creation and the Last Judgment, and that medieval historians treated individuals as "passive spectators rather than active agents," considered secular affairs important only as they reflected divine affairs, and could see connections between events only if explicable in the words of prophets. Cochrane avoids judging these characteristics, and perhaps they were not necessarily detrimental, but in practice they generally were. Spiegel (1983:43–44) gives a concise list of the "errors" of which medieval historiography stands accused, and does not attempt "entirely to dispel" them.

Among the characteristics of medieval historiography are the following: an undue concern with myth, forgery, and fabulous genealogy; an uncertain grasp of the distinction between real and ideal, combined with some problems in reasoning or in understanding causation; almost exclusively religious authorship; a strong tendency for the individual to be effaced, both as subject and author; a tendency to ignore or distort the history of the pre-Christian era; and an absence of the notion of anachronism. These and a few less important characteristics are worth discussing before we examine specific historians.

It is important to realize that men of the medieval period did not lose all interest in the past. But the sources available to them, as Marc Bloch pointed out, were "more copious than exact, . . . forgery and myth-making . . . were exceptionally flourishing, . . . [and] people came to reconstruct [the past] as they considered it ought to have been" (1961:I, 90–92).

Genealogical matters were particularly prone to historical falsification or fabrication. Without attaching any sociological significance to it, Sanford (1944:40), for example, notes that in the Middle Ages "Frankish and Flemish nobles . . . traced their descent from Priam, Adam, or both." Bloch (1961:II, 284) adds, "The most striking feature of the history of the dominant families in the first feudal age is the shortness of their pedigrees—at least if we agree to reject . . . the fables invented by the Middle Ages themselves." Those fables should not be rejected, however, because they do form part of the medieval view of the past (Spiegel 1983) and because they provide crucial evidence as to why European society in the Middle Ages was not historically minded. If it was the dominant families who promulgated fabulous accounts of their past, surely it is no mystery that the historian had little incentive to correct those accounts.

Later I will try to show that the forgery and mythmaking were closely linked to the structure of society in the Middle Ages. This is not a novel idea. In medieval historiography, Heinrich von Sybel observed,

No distinction was made between ideal and real. . . . Heroic poems were considered a true and lofty form of history and history was everywhere displaced by epics, legends or poetical fiction of some kind. . . . Almost no one felt any scruples in giving to existing conditions the sanction of venerable age by means of fabricated history or forged documents. The question whether the ascribed derivation was true interested no one; it was enough if the result harmonized with existing rights, dominating interests and prevalent beliefs. (Quoted in Barnes 1937:56)

For the moment it will suffice to mention perhaps the most famous medieval forgery, the Donation of Constantine. This document was fundamental to the positions of both pope and emperor in medieval Europe, and also to the status of the clergy. The exposure of the document as a forgery during the Renaissance was one of the key exercises in critical history that marked the shift from medieval to Renaissance historiography. By showing that the meanings of words and the character of institutions changed with time, the Renaissance introduced the idea of historicism. Prior to the development of this revolutionary idea, European historians tended to see the past largely in their own unreflective terms. Thus "a serious deficiency of much of medieval historical writing was the absence of historical sense; . . . anachronisms abounded" (Russell 1954a:44).

Though sponsored by reigning families as well as monastic houses (Russell 1954a), nearly all medieval literature was written by churchmen and strongly projects theological concerns. Probably linked to theological concerns was the poor sense of time (Thompson 1942:I), but more clearly connected to theology was the considerable development of hagiography—biographies of the saints. Hagiography, as will be described in a later section, became one of the important mechanisms in the legitimation of Europe's medieval nobility.

Whether in hagiography or in other forms of medieval historical writing, one of the peculiar features of the period's historiography is its striking impersonality:

It is assuredly not without coincidence that we know so very little of the personal traits of most of the men who directed the path of medieval society. Hardly any personal correspondence has survived; no personal anecdotes are there; none of the stories which grow round great men exist; there are few biographical data; above all there is hardly any worthwhile contemporary biography or pictorial representation of the great kings, popes, or emperors. (Ullmann 1966a:43–44; see also Ullmann 1966b)

What mattered was not the man but the office he occupied. Closely related to this concern for office or status, and not individuals, was an extraordinary elaboration of ritual and etiquette (Huizinga [1924] 1950).

In spite of the medieval concern for the past, there were no professional historians (Russell 1954a, 1954b), and history per se was not a part of the period's university curriculum, except insofar as it was covered under the heading of grammar (Holmes 1975; Lacroix 1954a; Sanford 1944). This was unfortunate, because medieval scholars were accustomed to "taking a limited subject matter and by scholastic processes . . . extracting all that could be drawn from the evidence," which "is precisely what historians have to do" (Russell 1954b:55). One of the marks of the end of the Middle Ages is the Renaissance's introduction of history into the educational curriculum.

While his reference is to the "waning of the Middle Ages," and therefore includes some characteristics I judge to be more connected with the early Renaissance than with the central features of medievalism, Huizinga (1950) isolates many of the features of medieval historiography. As did Ullmann, Huizinga found rulers and officials depicted in idealized stereotypes. Moreover, as a means of defending medieval ideas of hierarchy, the individual was deliberately ignored; even eye-witness accounts reflected the "hieratic" view of the time (1950:7). Huizinga also found in medieval historiography a strong tendency to overgeneralization, weak reasoning, and a surprising inexactness (1950:214, 216). Lacroix (1954b:20) also notes the "disconcerting" weakness of medieval historians in the "interpretation of facts," while Russell (1954b) adds that the rules of logic were not applied to history.

Huizinga was especially impressed by the stark contrast between the

Middle Ages' chivalric ideals and the realities of the period. The attempt of chroniclers to impose chivalric notions on history and biography was at the root of the distortions so characteristic of the age's literature. And the fact that when honestly recording real people's real behavior they exposed such a gap between ideal and real—without noting the startling incongruity—was the basis for Huizinga's doubts about the chroniclers' reasoning ability. "As a principle of historiography," he said, the chivalric political theory of the time was "very inferior" (1950:57).

Although much of Latin literature was known throughout the Middle Ages, some texts did effectively disappear; most others were used only insofar as they could be interpreted to fit prevailing ideological concerns. Texts that could not be so interpreted were "consigned to oblivion" (Ullmann 1966a:142; see also Shotwell 1923). The writings of Cicero provide an illuminating example. In the Middle Ages the promotion of a few excerpts from his writings and the suppression of the great bulk of them allowed him to be presented "as if he had been himself a monastic scholar— a recluse who seemed to teach contempt of marriage and women, and of all the passions and burdens of life in this world" (Baron [1938] 1968a:294). This was not a caricature, it was the opposite of the man's views. Greek literature, except where known from Latin translations or epitomes, was even more effectively lost to western Europe.

In some respects the difference between medieval historiography and that of ancient and modern Europe is one of degree. Some features of medieval histories are good, some biography was written, some historians of the period do stand out. Perhaps the most frequently cited exceptions are Gregory of Tours, Bede, Einhard, and Otto of Freising. An examination of these historians will set forth the high points of medieval historiography.

Gregory of Tours (539–594) wrote a history of the Franks down to his own time. Gregory consulted the relevant sources for earlier periods, but he shows his greatest strength in narrating events that he witnessed or was involved with (Dalton 1927). Insofar as he describes the actions of peoples from all walks of life, he provides a vivid picture of his times, but for all the vividness of events and action, he provides almost no physical descriptions, either of people, things, or places (Dalton 1927). Similarly, Gregory provides very little information, except unintentionally, about his private life, his family, his kin, or the bishopric he headed (Dalton 1927). Gregory never intentionally falsifies, but he often quotes inaccurately, and he is highly biased toward kings (as opposed to "landed aristocracy") and toward religious orthodoxy; he will believe anything about saints, and he often sidetracks issues of cause and effect in order to shift more credit for events to the saints (Dalton 1927). The structure of Gregory's *History* is irregular, the narrative often broken; it lacks logical arrangement and is weak in causal analysis (Dalton 1927). Nonetheless, O.M. Dalton concluded that "the *History of the Franks* shines with a lonely brilliance in exceptionally dark skies. There is nothing like it [at the time] or second to it" (1927:31).

For all its importance in reconstructing the history of the Merovingian period, Gregory's *History* is judged a "true history" only by comparison with the dry recitals of medieval chronicles or annals (Dalton 1927:25). It is not described as a great history, and it is not compared with the histories of the Greeks and Romans or the Renaissance historians. Dalton (1927), who translated and provided a lengthy introduction to Gregory's *History*, compares it only with Bede's *History*, saying that Gregory's Latin was poorer, but his account was livelier and more full of human interest than Bede's.

The Venerable Bede (673–735) completed his *Ecclesiastical History of the English People* in 731. Bede, too, produced more than a bare chronicle, more than popular hagiography: "He set himself to examine all available records, to secure verbal or written accounts from reliable living authorities, to record local traditions and stories, to interpret significant events, and, in short, to compile as complete and continuous a history of the English Church and people as lay within his power" (Sherley-Price [1955] 1977:25). He was remarkably successful in this large and pioneering project. It contains many lively character sketches, is relatively free of inaccuracies, and remains an indispensable sourcework (Colgrave 1969; Sherley-Price [1955] 1977; Thompson 1942:I). So exceptional was Bede that Barnes (1922:219) considered his work "a fine product of the lingering classical culture in the north of Europe" rather than a product of the Middle Ages, and Lacroix (1954b:22) calls him "one of the greatest historians of all times." Campbell (1966:167), calls him "almost a modern historian."

Sound as Bede's work may have been, its flaws were characteristic of the age. The nearer Bede came to his own time, the less he wrote, and he by no means entirely escaped from the tradition of hagiography, the principles of which "were largely contrary to those of scholarship" (Campbell 1966:182). Bede's partiality to miracles in the lives of the saints is only slightly less of an embarrassment than Gregory's (Colgrave 1969; Sherley-Price [1955] 1977). Bede was unduly circumspect in treating the authorities— sacred or secular—of his time (Campbell 1966). He was truly an exceptional historian, but the baseline from which he is compared is not a high one.

Bede was not alone, however, in producing relatively good history for the time; the north of England showed an unusual interest in both history and biography in the eighth century (Stenton 1971; Thompson 1942:I).

Einhard (c. 770–840) served for decades in the court of Charlemagne. From this ideal vantage point he wrote the first and the best biography of a lay figure in the Middle Ages (Painter 1960; Thorpe 1969; Zeydel 1972). It is very brief (about ten thousand words in English translation), it was written without any apparent author's perspective (Einhard never mentions his own name), it is occasionally careless with facts, and it omits or glosses over material that would detract from Charlemagne's image, but on the whole it is reliable and has been very influential (Painter 1960; Thompson 1942:I; Thorpe 1969; Zeydel 1972). Opinions vary considerably on Einhard's stature as a historian (see especially Zeydel 1972). But one thing seems certain: no one claims that Einhard was a better historian or biographer than his counterparts in the classical world or the Renaissance. He modeled his biography on those of Suetonius, yet no one unambiguously says that he was the equal of Suetonius. It follows that if Einhard is the best biographer of the Middle Ages, medieval biography was either inferior to or only equal to that of classical Greece and Rome. The indications are that it was inferior.

Einhard was not an exception but was instead part of the Carolingian Renaissance, which persisted well into the ninth century in spite of the troubled conditions that followed the death of Charlemagne in 814. Next to Einhard, Nithard (d. 844) was perhaps the best historian, but there were others too. The quantity of historical materials increased, and much of the Latin literature that has survived was copied at this time (Lacroix 1954b; Thompson 1942:I).

With Otto of Freising (c. 1113–1158) we jump a few centuries ahead into the early stirrings of the Renaissance, the "renaissance of the twelfth century" (Haskins [1927] 1966). By wide consensus, Otto was "a careful and critical historian" (Mierow 1928:3). His major work was *The Two Cities: A Chronicle of Universal History to the Year 1146*. He began, but did not live to complete, another important work, *The Deeds of Frederick Barbarossa*. Highborn, a bishop and a territorial lord, Otto was in a good position to observe the events of his time (Haskins [1927] 1966). His *Chronicle* attempted to present the entire history of the world in a narrative style and comprehended as the eternal conflict between good and evil (Mierow 1928). Otto had, as Mierow observed, "absolute faith in an ever-active divine will, busying itself with the course of human events"; "everything is judged and explained according to its place in the divine plan" (1928:52, 62). Otto was not, however, a miracle mongerer. Although he did not subject Christian legends to criticism, he generally refused to believe the improbable or impossible (Mierow 1928).

Otto usually showed a genuinely critical attitude, he could see the effects of political partisanship in producing conflicting accounts, and he attempted to record impartially rather than pass judgment (Mierow 1928; Thompson 1942:I). Rudimentary elements of social science appear in his writings: attempts to account for human development from primitiveness to civilization in the *Chronicle* (Mierow 1928), and for the rise of Lombardy's wealthy and powerful city-states in the *Deeds* (Haskins [1927] 1966; Thompson 1942:I). Otto was "ahead of his time in regarding history as a teacher of men" (Mierow 1928:22).

In addition to his lack of scruples about introducing "transcendental materials" into his history (Mierow 1928:76), Otto showed further characteristics of his age. Otto rarely mentions himself, and he did not regard "the individual as a principal factor in historical development" (Mierow 1928:61), though he did give more attention to individuals than was common in the Middle Ages (Ullmann 1966a). He was not very original (Mierow 1928). According to Haskins ([1927] 1966:243), "one enthusiastic writer" ranked Otto with Tacitus and Thucydides, but Haskins does not concur.

By Otto's time, broad improvements in the quality of medieval historiography had been underway for some time. In order to put this improvement into perspective, let us review the major outlines of the fall and rise of historiography before Otto's time. As we saw in the last chapter's discussion of the late western empire, a decline in historiography began before the Middle Ages. The quality and quantity of historical writing then dropped to a low point in the seventh century (Thompson 1942:I), but signs of improving historiography were apparent in various parts of Europe well before the period normally indicated by the term Renaissance. In the Saxon dynasty in Germany (919–1024), which was one of the first to achieve some stability after a period of turmoil, historiography began to revive (Thompson 1942:I). In the succeeding Salian dynasty (1024–1125), "for the first time since antiquity history began to be written with strength, clarity, and even literary artistry" (Thompson 1942:I, 185). Wipo's *Life of Conrad II* is the outstanding example. It even included an analysis of the social classes of Lombardy. The period's historical writing in general was marked by increasing and more careful use of archival sources and official

documents, more interpretation and explanation, more analysis of individual action, an increasing sense of the connections between events,
and a growing awareness of the nature of historical change (Thompson
1942:I).

Roughly coincident with these developments in Germany, historiography also showed strong development in Norman France and Angevin
England (Haskins 1915, [1927] 1966). The Norman conquest gave a considerable impulse to historical writing, and Thompson concluded that the
standards set in England between 1066 and 1215 were "unmatched anywhere
else in medieval history, except possibly in Germany in the same centuries"
(1942:I, 247). The outstanding historians of the time and place were Or-
dericus Vitalis (d. 1142), William of Malmesbury (d. 1142), and William of
Newburgh (d. 1198). In the works of the latter two we find, among other
signs of historiographic quality, the "fundamental principles of modern
historical criticism, even the distinction between external and internal criticism" (Thompson 1942:I, 251). The Angevin rulers were exceptional in
promoting historical writing. Under Henry II (r. 1154–1189) historians
received quasi-official support (Thompson 1942:I, 257). Legal history was
recorded in England in far greater detail and quantity than on the Continent
(Ullmann 1966a).

In Italy historiography was slower to improve, but by the eleventh
century the north Italian communes had begun to produce historians, who
were usually laymen connected with the cities' archives. Genoa was the
first to officially recognize civic history (Russell 1954a, 1954b; Thompson
1942:I).

Thus in the overall sweep of medieval history, Otto of Freising may
have been exceptional, and he may have been an outstanding historian for
his century, but clearly historiography was on the mend, and Otto was
much less an exception than were Gregory or Bede. By the twelfth century,
biography and autobiography had become more sensitive and common,
and their subjects were more likely to be secular. History was beginning
to have a popular audience, the vernacular was coming into use, the universal chronicle was going out of fashion, and hagiography was in decline.
Methodological awareness had developed too: Leo Marsicanus of Ostia
(c. 1046–1117) had described his method, and Hugo of St. Victor (d. 1143),
of whom Otto had been a student, had written a book on *The Three Most
Important Factors in Events*, that is, time, place, and circumstance. Historical
writings in general had become more common. In the eleventh century

there was a general explosion of intellectual development (Murray 1978; Russell 1954a; Thompson 1942:I). From Otto's time it was but a short leap to the more definitive dissolution of medieval historiography in Renaissance Italy.

Social Stratification

During much of the Middle Ages, Europe was highly decentralized, and travel between its regions was relatively difficult. Conditions found in one time and place may not have been found elsewhere at the same time, or in the same place at a different time. No doubt this accounts for the discrepancies in the views on medieval stratification, which now need to be reviewed. In the course of this review I will attempt to answer the following interrelated questions: If caste was found in medieval Europe, was it a continuation of conditions in late antiquity, or did it develop later? When was caste most typical of medieval Europe, or when was social mobility least common? When did social mobility pick up and caste decline? What were the ideological stances of medieval Europeans on the matters of nobility and social mobility? Were there important regional differences in all these matters?

Judgments of when medieval Europe became, or was most, castelike cover a wide spectrum. At one extreme, Bloch (1961:II) argued that on the continent the period from about 1250 to 1400 saw the greatest rigidity of social stratification. A de facto nobility had developed earlier, but only in this period did nobility acquire legal definition in feudal Europe (England excepted). On the other hand, Bloch notes that violent opposition to the nobility had already developed in the twelfth century, at least in France. It is possible, therefore, that the evidence on which Bloch's argument rests resulted from belated reactions to forces working against nobility. For considerable evidence of a much earlier development of medieval Europe's nobility is presented in two collections of major essays on the topic (Cheyette 1968; Reuter 1978).

While some of the contributors to these volumes largely agree with Bloch, the predominant view in the relevant chapters is that hereditary stratification emerged much earlier as an amalgam of late Roman and barbarian institutions but that it was never rigidly hereditary and showed considerable regional variation. Reuter (1978:28) attempts a summary of the complex issues: "If one wished to sketch a picture of the nobility which would remain valid for the whole of the middle ages, one would have to confine it to a few characteristics: in particular the importance of blood." Let us look at some of the evidence for this.

There is good evidence that the old Germanic chiefs enjoyed a certain religious charisma (*Heil*), but the evidence, while suggestive, is not clear that Germanic leadership was hereditary (Reuter 1978; cf. Schlesinger 1968). Be that as it may, a number of authorities stress the essential similarity of Germanic and Gallo-Roman lordship, so that the transition from late Roman to Merovingian lordship would have entailed no essential change (Irsigler 1978).

Genicot 1968 argues that in Merovingian, Carolingian (eighth to tenth centuries), and post-Carolingian times, the term *noble* definitely referred to a class or caste, not to personal qualities. He admits the difficulty of tracing the origins of medieval nobility but suggests that they lie in the Germanic kings (*principes*), in the right-hand men of the barbarian kings, and in the descendants of the Gallo-Roman senators, with considerable regional variation. Whatever its origin, the nobility became a legal and hereditary class (Genicot 1968).

Duby 1968 traces similar developments in the region of the Macconais. Whereas theoretically knighthood could be gained, and in fact was at times lost, it "contained the seed of inheritance" from the beginning (Duby 1968:151). Thus knighthood was rapidly confined to a closed, hereditary class. By 1050–1075 it was strictly hereditary, the title being taken by all male heirs of a knight who were not clergy.

In Werner's view (1978:141), landed lordship, "the decisive factor in the economy of the early and high middle ages," developed in late antiquity and was fully established in Gaul when the Franks took over. But the Gallo-Roman landlords, of senatorial rank, were not displaced by the Franks. The Roman and German elements quickly and easily blended into a state neither German nor Roman but Frankish. Werner did not think that the Gallo-Roman nobility had "racial" origins, but he was struck by

how strong the dynastic sense of this new late Roman hereditary nobility was. Bishops of senatorial rank concerned themselves with the survival of their families. . . . Add to this the nepotism which enabled families to hold on to episcopal office . . . and we can see the enormous gulf between the *potentes* . . . and the remaining mass of the population. All this must mean that the culture, the life style, the political and economic position of the class which dominated the medieval centuries were all translated with no break in continuity from the world of late antiquity. (Werner 1978:145–46)

For Werner, the Germans only intensified and modified the basic pattern of the late empire, and within a century of the beginning of the Frankish kingdom, "the leading families of Roman and German origin in Gaul, the *optimates* of the court and the *potentes* of the provinces had intermingled to become a single class" (1978:146).

Irsigler 1978 traces a Frankish ruling class back to before the middle of the fifth century. Among its characteristic qualities was "membership by birth of a family of high reputation" (1978:123). Irsigler found that the process of assimilation of the Roman senatorial nobility began before the middle of the sixth century but was not entirely complete in the seventh.

Whether or not Germanic and Roman nobility had originally been hereditary, as time went on they were presumed to have been; hereditary claims were traced to them. Thus Tellenbach (1978:207), treating the Carolingian period, mentions that "the Germanic belief in royal charisma and the Christian and theocratic conception of kingship as an office made the king a member of a supernatural order." Moreover, "the nobility also possessed their own distinct powers. According to Germanic thinking not only the royal but also other kin groups had a heritable charisma." For Tellenbach (1978:204), "nobility was acquired by birth, certainly." Not only did the nobility share the charisma of royalty, but according to Bosl (1968) the rule of the nobility was more fundamental than kingship in tenth- through twelfth-century Germany. Finally, Hauck (1978) shows that in the literature of the eleventh and twelfth centuries, noble families traced their origins to pre-Christian sources, in one case probably back to Woden.

Although Reuter (1978) reports that there is considerable biological continuity demonstrable between the nobilities of the eighth and ninth centuries and those of the eleventh and twelfth, most of the contributors to his volume stress the enormous difficulties presented by genealogical research in the medieval period. Werner 1978, for example, notes the frequency of missing genealogical links, which can only be filled in by guessing. "From the viewpoint of the critical historian, this is to tremble on the brink, not just of error, but of catastrophe"; the man who tries to use guesswork to fill in genealogical lacunae "is no longer dealing with history, but fiction" (Werner 1978:151). Although modern historians may shrink from the problems of establishing the continuity of noble lines, medieval authors were often much less circumspect, as will be seen below.

Most modern authors seem to argue that the nobility was never rigidly closed. Genicot, for example, tried to show that some noble families seemed to vanish, replaced by others not previously recorded. He thought it advantageous to kings to favor new nobility over old. The process of the renewal of nobility probably increased its pace through the Middle Ages (Genicot 1978).

Bosl traces the slow process whereby the *ministeriales*, unfree officials of the German emperor, had by the twelfth century slowly been converted into a new nobility as emperor and court sought allies against the lay and ecclesiastical lords (1978, see also Genicot 1968). The *ministeriales* used "ideology, history and myth" to legitimate their rise (Bosl 1978:300). A sympathetic chronicler alleged, for example, that the *ministeriales* received their high status from Julius Caesar (Bosl 1978). In spite of the power and prestige they ultimately achieved, the humble origins of the *ministeriales* were long remembered by the old nobility. Thus certain monasteries, which "were mostly noble foundations with an advocacy restricted to the 'caste' (*Hirsch*) of nobles, rejected *ministeriales*" (Bosl 1978:308). This is very reminiscent of the ponderous motion of the upwardly mobile caste in India.

Schlesinger 1968 argues that the Germanic and Frankish kings often sought to turn the nobility into a class of officials who could be dismissed or promoted at will. Charlemagne for a time curbed the nobility and elevated to office whom he would. He thus made a start on the creation of a true "administration," but on his death the nobility reasserted itself. On the other hand, when non-nobles did succeed in achieving high status, they quickly claimed to be ancient nobility. Although the evidence is poor, there also appear to have been ways in which nobility could be lost, resulting in downward social mobility. Loss of territorial jurisdiction is thought to have been decisive, and *dérogeance* (akin to outcasting) allegedly lowered the status of those who violated the code of nobility (Bitton 1969; Duby 1968).

Virtually all sources agree that there were substantial regional as well as temporal variations in social stratification in medieval Europe (see, e.g., Genicot 1978). In Germany and in most of France, nobility was more hereditary; to the south, less so. Indeed, the whole first rank of territorial nobles was gone from much of Italy by very early in the twelfth century (Reuter 1978:9; Genicot 1978). Most authorities also note that the hereditary principle was much less in evidence in England (Reuter 1978). Although a de facto nobility developed there as on the Continent, it never achieved legal definition, nor did it become really closed (Bloch 1961:II). In contrast to the situation across the Channel, "English society was an astonishingly egalitarian structure" (Bloch 1961:II, 331). Ullmann (1966a:85) linked England's difference to a more perfect feudalism, which prevented the full rationalization of the theocratic-hierarchic structure of medieval society: "Feudal law . . . was applicable to all conditions of man in England . . . and through its equalizing effects it prevented, above all, the emergence of a caste." On the Continent, by contrast, medieval society was divided into estates that were entirely a matter of "custom and tradition" (rather than Roman-canonical law), that were distinguished by "sharp cleavages," and between which individuals could not move (Ullmann 1966:41). The norms of behavior for the various estates governed their members in different ways.

Feudalism was also a matter of custom, but it contained a feature that Ullmann (1966a) concluded ultimately facilitated the demise of medieval estates: the idea of contract that was central to feudal relations. Whereas in the prevailing theocratic ideal there was no right of resistance against a superior, the feudal vassal was allowed to repudiate his contract with a lord who did not fulfill his obligations to him. In England, feudal contract was given freer reign, or was given it earlier, than on the Continent. In sum, it is necessary to admit whole or partial exceptions at various times and places, yet there is substantial agreement on significant degrees of hereditary closure in medieval Europe.

Complementing the primary concern with nobility in Reuter 1978 and Cheyette 1968 is a recent work (Murray 1978) that is primarily concerned with medieval European social mobility, its temporal profile, indices, causes, and consequences. Murray sees some signs of social mobility in the tenth century, but he sees more substantial signs of "an acceleration of up-and-down mobility . . . after the millennium" (1978:18). As indices of social mobility, Murray focuses on depictions of the wheel of fortune; satirical and moralistic criticism of ambition, avarice, and simony; increasing concern with the virtue of prudence; and other more direct indications. Murray is particularly concerned with the monetization of the economy and the rise of centralized states as causes of increasing social mobility, but he also gives considerable importance to the universities once they were established. Finally, Murray sees a whole new civilizational orientation emerging as a consequence or concomitant of the rise of social mobility. In the early medieval period, European civilization was marked by a "Hebraic" emphasis on will and by innumeracy, monasticism, and a belief in miracles; after the millennium the orientation was increasingly numerate, and "Greek" in its rationality or intellectualism (1978).

Relying particularly on the works of Karl Werner, Murray rejects the idea (attributed to Bloch above) that social mobility was substantial until the second half of the eleventh century. While it is true that the narrative histories of the time suggest this, in that several of the most noble French families trace their descent from earlier upstart heroes, these histories were apparently fabricated. When attempts are now made to trace the noble lineages back in time, they go not to upstarts but simply further and further back—to Carolingian and possibly even Merovingian times—while remaining noble. Murray speculates that the nobles adopted shorter genealogies and heroic but human apical ancestors because of "a fashion, growing in the eleventh century, for the acquisition of rank by virtue" (1978:94).

The main focus of Murray's work, however, is not on the centuries before the millennium. He is mostly concerned with the period from about 1100 to about 1300 and the evidence that social mobility was then on the increase. Laying groundwork for the changes he documents in that period was a "generic change in the European economy" between 975 and 1125 that "intensified up-and-down social mobility by way both of money and political power" (1978:18). The "explosive" changes in the economy were in large measure reflections of the tremendous monetization of the Islamic world, a monetization that penetrated Europe first along its southern and western rims, then into its "nerve centers," and finally into all its parts (1978:51, 57). This monetization had many consequences. Importantly, "liquidity in wealth" made for "social liquidity" and for an "abstraction of power," meaning that power that was based on monetary wealth could be greatly centralized (1978: 60, 84). Money needed to be counted. Those who handled money, and those who administered it and the projects it paid for, needed mathematical skills that had long been ignored in Europe. Those who acquired these skills could rise on "society's two main staircases": commerce and government service (1978:206). Murray thinks that those who rose in government—the German *ministeriales* referred to earlier and the aristocracy that formed around the dukes of Normandy, for example—were more numerous or successful. Numeracy was but one of several intellectual skills that were then perceived as valuable to centralizing rulers. The idea that reason in general could have value strengthened measurably between 1100 and 1300. Both church and state began to provide education for promising men regardless of their background, a movement that culminated in the formation of the medieval universities.

The nexus between the state, money, numeracy, and rationality is illustrated in the *Secretum Secretorum*, a pseudo-Aristotelian text translated into Latin from Arabic and widely circulated between the early twelfth and the mid-thirteenth centuries. It made shrewd observations on politics and noted the necessity of money in a centralized state. It extolled the role of reason in the state and advised the ruler to stress intellectual skills in choosing ministers. Of the sciences that a ruler should cherish in his officials, it said, arithmetic was the most important. Men did in fact rise on the basis of mathematical skills. The *Secretum* made no mention of birth qualifications. Running to some forty printed editions, it was read in high as well as low political circles (Murray 1978).

The twelfth and thirteenth centuries saw the rise of a more rationalistic culture "mainly borne by the upward-moving battalions on the Wheel of Fortune; by those who responded . . . to the pulling power of social rank" (Murray 1978:137). In this environment, history began to defend itself for its "prudential value," for its aid in avoiding mistakes: "the past, . . . not unlike the astrologers' stars, revealed the future" (1978:131–32). Murray sees an awareness of the existence of social mobility in a strong twelfth-century concern with the rise and fall of empires, and in the above-mentioned depictions of the Wheel of Fortune, the first to survive being one from England around 1170. Further evidence was found in the considerable discussion of avarice and ambition, the latter "in the sense of a desire to climb to the top of the social scale" (1978:81). John of Salisbury's *Policraticus* (c. 1159), for example, devoted fifty pages to a discussion of ambition, came close to approving it in lay politics, and said that "the same yearning for power and prestige affects high and low" (Murray 1978:81). An awareness of social mobility was, however, not the same as approval. According to Murray (1978:274), the attack on hereditary nobility "was not spelt out fully before the fifteenth century"—and was largely connected with events in Italy to be explored in the next chapter—but the discussion was underway much earlier.

Murray devotes considerable space to an analysis of the ideological stances toward nobility and merit in medieval Europe. His main conclusions are that Biblical references, being contradictory on the issue, could never settle it firmly one way or the other but that the Church was legally open, though in practice often closed, and that the tripartite ideology of society divided into those who fought, prayed, and worked was probably a reaction to the perception that social mobility was taking place. These and other points concerning the ideology of stratification in medieval Europe will be taken up in the next section.

First, however, I will close the discussion of social stratification by noting that the exceptionally sound medieval historians can be shown to have been writing during periods of comparative stratificational openness. By way of an introduction to his translation of Gregory of Tours' *History of the Franks*, for example, Dalton (1927) provides an extensive discussion of early Merovingian society. He explicitly indicates that in this period strata were not as rigidly hereditary as they had been and were to be: "A real hereditary nobility was not . . . found until later than the sixth century, it did not exist in the fifth" (1927:386n). He adds that

Merovingian society was stratified, but not so rigidly as in the later days of imperial power. Under the Empire a man born in one stratum had no chance of rising to another. Under the Franks, though in the main recognized divisions were kept apart, the individual might improve his position if he found favour with the great or could amass a certain amount of money. A man of servile origin might become a count. (1927:383)

Gregory himself was born to a "senatorial" family that had a long tradition of providing many of the bishops of Tours (Dalton 1927:4). In spite of his connection with nobility, Gregory firmly sided with royal power in its attempt to weaken the landed aristocracy, as I noted earlier. The landed aristocracy was destined to prevail, however, and early in the seventh century—after Gregory's time—they won the upper hand (Dalton 1927). Thus Gregory's time seems to have provided a window of stratificational openness sandwiched between more closed periods. In many respects, however, Gregory's *History* shows the signs of European medievalism; he neglected education, for example, and the sciences (Dalton 1927).

The family background of Bede, who lived in a monastery from age seven onward, is unknown (Sherley-Price [1955] 1977). Unusually numerate for his time, he was one of the five great mathematicians of the Middle Ages, all of whom became friends of kings (Murray 1978). Stenton 1971 provides an extensive discussion of stratification in seventh- and eighth-century Anglo-Saxon England. Excluding royalty, society was basically divided into two strata. At the lower level was the ceorl, the free peasant landowner. He was armed, was accustomed to adjudicating law in local assemblies, owned property individually, and generally recognized no lord between himself and the king. "Throughout early English history" Stenton points out, "society in every kingdom rested on men of this type" (1971:278). Ranking above the ceorl, in a generally rank-conscious society, was the *gesith*. The root meaning of the term is "companion," and "there is little doubt that membership of a king's bodyguard had formed the primitive test" of *gesith* status in most of the kingdoms for which information is available (Stenton 1971:303). The one exception is the southerly kingdom of Kent, where somewhat stronger traces of an old hereditary nobility persisted (Stenton 1971). Elsewhere, if there had been an indigenous nobility, it had largely disappeared, and if the invading Anglo-Saxons had possessed a nobility, "it would seem that the circumstances of the migration to Britain had disintegrated" it (Stenton 1971:304). A landed elite was coming into being, with land as the reward for service to the king, but it was far from a dominant element in Bede's time (Stenton 1971). In spite of the later development of a landed elite, there are various indications that conditions in the British Isles remained generally less castelike than on the Continent (see, e.g., Ullmann's comments on feudalism above, Tocqueville [1856] 1955, and Macfarlane 1978). The work of Bede and his colleagues may also have been stimulated by learned refugees from Syria and Africa who reached England in 669 and 670 (Murray 1978).

Einhard was of noble or "comparatively noble" lineage (Thorpe 1969:13; see also Zeydel 1972), yet, like Gregory, he lived in a period of relative openness. Charlemagne's reorganization of the empire rested on the use of men of talent without regard for their birth status: "Plebian or patrician, it mattered nothing to Charles: he singled out the most proficient with rare impartiality and promoted them to vacant offices or preferments" (Thorpe 1969:10). Thus under Charlemagne social stratification was opened for a while. Historical and other studies flourished for a period, too, giving rise to the Carolingian Renaissance.

Otto of Freising was definitely of noble stock and was very highly placed (Mierow 1928), but he lived at a time when, in the wake of the Crusades and the resulting reentry of Europeans into East-West trade, the stirrings of social mobility and its concomitants were felt, especially in southern Europe (Haskins [1927] 1966). While he apparently did not approve, Otto was well aware of these new conditions: "He was oppressed by the fact that the great sink into insignificance and the strong fall down from their power and their pride" (Mierow 1928:58). In his *Deeds of Frederick Barbarossa* Otto analyzed the class system of the city-states of Lombardy, in which men of humble birth were promoted to high office if they served their city well, and added that "to this practice it is due that they surpass the other cities of the world in riches and power" (quoted in Haskins [1927] 1966:243). For the reasons spelled out in Murray 1978, Otto is simply too near the Renaissance to count as a serious exception.

Serious or not, these exceptions can be put in perspective by taking stock of what has so far been said about stratification in medieval Europe. First, there is good evidence of legal and actual caste, even though there are real problems in interpreting the way in which these two aspects of closure tracked one another. Second, there were three situations in which caste tended to be absent or to break down: (1) certain regions—particularly peripheral ones—were less castelike, (2) centralizing states were less caste-like, and (3) the period after the millennium showed a general trend to increasing social mobility. As mentioned above, England was one of the regions more prone to openness, and there is also some evidence of stronger historiographic traditions there. The Norman regions were also exceptional. The Normans were, of course, the recent descendants of Viking raiding bands and hence in some sense an upstart aristocracy in all their areas (Douglas 1964; Haskins 1915). Moreover, the bureaucracies of Norman administrations (Haskins [1927] 1966) suggest meritocratic principles. Murray 1978 cites the Normans as an example of a centralizing state creating scope for social mobility, mostly after the millennium. Correspondingly, the historiographic tradition of the Norman areas was relatively sound.

Ideology and Linkages

However poor medieval European historiography may have been, it was never as absent as in India. We can, as a consequence, speak with more confidence about the linkages between social stratification and historiography in medieval Europe. This section explores relationships between social stratification and the doctrines and institutions of the Middle Ages, particularly those of Christianity. There is no denying the role of clerics in composing medieval history, or in imposing theocratic perceptions on historiography. The intervention of churchmen is direct and obvious. What is much less obvious, in terms of modern conceptions, is what Christianity could have to do with hereditary stratification. One key to this problem, scarcely imaginable in modern Euro-American Christian terms, was the alignment of Europe's noble pedigrees with the sources of Christian charisma, especially with the early Christian saints. Another key is the extent to which religion was the handmaiden of the nobility of medieval Europe. Finally, the chivalric code provided links between hereditary nobility and fictive history, links that were largely mediated by clerics, though more because of their literacy than their religious functions.

When one recalls that Constantine was particularly involved in the legislation of caste and the promotion of Christianity, it is tempting to ask whether there may have been some direct connection between these policies. Perhaps the Christian doctrine of acceptance, in the form of "Render therefore unto Caesar the things which are Caesar's; and unto God the things that are God's," facilitated the imposition of caste. Whatever the case, over the centuries "the things which are Caesar's" and "the things that are God's" came to mean empire and Church. An ideology profoundly authoritarian, hierarchical, and organismic was constructed upon these twin pillars, but in spite of inspired defenses of the idea that men are by nature unequal and that this is part and parcel of the great scheme of things (Lovejoy 1942), the idea that these inequalities are inherited was by no means clearly and consistently elaborated as a point of doctrine. Saints Ambrose and Augustine stressed faith and conduct above birth, and Boethius said that all mankind are one (Murray 1978). Yet there is Biblical support for nobility, as in: "By me princes rule and nobles govern the earth" (Proverbs 8.6). And while some proclaimed Christ's common status, others pointed to his genealogies in Matthew and Luke and declared him noble (Murray 1978). The Church was thus either ambivalent on the matter of equality and nobility or managed to accommodate both principles (Murray 1978).

An obscure feature of medieval culture—its fascination with "monstrous races"—illustrates the way in which Scripture could be used more directly to defend hereditary stratification. The monstrous races included such creatures as the Blemmyae, who had no heads and whose faces were on their chests, the Cynocephali, who had the heads of dogs, and the Sciopods, who had one large foot with which to shade themselves from the sun. The monstrous races have definable connections with the Germanic biological and racial theories that "shaped the middle ages" (Werner 1978:142). Monstrous races were known to the Greeks and Romans—Pliny produced an influential catalogue of them—but interest in them increased in late imperial Rome, reached a peak in the Middle Ages, and then diminished in the Renaissance (Friedman 1981). Furthermore, medieval Europeans, "obsessed as they were by genealogies," had a strong genealogical interest in the monstrous races (Friedman 1981:92). Friedman argues that belief in monstrous men met some sort of "psychological need" of the medieval mind (1981:24). The idea of monstrous races seems to have had its origin in Greek contacts with India (Friedman 1981), which suggests that Indian notions of caste and the visual representations of gods are part of a system of classification—stretching from monstrous races through the castes to the gods—that is analogous to medieval notions about racial and species differentiation (and possibly of Egyptian representations of gods and men too). In each case an attempt to assert elaborate speciation where it does not exist accounts for specieslike hierarchical differences among humans in a scheme of classification that stretches above and below humanity.

The basic attitude of medieval Europeans was that the monstrous races were in some sense men (i.e., descendants of Adam and Noah), yet they were inferior. With a few exceptions they were depicted in ways that illustrated their inferiority; for example, they were shown using crude clubs as weapons, rather than the equipment available to a medieval warrior (Friedman 1981). The inferiority of the monstrous races was explained in specifically Biblical and genealogical terms: in the Middle Ages "genealogy offered the most direct approach to any problem of identity, and the monstrous races were no exception in this regard" (Friedman 1981:88). Accordingly, the monstrous races were explained by a "concept of the decay of species [that] was natural to Judeo-Christian culture," even though the scriptures themselves exhibit no interest in monstrous races (Friedman 1981:89). Adam had been made in God's image, but clearly many of his descendants fell short of that ideal. These deviations were explained either by "alien strains" entering the line of descent or by divine punishment (1981:89). The monstrous races were considered to be descendants of Cain or Ham, the sons cursed by Adam and Noah. This line of reasoning was applied to the medieval social order by exaggerating the difference between the high- and the low-born and by stereotyping the latter as "comic, crude, and even monstrous" (Friedman 1981:102). Friedman cites a series of works on heraldry that explained the difference between "churls" and "gentlemen by nature" in terms of the hereditary curses upon Cain and Ham. To complete the connection between monstrous races and medieval Europe's lower orders, Friedman says that peasants (as well as giants and non-Christian warriors) were often depicted in twelfth-century literature defending themselves with clubs, the symbol of the inferiority of the monstrous races.

The most elaborate moral discussion of the monstrous races occurred in a late-thirteenth-century poem, "De Monstruosis Hominibus," written by a cleric, and for a "probably aristocratic audience" (Friedman 1981:127). The authorship and audience of this poem suggest the ideological importance of the line of reasoning connected with monstrous races. According to this ideology, humanity was subdivided into strata, each at a distance from divinity that indicated the extent to which it had fallen from an original high state.

While the warfare that brought about the ascendance of secular over religious authority bulks large in the memory of most modern Europeans, these two forms of authority were closely aligned in much of the medieval world, with the nobles in a commanding position. The nobility "controlled the Church, and hence the spiritual and to a large extent intellectual life" from the Carolingian period to the later Middle Ages (Werner 1978:138; see also Bosl 1978; Irsigler 1978; Lot [1937] 1961; Murray 1978; Tellenbach 1978). Noble control of religious life took two forms. First, and probably most important, the high positions in church and monastery were in practice confined to nobles—although an occasional plebian did climb to high position. Pope Leo said that priests who had been serfs "polluted" holy orders, while nobles honored church office (Murray 1978:323). Second, many religious institutions were open only to nobles. Given this sort of representation in or patronage of religion, noble points of view were unlikely to be very directly attacked or undermined by theologians. On the contrary, religious views were likely to take on a noble slant, which they did. Hagiography, wherein "the stereotypical reaches its apogee" (Ullmann 1966b:299), was the main vehicle, according to Irsigler:

> One is forced to agree with the theory which has been put forward again and again in recent research, that noble families or kin-groups were credited with a particular *Heil* or charisma. . . . F. Prinz' thesis that Merovingian and Carolingian hagiography had a quite specific role of "giving a new religious and specifically Christian sanction to noble leadership in Francia, which had lost the old pagan charismatic sanction . . ." (Prinz 1965:548), can scarcely be demonstrated . . . as far as the loss of the pagan charisma . . . is concerned. . . . The second part of the thesis, however, can be verified. The hagiographers of the seventh to ninth centuries, many themselves of noble origin, . . . provided a justification of the aristocratic organization of early medieval society, at least unconsciously, by creating a new ideal of the noble saint. . . . Prinz cites as evidence their regular stress on noble origin . . . and the fact that the earlier political and governmental activities and the family connexions of saints were given an emphasis unusual in this type of source. (Irsigler 1978:112–13)

Hagiographers, Irsigler says, showed an "extraordinarily positive attitude" "in their descriptions of the typical forms, contents and symbols of the noble way of life" and frequently suggested "that the nobility above all were the ones who adopted the monastic ideal" (1978:113). Hagiography thus effected a gradual shift in the image of the saints. In early Merovingian hagiography, saints were only metaphorically warriors; as in late antiquity, they rode donkeys. Before the end of the Merovingian period, we see the "Saint on his charger, the owner of bloodstock envied by princes" (Irsigler 1978:122). Even accounts of the people saints wined and dined with served as vehicles for linking saintliness with nobility (Irsigler 1978). The "self-sanctification" of Europe's medieval nobility was "by no means unconscious" (Irsigler 1978:113). To summarize, the "strictly ascetic and monastic [saintly] ideal of late Roman Gaul" gave way by the seventh and eighth centuries to the ideal of the "noble saint" (Irsigler 1978:112; Genicot 1978). Once the saints had been made nobles, the next step was to incorporate them into noble genealogies.

Irsigler gives various examples of kingly and noble families stressing their genealogical ties with saints and saintly bishops in order to associate themselves with sanctity and "blood-charisma" (1978:114; see also Schlesinger 1968). Hauck 1978 cites similar material (such as the *Nibelungenlied*) from the eleventh- and twelfth-century literature of noble house and kindred. Some, perhaps even many, of the genealogical claims may have been valid; in the long run, nobles did achieve sainthood in very disproportionate numbers (Murray 1978). But other of the claims have helped to earn medieval Europe its reputation for fabulous genealogies. I have already mentioned the noble family that appeared to trace back to Woden. Schmid ([1959] 1978:49), in a study of the nobility in the earlier Middle Ages, found "a general pride in being able to trace oneself back to an especially famous 'chief ancestor'. . . . Such pride was not always justified. At times such 'chief ancestors' were invented or simply appropriated for one's own family; this was notably true in late antiquity, and in the later middle ages." Indeed, it would be very surprising if the caste legislation of late antiquity had not clogged the courts with people trying to prove their descent from persons of high status and generally set off an orgy of genealogical research and fiction writing. If so, the orgy was to last for a long time. Werner (1978:200), for example, cites "the extraordinary success" of a set of fictitious genealogies in Carolingian times, while Baron (1966:422n) takes note of a "fabulous" pedigree that claimed as late as the 1400s descent from Abraham, Aeneas, and Romulus. Such claims were not exceptional, nor were they quickly forgotten in the Renaissance or later. Florence King, in *Southern Ladies and Gentlemen* (1976) quite precisely, and amusingly, dissects the mental links between overzealous genealogical research and status based on blood in the American South of our own time.

Bogus genealogy was not the only tactic of noble self-sanctification that involved reconstructing the past. Hauck 1978 describes the quests of nobles for holy relics that they might use as the new core of family traditions, supplanting the quasi-divine status relics possessed in the old cult festivals of the pagan period. In the place of natural causation, for which they showed little concern, medieval historians saw "nobility of blood and heavenly aid" as the requirements of political success, with relics "as the commonest channel of divine favour" (Southern 1970:190, 191). The transfer of powerful relics from one location to another, for example, was used to account for transfers of authority. The quantity and variety of relics obtained at this time remains a scandal to this day.

The lay literature that embodied fictitious genealogy, relic quests, and the like, though probably written by religious figures, is thought to have been read aloud in the households it eulogized, possibly by the dynasts themselves. The noble members of these households were not "passive recipients of intellectual . . . culture," but were instead patrons (Hauck 1978:79). Hauck thinks that a careful consideration of the implications of noble patronage of medieval culture might go a long way toward making the medieval period more intelligible. He also thinks that the oral tradition, as opposed to the written materials still available to us, was probably even more lavish in its praise of nobility.

Huizinga's discussion of late medieval chivalry, mentioned earlier, provides further insight into the linkage between medieval nobility and historiography ([1924] 1950). He stresses the great social distance between the ranks of society and says that the chronicles and literature of the period gave more attention to nobility and its code of chivalry than we now realize. Even "in the fifteenth century chivalry was still, after religion, the strongest of all ethical conceptions which dominated the mind and heart" ([1924] 1950:47). Since the social hierarchy was seen as a set of steps leading up to God, each order's value depended not on its utility "but on its sanctity—that is to say, its proximity to the highest place" ([1924] 1950:48). The unworthiness of the individuals comprising it in no way detracted from the "sacred character" of the nobility (1950:48). Chivalry was the code of the upper caste and did not mitigate the condition of non-nobles. But chivalry, as the basis of society, was an illusion, consistently clashing with reality. The clash is glaringly visible in the chronicles of the time, as already noted. According to Huizinga, the discrepancy between the chivalric ideal and reality was so great that the ideal was only realized in the tournament, that is, in a make-believe world of ceremony. In a related consideration, Huizinga notes the great social distance between medieval ranks and draws attention to the associated elaborate ceremony which, veiling "cruel reality under apparent harmony, made life an art" (1950:44). Substituting art for reality is a common feature of the caste-organized society.

Among the arts that flourished in medieval Europe was forgery (Ullmann 1965). Forgery reflected the tendency to explain social institutions in terms of the authority of Rome and the early church fathers, and the willingness to produce false documents. The previously mentioned Donation of Constantine was the most spectacular example. It falsely bolstered both popes and emperors, but it had a more-than-casual connection with nobility too (Valla [1440] 1922). It gave to the clergy the status of Roman senators (Valla [1440] 1922), a status no doubt widely understood as hereditary at the time of the forgery. Forgery, fictitious genealogy, mythical history, the sanctification of early nobles, the nobilization of early saints, the acquisition of alleged relics—all these have in common the presentation of the past in a way contrary to what actually happened, and all were linked in that this presentation of the past was in substantial measure dictated by the political needs of a hereditary nobility that, precisely because it was hereditary, could only be legitimate if it had illustrious ancestors and other proofs of nearness to divinity. The fiction of the tournament and the fictions created about the past were two facets of the same phenomenon. All were further linked in that the ideologues who put the past in writing were mostly churchmen, who in turn generally were nobles themselves, were under the control of nobles, or were under noble patronage. Lastly, scriptural authority itself was put to use in defending nobility and caste. Hence the links are definable between hereditary nobility, ahistoricity, and the Christian character of the Middle Ages.

Concomitants

Ideological considerations of the sort that underpinned medieval conceptions of monstrous races suggest that the period was not characterized by a uniform conception of human nature, or that the uniformities were minimized in defense of caste. A twelfth-century abbess who excluded non-noble women from her convent neatly expressed the idea that mankind is composed of a set of separate races or species: "Who, unless he courts ruin, puts all his farm-stock into one shed: oxen, asses, sheep, and kids all together?" (quoted in Murray 1978:325).

Individualism was noticeably absent, as was shown earlier. Biography was largely replaced with the pious stereotypes of hagiography. The tendency to portray the status rather than the individuality of humans was characteristic of medieval art. "The artist," Ullmann asserts, "took infinite pains to depict the garments and paraphernalia of the office which his subject occupied. He also devoted great attention to any symbolic gestures or symbolic elements or ritual features" (1966a:44). Medieval thought gave little attention to real human nature, or even to nature in general (Ullmann 1966a, 1966b). These characteristics of the medieval period were not due to a lack of ability but, according to Ullmann, to a lack of interest.

Only in the twelfth and, more noticeably, the thirteenth century was a beginning made in considering the human individual—as a *human*—in his capacity for making history. At the same time, naturalism began to develop in the arts and sciences (Ullmann 1966b). Only with the full-blown development of humanism in the Renaissance was the real man to emerge from the obscurity of medieval stereotypes (Ullmann 1966b). Huizinga disagrees, saying that "naive" realism was a characteristic of medieval art that the Renaissance transcended ([1924] 1950:243; Huizinga 1959). But his examples of naive realism are all from the late Middle Ages—the fourteenth and fifteenth centuries—and especially from the Lowlands, where opportunities for social mobility and the breakdown of caste were very similar to what will be described in the next chapter. The movement from stereotype to a naive realism and on to the sort of realism that penetrates character was a continuous process that is temporally coincident with increasing social mobility after the millennium.

In the near-millennium, when the individual was unimportant, there was no political science, either (Ullmann 1966a). The innumeracy of the Middle Ages (Murray 1978) was a barrier to all sorts of scientific development, and certainly to any sort of economics. While it is now established that technological developments of enormous import took place in medieval Europe, the comparative hostility of the period to the sciences, natural or social, is beyond dispute:

The period between the decline of Rome and the twelfth-century "renaissance" has traditionally been looked upon as the "dark age" of theoretical science. There is some accuracy in this view. Compared to the earlier achievements of the Greeks and the contemporary activities of the Arabs, Latin natural philosophy remained at a rudimentary level. (Stock 1978:32–33)

Until the development of the universities, education tended to be very limited—in effect a monopoly of the clergy, with the clergy in effect a monopoly of the nobility. Humanistic secularism was absent too, supplanted by an intense religiosity that requires no documentation. Divination was not entirely absent, and in the later Middle Ages it exercised good minds (Murray 1978). But the Church was hostile to many forms of divination (Lessa 1968), and it would be difficult to support the proposition that divination had the importance it possessed in most of the classical world and later in the Renaissance.

Thus the Middle Ages, particularly if we confine ourselves to its earlier centuries, shows the full spectrum of concomitants of caste. But in spite of a general decline in science, technological development did take place, and the pattern of concomitants began to change as social mobility increased after the millennium. Murray 1978 discusses at length the broadly developing front of reason (in the Greek sense) after the millennium, citing the twelfth century as the turning point in the "balance of power between man and nature" (1978:116). The twelfth and thirteenth centuries saw a realization that intellect could be used not only to control nature but also as a weapon against other men; hence the value both of history and a budding political science (Murray 1978). At the same time, a beginning was made on the other social sciences, as in Otto of Freising's discussion of social stratification in Lombardy. Ullmann (1966a) found the beginnings of new concepts of the individual, art, and historiography to be perceptible in the twelfth century and clearly underway in the thirteenth. These changes in the concomitants are precisely what is to be expected from the changing pattern of social mobility.

Summary

To summarize the medieval period, we may say that its generally unsound conceptions of historiography and its castelike social stratification maintained a pattern created in the late western empire. The subsequent development of the Church necessarily served to link social structure with historiography, since virtually all literary productions issued from clerics. But the Church was closely identified with hereditary nobles, so that history—whether secular or religious in content—was stamped by views compatible with noble dominance. On one hand, this took the form of identifying noble lineage with saintliness; on the other, it took the form of false claims of genealogical ties to persons of high status in the past. In either case, sound history suffered, and there was no alternative set of patrons to set the record straight. Such sound history as was written tended to be associated with relative openness in an otherwise relatively closed period. In the later Middle Ages, after the millennium, there was a general tendency for social mobility to increase and for historiography to improve. But some of the clearest statements of caste ideology that survive today come from this late period, presumably (this point is not as demonstrable as I might wish) as reactionary defenses of a nobility that no longer held its position as securely as it had before the millennium. All the concomitants of caste are well documented before the millennium, but they begin to change thereafter.

BYZANTIUM

Historiography

When Constantine founded Constantinople as a new co-capital (in the fourth century) it became the administrative center of the eastern half of the empire, while Rome remained the capital in the west. A system of dual emperors was created, with all laws being promulgated in the names of both. From the very beginning there were important differences between the eastern and western halves.

In the fifth century the western half of the empire was shattered by the barbarian invasions, and Rome was sacked. The eastern half stood fast, the Roman Empire persisting there until brought down by the Ottoman Turks in the fifteenth century. In the meantime, the western half of the empire was revived. From the middle of the eighth century, when the pope recognized and assisted the rule of Pepin the Short, it is more correct to speak of two empires, the western and the eastern. The differences between the two were now much greater, as shown, for example, by the fact that Greek had become the dominant language in the East, while Latin retained dominance in the West.

The Byzantines called themselves Romans and retained much of the Roman culture that disappeared in the West. Nonetheless, at some point the civilization centered on Constantinople acquired sufficient distinctiveness to warrant a separate designation: Byzantine. Its peculiar blend of Greek, Roman, and Christian civilization, all developing under conditions increasingly different from those in western Europe, provides the setting for the materials discussed in this section.

Byzantine historiography is almost universally judged as "far superior to that of the medieval West" (Ostrogorsky 1957:24). The stimulus provided to the Italian Renaissance when works in Greek—hitherto lost in the West but preserved in Byzantium—made their way to western Europe in the late fourteenth and early fifteenth centuries forcefully reminds us of the Byzantine attachment to history. Yet in many ways Byzantium shared in and grew from the conditions of the late Roman Empire. Byzantium would seem to have set off on the same path out of the classical world as did the medieval West, yet the courses of the two civilizations were long to diverge, and were only fleetingly to meet again when Byzantium faced destruction and the Western world began its Renaissance metamorphosis.

The least charitable statement about Byzantine historiography—that it showed little originality and merely carried on the classical tradition of historiography (Vryonis 1966)—is precisely equivalent to the most charitable statement about medieval historiography in the West, that is, that it did not seriously decline from the classical standards but did not improve upon them either (Sanford 1944). Vryonis, and all other sources that I have consulted and that explicitly compare Byzantine and Western medieval historiography, state emphatically that the former was superior. Vryonis (1966:117) says that Byzantine "historiographical production was superior to its contemporary counterparts in the West." In a concise and comparative description of Byzantine historiography (1968:130) he begins by quoting Carl Krumbacher (whom he calls "the founder of modern Byzantine studies") as follows: "No other nation, with perhaps the exception of the Chinese, has such a rich historical literature as the Greeks." Vryonis goes on to describe the Western medieval historical writings as rudimentary in comparison with the "competent histories and chronicles" of Byzantium. In his grand historical and comparative study of historiography, Thompson, as noted earlier, says that the Byzantine historians "were better observers and recorders of events than those of the West." Rosenthal (1968:75) adds that "the Byzantines showed a very deep interest in historical literature, and Byzantinists seem to be agreed that historiography occupied a preponderant position in Byzantine literary activity."

Byzantine historical writing shared a number of features with the great classical and later Greek historians, notably an emphasis on contemporary or recent history. As time went on, excessive attachment to the classical models led to the use of increasingly archaic language by historians (Vryonis 1968), but this in turn may have helped maintain the eastern empire's greater sense of the continuity of history, which is noted by Thompson (1942:I).

Rather than being the work of professional historians or scribes, Byzantine history was often the work of men of affairs, including several emperors (and at least one extraordinary woman). As was to be the case in Renaissance Italy, the historians were often lawyers (Diehl 1957; Ostrogorsky 1957; Thompson 1942:I; Vasiliev 1952; Vryonis 1968). Historical writing was not only the product of the Byzantine elite, it was also the most developed form of Byzantine literature, surpassing even theology (Diehl 1957; Vryonis 1968). Moreover, relatively little of the great historical writing of Byzantium was produced by monks, although for certain periods monastic records are important historical sources, and a chronicle form of history produced by monks enjoyed wide popularity among the masses. Besides employing popular language, the chronicles were full of the miraculous, in these and other respects showing much in common with the medieval chronicles of western Europe. Indeed, the Byzantine chronicles were often translated, and widely borrowed, while the finer works of history had little appeal beyond Byzantium (Bury [1911] n.d.; Diehl 1957; Ostrogorsky 1957; Thompson 1942:I; Vasiliev 1952; Vryonis 1968).

In spite of the overall sense of high quality in Byzantine historiography, it developed over a very long span of time, not all periods of which were equally illustrious. According to Vasiliev (1952), there already was sound contemporary history by around A.D. 400, with a good eye-witness account of Attila and of Hun customs dating to the time of Theodosius II (A.D. 408–450).

The age of Justinian (r. 527–565) gave further impetus to historiography, which flourished until the seventh century (Lichtheim 1966; Thompson 1942:I; Vasiliev 1952). By far the most important historian of the period was Procopius, born at the end of the fifth century. He wrote three works on the age of Justinian: one dealt with wars, one vilified Justinian and his empress, Theodora, and the third presented a favorable view of Justinian and his extensive building activities. Besides the obvious biographical and political emphases, Procopius provided, especially in his book on wars, the sort of ethnographic, geographical, and historical background to his writings that links them firmly with the classical Greek tradition (Vryonis 1968).

Others continued the history of Byzantium until the early seventh century. Throughout the eighth century, Byzantium underwent a dark age, from which very little historical material survives (Bury [1911] n.d.; Charanis 1944–45; Ostrogorsky 1957; Vasiliev 1952; Vryonis 1968). Chronicles, which had hitherto been rare in Byzantium, began to fill in the historical record in the early ninth century, and within another century historical writing—

history and chronicle—received patronage from Constantine VII (r. 913–959), who himself wrote a biography of the founder of the Macedonian dynasty (867–1056) of Byzantine emperors (Vryonis 1968).

The outstanding historian—perhaps the outstanding intellect—of the period was Michael Psellus (1018–1078). He led an extraordinarily successful political life while simultaneously writing at length on many subjects. When a university was reconstituted in Constantinople in 1045, Psellus became the head of its illustrious school of philosophy. In a major work, the *Chronographia*, he treats Byzantine history from 976 to 1077. This work is remarkable both for its style and for the portraits of emperors it provides. Vryonis (1968:137) sees Psellus as "the Byzantine equivalent of the highly cultured professor who in modern times has left the university to serve the government, and who has combined his educational and literary talents with government service to produce a valuable and sparkling memoir, not history, not biography, but a combination of both." Ostrogorsky (1957:290) says of Psellus that "his whole existence was, and remained, bound up with the things of this world; he thirsted after secular learning with an unquenchable craving and he observed and analyzed the motives of his fellow-beings with unerring accuracy." An avid classical scholar, "he was," Ostrogorsky continues, "the greatest Byzantine philosopher and the first great humanist." As a historian, Psellus was a "master of his art," and his *Chronographia* is "the outstanding memoir of the middle ages," showing "discriminating psychological insight and . . . clear-cut and brilliant characterizations" (Ostrogorsky 1957:280). Thompson (1942:I, 307) describes Psellus as "the ablest of all Byzantine historians" and notes that he was a lawyer.

Ostrogorsky (157:311) describes the Comneni dynasty (1081–1185) as "one of the most flourishing periods of Byzantine historiography, largely thanks to the works of Anna Comnena" and others. Vasiliev (1952) agrees on the favorable judgment of historiography under the Comneni. He also describes Anna Comnena's *Alexiad*, which covers the period from 1069 to 1118 (the reign of her father), as an important historical work, based on her own memories, oral reports, and documentary evidence. Vryonis (1968:137) says of Anna Comnena (1083–1148 or later) that she "heralds the series of gifted Byzantine historians who recorded the decline of the empire from the twelfth century." They were well educated and were versed in the classics. They copied the style of the classics, including its by-then archaic language, but also maintained classical "standards of accuracy [and] objectivity."

In a somewhat later period, Nicephorus Gregoras (1290/1–1360) carried on the high standard of Byzantine historiography. He was, Ostrogorsky said, "one of the outstanding figures of the fourteenth century and one of the most remarkable and prolific scholars of Byzantium, who wrote on all aspects of contemporary knowledge. His history is full of information and throws considerable light on constitutional, administrative and economic questions often neglected in historical works of the middle ages" (1957:415). Ostrogorsky judges his history to be generally reliable. Perhaps in its consideration of economic matters we see the clearest sign of the historiographic development that was taking place simultaneously in Florence, described in the next chapter.

Historiography, and humanistic studies in general, continued to thrive through the final dynasty of Byzantium, the dynasty of the Palaeologi (1261–1453) (Diehl 1957; Vasiliev 1952). It was a period that "produced a group of important and gifted historians who endeavored to describe and to explain the tragic events of the time" (Vasiliev 1952:693). Philosophical inquiries on the nature of man, rich autobiographical material, some ethnographic notes, treatises on political science (and on science in general), developments in medicine, significant developments in art—added to the above-mentioned burst of historical writing and the simultaneous virtual disappearance of the chronicle form—all mark the development of that humanism better known to us in its Italian form (Ostrogorsky 1957; Vasiliev 1952). Finally, it should be recalled that in addition to maintaining the classics of Greek literature, the Byzantines preserved priceless items in the Latin language long unknown in the West, most notably the great legal texts, such as the Justinian Code.

Social Stratification

The term "caste" is conspicuously absent in the descriptive and historical literature on Byzantium. I found only a single use of the term, and that confined to the late period in the thirteenth century when western European nobles who remained in the East after the Crusades intermarried with the Byzantine elite. The result of that intermarriage is described as having "formed a single caste" (Diehl 1957:162). This is in sharp contrast to the common use of the word "caste" in the literature on western Europe, both in late Roman times and in the Middle Ages. Furthermore, clear statements on a normal pattern of social mobility are readily found. Runciman (1948:196), for example, says that "there was nothing closed about the ranks of the aristocracy. Anyone with enough money . . . might found a noble family." He adds that "to the last the aristocracy remained an aristocracy of wealth." Elsewhere he says that "ambition was a common characteristic in Byzantium" (1948:202) and that there was a "general fluidity of society," "helped by the interest that everyone took in trade" (1948:204).

As we saw in the last chapter, there is evidence that from its beginnings Constantinople was more open than Rome. The absence of hereditary occupations in the East is asserted with particular confidence, because we are fortunate in having a Byzantine source, *The Book of the Eparch* (tenth century), that describes guild organization and regulation in Constantinople in detail (Charanis 1944–45; Ostrogorsky 1957; Runciman 1948; Vasiliev 1952).

At the upper end of the social scale, the Senate of Constantinople was created de novo. Its members lacked the great wealth (particularly in landed estates) and the genealogical pretensions of the western senators. Mobility into the Senate of Constantinople seems to have remained high, its powers weak, and its titles continuously degraded. All in all, the eastern senate, and the highest ranks within it, never became as closed as that in the West (Jones 1964; Ostrogorsky 1957; Runciman 1948).

The relative insignificance of the senate in Constantinople was a reflection of at least three major factors: (1) the extraordinary power of the Byzantine emperors, exercised through an efficient and dependent bureaucracy; (2) the resulting ability of the emperors to curb the power and cohesion of a nobility; and (3) the related success of the emperors in maintaining a relatively free armed peasantry. From the top to the bottom of the administrative hierarchy "promotions were entirely at the discretion of the Emperor" (Diehl 1957:68), and the emperor consistently had more power than the Church (Diehl 1957; Ostrogorsky 1957). Leo VI (886–912) illustrated the extreme of Byzantine power when he successfully revoked the ancient rights of the curia and the senate, thus bringing all the power of the state into the hands of the emperor and his bureaucracy (Ostrogorsky 1957). Only "common justice," existing law (which, however, he could change), and certain privileges of the Church limited his authority. In most periods, the Byzantine ruler was stronger than any of his Western (or Muslim) counterparts (Runciman 1948).

Curbing the power of the nobility and promoting a free and vigorous peasantry were intimately associated with imperial land policy. Basically, the emperors sought to prevent the development of large landed estates and to defend the holdings of small to middling farmers, whose interests in their farms would make them a militarily effective citizenry. In the late Roman period, from at least the fourth century, most peasants may have been hereditarily bound to their occupation (Ostrogorsky 1957). However, the much greater size of landed estates, and the resulting greater entrenchment of the nobility in the West, may have reduced the significance of the colonate in the East. Moreover, in a few centuries Byzantium took firm steps to free its serfs. Sometime between the seventh and eighth centuries—under the pressure of severe military encroachments from almost all sides—the administrative structure of Byzantium was thoroughly overhauled, and its social structure underwent an extensive transformation (Bury [1911] n.d.; Charanis 1944–45). The best-known document of this dark age in Byzantium is the Farmer's Law, which established the free village community as the mainstay of Byzantine society (Charanis 1944–45; Ostrogorsky 1957). The Farmer's Law was "plainly designed for a free and mobile peasantry" (Ostrogorsky 1957:120). By its terms, "the local peasantry was given plots of land, salaries, and tax exemptions in return for which it was to perform military service, and so henceforth, a free peasantry came to constitute the backbone of the Byzantine military strength" (Vryonis 1966:106). There was a hereditary element in the new arrangement, but it nonetheless resulted in "a large class of free and free-moving peasants" that "became a characteristic feature of the provinces" (Ostrogorsky 1957:120). There was, of course, no parallel development in the West, where the serfs generally did not achieve much freedom (except by fleeing the countryside) until the late Middle Ages.

The free peasant and free peasant village were to remain a part of Byzantine social structure until the thirteenth century or later, and a strictly hereditary form of serfdom such as the colonate never developed again (Charanis 1951). On the other hand, there was a nearly continuous seesawing between the policy of strengthening the peasantry and a countervailing tendency of a landed aristocracy to attempt to reduce the peasants to dependent status. In hard times peasants sought or accepted dependent status in return for the protection and security provided by the holders of larger estates. Alternately, the emperors took action—often extreme and effective action—to undo peasant dependency and return their lands to them (Charanis 1944–45, 1951; Diehl 1957; Ostrogorsky 1957; Runciman 1948). Although Vasiliev (1952:577) described large landowners as a "social anomaly" in Byzantium, they began to get the upper hand in the eleventh century (Diehl 1957). Basil II (r. 976–1025) was the last emperor with the power to roll back the rising tide of landed aristocracy and legislate firmly and effectively in favor of the free peasantry (Ostrogorsky 1957). After him, the dynasty of the Comneni (1081–1185) came to represent and promote the interests of a landed and military elite at the expense of the free peasant and free peasant village (Ostrogorsky 1957). However, as already mentioned, the free peasantry declined but did not disappear (Ostrogorsky 1957). Indeed, in the twelfth century Emperor Manuel I (r. 1143–1180) put up the money to buy back the lands of peasants who had surrendered their freedom for the security provided by great landowners (Ostrogorsky 1957), and in the thirteenth century the free peasant village was still legally protected (Charanis 1951).

Moreover, although a landed military aristocracy was on the rise from the eleventh century, it was by no means a hereditary nobility. The principal form of the landed estate became the *pronoia*, an estate granted to an individual in return for service to the state, generally military service. These grants of land varied in size—commensurate with their holder's obligation to the state—but were generally larger than the grants made after the seventh and eighth centuries to the peasant-soldiers called *stratiotes*. The recipient of the *pronoia*, the *pronoiar*, often received peasants with the land. These peasants were the *paroikoi* of the *pronoiar*. Clearly this is an institutional complex much akin to feudalism. But in the eleventh century, under the Comneni, the *pronoia* remained the property of the state, the grant being made only for a determinate period of time, usually for life. Only exceptionally, and only if clearly specified, were the grants hereditary (Charanis 1951; Ostrogorsky 1957).

The *pronoia* remained the dominant element in the Byzantine social structure until the end of the empire, and under the Palaeologi (1261–1453) it was often put on a hereditary basis. Probably most peasants were in a dependent status—i.e., were *paroikoi*—by the thirteenth century, and the balance of power had shifted firmly into the hands of a landed aristocracy (Charanis 1951; Ostrogorsky 1957; Runciman 1948). But the peasantry and the poor did not everywhere acquiesce in this state of affairs. Violent anti-aristocratic revolts racked the state in the 1340s, though the aristocracy was ultimately able to crush them (Charanis 1951; Ostrogorsky 1957; Vasiliev 1952). In sum, a landed nobility rose to power only very late in Byzantine history and had too little time to convert itself into a legitimate hereditary estate.

The ability of the Byzantine emperors to forestall for so long the growth of hereditary nobility is closely linked to the nature of the Byzantine bureaucracy, which created an administrative elite (Diehl 1957) that was rarely hereditary. While focused on the ninth century, Bury's description of the Byzantine bureaucracy generalizes for a wider space of time, and it rarely if ever mentions hereditary qualifications for office ([1911] n.d.). As early as the sixth century, the establishment of a law school provided a route for considerable social mobility into the bureaucracy and upward within it (Diehl 1957; Runciman 1948). As mentioned earlier, promotion within the bureaucracy was basically at the emperor's will. At the highest levels this gave rise to notorious palace intrigues and the meteoric rise and fall of individuals that is characteristic of despotisms (Diehl 1957; Ostrogorsky 1957). Eunuchs, allowed to hold any office save that of the emperor and much used in the Byzantine court, were prominent in palace intrigues (Ostrogorsky 1957; Runciman 1948). The use of eunuchs was another key practice in preventing the rise of a hereditary nobility in Byzantium (Runciman 1948).

From 1025 to 1081, before the landed aristocracy took control, the dominant group in Byzantium was an aristocracy of the civil service. Its ascendancy gave another boost to the legal profession, at the expense of the military, but this was relatively short-lived. In the last few centuries of the Byzantine empire the civil bureaucracy increasingly came under the control of the landed military aristocracy. But as late as the 1180s there was an attempt to restore meritocratic principles to the state's bureaucracy (Charanis 1944–45; Ostrogorsky 1957). Even in the final years of the empire, when the aristocracy had lost most of its lands to foreign invaders and when the bureaucracy was thus the aristrocracy's only remaining bastion of power, "government service remained open to all; the meritorious plebian could still climb to prominence" (Runciman 1948:104). Furthermore, the administration retained to the end an efficiency "unknown in Western Europe" (Runciman 1948:104).

In addition to the bureaucracy, the army and the church also provided channels of upward mobility in Byzantium (Diehl 1957; Jones 1964; Ostrogorsky 1957). Even in the final stage of the empire, when its aristocracy had grown as rigid as it ever would, the emperor Michael Palaeologus advised his son to reward good soldiers with extra land and to take away the lands of soldiers who performed poorly (Charanis 1951).

The position of emperor itself was not always conceived of as hereditary (Ostrogorsky 1957). Runciman (1948), in a discussion of the rapid and easy assimilation of foreigners into Byzantine society, said that newcomers might be emperors in two generations. At least six emperors were sons of peasants: Justin I (r. 518–527), Justinian (r. 527–565), Leo III (r. 717–741), Basil I (r. 867–886), Romanus Lecapenus (920–944), and Michael IV (r. 1034–1041). Some of the late western emperors had been of obscure background, but the pattern is more noticeable in the East. The Angeli dynasty, which came to the throne in 1185, was of obscure origin but rose rapidly to power when a daughter of an emperor fell in love with and married Constantine Angelus (Ostrogorsky 1957).

The absence of restrictions on marriage between the strata of Byzantine society is an important indicator of open stratification. So too is the absence of a simple and clear-cut system of titles (Ostrogorsky 1957). It should also be noted that a system of co-emperors was maintained within Byzantium and that this institution itself facilitated mobility to the highest post in the land. The position of second emperor was more likely to be occupied by persons with less-than-impeccable claims who yet had an opportunity to hold the lesser office long enough to win acceptance should they usurp or succeed to the throne (see, e.g., Ostrogorsky 1957).

Finally, it should be noted that although an aristocracy succeeded in gaining power late in the empire's life, the popular revolts mentioned earlier were not the only signs that a caste mentality was not imposed on the Byzantines. In earlier periods and again from the eleventh century onward, the "people" of the cities were a real political force. By the end of the twelfth century, the people had not only claimed the right to acclaim the ruler, which they already possessed, but also to elect him (previously he was in theory elected by the army and the senate). Also in the late twelfth century, an assembly was formed, composed of the senate, the clergy, and the commercial and industrial segments of the population. In 1347 an even more democratic assembly was formed (Charanis 1951).

The importance of the people of the cities was itself a reflection of the greater importance of cities in Byzantium than in the West. In Byzantium the cities were almost as important as the rural areas (Charanis 1951), and this in turn reflected the far more lively economy of Byzantium. In the third century the economic situation of the West was worse than that of the East, and conditions improved more quickly thereafter in the East. For eight centuries Constantinople was the wealthiest and most cosmopolitan city of Christendom (Vryonis 1966).

Thus, although the Byzantine Empire was in a constant state of flux (Ostrogorsky 1957), its elite, although in some senses coming to be feudal, was rarely or only imperfectly hereditary (Diehl 1957). In most periods there was legitimate and actual mobility at all levels of society and in both rural and urban settings. However familiar the crusading Latins may have found Byzantium (Charanis 1951), it was only because for a fleeting period late in its life Byzantium drifted toward the form of social structure that had long prevailed in the West but that was soon to fade there. The Italians had insinuated themselves into the economy of late Byzantium (Charanis 1944–45, 1951). Fortunately, therefore, when Byzantium fell to the Turks, some of the Italians were prepared to profit from their contact with a civilization long actuated by different forces from those equally long prevalent in the West. We will turn to the Italians in the next chapter.

Concomitants

Most of the concomitants appeared in the expected pattern in Byzantium. Biography and autobiography were major components of Byzantine historiography, and few of the important works are anonymous (Lichtheim 1966; Ostrogorsky 1957; Thompson 1942:I; Vasiliev 1952; but cf. Runciman 1948, which notes that the bulk of the biography is hagiography). In Byzantium, even illuminated manuscripts were signed (Vasiliev 1952). All this argues for a strong sense of the individual. On the other hand, while some items of Byzantine portraiture show considerable naturalism, increasingly so after 1150, it is not clear that it was significantly more naturalistic than portraiture in the West (Diehl 1948; Grabar 1967; Runciman 1948; Vasiliev 1952). Artists rarely signed their paintings, though in later periods they painted in individual styles (Grabar 1967).

Vryonis (1968:131) points out that Byzantine historiography was much concerned with political experience, had a "pragmatic educational value," and recognized the impropriety of partisanship, and hence strove for and achieved a degree of accuracy and objectivity greater than that in the Latin West (see also Thompson 1942:I; Vryonis 1966). Political science in general was a substantial ingredient in Byzantine writing, though it was not very original (Barker 1957; Ostrogorsky 1957; Thompson 1942:I; Vryonis 1968). In its later stages, even economics was included (Ostrogorsky 1957). The finest products of Byzantine historiography showed keen psychological analysis, a materialistic sense of history, and a naturalistic sense of human nature that probably marked the earliest stirrings of the humanism more commonly associated with Renaissance Italy (Jenkins 1967; Ostrogorsky 1957; Vasiliev 1952).

Byzantine writings on education are rare, apparently because the Byzantines relied on the classical educational treatises (Buckler 1948). But education was open to whoever could afford it, and the ambition to be educated was very widespread (Buckler 1948; Jenkins 1967; Runciman 1948). Because of its contribution to bureaucratic needs, education received strong state support and was apparently uniform in its steps or stages (Buckler 1948; Jenkins 1967). The first Byzantine university was established in Constantinople in 1045, well before universities developed in western Europe. However, like its medieval counterparts, the Byzantine university did not have history in its curriculum (Ostrogorsky 1957; Vasiliev 1952).

As was true in classical Greece, geography and ethnography were prominent in Byzantine writings (Vryonis 1968). Science in general was more interesting to the Byzantines than it had been to the later Romans or the medieval western Europeans (Diehl 1957; Jones 1964; Lichtheim 1966; Ostrogorsky 1957; Vasiliev 1952), but it was essentially preservationist, advancing little from classical standards (Runciman 1948; Vogel 1967). The pseudoscience of divination, which employed a variety of methods and was of concern to intellectuals and clerics as well as the masses, was pervasive in Byzantium (Diehl 1957; Jenkins 1967; Runciman 1948; Vasiliev 1952; Vogel 1967). No one, however, specifically argues that it was more important than in western Europe.

A uniform conception of human nature is strongly indicated by such statements as, "There was extraordinarily little racial prejudice among the Byzantines" (Runciman 1948:182), and, "In theory the Empire was ecumenical, and recognized no separate nationalities within its borders" (Hussey 1967:80). Religion alone qualified citizenship, and for the orthodox there were no restrictions on intermarriage (Runciman 1948).

Thus, only three of the concomitants deviate from expectations. Most notable is the rarity of realistic portraiture, which to some extent detracts from other signs of individualism. And although Byzantium's interest in science may have been greater than medieval Europe's, it was not as strong as it was among, say, the Muslims.

THE ISLAMIC NEAR EAST

Historiography

The Arabian peninsula was a backwater when, around A.D. 570, the Prophet Muhammad was born. He began to prophesy in Mecca, where he made a number of converts but where he and his followers also faced persecution. Muhammad remained in Mecca until 622, when he yielded to a request of people in Medina that he come to their city. This proved a fortunate move: Muhammad, his companions, and followers launched the series of conquests from Medina that was to give their new religion a vast territorial empire within a scant hundred years. So decisive was the move (*hegira*) to Medina that the Muslim world adopted the year of its occurrence as its reference point for chronology. Muhammad was not only a prophet, he became the political leader of the community of the faithful. As the "Seal of the Prophets" he could have no prophetic successor, but when he died a successor as leader and "protector" of the faithful had to be chosen. Four persons, the "Rightly Guided Caliphs," who were both relatives and companions of the Prophet, were chosen in succession.

The fifth caliph after Muhammad founded a dynasty, the Umayyad, which moved Islam's capital from Medina to Damascus. Under the Umayyad caliphs, who ruled from 661 to 750, the Islamic empire reached very nearly its fullest extent as a single, unified political community. From their homelands the Arabs had swept across North Africa and into Spain. To the east they had gone as far as the Indus valley of India and the southwest areas of China and central Asia.

Shortly after its collapse, the Umayyad dynasty was replaced by the much longer lived Abbasids. The Abbasid caliphs moved their capital to Baghdad, remaining there until the Mongols sacked it in 1258. Under the Abbasids, it is generally agreed, Islamic civilization crystalized and reached its zenith. In the meantime, the Islamic community began to divide politically, with competing regional dynasties springing up in various locations. As a community of converts, however, Islam continued to spread, and Islamic culture proved to have extraordinary assimilative powers, so that a remarkably homogeneous culture—with Islam as its religion and Arabic as its language—unified much of the Near East. The Muslim culture or civilization of the Near East, in the period roughly coincident with Europe's Middle Ages, is the subject of this section.

Before the coming of Islam there was relatively little in the way of Arabic literature (Obermann 1955; Rosenthal 1968). But in the distinctive Muslim civilization that developed in the Near East from the seventh to the tenth centuries—and that persisted long thereafter—historical writing was to flourish. Franz Rosenthal's *A History of Muslim Historiography* is the major work on the topic. According to Rosenthal (1968:196), "it may be doubted whether anywhere in earlier history, there existed so large a historical literature as we find in Islam. The Greek and Latin historical production may have been equally large, but there certainly was nothing to be compared with it in sheer bulk in medieval Byzantine, European, or even Far Eastern literature." Muslim historical writings were not only quantitatively impressive but were qualitatively sound too: "For many centuries, Muslim historiography was superior to contemporary non-Muslim works" (Rosenthal 1968:197). Obermann (1955:306) concurs in this judgment, crediting Muslim literature with presaging "the dawn of modern culture" and saying that historiography, because of its "vastness of volume and monumentality of structure," was the most remarkable branch of Islamic literature. Others express a more cautious estimate of Muslim historiography, but none judges it inferior to that of medieval Europe (see, e.g., Arnakis 1954 and Thompson 1942:I).

Historical writing had not really begun at all among the Muslims until the second half of the seventh century, or a bit earlier, so that a "darkness surrounds the earliest period of Islam's intellectual and literary history" (Rosenthal 1962:45; Rosenthal 1968; Thompson 1942:I). By the end of the first century of the Muslim era, record keeping had begun and a start had been made on pulling together a biography of the Prophet (Duri 1962). Historiography was to become the main element in Muslim literature in the eighth century (Obermann 1955; Rosenthal 1968). "With the rise of the dynasty that founded Baghdad, . . . Muslim historiography displayed a new dignity and magnitude. . . . The last decades of the eighth century and the early decades of the ninth were a brilliant period in Abbasid historiography" (Thompson 1942:I, 340).

Although the Muslims were to borrow much from the Greeks, there is no evidence that any of the Greek historians were translated or in other ways stimulated the development of Muslim historiography. Persian literary traditions, and perhaps Persian perceptions of the past, influenced Muslim historiography, but for the most part it was an independent development (Gibb 1962; Lewis 1962; Rosenthal 1968; Spuler 1962; Thompson 1942:I). All the major forms of historical writing developed early, and they underwent little further development except by combining the forms and altering their content (Rosenthal 1968). While the emphasis placed on one genre or another, or even on historical writing in general, varied from place to place and time to time in the Muslim world (see the various essays in Lewis and Holt 1962), the diverse historiographic genres were remarkably homogeneous in form throughout the Muslim area (Pellat 1962).

The oldest form of Muslim historical writing is the *khabar*, a "well-rounded description of a single event, usually no more than a few pages"

(Rosenthal 1968:66; Duri 1962). The *khabar* appears to be descended from "battle day" narratives, which were anonymous and relatively impartial (Obermann 1955), and it is found as an element in all Muslim narrative historical works (Rosenthal 1968).

An annalistic form also developed early, consisting of bare facts recorded contemporaneously and not subsequently altered (Rosenthal 1968). The early adoption of A.D. 622 as the uniform reference point for Islamic chronology, in lunar years, gave Muslim historiography an advantage not found in contemporary Europe, where there was no agreed-upon chronology (Thompson 1942:I). The Muslim chroniclers superimposed a reign scheme on the annalistic form and usually supplied biographical information for each ruler, stressing moral and ethical strengths and weaknesses. Often there was a description of the physical appearance of the ruler, along with lists of his wives, children, and officials. Considerable information on administration, and on astrology too, was often included (Rosenthal 1968). A related but less frequent form of periodization was the *tabaqah* (literally, layer—but usually translated as *generation* or *cohort*), which refers to all the companions of a single ruler, analogous to the companions of the Prophet. This form of periodization appears to have been original with the Muslims and was generally used in biographical collections (von Grunebaum 1961; Rosenthal 1968).

Biography is a very important genre in Muslim literature, and it is an important element in almost all forms of Muslim historical writing. To some extent the Muslim interest in biography sprang from an earlier interest in genealogy. But although the Muslims retained a healthy respect for the role of genealogical relations in human history, and although genealogical studies were consulted by historians (Obermann 1955), genealogical history had little impact on Muslim historical forms (Rosenthal 1968). Having been a part of Muslim historical writing from the beginning, biography came to dominate it, largely because of the distinctive Muslim method of reconstructing details of the Prophet Muhammad's life (which was, of course, the subject of the first major biography) from oral traditions handed down by his companions through various lines of transmission. In order to flesh out the Prophet's life accurately, it was necessary to assess the lives of all the transmitters, so that the reliability of each could be judged with respect to various parts of the traditions (Rosenthal 1968). "In addition," according to Rosenthal, "all Muslims shared in the firm conviction that all politics was the work of individuals and understandable in the light of their personal qualities and experiences. In many Muslim minds, history thus became almost synonymous with biography" (1968:101). The earliest

biographies were oriented to the needs of religious scholars, but the genre
was gradually widened to include men of secular affairs. Collections of
biographies (of men of science or of poets, for example), became popular,
and by the eleventh century "biographical dictionaries" were produced, in
which the biographies of prominent men in all fields were collected. The
Muslim biographical dictionary is quite unlike the biographical sections
of Chinese histories (Lewis and Holt 1962) but instead appears to be "a
wholly indigenous creation of the Islamic Community" (Gibb 1962:54). It
was peculiarly associated with the Arabic provinces of Islam, and it culminated in the *Obituaries of Eminent Men* by the thirteenth-century biographer Ibn Khallikan (Gibb 1962; Thompson 1942:I).

Except in the very oldest biographies, the subject's date of death is
always given (Rosenthal 1968). As mentioned above, the physical features
of the subject were often given. The early biography of the Prophet himself
mentions his physical features, and a whole monograph on the physical
appearance of rulers was also compiled early in the Muslim era, possibly
in imitation of similar Greek works (von Grunebaum 1961; Rosenthal 1968).
Rosenthal considers Muslim personality characterization to have reached
a peak in the tenth century. Later biographies gave better overall descriptions of the course of the subject's life, but they lacked psychological
penetration. Rosenthal (1968) mentions that the "human personality" of
the famous Saladin (1137–1193) comes through in his biography, even though
it was written well after the tenth century. Without denying the emphasis
on the individual in Muslim history, and of course in biography, Gibb
1962, von Grunebaum 1961 (221ff, but cf. 280–81 and 284–87), and Walsh
1962 all agree on the lack of psychological depth in Muslim descriptions
of individuals (this is similar to the Chinese case).

Among the other important historical genres were the local history and
the "world" or "universal" history. In addition to containing lists of local
officials, and of course biographies, local histories often provided important
geographical information (Rosenthal 1968). Local histories became more
common when the Muslim community broke up into its separate political
units (Thompson 1942:I). World history—by which was generally meant
the history of the entire Islamic community—was a major genre and
eventually illustrated the Muslim's "truly human concept of the world"
(Rosenthal 1968:150; see also Pellat 1962). Among the outstanding world
histories were those of al-Beruni (973–1048) and Rashid al-Din (c. 1247–
1318). Al-Beruni was a great natural and social scientist and the leading
historian of the eleventh century. His *Vestiges of the Past* ([1000] 1879) is

primarily a vast exercise in comparative chronology. Al-Beruni mastered several languages, including Sanskrit. His *History of India*, written in about 1030, is a work of immense and lasting value. As a historian he showed a commendably scientific and critical spirit (Arnakis 1954; Lewis 1962; Rosenthal 1962; Thompson 1942:I). Rashid al-Din was apparently the first historian ever to have a truly universal perspective, in the sense that his coverage swept from western Europe to the Far East. In the wake of the Mongol conquests he was able to assemble a team of collaborators that included two Chinese scholars, a Buddhist hermit from Kashmir, a specialist in Mongol tribal tradition, and a "Frankish traveler" (Lewis 1962).

History for the Muslims was both practical and entertaining. The Prophet himself had stressed the importance of history (Obermann 1955; Rosenthal 1968), but the influence of his particular view of history on the development of Islamic historiography was not, according to Rosenthal (1922:39), "altogether beneficial and productive." Historical instruction was considered specially appropriate for future rulers, as "the best way to imbibe political wisdom" (Rosenthal 1968:48), and many caliphs were personally interested in history (Rosenthal 1968). "From this, the highest layer of society, the knowledge of history trickled down the whole social scale of officials, scholars, and all those who wanted to be considered educated. It became the hallmark of general culture" (Rosenthal 1968:51).

Although Walsh (1962) cautions against accepting the professed claims for the uses or purposes of histories, Rosenthal's comments are particularly relevant to this book. Muslim historians, he said, sought "to produce works which would be useful and improve the social position of the individual acquainted with them. The knowledge of historical works, they contended, brought with it the political wisdom and conversational skill which assured success in this world" (1968:60). No educated man or government secretary could lack a cultivated knowledge of the past (Rosenthal 1968). Von Grunebaum (1961:171) makes a similar observation: "The value of culture for social advancement is stressed and the advice is voiced to study history, literature, and astronomy, as the kings are interested in these kinds of information." If Rosenthal and von Grunebaum are correct, the connection between historical writing and social mobility was conscious and direct.

On the other hand, history was not a major part of higher education. History was classed as an "Arab science" rather than a "Greek science," and was also classified among the "practical sciences" (as was divination). In another classification, history was lumped with religious law and linguistics as a "relative science" (relative to a specific group of people), as opposed to the fixed sciences of astronomy, mathematics, medicine, and philosophy (Rosenthal 1968). In elementary education, however, history was in a stronger position. It was sometimes formally taught and was always "the favorite reading matter for school boys and an important element in their intellectual formation" (Rosenthal 1968:45). Thus Rosenthal asserts that "historiography . . . was richly compensated for its theoretical inferiority by the domination it exercised over the minds of young men and the thinking of men of political influence and general culture. And the Muslim historian had the right to feel and, as a rule, did feel confident about the value of his work" (1968:53; see also M. Hilmy 1962). Concerning the entertainment function of history, he observes that "the novel (or romance) in Arabic literature is largely represented by historical novels. . . . [T]heir very existence and popularity are indicative of a strong historical consciousness in the Muslim masses" (Rosenthal 1968:186).

Professional historians existed but were relatively rare. Often they were connected with the courts. Though usually he was highly placed, the position of court historian in the Muslim world had its risks, as did most court positions. Amateur historians were more common than official ones, and no sharp line divided one from the other (Rosenthal 1968).

In addition to the practical and biographical concerns already mentioned, other characteristics of Muslim historiography need discussion. These include its emphasis on contemporary history, its extensive use of documentary sources, its emphasis on facts rather than interpretation, its concern for accuracy, its tendency to allocate praise and blame, its sober prose style, and its close connection with religion in combination with a humanistic orientation.

Turning to the first of these characteristics, note that antiquarian works, except for biography, were rare among the Muslims; virtually all their historical works were "keyed to the time of their individual authors," and "in all genuinely historical production, the author would use past history merely as a background for the present" (Rosenthal 1968:172). All histories contained information on the present, and contemporary history differed little in form and content from general history. The most common of the contemporary histories were those ordered by rulers, generally to record their deeds. Diaries were relatively rare (Rosenthal [1968] attributed this to the risks of officeholding), but the diary of Saladin's secretary, for one, was excellent and comprehensive (Rosenthal 1968).

Muslim historians used contemporary sources extensively, including various kinds of government documents, letters, and speeches (Rosenthal 1968:119). Documents were sometimes included verbatim in the texts, both because there was considerable concern for accuracy, and because "the historian was under the obligation to reproduce his sources literally and to avoid any arbitrary tampering with them" (Rosenthal 1968:177). But almost no one sought out old documents or examined relics for the information they could have supplied, nor were court records exploited as much as they could have been (Rosenthal 1968). Poetry, though, was sometimes consulted for its dates and details (M. Hilmy 1962).

Except for standardized criteria for fixing praise and blame—often according to religious considerations that proved detrimental to the quality of historiography—Muslim historians were generally committed to transmitting facts, not interpretations (M. Hilmy 1962; Rosenthal 1968; Walsh 1962). There were, however, notable exceptions. Von Grunebaum (1961:281) says that Muslim historians' standards "of accuracy and conscientiousness" were "astoundingly high." At least in part because of its concern for accuracy, Muslim historiography was spared the damage so often inflicted by poetical or belletristic standards. The epic historical poem, for example, seems to have been unknown to Arab literature (Rosenthal 1968). "Its concern with concrete data and observations from daily life brought with it a factual and concrete form of linguistic expression," and the concern for literal transmission maintained "the sober style of the early authors" (Rosenthal 1968:176–77). An exception occurred in certain forms of panegyrical biographies, written in a "rhymed prose" style that was popular in nonhistorical literary genres. "The stylistic brilliance displayed in these works reconciled the reader to the difficulties he encountered in trying to figure out their meanings," and "the rhymed prose style always showed a considerable disinclination for facts and conciseness" (Rosenthal 1968:177, 178–79). These are observations that, suitably generalized, describe the relationship between artistic and scientific accounts of the past in circles much wider than the Muslim world.

In its purposes and its method, Muslim historiography grew in large measure from religious concerns (Rosenthal 1968). The principal duty of historical writing was "to illustrate the truth of Islam" (Rosenthal 1968:90). Islam is itself distinctly historically oriented, and the religious element was always prominent in Muslim historiography (Lewis and Holt 1962; Rosenthal 1968). Yet religious concerns did not stifle an interest in individuals as individuals and a lively interest in human affairs, nor, as mentioned above, did it suppress the notion that history and human culture are made by individuals. The Muslims, Rosenthal asserted, had a "truly human concept of the world," in which conception historical writing was a key element: "[I]n its close association with biography, historiography was the only effective vehicle in Islam for concrete self-expression and for the factual observation of life, for looking at life as it was and for analyzing . . . man and his aspirations as the sole source of cultural development" (1968:195).

Gibb (1962:54) says that the conception underlying the oldest biographical dictionaries "is that the history of the Islamic Community is essentially the contribution of individual men and women, . . . that it is these persons . . . who reflect the active forces in Muslim society, . . . and that their individual contributions are worthy of being recorded for future generations." Although his principal concern is with a very late period, Walsh (1962:198) attributes to "essentially Islamic origins" a "preoccupation with events in themselves, and [that] these events are invariably given an individual human motivation." For all the religiosity of the Muslim historians, therefore, there is more than a touch of humanism in their writings, which exhibit "a keen interest in the human element, . . . hard to find in Europe before the Renaissance" (Arnakis 1954:85). So in spite of the unquestioned religious emphasis in most Muslim thought, the Islamic world analyzed itself in a surprisingly humanistic-secular way. One Muslim historian "completely eliminated God from history by the simple expedient of declaring the doings of the Prophets . . . something outside human experience, that is, history, and, therefore, not deserving the attention of the historian" (Rosenthal 1962:40). Ibn Khaldun (1332–1406), while he certainly believed in the supernatural, generally "relegated its influence to a realm outside, or beyond the ordinary course of human affairs" (Rosenthal 1958:lxxiii). However, von Grunebaum disagrees, describing Islam as humanistic: "Islam is eminently human in that it takes man for what he is, but it is not humanist in that it is not interested in the richest possible unfolding and evolving of man's potentialities, in that it never conceived of the forming of men as civilizations' principal and most noble task." In short, the humanism of Islam is not that of the modern, secular West, but it does seem to have been greater than that of medieval Europe.

Rosenthal (1968:195–96) sums up his assessment of Muslim historiography with the opinion that it never "reached the depth of penetration and artistic expression of classical Greek and Roman historiography, although it eventually achieved a definite advance beyond previous historical writing in the sociological understanding and the scientific systematization of historiography." Ibn Khaldun, the greatest of all Muslim historians, was unquestionably involved in earning good marks for Muslim historiography in sociological understanding.

Ibn Khaldun has been called the "first critical culture historian" (Thompson 1942:I, 360) and the "greatest of early modern . . . sociologists" (Becker and Barnes 1961:266)—titles he richly deserves. His fame rests largely on the *Muqaddimah*, the introduction to his universal history, which gives special attention to northwest Africa and Muslim Spain, though it covers a much wider area too. The sections of the history dealing with northwest Africa are of great value (Rosenthal 1958), but it is the introduction, the *Muqaddimah*, that warrants the most attention. It is described by Arnold Toynbee as "undoubtedly the greatest work of its kind that has ever been created by any mind in any time or place . . . the most comprehensive and illuminating analysis of how human affairs work that has been made anywhere" (1959:21).

It was Ibn Khaldun's position that error naturally creeps into the historical record due, among other things, to partisan reporting. But the most powerful cause of error is ignorance of human social organization and culture (Khaldun 1958). The historian, faced with the task of critically evaluating the historical record, therefore needs an understanding of human social organization (which for Ibn Khaldun is synonymous with civilization or culture). In the *Muqaddimah* Ibn Khaldun essayed to provide, comprehensively yet in detail, an understanding of human social organization (which, however, is primarily applicable to the Maghrib).

A key term in the *Muqaddimah*, and perhaps its author's most brilliant innovation (Rosenthal 1958), is *asabiyah*, variously translated as esprit de corps, group feeling, or solidarity. Etymologically, the term derives from the word for paternal kin, and it was generally used in the somewhat pejorative sense of clannishness. Ibn Khaldun gave it a positive connotation and identified it as a key to political power. In addition to that arising from the ties of kinship, Ibn Khaldun also identified group feeling arising from territoriality, propinquity, religion, property interests, rank, and clientage. Ibn Khaldun (1958, 1967) describes at length the conditions that give rise to or diminish group feeling in each of these modes.

The fruit of group feeling, he said, is political power, and Ibn Khaldun's dispassionate, generally secular analysis of the role of power in society almost certainly had no rival until Machiavelli (Becker and Barnes 1961). One of the great sources of group feeling and hence of power, Ibn Khaldun wrote, is the hardship of desert life, because life is so demanding in the desert that one must cooperate or perish. Under these conditions, groups of men of unusual bravery and fortitude are continuously produced. They may become so powerful that they can successfully attack and defeat the larger and richer populations of the cities. But the environment of the city is altogether different. In the city there is luxury, for which men naturally yearn. Luxury, however, is the great solvent of group spirit. Men in cities lose their group feeling and thus normally grow politically weaker with the passing of time. Ibn Khaldun describes the normal stages in the growth of group feeling—the rise of kin groups and of dynasties—and their normal stages of decline, with the mechanism of decline being differential socialization from generation to generation, in a manner similar to that set forth by Polybius to explain the succession of Greek states.

Yet, in spite of a ceaseless and generally cyclic flow of people from rural to urban areas and back again, the cultures of the two areas persist unchanged. Environmental constraints are paramount in the rural areas, while in the cities the newcomers learn the habits or aptitudes, crafts, and sciences of their predecessors, and hence perpetuate the sedentary way of life. Thus Ibn Khaldun had a clear grasp of the notion of culture, and though he may have overstated the case, his grasp of cultural ecology is evident too. Since he correlated changing individual and group psychology with stages in the various cycles of social flow, he was also a social psychologist.

Economic factors receive considerable attention in the *Muqaddimah*. Ibn Khaldun had a sure grasp of the roles played by capital and labor. Because of the emphasis he placed on the environment and the mode of livelihood in shaping social organization and culture, he has been credited with anticipating the materialist view of history (Rosenthal 1958).

Rosenthal (1958:lxxxiv) says that for Ibn Khaldun "political and cultural life was moving in never-ending, always repeated circles." There can be no doubt but that he saw in human affairs—in the natural life spans of families, dynasties, and civilizations—a profound tendency to cyclicity. But at the same time as he described the normal cycles and their various stages of rise and decline, he detailed the many conditions that for a time can forestall the normal course of change. Things may repeat themselves in the long run, and in essentials, but in the particulars of each case there is much room for variation. Perhaps the most accurate view is that for Ibn Khaldun "history is but a composite of processes of social change" (Becker and Barnes 1961:266).

"In Ibn Khaldun's view of history," says Rosenthal (1958:lxxx), "the whole world and everything in it depends upon man." Ibn Khaldun was a deeply religious man who believed in many manifestations of the supernatural, yet he considered the normal course of events to proceed in accordance with objective conditions of the environment and in accord with the mundane actions of men (Rosenthal 1958). He was a natural scientist (Becker and Barnes 1961), whose object of study was the affairs of men. And he brought it all together in a work as incisively organized structurally as it was historically. While profoundly theoretical, it is all phrased in terms of testable generalizations that are derived from or illustrated by actual situations clearly located in space and time. If Ibn Khaldun had serious flaws as a historian, they were ones he shared with Muslim historians in general: a failure to grasp the importance of permanent change in general and the lack of a theory of progress in particular (Rosenthal 1958, 1968).

It is important to note that Ibn Khaldun's genius was essentially of a synthetic nature. Except for his notion of *asabiyah* and the idea that a knowledge of social organization is indispensable to historical criticism, there is little in his work that had not already been set forth somewhere in Muslim literature. But he raised historiography to a level that was not matched until the time of Machiavelli and Guicciardini, and he sparked a flurry of sophisticated socioeconomic historical studies in fifteenth-century Egypt (Gibb 1933; Rosenthal 1958, 1968). His work was especially well regarded in later Ottoman times. No less than four copies of the *Muqaddimah* prepared in Ibn Khaldun's own lifetime have been preserved, but it is only recently that he has come to Western attention.

In addition to his history, Ibn Khaldun also wrote biography and autobiography. After an audience with the great conqueror Tamurlane, Ibn Khaldun wrote a "well balanced estimate of . . . [his] personality" (Rosenthal 1958:lxiv). His autobiography is "the most detailed . . . in medieval Muslim literature" (Rosenthal 1958:xxix). The work contains less detail on his early childhood, his family situation, and psychological matters in general than would be desirable, but it has a more personal style than was usual at the time (Rosenthal 1958).

Ibn Khaldun well illustrates the connection between historical writing and the social sciences, but it needs to be reiterated that political science and economics were cultivated by Muslim writers before Ibn Khaldun's time. Political matters, always subordinate to religious issues, never received among the Muslims the central attention that the Romans gave them (see, e.g., Gibb 1962), but handbooks for rulers and histories focusing on administrative and dynastic elements were standard exercises (Rosenthal 1968). For example, in the ninth century Ibn Qutaibah wrote a history of the Islamic state entitled the *Book of Sovereignty and Government* (Thompson 1942:I). Rosenthal (1968) considered Greek economics to be the most developed part of medieval Muslim social science (see also Thompson 1942:I). Taxation was effectively analyzed, and statistics were commonly compiled and used.

Geography and ethnology, often integrated into histories, were well represented in Muslim literature (Rosenthal 1968), as in the cases of Tabari (839?–923) and the great early-tenth-century historian Mas'udi (Arnakis 1954). Al-Beruni's ethnology is so valuable that he has been called the first anthropologist (Ahmed 1984). The greatest surviving geography, according to Thompson (1942:I), was produced in the thirteenth century by Yaqut and is an invaluable source for the history of western Asia. Geographical and historical writings reflected considerable intellectual interest in travel. The greatest of the Muslim travelers, "indubitably the greatest traveler who ever lived, excelling even Marco Polo" (Thompson 1942:I), was Ibn Battuta (1304–1377). His travels stretched from Spain eastward to China and to insular as well as mainland Southeast Asia. To the north he went far enough into Russia to see the midnight sun, while to the south he crossed the Sahara to visit the Muslim lands on the Niger (Thompson 1942:I). One of the most famous and, from a Western viewpoint, influential Muslim geographers was al-Idrisi. He composed his geography, *The Book of Roger*, in the first half of the twelfth century for Roger II, the Norman king of Sicily (Thompson 1942:I).

In a few cases the wide-ranging interests of Muslims produced a rudimentary start on linguistics, as when al-Beruni ([1000] 1879) listed select vocabularies as specimens of certain old dialects (Thompson 1942:I). Ali ibn Hazm (994–1064), an Andalusian, is said to have been "the first scholar in the field of comparative religion," in addition to allegedly having written four hundred volumes of history (Hitti 1968:133).

Social Stratification

Pre-Muslim Arab society contained a hereditarian element that persisted to some degree into early Islam. But in the period in which Islamic culture in the Near East reached its full stature, the hereditarian element was submerged by the notion of the basic equality of all Muslims. Ancient Arab society was composed of groups based on common descent (Obermann 1955). The solidarity (Ibn Khaldun's "group feeling") of descent groups, manifest in their feuds and preferential endogamy, was a fundamental principle of Arab social organization (Watt 1968). Poets, who were often the chiefs of their descent groups, proclaimed the nobility of their lineage in a manner "violently partisan" (Obermann 1955:257). The poets put great stress on the inheritance of nobility, and at times there was a degree of consensus about which descent groups were most noble (Obermann 1955). However, it appears that the rank of descent groups depended partly on descent "but even more on their current wealth and prosperity" (Watt 1968:47, but cf. p. 90). Hence claims to nobility often were just that: claims, not demonstrations (Obermann 1955). At maximal levels of segmentation, descent groups seem typically to have been structural and functional equivalents of each other rather than the functionally interdependent and hierarchical units of a caste system; each "was independent of every other and acknowledged no political superior" (Watt 1953:17). However, one group, the tribe of the Quraysh, was destined for a lengthy position at the top. From a previously "disunited and uninfluential" status (Watt 1953:5), they rose to a powerful position in Mecca. Muhammad was born to the Quraysh, who have therefore retained hereditary prestige to this day (to be discussed again later). In the short term, however, influential leaders of the Quraysh turned against the Prophet (Hitti 1968; Watt 1953).

Perhaps as a reflection of the individualism induced by commerce, Watt 1953 suggests, the Prophet Muhammad spoke out in the earlier Meccan period of his life against the ties of kinship, saying that they would be irrelevant on the Day of Judgment (see also Obermann 1955). Perhaps in part because of opposition from some of his own kinsmen, he continued to de-emphasize kinship in his pronouncements after the emigration to Medina—"lo, the noblest of you, in the eyes of Allah, is the most pious" (Sura 49:13, cited in Obermann 1955:276). Rosenthal (1968:29) says that Muhammad's "low opinion of genealogy . . . must be understood in the light of his efforts to tear down the social barriers . . . which had been created by ancestral pride." In the long run, therefore, "old barriers fell, and there was a rare opportunity for all the different peoples and civilizations to start a new intellectual life on the basis of absolute equality and in a spirit of free competition" (Rosenthal 1968:31). But in the short run, matters were different, for in practice the old Arab pattern of organization into solidary units based on common descent became the basis of order in the early Muslim polity (Obermann 1955; von Grunebaum 1970). Taxation was by descent group, as was warfare and even conversion to Islam (Obermann 1955). Converts were either incorporated into the Muslim community as descent groups (rather than individually) or, if they were not Arabs, were required to enter one of the existing Muslim Arab descent groups as clients, *mawali* (von Grunebaum 1970). Given the extraordinary expansion of Islam, the clients—clearly in a second-class status—probably soon outnumbered the aristocracy formed from the old Arab lineages. Moreover, among the Arabs an even higher elite or nobility existed, based either on pre-Muslim high status, kinship with the Prophet, or participation in important early Muslim conquests (Hitti 1968; Levy 1957).

Thus, from the Medinan period through the Umayyad dynasty a caste system, or something closely resembling it, emerged. To the extent that it was not possible for clients to move upward and lose their client status, the Muslim Arabs, often described in the period as a "racial" aristocracy, were a dominant "military caste" (Obermann 1955:290–91, 301; von Grunebaum 1970:57; Rosenthal 1968; according to Levy [1957], some of the clients changed their names and adopted fictitious genealogies, thus raising their status by passing for Arabs). However, in spite of its de jure and de facto caste system, not everyone agreed that this was the proper way to organize the Muslim community. The pious of many backgrounds spoke out on behalf of the equality of all Muslims (Levy 1957; Obermann 1955). The development of the *sunna*—traditions of the life of the Prophet collected as a guide to correct behavior—was largely in the hands of those who followed the early, Meccan preachings of Muhammad and who therefore had "freed themselves from the shackles of clan and tribe, from the passions of partisanship, and [who were] intent on serving the one God of the world as individuals" (Obermann 1955:285). To the pious, Islam was greater than kinship; thus Obermann (1955:298) quotes the great historian Tabari: "For one who is held back by his works will not advance by his pedigree." Even one of the Umayyad rulers, the caliph Omar bin Abdal Aziz, held that all Muslims were equal (Obermann 1955). The ideological seeds of a new order had been sewn and were sprouting here and there.

In spite of what the Prophet said about kinship, it has been said that in the early Islamic period, genealogy was more important than the Koran and the Hadith (the record of the words and deeds of the Prophet and his companions). But the Prophet Muhammad, by accepting and including within the Muslim tradition the Biblical accounts of Adam and of Noah, had sewn further seeds of trouble for the genealogist. Whereas the old Arab genealogies went back to a few individuals and accounted only for the Arabs, for the pious Muslim all mankind must go back to a single source. Ultimately, this new conception of genealogy eroded, but did not entirely efface, both Arab racialism and the concept of hereditary nobility (Obermann 1955).

When the Umayyad dynasty was replaced by the Abbasid caliphate, the

Arabs lost their dominance. The former clients were fully enfranchised, and merit became the route to high position. According to most authorities, this brought Muslim society into accord with Muslim doctrine. Levy (1957:67) quotes a ninth-century geographer on social stratification in the Abbasid caliphate: at the top are the rulers, "elevated to office because of their deserts"; then come the viziers, "distinguished by their wisdom and understanding"; then the upper classes, "elevated by their wealth"; next are the middle classes, "to which belong the men marked by their culture"; "the remainder are filthy refuse." Levy then notes that "the pre-Islamic ideals of birth had almost entirely vanished, for . . . the struggle for 'equality' had been won" (1957:67).

According to Watt (1968:79), "Islam is essentially a universalist religion in which all the believers are brothers on a footing of equality; and the privileged status of the Arab Muslim was an 'innovation' which had crept in unperceived." Watt goes on to suggest that governing through an Arab nobility had also proven inefficient, and this too led the Abbasid caliphs to squeeze the nobility out of their position. The nobility was

replaced by a new kind of courtier, largely created by the caliph and dependent on his favour. . . . Such men might be rapidly promoted to the highest offices and to great wealth, but might just as rapidly lose everything. Unless their sons were equally gifted they were unlikely to retain the position and privileges of their fathers. Thus through all the centuries of Islamic history from the accession of the 'Abbasids in 750 there was little that could be considered a permanent aristocracy. (Watt 1968:79)

So, barring the period of about 130 years before Islamic principles were freed from the earlier Arabic principles of social organization, Islamic civilization in the Near East has generally been open. Von Grunebaum essentially concurs. He notes the de facto conflict of stratificational principles while emphasizing the ideological commitment to fundamental equality and openness: "Political influence, military power, administrative rank, wealth, birth, and schooling, in every possible combination, strengthened or counteracted one another in assigning a given individual his place in society" (1961:212). In some respects, rank was stressed, yet "this emphasis on social inequality . . . does not touch the core of the personalities involved. The ceremonial registers the accident of their relative position at any given moment. It implies recognition of a social fact that may be short-lived, but it does in no way suggest inequality of substance" (1961:170). Von Grunebaum stresses that "the fundamental assumption of Islam [is the] leveling [of] all distinctions of birth" (1961:171).

From von Grunebaum's statements we see that the idea of equality in the Muslim context, as in most modern Western democracies, merely denies the relevance of descent and does not imply that society is not stratified. Von Grunebaum's choice of the word *substance* is also revealing; it points to a de-emphasis of racism in Islam. Thus the Muslim population is a "harmonious fusion of various human strains" (von Grunebaum 1964:284). So, too, Hitti (1968:76, 77) speaks of "the melting-pot process which resulted in the amalgamation of Arabians and foreigners," and of how an Arab "became one who professed Islam and spoke and wrote the Arabic tongue, regardless of his racial affiliation." In post-Umayyad times the Muslim world has had an essentially uniform conception of human nature.

There are, however, important exceptions to this generalization. As mentioned earlier, the tribe of the Prophet, the Quraysh, has retained hereditary prestige to this day (von Grunebaum 1961; Levy 1957; Obermann 1955). The founder of the Umayyad dynasty was of the Quraysh; so too was the founder of the Abbasid dynasty. The latter, moreover, was even of the Prophet's clan, the Bani Hashim. Some present-day Muslim kings are also descendants of the Bani Hashim clan. In two of the four major schools of Islamic legal thought the superior status of the Qurayshites, and to some extent of Arabs in general, is explicitly recognized. The other schools do not recognize these inequalities (von Grunebaum 1961; Levy 1957). Even during the Abbasid period the Bani Hashim were granted special privileges (Levy 1957). In these and other ways the various descendants of the Prophet, or of others associated with him, continue to hold positions of prestige, power, and wealth in various parts of the Muslim world (Levy 1957). Present-day Moroccan folk belief holds descendants of the Prophet to be a breed apart (Henry Munson, personal communication). Yet this is a contradiction to the generally accepted premise of the equality of all Muslims. Further, in spite of their prestige the descendants of the Prophet "in no sense . . . form a separate priestly caste or any particularly pious community. Out of their ranks have risen such secular monarchs as the kings of [Morocco] and Jordan, who, as far as their religious origins are concerned, stand no higher in public esteem than the ruler of Sa'udi Arabia, whose kingdom was gained largely by the sword" (Levy 1957:68).

At the lower end of society there were exceptions too. Levy (1957:73) cites a report of outcaste "gypsy" groups in the Arabian peninsula. But it is not clear that this condition can be projected into the past, and it is reasonably certain that only a small minority is involved. A more substantial case is that of Islam's ambivalent attitude to black Africans, in spite of a general commitment to equality. In his analysis of the "curse of Ham" as an ideological prop for antiblack prejudice, Friedman (1981:101) says that perhaps its "most sweeping account" was set forth in an eleventh-century work by a Muslim traveler, and it "reveals most strikingly the deeply rooted and early hostility toward black men on the part of Arab geographers." Both von Grunebaum (1961) and Levy (1957) treat at length the ambivalence of Muslims toward blacks but indicate that law and religion have generally promoted equality. Slavery was a normal part of the Islamic world, but slaves could and did pass out of their condition to freedom (Levy 1957).

In sum, hereditarian principles have persisted in various parts of the Islamic community from early times. Yet the views of the Prophet on the matter are clear and have generally provided a basis for the legitimation of inherent equality, and hence of much social mobility, throughout the Muslim Near East. The descendants of the Prophet are often spoken of as a nobility, but they are properly viewed as a nobility in the sense of the nobility in modern Europe: a group that still retains considerable prestige and is often wealthy and powerful but that falls short of exercising the dominance of a true nobility (von Grunebaum 1961).

Obermann sees a close relationship between the Abbasid reforms—which eliminated the castelike structure of Umayyad times—and the rise of Muslim historiography. He notes that except for the Koran itself, almost all our knowledge of early Islam to the fall of the Umayyads was actually compiled in the classical period, marked by the rise of the Abbasid caliphate in A.D. 750 and lasting for about three hundred years thereafter. In this period the Arabs no longer dominated. Instead, "those who wield the pen [were] for the most part devout Moslems of non-Arab descent; . . . in the main, it is they to whose efforts and genius we owe the incomparable literature of classical Arabic prose—a literature that brought to new life and blossom the whole realm of medieval culture, and to a good extent, even presaged the dawn of modern culture" (Obermann 1955:306; see also Hitti 1968 and Thompson 1942:I). As noted earlier, Obermann thought historiography was the largest and most monumental element in Muslim literature.

The social backgrounds of the Muslim historians were highly various. Ibn Ishaq, the first biographer of the Prophet, was the grandson of a Christian prisoner taken in the Medinan period (Hitti 1960; Thompson 1942:I). Yaqut, the geographer, was born an Anatolian Greek and was enslaved in his youth to a merchant of Baghdad (Thompson 1942:I). Rashid-ad-din was a convert from Judaism, as were other famous historians (Rosenthal 1968). In the classical period, beginning with the Abbasids, most eminent historians were Persians (Thompson 1942:I), which indicates at least that they were not part of the old Muslim aristocracy. Among prominent historians mentioned by M. Hilmy M. Ahmad (1962) for the twelfth and thirteenth centuries, one was the son of a slave and one the son of a carpenter, but also one was the son of a Coptic family that had been in civil service for 150 years. As for the upper levels of society, Thompson (1942:I, 354) mentions an early-fourteenth-century historian of "princely rank." Ibn Khaldun was descended from a family that for centuries had been one of the dominant elements in Seville. His more recent ancestors were well connected with rulers of northwest Africa.

Some sort of "nobility" or prestige attached to Ibn Khaldun's ultimately Arabian origin too (Rosenthal 1958). But Ibn Khaldun did not have an exaggerated notion of the value of pedigree, and his *Muqaddimah* is saturated with a motif of social mobility. It is true that he disliked one of his occupations because it entailed work that he "had never seen his ancestors do" (quoted in Rosenthal 1958:xlvii). But he is unequivocal in saying that a pedigree of itself is meaningless; it has significance only if, through propinquity, it is a basis for group feeling (Khaldun 1958:I). For Ibn Khaldun, "nobility and prestige are the result of (personal) qualities," and nobility in a family or group dissolves when it loses its group feeling; when group feeling is gone, nobility is a "delusion" (1958:I, 273–74). On the other hand, persons without nobility may acquire it, and have done so, through attaching themselves as clients to ruling dynasties (Khaldun 1958:I). Generally, prestige in a single lineage lasts but four generations, due to a developmental cycle in which each generation is socialized differently from those that succeed or follow it (Khaldun 1958:I). And this is but a single instance of those processes whereby not only lineages but also dynasties and nations rise and fall in generally predictable and ceaseless fashion, clearly making social mobility one of the dominant facts of human life. Finally, while it would no doubt stretch matters to say that Ibn Khaldun was an egalitarian—on the contrary, he considered social ranks a part of "God's wise plan" (1958:II, 328)—he judged it unnatural for the master-servant relationship to exist, "since it is a sign of weakness to rely on persons (other than oneself). It also adds to one's duties and expenditures, and indicates a weakness and effeminacy. . . . However, custom causes human nature to incline towards the things to which it becomes used. Man is the child of customs, not the child of his ancestors" (Khaldun 1958:II, 318).

As the last sentence clearly indicates, Ibn Khaldun's thought had no place for the hereditarian ideology associated with caste. On the contrary, his determinants of human behavior are the universals of human nature, combined with culture, society, and environment. His views do not seem to have differed in these respects from those of most other Muslim thinkers. Indeed, one of the popular philosophical themes of Muslim writers was "the short duration of worldly glory," and this same theme was thus a "keynote of historical investigation" (Rosenthal 1968:114). What this investigation showed was "the instability of all human greatness" (Rosenthal 1968:181). Thus the connection between social mobility and historiography was especially close in classical Islam, and as noted earlier, was consciously perceived, in the sense that a knowledge of history was considered a means of personal advancement. Von Grunebaum (1962:459) says "that between a society's motivation to support historiography, usually of a clearly defined type, and its self-image there exists a definite link." The image of the Islamic community as an open one, I suggest, was decisive in the development of Muslim historiography, particularly after the Abbasids gave substance to the image.

Concomitants

Many of the concomitants have already been mentioned. The remainder may be dealt with briefly here. Medieval Muslim contributions to the natural sciences have long been acknowledged as outstanding (Stock 1978). Hitti (1968:113) even credits Islamic science with the introduction of the "objective experiment" in chemistry and other physical sciences. That Muslims classified divination as being among the sciences, as noted earlier, suggests substantial interest in divination. Ibn Khaldun (1958:I) discusses a variety of divinatory procedures at considerable length, with little skepticism.

Whether or not treatises on education were a major genre in Muslim literature, Islam prescribes that education be open to all, rich and poor. Education was seen as a means of social mobility (Ahmed 1968; von Grunebaum 1961; Shalaby 1954; Totah 1926). Equal access to education implies a uniform conception of human nature, but Muslims have shown considerable ambivalence on the subject (as was discussed above). The great efflorescence of Muslim biography is evidence in itself that the individual per se was important to Muslims. Some authors specifically draw attention to individualism, at least among the Arabs: "The unsocial features of individualism and the clan spirit were never outgrown by the Arab character after the rise of Islam" (Hitti 1968:15). Watt 1953 identifies the origins of individualism, at the expense of tribal or clan unity, as a consequence of the development of a mercantile economy in places such as Mecca.

It remains only to note that portraiture is the one point at which medieval Islamic culture most clearly does not conform to the general syndrome of the open society. However, it must be recalled that the Muslims generally did not produce *any* representations of human or supernatural figures, neither realistic nor unrealistic. Also, as I observed above, Muslim biographies described the physical appearance of persons, suggesting an interest in realistic presentation of individual personalities even if not expressed plastically. Finally, it should be recalled that in western India, where Muslims did produce or commission portraits, their portraiture showed considerable realism, certainly more realism than that of contemporaneous Hindu Indians (see chapter 2). Mughal portraiture thus provides us with a natural experiment, verifying the hypothesis that *if* the Muslims were to produce portraits they would be realistic.

SASSANID PERSIA

Most authorities agree on the basic originality of Muslim historiography; if it had any stimulus, however, it is most frequently alleged to have come from Persia. The problems presented by pre-Muslim Persian historiography deserve brief comment. Because I found judgments of Persian historiography somewhat inconsistent, I did not originally include Persia among the cases to be analyzed. But if I am to argue that the development of Muslim historiography was linked to the nature of Muslim society, any argument that, on the contrary, the Muslims simply absorbed an existing historical tradition should be addressed. Only the last pre-Muslim Persian dynasty, the Sassanid, which lasted from the third century A.D. until the Muslim conquests in the eighth century will be covered.

On the question of the degree to which Islamic historical writing was independent or was influenced by other traditions, Pulleyblank and Beasley (1961) listed the Muslims—along with the classical Greeks and Romans, and the Chinese—as independent inventors of historical writing. Some features of Muslim historiography—such as the *khabar*, the *tabaqah*, and the biographical dictionary—seem indisputably original. On the other hand, the descriptions of physical appearances in Muslim biography seem just as indisputably modeled on a Greek pattern. But this is a minor factor;

generally, Greek influence was minimal. Thompson (1942:I, 339) says, "There is no evidence of any translation of any Greek historian into Arabic. Muslim historiography is without a trace of classical influence. It is as if historiography began with a clean slate." Lewis (1962:181) says of the Muslims that "at no time did they attempt to consult Greek historical sources." Rosenthal (1968:74n, 75) cites the case of a tenth-century Muslim historian who obtained an oral translation of a Greek work, but he then says, "It is common knowledge that none of the classical works of Greek historiography ever reached the Arabs." Thus, although the Muslims borrowed much from the Greeks, little historiography was included. According to Hitti (1960) the concept of world history goes back to Judeo-Christian models, but the specific form of the Muslim world history is its own invention. Von Grunebaum (1970:93) describes early Muslim historiography "which dealt with the appearance of the Prophet and the rise of the Islamic empire," as independent.

References to Persian influence are more numerous. Whereas at one point Thompson, as just noted, describes the independent nature of Muslim historiography, elsewhere he credits Persia with providing that "decisive influence" that made the Arabs historically minded (1942:I, 336). It is beyond question that Muslim historiography flourished after the caliphate was moved to Persian Baghdad and that many great Muslim historians were Persians. Thompson (1942:I, 341) says that "Muslim historiography, under Persian inspiration, grew stronger and sustained its quality as well as quantity." Arnakis (1954:85) agrees that Muslim historiography was influenced by Persian "sources and prototypes," especially the *Book of Kings*, which covers the first three hundred years of the Sassanid dynasty. This work was translated into Arabic in the eighth century. Hitti (1960:388–89) also says that the *Book of Kings* was one of the models that Muslims "evidently" looked to when they first undertook "formal historical composition." Von Grunebaum (1961) acknowledges Persian influence on Muslim historiography and biography, particularly in the grouping of events around individual kings, but considers the Arab element predominant. Rosenthal (1968) says that a diffuse Persian historiographic influence may have been present among Muslims from earliest times, but he notes the paucity of Persian sources and will only credit Persia with having had a limited influence. He notes that the reign scheme of ordering history is "very ancient and widely used" (1968:88).

In spite of this alleged influence of Persian historiography, there is good evidence that Sassanid Persia should be classified as ahistorical. Thompson (1942:I, 337) mentions the "huge gap in our knowledge of Sassanid Persia due to the destruction of the archives and literature in the first furious conquest of the country by the Arabs." This is suspiciously similar to Indian claims that their historical writings were stolen by the British and to similar claims made by the Bruneis. Thompson (1942:I, 337–38) continues:

After the Muslim conquest of Persia, Persian historical tradition was badly preserved by the Persians. The medieval Persians offer the remarkable example of a people which completely forgot its past, and which replaced history with a perfectly imaginary one. Neither Cyrus, nor Cambyses, nor Darius, nor Xerxes were known to medieval Persia except from Greek sources. Instead a mythical dynasty of ancient gods and demons was invented.

Thompson is not alone in drawing attention to the scarcity of Persian historical material (see, e.g., von Grunebaum 1961 and Rosenthal 1968). But the most emphatic statement comes from Bertold Spuler (1962:126), who asserts that "historiography seems to have been of no great importance to pre-Islamic Iranians. We know of no real historical work of this period." He goes on to say that there probably were some notices of kings' deeds from an early period, and perhaps even rudimentary archives. But from the third to the seventh centuries,

legends originated covering the whole of the known Persian history, but omitting most important events and presenting historical events as actions of a few principal figures, heroes and their wives, representing the mythical self-appreciation of the leading classes of this people. These legends present just as little actual history as, for instance, the *Nibelungenlied* and the *Chanson de Roland*. Thus we may state that apparently no real historiography existed in pre-Islamic Persia. (Spuler 1962:126)

Spuler continues by noting that there were no real histories among the post-Islamic Zoroastrians in Persia, nor among the Parsees in India. He also notes that the lower or middle level of the old Persian elite, the Dihqans, took no interest in Muslim historiography, preferring the legends of their "alleged ancestors." "It was useless to describe the history of Islamic Persia to them, even in Persian." The Dihqans "felt, spoke, and acted" in the same way as their "alleged ancestors"; for this reason, Spuler continues, Persian was neglected in "historical and other scientific works" (Spuler 1962:128). Lambton (1962) draws attention to the relative neglect of biography in the Persian areas of the Muslim empire.

Given the foregoing remarks, it is also of interest to know whether

Sassanid Persia was caste organized. There is some evidence that it was (though it may, significantly, have opened up on the eve of the Muslim invasions). Al-Beruni's *India*, written in the eleventh century, has a chapter on its castes in which the author digresses on Persia:

All this is well illustrated by the history of the ancient . . . [Xerxes], for they had created great institutions of this kind, which could not be broken through by the special merits of any individual nor by bribery. When Ardashir ben Babak [founder of the Sassanid dynasty] restored the Persian empire, he also restored the classes or castes of the population in the following way:—

The first class were the knights and princes.
The second class the monks, the fire-priests, and the lawyers.
The third class the physicians, astronomers, and other men of science.
The fourth class the husbandmen and artisans.

And within these classes there were subdivisions, distinct from each other, like the species within a genus. (al-Beruni [c. 1030] 1910:I, 100)

In short, al-Beruni considered the Persians to have had a caste system similar to India's. He also considered it quite unlike Muslim stratification: "We Muslims, of course, stand entirely on the other side of the question, considering all men as equal, except in piety ([c. 1030] 1910:I, 100).

Dhalla (1922:295) provides a brief summary of the fourfold division of Sassanid society, noting that each part, as in India, was likened to higher or lower parts of the human organism. "It was thought desirable, it seems, for all to follow the professions of their ancestors," except that the king could allow a person, duly examined by the priests and found fit for it, to assume a profession outside his birth status (Dhalla 1922:296). Huart (1927:139–43, 153–54) provides another description of the four "classes" and their subdivisions in Sassanid Persia, noting various hereditary posts and the fact that the priests were drawn from a distinct "tribe," the Magi, while the "knights" were apparently descended from Aryans who had conquered the aborigines of the area (1927:139, 142–43). The priests were influential partly because they owned great landed estates. They "lived by their own laws," and "were accepted as a state within the State" (1927:153). Even the "smallest events of daily life" were governed by ritual matters over which the priesthood alone had authority, which necessitated their constant intervention (1927:154). "Teaching was done by the priests alone," and it is not certain whether their teaching extended to "the middle class and the people" (Huart 1927:154). Priestly knowledge was locked in a writing system of unusual complexity, "the most inconvenient alphabetic script ever devised" (Thompson 1942:I, 338). Dhalla (1922) notes that the Sassanid dynasty was founded by a priestly family that eventually claimed divinity. It is not certain, however, that the priesthood was therefore seen as divine or semidivine. Dhalla does go on to say that the union of church and state was very close. Huart (1927:143) describes the strata of nobility down to the Dihqans and says that "the nobility, thus graded, was divided from the people by an impassable barrier." "It was an exception for anyone to pass from one caste to another" (Huart 1927:143–44). But Huart also mentions the provision for promoting a distinguished commoner, while Peter Brown notes that little more than a generation before the Muslim conquests the "caste-ridden" structure of Persia was loosened (P. Brown 1971:166).

Concerning the concomitants, the foregoing account of Magian priests, Aryan nobles, and aboriginal masses suggests a racialist order of society. Priestly control of education, in an arcane writing system, also fits expectations for a castelike society (but Dhalla 1922 speaks of a widespread duty to educate children in Sassanid Persia, without specifying a social context). The penetration of religion deep into everyday affairs may well have eliminated humanistic secularism, and the absence of any discussion of science in general works such as Huart's and Dhalla's suggests its reduced importance. Rosenthal 1968 often mentions Persian handbooks for kings as sources on Muslim political science but also says that it is uncertain whether they really were Persian in origin. Perhaps it is best to leave that question unanswered. It is unlikely that social science developed, or it would have been mentioned. No strong indications of individualism or its absence are indicated. No remains of realistic portraiture exist, and it almost certainly was not a significant part of Sassanid art. But the Muslim historian Mas'udi reported that he saw copies of death portraits of the Sassanid kings that included the "expression of [their] features" (Huart 1927:145). Perhaps we should reserve judgment on this topic too. Dhalla (1922) describes a great emphasis on fate and a widespread interest in divination, but almost exclusively in the form of astrology. There is thus only an incomplete tendency to manifest the closed-society syndrome.

To summarize, if Sassanid Persian historiography had sparked the efflorescence of Muslim historiography that took place after the rise of the Abbasids, as some authorities suggest, it would be difficult to judge the Persians as historiographically unsound. Yet there is evidence that it was unsound, and the evidence that Muslim historiography was decisively influenced by Persian historical writing is far from ironclad. Correspondingly, the evidence for caste in Sassanid Persia is rather strong, weakened by only two considerations: the reported provision for at least some upward mobility with priestly and kingly permission, and the opening of Persian stratification just before Islam came. What this suggests, then, is that although Muslim historiography may indeed owe something to Persian historiography—perhaps that sense of time depth that the Greeks discovered in Egypt, perhaps some literary motifs or models—the decisive influence came not from borrowing but from social conditions. The flourishing of Muslim historiography in Persia is something of a mystery when one looks to Persian models; it is much less so when one bears in mind that the last generations of the Sassanid dynasty and the first generations of the Abbasid witnessed the opening of previously closed societies.

THE FOUR CASES FROM THE MIDDLE AGES:
A DISCUSSION

In spite of their common origin in the Roman Empire, medieval Europe and Byzantium developed markedly different societies. Medieval Europe was relatively closed, while Byzantium was relatively open. All the concomitants of caste are well documented for the former, while most of the open syndrome was found in Byzantium. Of special interest is the intense religiosity both in Europe and Byzantium, which weakens the usual claim that the religiosity of medieval Europe is the principal feature underlying its distinctive characteristics. It is also difficult to avoid the conclusion that Sassanid Persia and the Islamic Near East were no less religious in their outlook and activities, yet the Muslims developed a civilization remarkably similar in many respects to the more secular civilizations found in Renaissance Europe and in China. Of course, the Muslims no doubt borrowed much from the Chinese, and the modern Western world in turn borrowed much from the Muslims. But the conditions that facilitated this borrowing most certainly have included the similarity of social order—and all that appears to flow therefrom—in those three civilizations. Sassanid Persia has perhaps been treated too briefly to yield a meaningful comparison with medieval Europe and Byzantium, but even a brief treatment suggests that it was the nature of Muslim social stratification, not so much the nature of preexisting Persian culture, that led to the development of sound historiography among the Muslims who conquered the Persian world. These cases, in short, support the principal hypothesis of this book and shed further light on the interrelation of social structure and the patterning of culture.

CHAPTER 6

The Renaissance

Italy was in the forefront of those changes that began in the Middle Ages and led to the Renaissance. Italy's greater urbanization, for example, was notable already in the twelfth century (Seigel 1968). In its earlier phases, Florence was the most illustrious exemplar of the Renaissance. Most of this chapter is therefore devoted to a description and analysis of Florence. But Venice, in many ways very different from Florence and destined to play a large role late in the Italian Renaissance, is briefly examined too. Florence presented a nearly perfect picture of the open society, with the expected correlates, while Venice was closed, was slow to adopt many features of the Renaissance, and particularly resisted the application of sound historiography to its own past.

FLORENCE

Historiography

Renaissance historians are far more likely to be counted as moderns than are their medieval predecessors. As with other features of the Renaissance, the homeland of the new historiography was Italy, and within Italy Lombardy was the first to change, though Florence was shortly to become of greater importance. Humanism is also strongly associated with Florence and with some of the more spectacular developments in historiography. There were three main streams of historiographic development in the Renaissance: chronicles, normally in the vernacular and written to commemorate one or another community; humanist histories, normally in Latin and modeled on works of the classical historians; and antiquarian studies. The latter two of these were closely linked to humanism.

Ullman (1946:45) says of the Renaissance historians that they "used our methods, more or less, on source materials; . . . we may think of them as earlier and less experienced incarnations of ourselves." Though the Renaissance historians' techniques were not yet perfected and they were at times carried away by rhetorical excess, they were, Ullman concludes, modern historians (1946:46). Similarly, Cochrane (1981) asserts that if they were not the fathers of modern history, they were at least its grandfathers. Ferguson (1948) concludes that the best of them were far superior to the medieval chroniclers.

This is not to say that everyone agrees on where to mark the boundary between medieval and Renaissance historiography. As we saw in the previous chapter, historiography began to develop Renaissance-like characteristics in the Middle Ages. Secular scholarship, which was to become an important feature of Renaissance historiography, began by insensible degrees in the centuries before the Renaissance, certainly by the thirteenth century (Ferguson 1948; Kristeller 1961), and by the fourteenth century, marked improvements in historiography were apparent in Italy (Schevill 1936:xvi; Becker 1971).

Different figures are cited as pivotal in the development of Renaissance historiography. For example, "in the history of the sense of history," according to Burke (1969:21), "it is difficult not to start with" Petrarch, who died in 1374. Certainly the humanistic side of Renaissance history has roots in Petrarch (Cochrane 1981), but for all his sense of history, he is not generally regarded as a historian. Leonardo Bruni (1369–1444) has been called "the first modern historian" (Ullman 1946:61; see also Garin [1947] 1965). Baron (1966:449) seems to agree, and he identifies a precise event signaling the change: the publication in 1403/4 of Bruni's *Laudatio Florentinae Urbis*, at which point "one realizes that . . . the threshold between the Medieval and the Renaissance has been crossed." Others who agree are Bouwsma (1973) and Seigel (1968). Cochrane sees "the real beginning of historical criticism" with Bruni (1981:5, quoting Momigliano). Rubinstein ([1942] 1965:225) considered Bruni's *History of Florence* (1415–29) to be "a remarkable achievement of the new historical method," in which the chapters dealing with ancient history "stand the test of modern research." Wilcox (1969:63), in a cautious analysis, sees Bruni as rising to a level previously matched only by "the greatest of classical historians."

Thompson (1942:I, 478) identifies "a critical change . . . in the spirit of Florentine historiography" by the middle of the fifteenth century, and he gives much of the credit to Bruni. But Thompson favors Machiavelli (1469–1527) as "the greatest of all Italian historians" (1942:I, 495). Dannenfeldt agrees and says that his *History of Florence* "marks the beginning of modern historiography" (1954b:101). While conceding considerable importance to Machiavelli, Cochrane (1981) sees his innovations as belonging more to political philosophy than to historiography. Gilbert (1965:301) prefers Machiavelli's contemporary, Francesco Guicciardini (1483–1540), whose *"History of Italy* is the last great work of history in the classical pattern, but . . . also the first great work of modern historiography." Thompson (1942:I, 498) quotes Eduard Fueter as saying that with Guicciardini's *History of Florence* (1520–1525) "begins the modern analytical history."

Everyone recognizes that Lorenzo Valla (1407–1457) produced a stunning demonstration of the effectiveness of the philological analysis of texts. Kelly (1970:45) is almost prepared to call him "the Copernicus of historical thought," because Valla "came closer than any other author to expressing the attitudes, presumptions, methods, and goals of historical scholarship as it would be practiced for centuries." For Bouwsma (1973:25), Valla was "probably the most profound thinker among the humanists of Italy." Valla was a Neapolitan subject, though a highly itinerant one; Bruni, Machiavelli, and Guicciardini were Florentine citizens.

In what way was the historiography of the Italian Renaissance new or improved, and what were its characteristics? First, Italian Renaissance historiographic development took place almost exclusively among laymen. Accordingly, Renaissance historians did not have the theological concerns of their medieval counterparts, and they wrote histories that did not start from theological premises or attempt to rationalize theological concerns. The Italian humanists, Ferguson claims, "took an essential step in the direction of sound historical thought when they abandoned the medieval habit of seeking supernatural causes for historical events" (1948:4). Renaissance historians were not irreligious, but they broke sharply and consciously with the traditions of medieval scholastic history (Becker 1971; Kristeller 1961; Reynolds 1953). Rather than seeing history as the unfolding of a divine plan, it was now conceived of as the product of human action; human affairs had been dignified (Cochrane 1981; Garin [1947] 1965; Kristeller 1961). It is safe to say that the term *secular humanism* was coined to describe the Renaissance, including its historiography (see Green 1972 for an extensive analysis of the progressive secularization of the Florentine vernacular chroniclers).

Thus Renaissance history was rooted in human affairs and was inclined to see history as the unfolding of the consequences of human will, impulse, and action. Machiavelli's cause-and-effect analysis of human motivation is a familiar example (Becker 1971; Dannenfeldt 1954b; Thompson 1942:I), but in general cause-and-effect analyses became more common (Burke 1969; Reynolds 1953), and the rudiments of the behavioral sciences developed on a broad front, generally in conjunction with historiography. In addition, Renaissance historians were less credulous than their immediate predecessors had been (and therefore more inclined to weed out what they saw as the improbably miraculous). Correspondingly, they were more realistic and naturalistic (Baron 1966; Wilcox 1969). A more critical evaluation of sources also developed during the Renaissance (Gilbert 1965).

It was especially important for its historiography that the Renaissance achieved a fresh understanding of the Roman Empire (Baron 1966). Whereas medieval history had glorified the Caesars, Renaissance historical studies produced good evidence for a glorious past that had preceded the Caesars. The kind of society that preceded them was similar to the kind of society found in some parts of Renaissance Italy, especially Florence, and the inspiration of this comparison, in conjunction with fifteenth-century political conditions, gave a distinctive stamp to the historiography then developing (Baron 1966; Holmes 1975). There was a decreasing emphasis on the dynastic and feudal concerns of medieval Europe and an increasing concern for city, state, regional, and national history (Baron 1968b; Becker 1968a, 1971; Ferguson 1948).

Political analysis was particularly emphasized in Renaissance historiography, as the familiar example of Machiavelli shows again. But others had earlier grasped the importance of politics. When Leonardo Bruni, for example, chose to write a political history of Florence early in the fifteenth century "he meant to choose the one significant factor which he considered the key to understanding all important historical events and human activities" (Wilcox 1969:38; see also Baron 1966 and Garin [1947] 1965). Rubinstein (1942), using early Renaissance Florentine materials, argues that political thought and sound history typically develop together. Initially this political thought was scarcely distinguishable from unreflective patriotism, or was nontheoretical. By the fifteenth century, however, theoretical analyses had developed (Baron 1968b; Becker 1968a; Brucker 1962; Ferguson 1948; Gilbert 1968).

Renaissance historiography profited greatly from the development or more consistent use of sociopolitical analysis in terms of institutional structures and their functions, and also techniques of writing that allowed the presentation of this analysis in a history. Gregorio Dati (1362–1435), for example, used fictitious dialogues to ask questions and provide answers concerning cause and consequence in historical events; he also described in detail the structure of Florentine government as part of its history (Baron 1966; Green 1972). But Dati's work was quickly overshadowed by Bruni's *Laudatio Florentinae Urbis*, in which he "analyzed the workings of a city-state constitution as the organic interplay of its agencies" (Baron 1966:196; but cf. Cochrane's 1981 criticism of humanist institutional analyses). By the sixteenth century, the analysis of structures and their functions was more commonplace and sophisticated (see, e.g., Gilbert 1965, 1968).

Structural-functional analysis, combined with the comparative perspective that is inherent in the difference between republican and imperial Rome (Thompson 1942:I) and in the apparent variation in custom described by travelers to the Orient (see, e.g., Hammond 1963), laid the groundwork for comparative sociology. A socioeconomic perspective was provided by compilations of statistics on population, commerce, and taxation (Becker 1968a; Burckhardt [1860] 1954).

Renaissance diarists, chroniclers, and historians were justly noted for the pungency and elaboration of their psychological analysis (Becker 1971; Holmes 1975; Struever 1970; Ullmann 1966b; Wilcox 1969). They embraced the notion of a uniform human nature, modified by the accidents of time and place (*fortuna*) and by education. The study of history was one of the means of discovering human nature (Garin [1947] 1965). Renaissance writers gave extraordinary attention to the conditions that differentiate people, and especially to the means of cultivating human virtues (Plumb 1961).

The distinctively personalistic, individualistic flavor of Renaissance historiography, with its emphasis on the role of individuals in history, was an important stimulus to biographical writing (Dannenfeldt 1954b; Thompson 1942:I). The rejection of medieval stereotypes can be seen in the writings of Boccaccio (1313–1375), and from Petrarch (1304–1374) onward biography became a major genre (Becker 1968a, 1971; Cochrane 1981; Holmes 1975; Reynolds 1953). According to Kristeller,

there . . . was a great contemporary demand for biographies, not merely of princes or saints, but also of statesmen and distinguished citizens, of poets and artists, of scholars and businessmen. Like the portrait painting of the time, the biographical literature reflects the so-called individualism of the period, that is, the importance attached to personal experiences, opinions, and achievements. (1965:11)

Personal and familial papers of extraordinary richness were produced, giving us ever more thorough biographical insight into ever-widening categories of people (Brucker 1962, 1967; Martines 1963; for diaries see, e.g., Pitti and Dati 1967). Contemporary biography set a high standard in such remarkable works as Giorgio Vasari's *Lives of the Most Eminent Painters, Sculptors and Architects* (1550). Benvenuto Cellini's autobiography, which was left unfinished in 1558, may be recalled in this context too, but autobiography was less successful than other genres during the Renaissance (Cochrane 1981). The Renaissance interest in biography "was much more a natural expression of the age than it was a reflection of antiquity" (Thompson 1942:I, 488).

Renaissance historians—particularly if we include among them the antiquarians who were pulling together information on all aspects of the past—drew on a wider range of source materials (Cochrane 1981; Seigel 1968). To some extent they used archaeological remains, such as inscriptions, coins, and medals (Thompson 1942:I), but they mostly utilized long-neglected textual materials from classical Rome and Greece. In the process of rediscovering the classical past, the humanists indefatigably sought out old manuscripts both in Latin and Greek, and thus brought to light almost all the texts that had survived from antiquity (Kristeller 1961).

The rediscovery of the past was accelerated by the visits of a few famous Greek scholars to western Europe from Constantinople (where Muslim pressure mounted and finally prevailed). Very few medieval scholars had known Greek, and some of the leading humanists quickly profited from their own translations of Greek works that had been forgotten or known only in distorted forms in the Middle Ages (Holmes 1975; Kristeller 1961). The example of Athens, whose glories as a city-state paralleled those of republican Rome, was also an inspiration (Baron 1968b).

It took more than Greek and medieval Latin to make sense of the texts the humanists brought to light; it was also necessary to develop methods of textual criticism and philology (Kristeller 1961; Thompson 1942:I). Philological developments in the Renaissance were particularly effective, not only for the historiographical insights they gave, but also for allowing historians to strip away medieval myth and forgery (Cochrane 1981).

Critical and philological exercises sharpened the sense of comparison between medieval Europe and the ancient past, between the republican era and the time of the Roman Empire, between the past and the present. Thus whereas "the Middle Ages had singularly lacked a sense of the reality of time," the Renaissance historians "achieved a new understanding of history," "a sense of perspective on the past, the ability to place oneself in time" (Gilmore 1952:201; see also Burke 1969 and Cochrane 1981). The notion of anachronism was now clearly perceived, and it was put to devastating use on medieval forgeries. Petrarch's notion of a "dark age" after the classical era was quickly supplemented by more useful periodizations, such as the five periods that order Bruni's history of Florence (Ferguson 1948; Ullman 1946). Periodization rested on the idea that ages in one way or another differed importantly from each other, and it was the task of the historian to discover and interpret those differences.

The bulk of Renaissance historical writing was not about the ancient past but rather the Middle Ages and contemporary events (Kristeller 1965). Whereas most medieval chronicles had begun with creation and were universal in scope, humanism ushered in a new form of history: "there appeared increasing numbers of direct personal accounts of contemporary episodes and experiences. . . ." Personal and secular, limited to the life span of the individual, these accounts are at the opposite extreme of the world chronicle" (Gilmore 1952:202). Thus in spite of their attraction to the past, Renaissance historians put what they learned from the past to use in matters of more contemporary concern.

Whereas medieval histories were generally in Latin, significant portions of Italian historical writing, produced by merchants or other secular figures, were in the vernacular. The motifs present in the vernacular chronicles of Florence before the flowering of humanism included an emphasis on voluntary association, a neglect of medieval political ideologies, the treatment of religion as a matter of faith, the idealization of the territorial state, support for public law, the presentation of individuals in the round (including their flaws), the idea of a fixed human nature, and the perception of history as a public enterprise (Becker 1971).

Since the vernacular historical writings predate or lie outside the mainstream of humanist historiography, they provide evidence that it was not merely an essentially literary and antiquarian phenomenon but rather that it had a broad sociological foundation. In this view—discussed further below—the Renaissance historians turned to the classics out of a sympathy bred by republican liberty. But turn to the classics they did. Cicero's views on history (and other matters) were central to the Renaissance, primarily because of his theoretical or philosophical statements on history, society, and the individual. Cicero had been important to the Middle Ages too, but in a form so distorted that it bore very little resemblance to the man and his thoughts rediscovered in the Renaissance (Baron 1968a). Polybius also provided theoretical guidelines and extensive historiographic models; both Bruni and Machiavelli were much indebted to him (Baron 1966; Gilbert 1965; Thompson 1942:I; Ullman 1946). Livy, Sallust, and Tacitus were the sources of often-copied models or important ideas (Baron 1968b; Struever 1970).

Virtually all humanists were much influenced by Cicero's view that history is a practical guide for life. The humanists liked to "extract from . . . [classical] writings a kind of common wisdom that could be learned, inherited and utilized" in moral and practical affairs (Kristeller 1965:37). In a humanist program for educational reform based on Roman rhetorical education, Pier Paulo Vergerio in 1400–1402 gave prominence to history because it gives "us concrete examples of the precepts inculcated by Philosophy," and shows "what men have said and done in the past, and what practical lessons we may draw therefrom for the present day" (quoted in Holmes 1975:304). Practical political lessons were especially emphasized. Machiavelli articulated the humanist view with special clarity, observing that "human beings are fundamentally the same at all times, and therefore it is possible to study the conduct of the ancients, to learn from their mistakes and from their achievements, and to follow their example where they were successful" (Kristeller 1965:28). The rapidity with which humanist historians were sought out in some courts is evidence that at least some rulers thought that the humanists could indeed provide practical lessons (Thompson 1942:I).

Renaissance humanist historiography showed a concern for rhetoric that is often judged unfavorably by more recent historians. But Cochrane 1981 defends the eloquence of the Renaissance humanist historians as an effective means of conveying the lessons of history to decision makers, and Struever 1970 defends rhetoric as a Renaissance science of the effects of words on human actions. Struever sees it as intimately and positively connected to the development of behavioral science, political science, and history. Given the importance of eloquence in the Florentine milieu of broad political participation, highly developed legal institutions, and extensive diplomatic negotiations, rhetoric clearly had a practical aspect. The Renaissance historians themselves were conscious of the potential for conflict between rhetoric and truth.

There seems also to have been a widespread feeling that humanist research would discover something deeper than practical knowledge. This was evident already in Petrarch, whose great interest in Scipio Africanus, the Roman general who defeated Hannibal, was based on the example he set of "a supremely good earthly life which combined glory with virtue" (Holmes 1975:152). Further illustration is provided by Cosimo de' Medici's patronage of Marsilio Ficino (1433–1499), who was engaged to translate Plato and related works. Cosimo thought that Plato's *On The Highest Good* would help him "to know what road leads most easily to felicity" (quoted in Holmes 1975:312).

Along with the emphasis on moral and practical lessons to be learned from biography and history went an equal emphasis on praise and blame. This had been an integral part of oratory and rhetoric in the ancient world, and it dovetailed with the speech-writing activities of many of the humanists (Kristeller 1965:11). An important term in the lexicon of Renaissance psychology was *virtu*, which Thompson identifies as the "positive spirit of power and achievement" that was "the breath of life" to the fifteenth century, "the identification of the individual with the greatest deeds and best culture" (1942:I, 489). Renaissance biographies sought to describe the virtue of great men past and present (Dannenfeldt 1954b). Bruni's special endeavor was to elucidate the connection between political institutions and *virtu*, arguing that it flourished most in republican systems such as that of pre-imperial Rome and late medieval to early Renaissance Florence (Baron 1966).

The counterpart of *virtu*, in explaining the fate of men and the course of human affairs, was *fortuna*. Again, Petrarch made the theme popular (Holmes 1975). Bruni was less concerned with the topic than other Renaissance historians (Wilcox 1969), but both Machiavelli and Guicciardini put great stress on the role of *fortuna* in history and politics (Gilbert 1965; Kristeller 1965). In the previous chapter we saw that the associated idea of the wheel of fortune, bearing men up and down, was seen more frequently in the centuries immediately preceding the Renaissance.

Something more than a rudimentary psychology emerged in the Italian Renaissance, with two points that should be noted here. One was the above-mentioned idea of a more or less universal human nature. The other was the specification of the content of human nature, its causes and consequences. Bruni used such notions as greed, revenge, lust for power, honor, and fear to explain both individual and collective behavior. He analyzed particular personalities in terms of objective features of their background, and he judged institutions with reference to their consonance with the basic elements of human nature (Wilcox 1969).

Finally, the study of history was given greater importance in the Renaissance. In the humanist conception of the humanities, the *studia humanitatis*, history became a central element in the curriculum of higher education, though it continued to be lodged under the heading of grammar. Some Renaissance historians received professorial chairs and were expected to continue writing history (Holmes 1975; Kristeller 1961, 1965; Momigliano 1982; cf. Cochrane 1981 and Gilbert 1967).

While we have seen that historiography showed signs of improvement in various parts of Europe even before the twelfth century, and while secular chronicles began no earlier in Florence than elsewhere in Italy (Haskins [1927] 1966; Becker 1971; Bouwsma 1973), many of the greatest leaps did take place in Florence. Thus most of the traits of Renaissance historiography that were just discussed were found earlier or with greater emphasis in Florence. In the following discussion of the sequence in which Renaissance historiography developed, only Florence will be covered.

Florentine historiography began to improve in the fourteenth century. At about the beginning of the fifteenth century, and again about a hundred years later, there were notable bursts of historical writing. The first was associated with humanist chancellors of Florence and the success of Florence in fighting off a threat to its republican liberty; the second was associated with Florence's declining years.

Medieval historical writing in Florence was in general undistinguished (see, e.g., Rubinstein [1942] 1965). By far the most frequently cited work that began to separate legend from history in Florence is the chronicle of Florence begun by Giovanni Villani (1276–1348) and continued by Matteo Villani (d. 1363). Schevill called Giovanni "the first authentic historian of Florence," and said he had a "feeling for factual reality which no medieval writer before him possessed in the same degree" (1936:xiv). He was in "command of the facts" and had the "power of critically evaluating them" (1936:xv). Unlike the works of his medieval predecessors, the individualistic tone of Giovanni's writing was unmistakable (Baron 1968b), and compared to medieval chronicles, Giovanni's was "obsessive" in its numeracy (Murray 1978:184). The Villanis provided a well-rounded analysis of the social structure, politics, and economy of Florence, along with discussions of its relations with its neighbors. Moreover, they showed remarkable candor in presenting the flaws of heroes as well as their strengths (Becker 1968a, 1971; Schevill 1936). In spite of this progress, much of the medieval was medieval was retained in Giovanni's initial effort (Ferguson 1948; Struever 1970). Matteo, in contrast, made notable progress in the restoration of contemporary history and was an astute political analyst (Becker 1968a).

Although not the pioneers that the Villanis were, other vernacular chroniclers played a part in Florentine historiography. One was Dino Compagni (1260–1324), a contemporary historian and political analyst who wrote a history of a major factional struggle that took place in Florence around 1300. This work broke even more with the medieval model, but it had little impact on the immediate development of historiography. Unlike the Villanis' chronicle, which quickly enjoyed wide circulation, Compagni's work was kept from the public for centuries (Schevill 1936). Another was Marchionne de Coppo Stefani (1336–c. 1385), who wrote a chronicle of events in Florence shortly before the beginning of the fifteenth century. This account is notable for its presentation of history as ceaseless struggles for power by individuals and groups, linked to an embryonic notion of a fixed human nature (Becker 1971; Green 1972; Schevill 1936). Yet another was Giovanni Cavalcanti (1381–c. 1450), a contemporary of Bruni and Poggio Bracciolini, who wrote memorials on the political events of his day, and also a history of Florence from 1420 to 1452. While Cavalcanti is often cited for his accurate coverage of the events of his time, his writings were disorganized and overly concerned with sacred and classical imagery (Becker 1971; Cochrane 1981).

Gregorio Dati, mentioned earlier for his methodological breakthroughs, was the last of the great Florentine vernacular historians. Dati's *L'Istoria di Firenze dal 1380 al 1405* is an account of Florence's wars with Duke Giangaleazzo. Becker (1968a:21) considers Dati "wiser and more insightful" than Bruni, primarily because of Dati's greater appreciation of the impersonal socioeconomic forces that affected the outcome of the wars. Although Dati was neither a member of the humanist circles nor a classical scholar, "the historical realism and some of the political-historical ideas which were to dominate the Florentine Renaissance" appear in his writings at about the same time as in Bruni's (Baron 1968b:138). After Dati the humanists put the Latin language and classical models in the mainstream of historiography.

"The essence of humanism is . . . a well-marked historical consciousness" (Garin [1947] 1965:14), and this consciousness was apparent already in Petrarch. Although Petrarch was a Florentine, there was at first no particular connection between humanism and Florence. But around the end of the fourteenth and the beginning of the fifteenth centuries, conditions in Florence stamped the development of humanism with enduring patterns (Baron 1968b; Bouwsma 1973). Because Italian humanism was associated with vigorous classical studies and with the adoption of classical genres and styles, it is often concluded that many of the Renaissance's characteristics were mere borrowings. But it is important to note the extent to which historians judge that classical studies can be seen as an effect rather than a cause of Renaissance developments. As Struever says, citing Fritz Saxl, "the men of the Renaissance returned to the pagans because they discovered types in their literature and art which expressed feeling similar to those which they wished to express" (1970:47; see also Baron 1968b; Becker 1968b; Dannenfeldt 1954b; and Seigel 1968). Many men of the Renaissance considered theirs to be a better world than there ever had been before (Gilbert 1967). When historiography became more exacting in the latter decades of the fourteenth century, the humanists borrowed from the past to polish and enrich trends set underway by the vernacular writers (Becker 1968a:77).

The humanist development of historiography in Florence is linked to Coluccio Salutati (1331–1406), the first humanist chancellor of Florence. While he was more a classical scholar than a historian, Salutati's theoretical contributions were important. He used the classics and developments in rhetoric and philology to conduct an extensive evaluation of the sources available for a history of Florence and to sharpen the distinction between fable and fact (Baron 1966; Becker 1968a; Bouwsma 1973; Struever 1970). Salutati "praised the advantages of history—the educator of mankind, the source of a knowledge more concrete than all the subtleties of theology and philosophy" (Garin [1947] 1965:7). Salutati's immediate influence was so great that from his time until long thereafter the center of gravity of humanistic studies shifted to Florence (Bouwsma 1973).

With Leonardo Bruni, as mentioned above, the historiographic quality of the ancient world was restored, and his humanistic skills were honed in the circle of scholars around Salutati. Like his master, Bruni became a chancellor of Florence. He was also one of the students of Manuel Chrysoloras (c. 1353–1415), a Byzantine scholar who was persuaded to make an extended stay in Florence, where he taught Greek and opened the materials of the eastern empire to the Florentine humanists (Holmes 1969). Among other things, Bruni translated Aristotle's *Politics*, which was no doubt part of what allowed him quickly to supersede Dati's functional analysis of Florentine institutions (Rubinstein 1968).

A few elements in Bruni's thought are critical to the evaluation of his historical writings. One is that he ordered his analysis of Florentine institutions around the theme of their being adjusted to the maintenance of republican liberty, as was mentioned earlier. According to Baron, Bruni "was the first to strive for careful selection of those aspects that showed organic interaction and a purposeful unity of the Florentine institutions" (1966:206). Baron goes on to say that Bruni tried to show how the Florentine constitution, by balancing powers, prevented tyranny and promoted liberty. Bruni also tried to show the relationship between external and internal politics, "that external power should be a function of internal political organization" (Wilcox 1969:45). Bruni used speeches, no doubt sometimes fictitious, in order to interpret and analyze historical events (Struever 1970). Methodologically, Bruni marked a considerable advance over medieval historiography. Another element was Bruni's development of the idea that the decline of Rome began when the advent of the Caesars destroyed Roman republican liberties and that the previous republican period of Rome (and Greek civilization) had seen the classical world's highest achievements. This was a radical interpretation of history, marking a sort of declaration of independence from the medieval world. Baron argues that it was this new interpretation that made Bruni pivotal (1968b; see also Cochrane 1981). A third element was that, like many of his contemporaries, and as mentioned earlier, Bruni had a full appreciation of the basic traits of human nature, the desirability of adjusting institutions to that nature, and the necessity of looking behind words to discover real motivation (Struever 1970). In his writing Bruni made extensive and critical use of archival and other materials (Gilbert 1965; Ullman 1946; Wilcox 1969). He was primarily interested in recent or contemporary history (Holmes 1975), and his *Vite di Dante e di Petrarca* were the first "full-blown humanistic biographies" in the vernacular (Baron 1968b:168).

The least favorable evaluation of Bruni is that he added no new facts (Schevill 1936), but also, he did not entirely purge his works of the miraculous, so long as the miracles benefited Florence (Wilcox 1969). Finally, Bruni's analysis of the social structure of Florence left much to be desired (Cochrane 1981).

Though in various ways overshadowed by his contemporaries, Giovanni Francesco Poggio Bracciolini (1380–1459) is rarely omitted from a discussion of Renaissance historiography. Poggio is usually cited for the unmatched zeal with which he collected ancient manuscripts (Thompson 1942:I), but Poggio was notable for other reasons too. He raised to a high level the appreciation of man as a material being (Garin [1947] 1965).

Francesco Tateo described his appreciation of the role that profit seeking played in bringing about the highest development of human culture as a "brilliant, materialistic vision of history" (quoted in Struever 1970:172). He was a keen analyst of public postures that hid private goals. Poggio arranged the publication of Niccolò Conti's account of his travels in Asia, a valuable contribution to ethnography and geography (Hammond 1963). Also a member of the humanist circle that formed around Salutati, Poggio, too, went on to be a chancellor of Florence and to write its history.

Flavio Biondo (1392–1463), whom Cochrane calls "the real founder of the scholarly investigation of Roman antiquities" (1981:38), brought archaeology into the historian's fold. He also conducted important philological studies, improved on existing historical periodization, presented the Middle Ages as a period worthy of study in itself, set history in a wider geographical scope, and produced enduring reference works (Cochrane 1981; Thompson 1942:I). Biondo was an itinerant scholar, but if he "was connected with any community at all, it was Florence," where he spent his formative years and established close ties with Bruni (Cochrane 1981:35).

Lorenzo Valla was the most effective philologist of the period, and he pushed his researches to their proper conclusions, though they were often an embarrassment to humanistic and other prejudices of the time. He pointed thoughtfully, for example, to the limitations of classical models for his time (Bouwsma 1973). Valla saw philology as a means of understanding the history of words, concepts, customs, and institutions (Garin [1947] 1965). He showed that the study of words was capable of "transforming manners and institutions in the present" (Cochrane 1981:148). He conceived of history "as the synthesis of all branches of human knowledge," says Garin ([1947] 1965:55), who quotes Valla's own words: "from history there flows a comprehensive knowledge of all things natural; . . . and a deep knowledge of customs and other kinds of wisdom." For Valla, Garin continues, history "is the method by which man takes survey of himself and which leads to the greatest possible enlargement of the horizon." Valla is best remembered for his decisive demonstration—on the basis of philological and historical data—that the so-called Donation of Constantine, one of the principal documents buttressing the medieval structure of pope and emperor, was a forgery (Valla [1440] 1922). The abstract study of language has profoundly influenced the understanding of mankind, much less the flow of human history, only a few times. Valla is responsible for one of those occasions.

Bartolomeo Scala (1430–1497), like Salutati, Bruni, and Poggio, was yet another humanist chancellor of Florence, and like the latter two, he also wrote a history of Florence (but died before completing it). Scala was better than most in citing his sources, and he showed unusual sensitivity to physical surroundings—both to produce history (through archaeology) and to give its events more order in space (Wilcox 1969). Scala reformed the Florentine chancery so that its valuable resources could be better preserved and more easily utilized for historical research (Brown 1979).

Most authorities, however, agree that in the period in which Scala wrote—the latter 1400s—Florentine historiography was less distinguished than in the earlier part of the century. The rise of the Medici, which put a damper on much political activity and discourse, is the usual explanation for the less exuberant historical writing of this period (Martines 1963). But there had been substantial continuity of thought in Florentine historiography from Salutati to Machiavelli and Guicciardini. Machiavelli and Guicciardini are generally regarded as the titans of the burst of historical writing in early-sixteenth-century Florence. Yet there were half a dozen other fine historians as well (Schevill 1936:xviii).

Gilbert 1965 sets the works of Machiavelli in the context of developments in Florence and elsewhere in Italy and Europe. From the 1430s until the 1490s Florence was dominated by the Medicis—first Cosimo, then his son Piero, then the latter's son, Lorenzo the Magnificent. It was a period in which Florentine intellectuals were more likely to discuss philosophy and literature than politics and history (Cochrane 1981; Gilbert 1965). But events took a decisive turn in 1494 when a French invasion destabilized Italy. The slow realization that a new epoch had been entered—an epoch that would see the rise of the European nation states and in which the affairs of Italy could not be understood apart from wider developments in Europe—turned Florence's thinkers toward historical and political studies with renewed energy (Gilbert 1965; Martines 1963).

Machiavelli served in Florence's chancellery, and like his illustrious predecessors there, he wrote a history of Florence. But he is best remembered for the *Prince* and the *Discourses upon Livy*, both written when he was out of office. They were written to convince the ruling powers that he should be reappointed to a position that would allow him to live the active political life he loved. Gilbert (1965:153) says of Machiavelli's the *Prince* and the *Discourses* that they "signify the beginning of a new stage—one might say, of the modern stage—in the development of political thought." The "dominating idea" in them "is an appeal to recognize the crucial importance of force in politics" (Gilbert 1965:154). They were intended "to reveal the laws which govern the world of politics" (Gilbert 1965:170). While he never clearly stated as much, Machiavelli's writings imply the autonomy of politics as a sphere of activity, but he clearly perceived that no state was an isolate and that each must "expand or perish" (Gilbert 1965:176–77, 178).

Machiavelli's search for general laws of politics rested on the idea, mentioned above, of the essential similarity of all men, especially their uniform egoism. He took a rationalistic and naturalistic approach to his subject matter (Gilbert 1965), and his aims were eminently practical. Machiavelli also perceived the limits of reason in political matters and drew attention to the role of *virtu*, in the sense of a "single-minded will-power" or "some undefinable inner force" (Gilbert 1965:179). The well-being of a state, he said, depended more on *virtu* than on any particular set of institutions (Gilbert 1965). He thought political action might result as much from instincts as from reason and that republican Rome's success rested on some harmony of institutions, *virtu*, and "life according to man's inherent natural instincts" (Gilbert 1965:191, 192). But institutions that work in one circumstance will not necessarily work in others: Machiavelli's views were relativistic (Gilbert 1965). Matters never being simple, Machiavelli shows more than any of his predecessors that "politics is choice and decision" (Gilbert 1965:200). With Machiavelli, history was subordinate to politics; history was studied to reveal its laws (Gilbert 1965). Some features of good historical writing were thereby slighted: Machiavelli's factual accuracy, critical sense, and honesty at times left something to be desired (Cochrane 1981; Gilbert 1965; Wilcox 1969).

Francesco Guicciardini shared many of Machiavelli's assumptions but initially had a greater faith in the role of rationality in political affairs. In an early work, the *Discorso di Logrogno*, Guicciardini systematically analyzed Florentine institutions in terms of the extent to which they corresponded to their original purposes (Gilbert 1965). The idea that government "ought to be organized on the basis of practical experience, historical knowledge, and human wisdom" informed the entire work, "one of the earliest . . . in which reasoning about politics is systematically based on the criterion of rational efficiency" (Gilbert 1965:98–99). Guicciardini, like Machiavelli, saw all governments as depending on force; the only important question was how well a government or institution promoted the well-being of the community (Gilbert 1965).

Guicciardini undertook two histories of Florence, in which he set new standards for factual accuracy and the use of documentary sources. He focused on political events and their causation, using history as an instructor in "the art of politics." He also provided excellent personality sketches, and he became a good judge of his sources. Finally, he began to perceive how all events in Italy were interconnected (Gilbert 1965).

Late in his life, Guicciardini undertook a *History of Italy*, the only work that he wrote not for his own edification but for publication (Gilbert 1965). He relied heavily on the standards for writing history set forth by Cicero (Gilbert 1965). By the time he began his work, Guicciardini had gained considerable respect for "passion, prejudice, blindness, and insight" in the conduct of human affairs (Cochrane 1981:299) and had lost much of his faith in reason, seeing *fortuna* as an all-powerful force. History, he said, might teach us something about war and government, but mostly it taught about the "inconstancy of all human affairs" (Gilbert 1965:289). Paradoxically, Guicciardini's stress on *fortuna*, which entailed a loss in the search for political laws, led to better history (Gilbert 1965). He showed a great concern for cause and effect: "why" took precedent over "what." This concern forced him to undertake more penetrating studies of personality, and he achieved a high level of psychological realism. He saw human nature as changed by events (Gilbert 1965:291–92). Guicciardini's *History of Italy* was novel in its scope of time and place, but it was all coherently structured by links of cause and effect (Cochrane 1981; Gilbert 1965). Guicciardini tried to obtain *all* relevant sources, and to weigh them critically. In this he approached the standards of the modern historian (Gilbert 1965).

Gilbert (1965) holds that historiography is primarily judged on the extent to which critical method has developed, especially with respect to the use of documentary rather than narrative sources. In the period of Machiavelli and Guicciardini, the standards improved. Guicciardini's *History of Italy* marked the point at which history achieved autonomy from political science and could focus on the "diverse and singular" and on "constant change" (Gilbert 1965:300–301).

Machiavelli's and Guicciardini's several contemporaries provided evidence for a wide development of historiography in the early 1500s. Giovanni Gioviano Pontano (1426–1503) was notable for giving attention to *how* to write history, though his views were set forth by Bernardo Rucellai (1448–1514). This was the first systematic discussion of the topic in the West (Cochrane 1981; Gilbert 1965). Bartolomaeus Fontius (1445–1513) gave a lecture that provided the world with what was perhaps the first brief history of historical writing (Gilbert 1965). Piero Parenti (1450–1519) wrote a history of Florence that emphasized the manifold connectedness of political events (Gilbert 1965). Bartolomeo Cerretani (1475–1524) wrote another Florentine history which, in accord with the general trend, was designed to provide an understanding of the present and be a guide to action. Cerretani stressed "factual accuracy and causal connectedness" (Gilbert 1965:233). Francesco Vettori (1474–1539) saw the interconnectedness of European history and wrote the first European diplomatic history (Gilbert 1965:248) He emphasized the role of force in politics and saw *fortuna* as all-powerful. Elsewhere, Gilbert (1968:492) draws attention to Donato Gianotti (1492–1573) for providing in 1525–26 a functional analysis of Venice, showing, with "a remarkable historical sense," the gradual development of its institutions (see also Bouwsma 1968). Except for Pontano, a Neapolitan, all the persons here mentioned by Gilbert were Florentines (Cosenza 1962). It should also be noted that these humanist histories and other histories in the narrower sense of the term were not the only accounts of the past being written in this time. Familial and personal records of various sorts were written by many people, implying that history in the broad sense must have been considered widely useful (Gilbert 1965).

Social Stratification

In the cities of Renaissance Italy, more than elsewhere in Europe, the differences between noble and non-noble first began to blur. Elements of the nobility joined in commerce with the rising bourgeoisie, giving birth to an elite defined by wealth and style of life. Inherited status lost much of the significance it had possessed in medieval Europe. These changes did not take place without reflection and planning. Indeed, because it was to a significant degree the product of "reflection and calculation," Burckhardt described the Renaissance state as "a work of art" ([1860] 1954:4), a generalization most applicable to Florence. Writing more than a hundred years after Burckhardt, Becker shifts the emphasis: "in the case of Florence, . . . [it] would have been better . . . to characterize the state not as a 'work of art' but rather as a work of public indebtedness and social mobility." The new class structure that Burckhardt described only implied social mobility; Becker makes it explicit and significant. Though it is seldom based on statistical data, the evidence for comparatively high rates of social mobility in Florence is strong, as a survey of Florentine social history shows.

Precisely when the opening of stratification began is not easy to say. We saw in the previous chapter that social mobility began to increase in the later Middle Ages and that many of the indices of an increasingly open society can be dated much earlier in Italy than in areas north of the Alps (Murray 1978).

There is some evidence that Italy, or major parts of it, may never have been as rigidly stratified as France and Germany in the Middle Ages (Bouwsma 1968; Seigel 1968). Moreover, there was a secular class of clerks (notaries, or *dictatores*) and scholars in Italy even in the Middle Ages (Holmes 1975). Notaries, frequently upwardly mobile, were the forerunners of the professional humanists (Seigel 1968). Further, there was considerable regional variation, due in part to the influence of the papacy in Rome and to Muslim kingdoms in the south. But in Tuscany, with Florence as its leading city, it is clear that sweeping changes in stratification occurred in the thirteenth and fourteenth centuries. Because Florence so often took the lead in Renaissance developments, I will continue to give it the greatest attention.

Before 1016 the Mediterranean had been a Muslim sea, but in that year the Pisans defeated the Muslims on Sardinia. Pisa, Genoa, Lucca, and other coastal towns of northwest Italy soon monopolized trade in the western Mediterranean, and from this time onward the merchant towns of this area began to contest the power of the great nobles. The merchants were often assisted by lesser nobles who took up residence in the towns and who themselves engaged in trade. An unprecedented, rudimentary self-government began to develop in the towns (Bouwsma 1973; Schevill 1936).

In the course of this development the Investiture controversy broke out between pope and emperor. Countess Matilda—then feudal ruler of the county that included Florence, Lucca, and Pisa—sided with the pope, and the merchants supported her. To gain the aid of Lucca and Pisa, the emperor granted them certain rights of self-rule in 1081. With or without such grants, Florence exercised similar autonomous rights at about the same time and also commenced to wage war without seeking the emperor's permission (Schevill 1936).

Although the emperor's nominal overlordship continued to be recognized by Florence (Brucker 1962), Countess Matilda had no effective successor. The emperor was henceforth heeded in Florence only when it was convenient for the Florentines or during the brief episodes when the emperor led substantial forces over the Alps to attempt to reassert his power in Italy. In 1107 Florence destroyed a castle of one of the lesser feudal lords of the area, the first of a long series of such actions that ultimately left *no* feudal strongholds in the whole of Tuscany. The contest

between pope and emperor provided the Florentines with many opportunities to eliminate their noble adversaries (Rubinstein [1942] 1965; Schevill 1936).

This was a period of remarkable experimentation in associational organization and in the organization of the communes, or cities, many of
which won varying degrees of autonomy, generally in northern Italy. The
communes were usually governed by councils composed of leading citizens,
who usually served brief terms. There were sometimes general assemblies
too. The clergy typically stood outside these organizations but were protected by them. The military force of the commune was divided into horse
and foot soldiers, with each citizen providing his own equipment and often
falling into one order or the other merely on the basis of which equipment
he could afford (Schevill 1936). The most influential of the new associations
were the guilds of great merchants and lawyers, which included many
knights too. Craft guilds developed, but they usually had lesser powers
(Schevill 1936).

Increasingly organized, wealthy, and powerful, the communes gained
control over feudal and private estates of the great nobles near them, gained
control of the bishops' estates, and in one place or another, won increasing
rights to self-rule. In Lombardy, for example, an alliance of communes
defeated a force under Frederick Barbarossa in 1177. In the subsequent
Peace of Constance, of 1183, the Lombard communes were given de jure
autonomy. Hitherto it had been clear that the communes could defeat
local noble forces, but they almost always yielded to imperial forces from
the north. This new turn of events was nearly the death knell of feudalism
(Schevill 1936:82). In Florence, city government continued to evolve. From
1250 to 1260 a genuinely popular government existed. In the latter year the
emperor's power was reestablished in Tuscany, ending the popular government but encouraging new efforts from the pope. He levied tithes on
the national churches throughout Europe, with the bankers of Florence
(and Siena) becoming his agents. In addition to whatever commissions
they received, the bankers made great fortunes by lending to the European
rulers the amounts they needed when they could not meet their tithes on
time, at 20 to 60 percent interest per annum. Moreover, alliances between
the pope, his European allies of the time, and the Florentine bankers gave
the latter equally lucrative commercial connections (Schevill 1936).

In 1282 the merchants and bankers of Florence succeeded in establishing
themselves as its constitutional authorities (Brucker 1962). Seven major
guilds (six of merchants and one comprising the legal profession), with

nominal representation from five lesser artisan guilds, chose six "priors" from among themselves. They served for only two months, living together in a single house. The chief executive officer was the *podestà*, an official instituted almost a century earlier. He was always a foreigner, served for one year, and functioned as a chief judge and head of the communal army. But now alongside the *podestà* another head of state was raised: a "captain and defender of the guilds." He led the twelve guilds organized as a militia to defend their interests. Members of the major guilds were clearly dominant. Though these guild-oligarchs were challenged from time to time, the basics of this system of government lasted from 1282 until the republic fell in 1533 (Kent 1978; Schevill 1936).

Because of the importance of its guilds, Florence is often referred to as a "guild republic," and its governing body the "priorate of guilds" (Becker 1960b:40; Becker 1967:218). While citizenship was not a simple concept in Florence (Kirshner 1971), membership in one or another of the guilds was in effect a requisite of full citizenship (Becker 1967, 1968a). Although the number of guilds expanded through time, the distinction between the greater guilds—*arti maggiori*—and the lesser guilds—*arti minori*—persisted. Generally the *arti minori* had less representation in the priorate (Becker and Brucker 1956). Succession to office was actually by drawing names of eligibles from a leather bag, but proportionately more eligible names were inserted from the major guilds' memberships. For a period in the mid to later 1300s, *arti minori* representation was probably numerically dominant (Becker and Brucker 1956). During this period substantial portions of the proletariat were also allowed to organize themselves, but in general they were rigidly excluded from any sort of effective organization (Becker 1967; Becker and Brucker 1956). With the establishment of the priorate of the guilds, antinoble sentiment ran high. Moreover, the interminable feuds of the nobles both prevented them from presenting a united front and gave the Florentines further excuses to curb their power (Schevill 1936).

In 1289 a law was passed freeing the serfs in all of Florence's dominions. While the rise of cities had already forced better treatment of the serfs, this law freed those who still suffered an unhappier condition in isolated upland districts. Most comparable acts north of the Alps came considerably later (Schevill 1936). But the nobles were soon to suffer even harder blows than the loss of their serfs.

In 1293 a broad constitutional document, the Ordinances of Justice, was put into effect. It widened the guild franchise, defined guild relationships, and established a seventh prior: the "Banner-bearer of Justice." It was his duty to execute sentences pronounced by the *podestà* against magnates, that is, nobles. He was assigned a force of one thousand men to follow his banner. The greater part of the ordinances concerned the magnates or grandees (*magnati* or *grandi*), who were defined as members of families that contained a knight. Using this criterion, a list of magnate families was drawn up, and some were given special disabilities. In the county controlled by Florence there were just under 150 of these "families" (*consorteria*; some were more like clans than families). There was a total of perhaps a thousand males in these magnate families (Schevill 1936). In the fourteenth century the number of magnate clans dropped to less than a hundred (Becker 1967).

Each male magnate had to swear obedience to the priors and put up a substantial bond that would be forfeited if the magnate did not keep the peace. In the event of crimes against commoners, fines would be assessed up to the amount of the bond. If a commoner were killed by a magnate, the penalty was death for the culprit, confiscation of his property, and destruction of his houses. In many respects the punishments were collective, making a wide range of relatives responsible for magnate behavior (Becker 1968a).

The Banner-bearer of Justice was soon called upon to take action against a magnate. The action was effective and marked "the Day of Judgment for the Magnates" (Schevill 1936:160). The skyline of medieval Florence had been studded by masonry towers that were the strongholds of the city's nobles, organized into "tower societies." The inexorable effect of the Ordinances of Justice was to level virtually all these towers by the 1400s, just as inexorably as the Florentine communal armies leveled the castles in the countryside (Becker 1967, 1968a). Draconian as the Ordinances of Justice were, they were repealed for only a few months in 1343 (Becker 1967). Though they were not always rigorously enforced and were rewritten at one point to lessen the scope of collective responsibility, they clearly demonstrate that the men in charge of Florentine affairs were far from slavish worshipers of noble blood-charisma.

The Ordinances of Justice also barred magnates from most of the positions of responsibility in Florence's communal government. However, legislation in 1295 enabled *all* members of constitutionally represented guilds to become priors (previously only those who actively followed a guild profession could so serve). This opened the way for certain lesser nobles to hold office even though they had no financial need to matriculate in a guild. But those designated as magnates were still barred (Schevill 1936).

In 1328 a revision of the Florentine constitution aimed (ineffectively) at broadening the base of power beyond the major guilds (Schevill 1936) contained a preamble declaring that public office should be open to all men whose conduct was appropriate. Such citizens, the preamble stated, should be able "gradually to ascend to and attain public office," while "those whose life does not render them worthy of it, should not climb up to government posts" (quoted in Rubinstein 1968:451). Not only had nobles lost charisma, but the meritocratic ideal was written into law.

The counterpart of the meritocratic ideal was that if magnates behaved in a lawful manner and were willing to renounce their noble status, and perhaps sever their connections with *consorteria* and move to another part of town to make the severance effective, then they could become commoners and hence achieve citizenship without magnate liabilities. Through the years a great many magnates did just that. In the 1340s "scores of noble clans . . . stood up in communal court and renounced their ancient ties and lineage" and were thus recognized by the Florentine councils as *populares et non magnates* (Becker 1968b:114).

The Florentines usurped the medieval powers of church and clergy no less than those of the feudal nobility. Autonomy was won from the pope, clerical immunities were eliminated, and the religious posts previously monopolized by the nobility were zealously taken up by Florence's new elite. The Florentines brought religious office and property fully under their control. Communal law became supreme, bowing neither to nobility nor clergy (Becker 1967, 1968a, 1968b, 1971; Becker and Brucker 1956; Martines 1963).

From 1343 to 1382 virtually all guilds participated in rule. Unprecedented numbers of "new men" (*novi cives* or *gente nuova*) entered government. Many of these new men were not even native-born Florentines, let alone members of old, established families. It has been called a "golden age of democracy" in Florence; even shopkeepers and artisans shared in government (Becker and Brucker 1956). This still left the mass of workers outside government, but for a brief period (1378–1381) a proletarian revolt resulted in something approaching genuinely popular rule (Brucker 1962; Schevill 1936). A woolen industry was the mainstay of Florence's economy, and from a quarter to a third of the city's populace worked in the industry. Generally the workers were rigidly controlled, but in 1378 the wool dyers revolted and achieved the right to form a guild organization for themselves.

However, oligarchy and tyranny of the sort made familiar to us by Machiavelli was to be the wave of the future.

Perhaps it is not correct to say that a true democracy emerged in Florence in the later 1300s (Martines 1963), yet by many standards the degree of popular participation in government was great. Given the rapid rotation of office, rules limiting repeat terms, and a further rule—the *divieto*— limiting the number of offices that could be held by members of a single family, several thousand men (out of an entire city population of 90,000 at most) necessarily held positions of responsibility in the government over the course of their lives (Baron 1960; Becker 1967; Brucker 1962). Certainly some Florentines regarded their republic as a democracy (Baron 1966).

In 1382 a more oligarchical regime established itself. In 1434 a party formed around Cosimo de' Medici came to power, stabilizing its position through manipulation of the process of choosing officials. Under Cosimo's son, Lorenzo the Magnificent, a new council became the instrument of Medician rule, but all the old councils continued to exist. Late in the fifteenth century, Florence, like the rest of Italy, was shaken as the great European powers invaded the peninsula and struggled for dominance. When conditions allowed, the Florentines sought to shore up their ancient governmental institutions by adopting one or another feature of the Venetian constitution. But in 1530 the republic finally collapsed; two years later the old governmental forms were swept away and Florence began two centuries of ducal autocracy under the Medicis (Schevill 1936).

Among the factors contributing to social mobility in Florence were the many wars the Florentines fought in their rise to greatness, the financial arrangements of the state, its burgeoning bureaucracy, and its mercantile-industrial economy. Florence initially employed a citizen militia under Florentine nobility, but the Ordinances of Justice destroyed the latter, and hired mercenaries took over the role of the former (Bayley 1961). Wars had to be financed, even though the benefits of empire were to be great. When, as in warfare, large sums of money were needed, the usual pattern was to borrow from the guilds or other great associations. But as time went by, the Florentine budget was put on a more stable basis by an institution called the Monte (the "mountain" of debt). Individual Florentines investing in the Monte received a guaranteed annual return, and shares in the Monte were negotiable. The state became a great stockholding corporation, with virtually the entire self-governing elite of the city as its investors (Becker 1967). Later, a related scheme, the Monte della Doti, financed state expenses. This was more on the order of a rotating credit system, which guaranteed the payment of the investors' daughters' dowries—in amounts varying with the shares invested. Both the Monte and the Monte della Doti linked the material interests of Florentines to the success or failure of their state. The Florentines were acutely aware of the significance of the Monte: it was referred to by the communal councils as "the heart of this body we call city, . . . [which] every limb, large and small, must contribute to preserving" (quoted in Becker 1968a:153). Since a Florentine woman without a dowry had, in those times, little chance of securing a desirable marriage, the Monte della Doti went beyond material interests in the usual sense to link the very reproductive interests of Florentines with their city (Becker 1968b). The elite of Florence were largely defined and graded in terms of their shares in the two *monti*.

In time the state became the principal consumer of capital, whereas earlier the great associations of Florence had collectively controlled far more wealth (Becker 1968a). The state effectively brought the old corporations under its control and reduced their significance. In the later 1300s even the guilds found their measure of autonomy increasingly limited. As the state grew, both its budget and its bureaucracy expanded (Becker 1967, 1968a; Seigel 1968). To make it more effective, it was progressively insulated from political interference through the development of impersonal law and the various steps taken to curb the powers of great families and associations that might try to pressure government (Becker 1967, 1968a).

Thus warfare and empire demanded a larger budget and a larger bureaucracy (Becker 1968a), and both of these in turn required a progressive expansion of Florence's elite. As investors in the *monti* and as bureaucrats and officials, ever-increasing numbers of new men were admitted to Florentine government and elite circles (Becker 1967, 1968a; Brucker 1962). It is for this reason that Becker emphasizes the role of social mobility in defining the Florentine state and in giving fifteenth-century humanism many of its peculiarities. The fifteenth-century humanists were the heirs of Florentine conditions in the mid to later fourteenth century (Becker 1960b).

Florence's severest test in the field of war came at the turn of the fifteenth century. Giangalleazzo (1351–1402), the duke of Milan, had brought much of northern Italy under his control. Florence was the last republican city-state to hold out, and it seemed doomed to go under too. But in 1402 Giangalleazzo suddenly died, and the threat dissolved. Hans Baron (1966) argues that this near-disaster made the Florentines acutely aware of their republican liberty and thus inspired them to hammer out the "civic human-ism" that stamped humanistic thought for well over a century thereafter.

Florence was industrialized to a degree unmatched elsewhere in the fourteenth and fifteenth centuries, and this necessarily entailed high rates of social mobility (Baron 1960). It was also in large measure a capitalist economy, which is "characterized by uncertainty, flexibility, risk, sharp rises and precipitous declines. . . . Inevitably, it contributes to social mo-bility and dislocation through perpetual redistribution of wealth" (Becker 1964:3; see also Brucker 1964). And while wealth was not the only factor, it was essential to high status in Florence (Martines 1963).

All these developments took place on a substantial scale. With a pop-ulation of about 90,000 in the early 1300s, Florence was one of the five largest and wealthiest cities of Europe (Brucker 1962). It drew much of its population, and many of its *novi cives* (Becker 1967, 1968a) from the surrounding countryside—not because of extraordinarily poor conditions there (compared to other rural areas) but because of the extraordinary opportunities in Florence. According to Marvin Becker, "This society was the creation of successive waves of immigrants who flocked to the cities in hope of increasing their patrimony and augmenting their status. This mass influx produced a quantitative change that is relatively easy to assess, for the phenomenal urban growth of the cities is a fact of number" (1968a:93).

I previously noted the growth of bureaucracy that accompanied Flor-entine expansion and prosperity. The extraordinary number of notaries who prospered in this setting—both as bureaucrats and as "lawyers" draw-ing up the ever more numerous contractual arrangements of commerce and industry—is often noted and is virtually identical to the situation in modern capitalist societies (Becker 1967, 1968a; Seigel 1968).

In sum, an order quite different from that of medieval Europe developed in Italy, a substantially urbanized order based on burgeoning commercial and industrial wealth. Wealth was important for a number of reasons. One was that it increased the general level of prosperity above that based more exclusively on medieval agriculture. This enlarged the class of people free from productive (or at any rate, agricultural) labor, allowed a more complex division of labor, gave more people the ability and need to support in-tellectual pursuits, and gave substantial numbers of people a sense of improving conditions and of the possibility of social movement (Gilmore 1952). Another reason was that this wealth went into hands other than, or in addition to, those of the old nobility. Thus patrons of learning emerged without the vested interests of the typical medieval nobility. Some of these patrons could perhaps only purchase books. Others, however, from humble beginnings grew fabulously wealthy, became more than rivals of the old nobility, and in fact patronized the era's distinctive ideologues—the humanists—to an extravagant degree (Holmes 1975; Russell 1954b; Trinkhaus [1940] 1965). Social mobility was a brute fact in much of Renaissance Italy, and it would have been extraordinary sociologically if the intellectuals of the day had failed to reflect it. It is not surprising that there was "an increasing questioning of the old order" (Gilmore 1952:69). Events in Italy had created a new class structure.

In order to assess further the significance of social mobility in Florence I will discuss three topics in greater detail: the social strata in Florence, the periods of greater and lesser rates of social mobility, and the attitudes of Florentines toward social mobility. Burckhardt ([1860] 1954:265) argued that social stratification in Renaissance Italy (Venice excepted) showed "the sharpest contrasts to medievalism." He drew attention to the fusion of classes, especially of the nobles and burghers dwelling together within the city walls. Starn (1971:427) expresses the extreme of a fusion argument: "In a political sense Florence, like most early modern European societies, was a one-class society; . . . even the very real economic and social differences within the office-holding class were bridged to some extent by common assumptions and common activities." Most modern authorities, however, use a three- or four-class system to describe Florentine stratification. The three-part scheme consists of *magnati* (nobles), *popolani grassi* (perhaps "people of substance" is an appropriate translation), and *popolo minuto* (little people). The fourteenth-century Florentine chroniclers "insisted" that these were the three classes of their community (Becker 1967:7). They were primarily legal classes. The *magnati*, as described above, were registered with the government and were subject to various onerous restrictions. This did not, of course, reduce their high social standing; nobles were often employed as envoys and were consulted by the government before certain kinds of policy decisions, and in times of war their military skills occasionally gained them temporary advantages (Becker 1967). Were it not for the government registration of *magnati* there is little doubt that the problem of defining them—deciding who was noble and who was not—would have been quite difficult. Intermarriage between *magnati* and *popolani* exacerbated the problem (Becker 1967). Brucker (1962:29n) cites E. Fiumi as having demonstrated "convincingly that very few Florentine magnate families were actually descendants of the feudal nobility."

The fact that the *magnati* could renounce their status, and that many petitioned and were allowed to do so, is itself convincing evidence that the Florentines had already adopted a definition of nobility in which descent gave way to behavior. In 1343 alone almost half of the magnates, 530 persons, were permitted to petition for the status of a commoner as a reward for their good behavior (Becker 1967). The logical extension of this was that if persons behaved like *magnati* (in the Florentine context this meant that if people *mis*behaved like *magnati*) they could be deprived of their *popolani* status and declared *magnati*. Brucker cites as examples the Cerchi, who "though not of noble descent, were designated as magnates in 1293 because they were rich, numerous and dangerous" and the Castiglionchi, who "though noble in origin, remained *popolani* because they were not sufficiently powerful to constitute a threat to the government of the guilds" (1962:29). In 1352 this procedure was regularized when a law was enacted allowing the priorate and the then twenty-one guild captains, by vote, to declare lawless commoners to be magnates (Becker 1967). In sum, the old feudal nobility of Florence seems almost to have disappeared by the thirteenth century, and their successors, the *magnati*, were increasingly defined by behavior rather than descent. By 1378 the magnates were all but eliminated as a political force in Florence (Becker 1967).

The *popolani grassi* seem to have been those legally nonmagnate persons who, having matriculated in a Florentine guild—especially one of the major guilds, the *arti maggiori*—had acquired essentially full citizenship rights. Most were reasonably wealthy, some enormously so. Some claimed ancient and respectable lineage in a manner little different from the magnates; others were clearly new men.

The *popolo minuto* formed the bottom of the social pyramid and were by far the most numerous. Although economic opportunities for the small man in Florence were no doubt better than in many other parts of Europe, the legal situation of the *popolo minuto* was unenviable. They were disproportionately taxed, were usually deprived of the right to associate for their own benefit (even for religious purposes), and were severely punished when they stepped out of line (Becker 1960b, 1967; Brucker 1962; Martines 1963). The *popolo minuto* had their day, however. During two periods in the fourteenth century, Florentines found their factionalism and fiscal problems so out of hand that they contracted with an allegedly experienced outside administrator, giving him virtually despotic powers, and allowing him to rule Florence. Brief as these despotic periods were, each one gave the *popolo minuto* somewhat better conditions and very much raised their ambitions. For example, under Walter of Brienne who for a period in the early 1340s was the despot of Florence, the wool dyers were allowed to form a guild and were even organized into companies and allowed to parade in uniforms. Within a short period of Walter's expulsion—he managed to alienate nearly everyone, including the *popolo minuto*—the wool dyers' right to organize was annulled. But they and other workers successfully revolted and for a brief period, as mentioned earlier, Florence enjoyed a semblance of democracy with genuinely broad participation. The number of new men admitted to office sharply increased under the dictator (Becker 1960a, 1960b, 1967; Becker and Brucker 1956).

Throughout the early Renaissance there was so much social mobility in Florence that, in spite of the chroniclers' insistence on its three-class structure, there is considerable evidence that it was far from adequate for all purposes. To solve some of the problems of understanding Florentine stratification, Brucker (1962:27–29) employs a four-class system, applicable after 1350. First came a patriciate of families long influential in Florentine affairs. Family ties and lineage were very important to them. Magnates formed the upper stratum of patricians, but decades of intermarriage with the more prestigious old *popolani* houses had welded them into a single socioeconomic (but not legal) class. Next came the *gente nuova*, men of newly acquired commercial wealth. Below them were "the petty bourgeois artisan-shopkeeper class," and finally there were "the unorganized and propertyless laborers."

While they by no means constituted a cohesive class in the sense that the patriciate did, the *gente nuova* did have certain common characteristics: obscure backgrounds, genealogies known only back to their grandfathers, sometimes no family name, generally no family (i.e., no cohesive kin-group affiliation), and hence an "isolated and vulnerable position" that led them to seek patronage and marriage alliances with the powerful. "What they all possessed in large measure was ambition" for wealth, influence, and social standing; it "was this quality which made their role dynamic in this period of Florentine history" (Brucker 1962:40). The life of Francisco de Marco Datini, a merchant of Prato but intimately associated with Florence (Origo 1957), provides an outstanding and massively documented example. Datini had sprung from membership in the lower guilds, as did many of the new men (Brucker 1962).

Brucker 1962 links his third class—the artisans and shopkeepers—primarily to immobile members of the lesser guilds. Except for their guild status, some members of the third class were scarcely differentiated from the laborers. "This mass of unorganized, unenfranchised, poverty-stricken humanity," Brucker concluded, "was the true *popolo minuto* of Florence" (1962:48–49). The bulk of the *popolo minuto* worked in the wool industry, the basis of Florence's productive economy (Becker 1967:195).

The problem of understanding Florentine stratification is complicated by two factors. One results from constitutional modifications. From 1282 onward the priorate of the guilds provided the fixed and central element in the Florentine constitution and was a key factor in the legal definition of social standing. But although the basic structure of guild stratification persisted, in time some new guilds were added to the *maggiori* category and many more to the *minori*. The boundary between *maggiori* and *minori* shifted, and elements once outside the guild system were shifted into it. The result was a significant amount of collective mobility (Becker and Brucker 1956).

The second complicating factor is that there was ample scope for individual mobility. The *novi cives*, so frequently referred to in all histories of Renaissance Florence, were individuals who moved from one stratum to another, often matriculating in the appropriate guilds either to achieve or ratify their new standing. Not only magnate families but also individual magnates, in amply documented numbers, voluntarily foreswore their high status. Brucker (1964:9) cites the case of a young petitioner in the wool trade who appealed "to be legally separated from his relatives 'who belong to a different rank and who lead less honorable lives and are not engaged in any trade.' This petition reflects a significant change . . . in the Florentine mentality, in which men now sought identification and status on their own merits, and did not wish to be judged by the condition and behavior of their kin." While perhaps poorly documented, individual men of the true *popolo minuto* no doubt also managed to move into the lower guilds. Becker (1967:180n) notes, for example, "that less than 5 percent of those communal office holders whose descent can be traced had immediate ancestors who were agricultural laborers." A figure anywhere near 5 percent for persons of that background alone—that is, not including urban laboring backgrounds—is not insignificant. In sum, the very discussion of classes in Florence repeatedly points to significant degrees of social mobility and a blurring of class lines generated by the ability to move from stratum to stratum rather than be confined by birth to a fixed station in life.

Let us now turn to the evidence for changes in the rate of social mobility in Florence. Within the guild structure and communal government there was a more or less regular *cursus honorum* (ladder of promotion, a term borrowed from ancient Roman usage). To some extent one passed through it merely as part of one's life cycle, but it was the channel for the upwardly mobile too, who would hold minor and then more significant offices in one or more guilds and move from there perhaps to provincial offices of ever higher grade or to lower offices in the city's administration. At the pinnacle was the priorate—also called the signory, a generic term for the highest magistracy in Italian towns (Becker 1967, 1968a). The very definition of a new man was one who, from his family, was serving in the priorate for the first time, particularly after 1343 (Becker 1968a; Brucker 1962). In 1343 the *divieto*, ancient legislation but often ignored, was put into effect. By its terms, as mentioned before, members of the same family could not hold high offices simultaneously and had to wait certain intervals before holding office again. This opened the floodgates to *novi cives*. In the selection of eligibles for the priorate in October 1343, the *majority* were new men. In fact, less than a third of the priorate from 1343 to 1348 were patricians (Brucker 1962), and in 1352 no less than two-thirds of the captains of the guilds were *novi cives* (Becker 1967).

Although the tempo of social mobility began to pick up much earlier (Becker 1967; Brucker 1962), the middle to later 1300s saw the highest rates of social mobility and the collapse of patrician resistance to ever-widening entry of new men into government (Becker 1967, 1968a). As mentioned earlier, during this period the wool dyers and other workers earned broader rights in guild and government too.

Between 1338 and 1346 economic conditions brought on a veritable wave of bankruptcies among the wealthiest and most prestigious families of Florence. Although some managed to hold their place in society, many went under (Becker 1967). The economy had begun to rebound by 1343 (Becker 1968a; Brucker 1962), providing the opportunity for new capitalist successes. Tax records from the year 1352 show that 40 percent of the households in the highest 2 percent of tax assessments were *gente nuova* households (Brucker 1962).

Martines (1963:75) says that by the middle of the fifteenth century, and probably by 1400, "the great age of social mobility in Florence was over." But elsewhere he says that "notable changes in the distribution of wealth" seem to have been a permanent feature of republican Florence, "throughout the fourteenth and fifteenth centuries" (Martines 1963:351). It should also be noted that the rates of social mobility in Florence were much greater than in Venice, Genoa, Siena, or probably most other comparable cities of the time (Baron 1960; Becker 1968a).

While there is some uncertainty about when social mobility began to decline in Florence, there is some agreement that it did decline, certainly by the middle 1400s, remaining comparatively low for long thereafter (see Litchfield 1971 for the sixteenth century and later). Correspondingly, a Florentine interest in genealogy burgeoned in the fifteenth century, presaging the "aristocratic society" of sixteenth-century Florence (Martines 1963:57). But in spite of greater de facto closure, the ideal of social mobility persisted. Thus Martines (1963:50, 278, 294), who speaks of "caste" in Florence by the late 1300s, says that the "illusion" of an open society was maintained thereafter; furthermore, he notes that the "optimistic climate" engendered by that illusion was the context in which the study of antiquity flourished. Trinkhaus ([1940] 1965:122) says that the theme of "social adjustment," of finding one's proper "career," remained an important element in humanist writings throughout the fifteenth and into the early sixteenth centuries. Baron, too, noted that social mobility and industrialization continued to "mold Florentine life" long after the fourteenth century (1960:448).

When the Medician party came to power in 1434, the meritocratic ideal was by no means abandoned. Cosimo de' Medici did not want his party to "harden into too close a corporation," a mistake he thought had been made by the oligarchs who had preceded him; therefore, as Schevill describes the situation,

In measure as the members of the lower ranks of society endowed with intelligence and energy amassed new fortunes they were to be admitted to the ruling circle. . . . [It] was Cosimo's intention that the reigning body of optimates should be constantly refreshed with new blood. As a result he had the ambitious, . . . rising young men of the common people on his side, for he placed no obstacle in the way of their aspiration. (1936:356; see also Cochrane 1981)

According to Kent (1978:115, n. 43), "a small but steady inflow of new families" into the ruling stratum persisted "at least to 1453."

In 1484, Piero Guicciardini, father of the great historian, described the continuing pattern of social mobility. Once newcomers achieve the lowest levels of office, he said,

they ascend from the lowest level and proceed to the next, always rising, and in their place are succeeded by even newer men to fill up the lowest ranks, and thus continually new men make the grade, and in order to gain them a place in the governing class it is necessary to eliminate from it long-established citizens; and that is what is actually done. (Quoted in Kent 1978:44)

In 1495, when democratic forces were prevalent again for a period, the Florentines established a Great Council, a borrowing from Venice. It had a hereditary component in that membership was basically confined to those who, within the last three generations, had had an ancestor who had served on one of the three principal magistracies. On the other hand, as many as sixty new members could be admitted each year. It was seen as a democratic council, presumably because of the large number of men who qualified for membership. In 1500 one in every four or five adult males was a member. It was not seen as a body of nobles, "as there no longer were any nobles in Florence and the very concept of nobility was unpopular" (Schevill 1936:439; see also Gilbert 1965). In the time of Machiavelli and Guicciardini it was still possible for men of talent to rise to high position, though it was rarer than it had once been (Gilbert 1965). In short, mobility declined during and after the 1400s, but it did not wholly disappear, and the ideal of social mobility was far from dead.

Let us look more closely at this ideal, first by assembling miscellaneous statements on the matter, then by examining the humanist debate on true nobility, and finally by assessing the extent to which Florentine historians were the products of social mobility and expressed opinions favorable to it. According to Becker, the idea that "true nobility was dependent upon deeds rather than birth" was the "capstone" of "consciously pursued ideals" in Florence (1967:3, 39). The "desire to attain high communal office," Brucker says, was a "sentiment shared by citizens of all classes" (1962:77). Martines found this desire to be understandable, for failing to enter politics "was to gamble with economic and social survival" (1963:178). One had not only to enter politics but to perform well, because "in Florentine life there was no room at the top for the leadership of men with mediocre political talents; rivalry was too keen, place too important" (Martines 1963:226).

The Florentines gave considerable thought to improving their positions: "Florentine diaries, memorials, and manner books are replete with prudent counsel for the social climber" (Becker 1967:26). Contemporary discussions of marriage also showed considerable concern for social mobility, pointing out the desirability of marrying up and the calamity of being forced to marry down (Brucker 1962, 1964; Martines 1963). Medieval notions on social mobility that stressed "meekness and contentment and minimized the competitive spirit" were "seriously challenged" in Renaissance Florence (Becker 1967:29n).

In an essay on the family, Leon Battista Alberti (1404–1472) noted that wealth led to familial stature but that wealth was difficult to maintain: rarely did it last more than three generations. "Many noble and honorable families of Florence . . . who formerly abounded in vast riches," he wrote, "have been reduced to misery and in some cases even to desperate need, owing to the injuries of fortune" (quoted in Martines 1963:78).

One of the major theses of a study of the humanists (Trinkhaus [1940] 1965) is that the precariousness of their positions gave them a sense of anxiety and pessimism. But this argument is partially refuted by a later study showing that most of the humanists were men of very considerable substance (Martines 1963). Nonetheless, there is ample evidence that Florentines in general *did* have a sense of anxiety, at least about their wealth and social position. Summarizing Origo's 1957 biography of the merchant Datini, Brucker (1962:45) says that his most striking character trait was an "overwhelming feeling of insecurity . . . manifested in every aspect of Datini's behavior." This was partly due to the "general instability of the age," but "it was much more the expression of the parvenu's rootlessness and isolation."

The intellectual discussion of social mobility is found primarily in the debate over "true nobility," a favorite topic of the humanists (Trinkhaus 1965). The question of whether true nobility depended on descent or was the result of personal virtue had been debated at length in classical antiquity. In the late medieval period there were already some who spoke out on behalf of personal merit (Murray 1978). But in Renaissance Italy the subject was to receive intense attention.

Hans Baron pointed out that "one of the most widely read and long remembered Renaissance treatises on true nobility was . . . the *Disputatio de Nobilitate*," the object of which was "to demonstrate the superior merit of the lowly born plebian who has risen by his own effort" (1966:419–20). The apparent author was Buonaccorso da Montemagno (1392–1429). The vehicle for Buonaccorso's argument is a contest between a Roman patrician and a plebian for the hand of a fair noble maiden (she chooses the plebian). Buonaccorso's "final standard is the confidence that Nature extends the same chance to become noble or ignoble to the high and lowly born alike, according to the fruitful use they make of their lives" (Baron 1966:420).

Becker (1967, 1968a, 1971) traces in considerable detail the changing attitudes toward social mobility in Florence, with special attention to the views of the historians. Initially there was a concern that the influx of rustics into the city would contaminate the "blood" of Florentines, that the rising merchant class was a threat to society, and that the poor treatment of the feudal nobility was an affront to morality and good government.

Although Dante (1265–1321) was ambivalent on the matter—he denigrated high lineage and appears ultimately to have opted for nobility of action rather than blood—he also decried the mixing of Florentines with the "beastly" immigrants from rural areas, and he deplored the cupidity of his age. Quite similar ideas were found in the early portions of the chronicles of Giovanni Villani (see also Rubinstein [1942] 1965). But by the latter half of the fourteenth century there was a marked shift in attitude. Giovanni, more so his brother Matteo, and also the chronicler Stefani, all stopped worrying about mixing blood and began to sing the praises of the new men, the merchants whose incomes underpinned the greatness of Florence, while blaming the magnates and other powerful old families for the city's ills. The humanists—with Salutati taking the lead—merely refined the ideas that the vernacular writers had already expressed. As Marvin Becker has said, "With Matteo, . . . Stefani, and the civic humanists from Salutati to Bruni, the old prejudices against the *novi cives* abated as they did against trade and the expansion of the polis. . . . Ambition, wealth, and energy were no longer so generally regarded as obstacles to virtue" (1968a:35–36). By the time of Bruni and Poggio, wealth, trade, and commerce were depicted in positive terms, as important to Florence "as blood is to the individual" (Becker 1968a:135). Salutati was one of the key links between the vernacular trends and the subsequent development of humanist ideas on nobility. He "spoke of Florence as governed by an aristocracy of deeds— the merchants and artisans—rather than by an aristocracy of birth" (Becker 1967:178), and he redefined nobility in terms of education and virtue (Trinkhaus 1965).

The *Disputatio de Nobilitate*, which interpreted the Florentine ideal of social mobility, was written by a member of Bruni's circle of Florentine humanists (Baron 1966:420, 455). For Bruni the possibility of upward mobility was an incentive for the public-spiritedness and industry that made Florence great:

Equal liberty exists for all; . . . the hope of winning public honors and ascending is the same for all, provided they possess industry and natural gifts and lead a serious-minded and respected way of life; for our commonwealth requires *virtus* and *probitas* in its citizens. Whoever has these qualifications is thought to be of sufficiently noble birth to participate in the government of the republic. . . . [I]t is marvellous to see how powerful this access to public office, once it is offered to a free people, proves to be in awakening the talents of the citizens. For where men are given the hope of attaining honor in the state, they take courage and raise themselves to a higher plane. (Quoted in Baron 1966:419; see also Becker 1968b; Struever 1970; and Wilcox 1969)

Bruni saw Florence's antinoble legislation (e.g., the Ordinances of Justice) as critical to its progress (Baron 1966). Poggio shared these views. He too wrote a treatise on nobility, in which the main protagonist defends achieved rank (Bracciolini [1440] 1978; Kristeller 1965). Poggio defended Florentine liberty as a "more solid and truer kind":

For not one or another single man governs here, nor does the arrogance of optimates or noblemen command, but the people are called on the basis of equal right to perform public functions in the commonwealth. As a consequence, highly placed and humble persons, members of noble families, and commoners, rich and poor work together with a common zeal for the cause of liberty. (Quoted in Baron 1966:408)

While in its results the aim of equality fell short of the mark (Rubinstein 1968), the ideal was clear, and the anticaste feeling was unmistakable. Finally, Scala apparently did not write at length on nobility, but his views were clear. He implied that even "the man in the street" might be truly noble, and the very decree that made him a Florentine citizen quoted Juvenal: "Virtue is man's only true nobility" (Brown 1979:282).

Machiavelli was opposed to the acquisition of high position on the basis of either birth or wealth. He thought that the truly great men of history were disproportionately of low, obscure, or otherwise unfortunate origins (Bondanella 1973). He thought that Roman history showed that *virtu* required poverty, or at least economic equality (Gilbert 1965). While Machiavelli had a sound humanist education, he wrote in the vernacular and was firmly in favor of popular government (Gilbert 1965). He considered the democratization of the 1340s to be a splendid achievement, though he regretted the loss of the Florentine nobility's martial spirit (Becker 1967, 1968a). Guicciardini took a more aristocratic view, condemning the rampant ambition that characterized his time (Cochrane 1981:295; Gilbert 1965). But Guicciardini was fully aware of the social mobility of the period. In his maturity, events cast him down, and he lamented that "from the extreme height of honors and esteem, of important affairs and general renown" he had been "suddenly thrown down to the other extreme into an idle, abject, and private life without dignities, without business," and "inferior to any small citizen" in Florence. Thus he discovered "what children and unlettered men know: that prosperity does not last and fortune changes" (quoted in Gilbert 1965:281). Later, Donato Gianotti (1492–1572), "drafting the last great program of democratic constitutional reform for Florence," still advocated a wide admission to government to satisfy men's "natural ambition" (Baron 1966:429). To my knowledge, no substantial Renaissance historian wrote a direct defense of caste.

In sum, there was a continuous development of the ideal of social mobility in Florence, traceable in the vernacular as well as the Latin humanist writings and common to all the historians. "The historically minded," Becker concluded, "subscribed to notions of an open society where talent and deeds, not birth and privilege, would triumph" (1971:157). Clearly Becker has seen in Florence the correlation that this book seeks to show was a much wider phenomenon. A corollary is stated by Plumb (1961:29) when he identifies the following questions for which the Renaissance historians sought answers in the history of antiquity: "What made men succeed? Or fail?"

It was not only in Florence that social mobility was championed. But there was a special connection between Florence (the ideal of social mobility) and historiography. Becker (1967:8) says all the vernacular chroniclers were *popolani*, that is, members of a class deeply marked by social mobility. Cavalcanti was the only possible exception. His family was indeed of the magnate class. But though an old Florentine family—coming into prominence in the twelfth century—it was not descended from feudal nobility (Martines 1963). Two factors make Cavalcanti's case ambiguous. First, he is not in fact very highly regarded as a historian, as noted earlier. Second, he had a very lively sense of his own personal social mobility. "I prefer to look after my own business affairs," he wrote. "This is what has raised me above the other citizens. I know that trade is the source and basis of my being honored by the Republic. . . . For when I was poor, far from being honored, not a citizen who knew me pretended that he had ever seen me" (quoted in Martines 1963:21).

Between 1427 and 1494 five humanists held the post of chancellor of Florence; four of them, including Bruni and Poggio, wrote histories. None of the historian-chancellors had actually been born in Florence, and all of them had obscure parentage. Scala even boasted "of having risen from the ranks of the underprivileged" (Wilcox 1969:6n; see also Seigel 1968). Bruni was a self-made man, a point that even Bruni's contemporaries stressed (Trinkhaus [1940] 1965:112; Martines 1963). Poggio, too, was of humble origins (Martines 1963:263). Since each was a product of the opportunities provided for social advancement in Florence, it should occasion no surprise that they championed open stratification. Machiavelli neither sympathized

with Florence's aristocracy nor was a member of it. Though the Machia-
vellis were an old and distinguished family, Niccolò "belonged to an impoverished branch, the decline of which he had experienced in his own
lifetime" (Gilbert 1965). Guicciardini was a member of the aristocracy and
sympathized with it, but as noted above, he considered social mobility to
be a normal aspect of life.

Generally speaking, the other cities of Italy lagged behind Florence in
the development of historiography, even though some of them began their
chronicle traditions earlier (Thompson 1942:I). It also seems likely that
none of them offered the opportunities for social mobility, nor championed
it as an ideology, as much as did Florence. Hence the connection between
improving historiography and social mobility is well illustrated in Florence.
Later, Venice will serve to illustrate contrasting connections within the
Renaissance.

Concomitants

Before turning to Venice we should note the extent to which Florence
and cities like it possessed the full complex of concomitants. The Renaissance conception of human nature as uniform has already been mentioned.
The humanist historians saw the attempt to understand human nature as
a principal task of historical studies (Becker 1971; Garin [1947] 1965; Kristeller 1961; Struever 1970). Because they saw human nature as perfectible,
education was a central preoccupation of the humanists (Bouwsma 1973;
Kristeller 1965; but cf. Cochrane 1981, which notes that the humanists
assumed that character was fixed at birth or conception). "Never in history,
except perhaps in our own time," according to Lewis Spitz, "has so much
been written on educational theory and practice as in the age of the
Renaissance" (1971:651). The humanists largely succeeded in convincing
the ruling stratum that it would only deserve its position if it were properly
educated (Kristeller 1965), but in Florence, education was not for the elite
alone. Marvin Becker concluded that in Florence "knowledge was not an
arcane preserve but a field for popularizing. Few generations of writers
had a higher estimate of the educability of their fellow citizens than did
these Florentines. From the humble materials of everyday burgher life they
created a formidable company of historical types" (1971:158).

Our term *humanism* came into being to describe Renaissance educators
and the educated, whose efforts centered around the *studia humanitatis*
(Grendler 1971; Kristeller 1961; Seigel 1968). The secularity of the humanists

was a matter of degree. According to Kristeller (1961:73), the Renaissance was a "fundamentally Christian age" in that the basic "convictions of Christianity were . . . never really challenged." But he also says that insofar as nonreligious concerns had achieved a place as large as or larger than religion in Renaissance thought, "the Renaissance was pagan." Compared to the Middle Ages, the Renaissance was much more concerned with secular matters (Kristeller 1965; Plumb 1961). In the specific case of historical writing, Ullman notes, "Everyone knows that Bruni and other historians of the Renaissance secularized history" (1946:55; see also Cochrane 1981 and Dannenfeldt 1954b).

The individualism unleashed in the Italian Renaissance has been a matter of common knowledge at least since the publication of Burckhardt's *Civilization of the Renaissance in Italy* in 1860. Renaissance thought and literature aimed "to a degree unknown to the Middle Ages and to most of ancient and modern times, at the expression of individual, subjective opinions, feelings, and experiences" (Kristeller 1965:65). While the state and family placed certain limitations on Florentine individualism (Becker 1968a; Cochrane 1981; Martines 1963), Burckhardt's thesis has not been seriously challenged.

Reflecting the period's individualism, biography and portraiture flourished in the Renaissance (Kristeller 1961, 1965). Reflecting the secular trend, many more secular biographies were written than biographies of saints (Kristeller 1965:27). Biography in the Renaissance "was much more a natural expression" of the age's "intense individualism" than it was a mere reflection of or borrowing from antiquity (Thompson 1942:I, 488–89; see also Dannenfeldt 1954b). The earliest influential biographers, Petrarch and Boccaccio, were Florentines, and Florence demonstrated a very strong interest in political biography (Martines 1963:281).

Realistic portraiture was no less particularly associated with Florence. The school of the Florentine artist Giotto (c. 1266–1337) "set art on a new course of realistic representation." Giotto's "figures are not, as in earlier medieval painting, symbolic emblems of biblical persons but men and women with perceptible body and weight, displaying visible emotions" (Holmes 1975:143). From Giotto onward there was progress in Florence in rendering facial expression (Berenson 1967). The Florentine painters were the most addicted to figure studies, particularly with conveying a tactile sense of the material solidity and motion of the body (Berenson 1967). The bane of Florentine painting, according to Berenson 1967, was an obsession with scientific naturalism and with the development of technique to render one's subject ever more naturalistically. There was, to be sure, still a symbolic element in Florentine art (Antal 1947; Becker 1968a), but the increased realism and aesthetic success of Florentine painting and sculpture throughout the Renaissance needs no further attention here (see the previous chapter's discussion of realism in art). Martines (1979) sees the distinctive features of Florentine art, including its naturalism and its emphasis on individuals, as a direct reflection of Florentine republican ideals (even though he thinks that by the fifteenth century the ideals were seriously divorced from reality). The importance of secular patronage for Florentine art is amply documented (Antal 1947).

The social sciences, too, developed in the Renaissance. Nicolai Rubinstein contended that "the beginnings of political thought are always closely related to the awakening of the interest in history" ([1942] 1965:198). We saw above the extent to which Renaissance historical writings merged with political science. From Dati's structural description of Florentine government, through Bruni's analysis of its functional cohesion, to Machiavelli's generalizations on political dynamics there is a clear and brilliant line of development. To some degree Renaissance political science overlapped with sociology. Bruni's *On the Politeia of the Florentines*, in which he argued that Florence ceased to be a full-fledged democracy when its citizens gave up the practice of arms in favor of hiring mercenaries, is, Hans Baron concluded, a "masterpiece of . . . sociological reasoning" (1966:427). Bruni and others also studied customs and ways of life, sometimes in the context of geography cum ethnology (Dannenfeldt 1954b; Garin [1947] 1965). The use of archaeology to rediscover the past was mentioned earlier. Also related to social science was the development of the science of statistics, which Burckhardt ([1860] 1954) said first occurred in the Italian Renaissance (see also Murray 1978). Psychology and social psychology were closely related to the humanists' efforts to study human nature, explore biography, interpret history, and understand political life (Becker 1971; Struever 1970; Wilcox 1969).

In the natural sciences, too, Burckhardt saw the Italian Renaissance as exceptional, concluding that it was unusual both in the widespread popular interest that science evoked and in the heights of its scientific achievement: "Italy, at the close of the fifteenth century . . . held incomparably the highest place among European nations in mathematics and the natural sciences" ([1860] 1954:214). But Petrarch, the Florentine founder of humanism, had been hostile to natural science (Garin [1947] 1965), and most of the outstanding figures in science date from the middle to the late Renaissance.

Florence produced Leonardo da Vinci (1452–1519); and Galileo (1564–1642), born in Pisa of an old Florentine family, spent his productive years in Florence.

Like China, Renaissance Italy presents a clear-cut case of the extraordinary growth of divination. According to Burckhardt ([1860] 1954) many popular superstitions did not vary much between the Middle Ages and the Renaissance. But in intellectual, ruling circles the differences were pronounced, especially with respect to astrology, which early in the thirteenth century

suddenly appeared in the foreground of Italian life. . . . Soon all scruples about consulting the stars ceased. Not only princes, but free cities, had their regular astrologers, and at the universities, from the fourteenth through the sixteenth century, professors of this pseudo-science were appointed, and lectured side by side with the astronomers. . . . [T]he astrologers might be highly respected and show themselves everywhere. There were also far more of them in Italy than in other European countries. . . . All the great householders in Italy, when the fashion was once established, kept an astrologer. (Burckhardt [1860] 1954:383, 384; see also Plumb 1961)

Astrology was not the only form of divination. There were various omens, prodigies, auguries, geomancy, chiromancy, the practice of opening a book to a chance passage, which was then used to divine, and other sorts of magic (Burckhardt [1860] 1954). Lessa (1968:175) found that body divination "was marked during the . . . Renaissance, when [it] received its greatest support from the intelligentsia." Burckhardt ([1860] 1954:392) also draws attention to divination's intellectual support, asserting that "we know positively that the humanists were peculiarly accessible to prodigies and auguries." He cites as an example the humanist chancellor-historian Poggio Bracciolini, the "same radical thinker who denied the rights of noble birth and the inequality of men" ([1860] 1954:392; see also Kristeller 1965). Before Poggio, the chronicler Giovanni Villani was much taken with astrology (Dannenfeldt 1954b; Green 1972; but cf. Burckhardt [1860] 1954). After Poggio, Francesco Guicciardini was no less concerned with it (Starn 1971). Villani, Poggio, and Guicciardini were all Florentines. So was the great humanist Marsilio Ficino, who defended astrology and drew horoscopes for the family of Lorenzo the Magnificent (Burckhardt [1860] 1954). But not everyone was a believer. The subject was hotly debated, and Pico della Mirandola (1463–1494), author of the famous *Oration on the Dignity of Man* and another product of the "Florentine milieu" (Martines 1963:298), effectively refuted the claims of astrology (Burckhardt [1860] 1954). Finally, linked to the Renaissance concern for astrology was an equally great concern with *fortuna* (Kristeller 1965). Lessa (1968) deals at length with the reasons why Renaissance men should have been more concerned with divination than their medieval predecessors had been, and the anxieties engendered by social mobility are prominent among those reasons. Not only is the nexus of concomitants clear in Renaissance Italy, then, but many of the connections among them have already caught the attention of specialists on the period.

VENICE

James Westfall Thompson once observed that "one of the anomalies of Renaissance historiography is that in spite of the enormous mass of its archives, Venetian historiography was so laggard in making its appearance" (1942: I, 482), which was noted even at the time (Labalme 1969). What Thompson refers to is the full-blown humanist historiography of the Renaissance. On the other hand, the Venetian chronicles had been of a high standard, but they were not public, were not even widely circulated, and were often anonymous (Bouwsma 1968; Cochrane 1981).

The Venetian patrician chronicles were similar to those of medieval Europe, particularly in the lack of individuality of their successive authors, whereas individuality was abundantly present already in Giovanni Villani's Florentine chronicle (Baron 1968b). Not only were the Venetian authors virtually without individual personalities, so too were the people they wrote about:

> Perhaps in no state of importance equal to that of Venice are we left in such obscurity as to personal details regarding its great men; material for biographies of leading Venetian statesmen and soldiers is singularly scanty. Venice demanded and secured the effacement of the individual, and impressed upon its citizens, one and all, that the state was everything, the individual nothing. (Brown 1907:84; see also Bouwsma 1968)

Later, an eighteenth-century Venetian noted "the curious paucity of biography" in the literature of his people (Bouwsma 1968:66). Brucker (1967) puzzles over the relative absence of biography in Venice and can only note that, whatever the cause, it did not affect Florence.

Although Burckhardt identified individualism as a key ingredient of the Italian Renaissance, he was fully aware that Venice was an exception to many of his generalizations, the exception showing most strikingly when the two cities of Florence and Venice are compared: "Florence, the city of incessant movement, . . . has left us a record of the thoughts and aspirations of each and all who, for three centuries, took part in this movement [i.e., the Renaissance], and Venice [was] the city of apparent stagnation and political secrecy. No contrast can be imagined stronger" ([1860] 1954:51). Note Burckhardt's phrase "apparent stagnation," for Venice did change over time; only in its mythology was it unchanging (Bouwsma 1968; Cochrane 1981). Note also the "political secrecy" Burckhardt mentioned. This myth of changelessness almost implies no political activity, and maintenance of the myth seems closely related to a virtual taboo on the public discussion of politics.

At the core of the myth of eternal Venice there were three important beliefs. The first listed by Cochrane (1981:65), and which he found support for in "all" the Venetian chronicles, was the thesis that Venice "had always been governed by noble families." Another was the belief that Venice had been Christianized directly by St. Mark (i.e., not through Roman proselytization) and that his relics, preserved in Venice, "guaranteed the survival of the Republic forever." This myth, buttressing Venice's claim to independence from pope and emperor, was a staple of official and unofficial histories of Venice (Bouwsma 1968; Cochrane 1981). No less important in the Venetian myth was an annually celebrated victory over a Roman fleet and a claim to have arranged a peace in 1177 between Frederick Barbarossa and Pope Alexander III. Celebrated in ritual, art, and literature, and thus ever before the people's eyes, these images of Venice seemed to place it almost "outside and above" Christendom (Bouwsma 1968:56). Venetians were aware that their location in the lagoons had insulated them from the centuries of turmoil on the Italian mainland (Bouwsma 1968). For all these reasons, Venice claimed an ancient and unchanging stability that reduced the significance of overt politics.

In Venice there was for long no "sophisticated tradition of formal political discourse" (Bouwsma 1968:52). When Francesco Barbaro, a Venetian patrician writing in the early 1400s, did discuss political matters, it was quite out of character for a Venetian, and it perhaps reflected Barbaro's visit as a youth to Florence, where he "probably came into contact with members of the ruling group" (Bouwsma 1968:71). Burckhardt ([1860] 1954:53) cites the story of a teacher, "accustomed to the frank loquacity of the scholars of his day" outside of Venice, who was astonished "that the young [Venetian] nobles . . . could not be prevailed upon to enter into political discussions." James C. Davis suggests that the shortage of political thinkers in Venice was perhaps the result of government censorship by men who "had little taste for thought-provoking political writing" (1962:139). Not until late in the sixteenth century was there significant political discourse in Venice (Bouwsma 1968; Grendler 1971).

Many features of the Renaissance that we associate with humanism were slow to develop in Venice or developed only weakly there (Bouwsma 1968; Burckhardt [1860] 1954; Cochrane 1981). The Venetians did not, for example, show that enthusiasm for classical antiquity so prevalent elsewhere in Italy (Burckhardt [1860] 1954). Renaissance art, particularly its concern with individualism, was slow to come to Venice (Bouwsma 1968; Berenson 1967). When individual portraiture was commissioned, it subdued individualism by, for example, avoiding the full face: "In the portraits of the Doges . . . Venice wanted the effigies of functionaries entirely devoted to the State, and not of great personalities, and the profile lent itself more readily to the omission of purely individual traits" (Berenson 1967:17). Even when the techniques of individual portraiture were fully developed in Venice, as in the works of Georgione (1478?–1511), "the least apparent object was the likeness, the real purpose being to please the eye and to turn the mind toward pleasant themes" (Berenson 1967:18). In subject matter, Venetian painting was markedly concerned with pageantry (Berenson 1967; Martines 1979).

Education in Venice served practical needs and was closely controlled. Physicians and jurists, rather than grammarians and rhetoricians, received honors in Venice (Bouwsma 1968; Burckhardt [1860] 1954). Although Venice patronized the University of Padua, such humanism as was taught there seemed to make little impact on Venetians. After 1434, Venetian citizens were legally forbidden to attend any university other than the University of Padua; academic titles obtained elsewhere were void. Efforts to create a university within Venice were discouraged by the government. Only in 1443 did the government decide to support the humanistic studies of grammar and rhetoric, and then principally to meet the needs of its chancellery (Bouwsma 1968).

Although Venice was no less prosperous and was more populous than Florence, it seemed to many historians, in sum, to be anachronistic, "still essentially medieval," and only adopting the intellectual and social features of the Renaissance "when the rest of Italy was entering the baroque age" (Bouwsma 1968:83–84).

Social Stratification

Corresponding with these intellectual peculiarities of the republic, Venice had a "caste-like . . . nobility" (Davis 1962:15). How did Venice acquire or maintain a castelike social system in the ferment of late-medieval and Renaissance Italy? Much of the early history of Venice is shrouded from view. In spite of the Venetian myth, however, we know that Venice was indeed under Roman imperial control and was later a part of the Byzantine Empire (Bouwsma 1968; Brown 1907). Nonetheless, it is true that as the medieval period came to a close, Venice had for long enjoyed a de facto if not a de jure autonomy, probably in part because of her geographical position. In a manner rather parallel to developments in Florence, a new aristocracy of commercial wealth arose in Venice between the late eleventh century and the early fourteenth. Venice became the preeminent power in the Adriatic Sea. The commercial aristocracy sought to crush the power of the doge (duke), for although his position was elective, he was the linchpin of the old feudal nobility, and frequently was one of them. Before the end of the fourteenth century, the doge had become a figurehead, while the power of both the old nobility and the rights of the people were sharply curbed too. At the same time, the new commercial aristocracy augmented its own power and organizational effectiveness. All this was the prelude to the *serrata*, the "closing" of the Great Council of Venice (Bouwsma 1968; Brown 1907).

When a ducal interregnum gave the new aristocracy an opportunity to consolidate its power in 1172, the Great Council (Maggior Consiglio) was formed (or reshaped; see Davis 1962). Both the new aristocracy and the old nobility acted in concert at this time to eliminate the people's role in electing the doge. Owing to the mode of election to the Great Council, it was not then closed; in fact, it even expanded participation in government. But the new aristocracy gained ever more of the Great Council's offices and positions of power. The new aristocracy already realized that its purposes would best be served by turning itself into a "caste" (Brown 1907:54). Thus, instead of repudiating blood nobility, as took place in Florence, the new aristocrats sought to turn themselves into a new blood nobility.

After the formation of the Great Council, the attempts to curtail the power of the doge moved on apace, accompanied by a marked increase in the ceremony attached to his office. Eventually he became not merely a figurehead but almost a captive within the palace. If elected, he was required to serve, and all members of his family lost most of their officeholding rights. The doge could never resign or quit Venice. A complicated system of electing the doge that was instituted in 1229 effectively deprived the old nobility of its power (Brown 1907). In 1286 an aristocratic scheme for closing membership in the Great Council was officially proposed but was defeated. Three years later the doge died, and the people attempted to reassert their right to participate in choosing his successor, by supporting a popular but timid noble. He wisely withdrew to the mainland, and a member of the new aristocracy was elected doge. In 1297 he moved closure of the Great Council. The motion carried, and a year later it was amended to even further restrict entry. To be a member of the Council, one had to "prove that a paternal ancestor had at some time sat in the Great Council" (Brown 1907:64). The result of these actions, James Davis points out, has "traditionally been considered a 'closing' of the Great Council by a group of men determined to become an exclusive political caste" (1962:17). Critics of the Venetian constitution saw the *serrata* as a reversal of the earlier trend toward greater equality (see, e.g., Bouwsma 1968).

A popular uprising in 1300 was brutally suppressed, and popular elements were quiescent for a long time thereafter. A decade later a party of old nobility attempted rebellion, but this too failed. When its exiled leader died, the old nobility died with him (Brown 1907).

A Council of Ten, which perhaps existed before 1310 but which in that year was commissioned to investigate the conspiracy of old nobles, gradually became the real ruling body of Venice. Its commission was renewed a few times, and in 1335 the body became permanent. With the old nobles quelled and the Council of Ten supreme, Venice's government was fixed in form for many years to come. In 1423 sovereignty formally passed to the Great Council, when it absorbed the long-moribund rights of the popular assembly; popular approval of a new doge was dropped as a formality. A "dense obscurity" overhangs many of these events, however, and they are not well understood (Brown 1907:77–78; Bouwsma 1968).

It is important to realize that the Great Council was not just one council among others. It was rather large—in the sixteenth century comprising 4 to 5 percent of the population and perhaps a higher proportion earlier. Council membership was a prerequisite to holding any office of political importance in Venice, and nobility and membership in the council were synonymous (Bouwsma 1968; Brown 1907; Davis 1962).

In 1315 the republic began to keep official records of all who qualified for membership in the Great Council. In the ensuing "rush of citizens to establish their nobility," enough "abuses appeared in the register" to require severe decrees to rectify them (Brown 1907:64–65). Various agencies and offices were set up to oversee these matters. Although new members were theoretically admissible (Davis 1962:16–18), "free circulation from the people . . . was effectively choked" (Brown 1907:65). Moreover, nobility that was traced to before 1172, the year when the Great Council was established, became meaningless too. Thus the people, and major elements of the old nobility, were hereditarily excluded from the Great Council, which itself became a hereditarily exclusive ruling caste. From 1328 until 1380 (when, after the War of Chioggia, thirty families were admitted) admissions seem to have ceased altogether (Brown 1907; Davis 1962). Even the families that were admitted because of their contributions to the war effort took no important part in government, and for the next 265 years virtually no new member was admitted. Davis concluded that this was a deliberate policy (1962:18). In the fifteenth and sixteenth centuries, "rules designed to preserve the body from contamination were perfected"; they involved the regulation of marriage, the exclusion of illegitimate sons, the careful scrutiny of alleged nobles from the provinces, and the recording of noble births and marriages in Golden Books (Brown 1907; Logan 1972). Somewhat similar developments occurred elsewhere in Italy, but Venice was unique in the early date and duration of its closure (Davis 1962).

In theory, all the nobles were equal and could sit anywhere in the Council. But nearly all had trade as the basis of their wealth, some were indeed more successful or wealthy than others, and some did rise or fall *within* the nobility. On the other hand, various government measures attempted to limit the amassing of great personal fortunes, and such major capital items as galleys were owned by the state rather than by individuals (Bouwsma 1968). As in Florence, wealth was essential to a successful political career. But the Venetian noble might become impoverished—and many were—without loss of his status (see, e.g., Burckhardt [1860] 1954; Logan 1972). This phenomenon had no Florentine counterpart.

Beneath the nobility was another somewhat larger category of "citizens," the most important being the *cittadini originari*, from whom were recruited the personnel for many routine government jobs, including the position of chancellor. Both Venetians of the lower classes and foreigners could enter this order. The *cittadini* and nobles in combination amounted to about 10 percent of the population. Some of the *cittadini* were extremely wealthy, and intermarriage in either direction between the nobility and them was not uncommon. Not surprisingly, when many of the humanistic developments at first did take root in Venice, it was in connection with the *cittadini*, and especially with their functions in the chancellery. In the long run, Venice was to make enduring contributions not only to humanism but also specifically to historiography. How did this take place, and how did it accommodate itself to a social system in which hereditary stratification was obviously significant? Briefly, the accommodation consisted of avoiding Renaissance historiographic developments as long as possible and then applying them to other peoples and places rather than to Venice itself.

Historiography

First let me repeat that the Venetians, like the medieval Europeans, were indeed interested in the past (Bouwsma 1968), but it was a past that partook greatly of myth, and Venetian authorities were loathe to rethink those myths. Even as the sixteenth century drew to a close, when some Venetians had developed a sound sense of history, the "old myth of an eternal and essentially unchanging Venice . . . was never attacked directly" (Bouwsma 1968:556), for "domestic history remained a state monopoly . . . entrusted only to historians already committed to [the] . . . 'myth of Venice' " (Cochrane 1981:479).

Attempts to gain support for an official humanist history in Venice did not succeed until the sixteenth century, though a shift away from the Venetian chronicle to the new types of history was perceptible in two histories published in the late 1400s (Bouwsma 1968). One of these was by a non-Venetian, Sabellico (1436–1506), but he was encouraged by the Venetian government. Bouwsma labels it "a rather mediocre example of humanist historiography" (1968:91), and Cochrane says that it "managed to combine the principal defects both of . . . humanist historiography and the Venetian chronicle tradition" (Cochrane 1981:84). Designed to buttress Venetian mythology, it was the first publication ever to be copyrighted (Logan 1972; Thompson 1942:I). The first of the humanist histories by a Venetian, *The History of the Origins of Venice*, by Bernardo Giustiniani (1408–1489), was published posthumously in 1492. It stressed the divine origins of the city, its perpetual autonomy, the greatness and antiquity of its nobility, and their extraordinary religiosity (Bouwsma 1968; Labalme 1969). While the form may have changed, the crucial role of myth was still evident.

By the middle of the sixteenth century, however, much began to change—

in political discourse, in historiography, and in art. Bouwsma 1968 links these developments, in a manner similar to Hans Baron's 1966 argument for Florence, to a great political crisis that Venice faced at the time. I accept his argument but I will try to show that although events forced Venetians to defend themselves by writing histories, these histories nonetheless support the main generalizations I wish to make.

The first official historian of Venice, Andrea Navagero (1483–1529) was appointed in 1515. The terms of his appointment made it clear that he "was to promote the 'reputation' of the state." He only partially completed his task, but the "work was so severely criticized—possibly because, as a man of some experience in public life, he understood politics too well for simple adulation—that (as it was reported) his will ordered that it be burned" (Bouwsma 1968:139).

Pietro Bembo (1470–1547) became the next official historian, in 1530. His father had been ambassador to Florence, and Pietro was probably introduced to the ruling circles there. He had a different background from most Venetian nobles, and he took no interest in politics and had no confidence in history. He looked on his job as historian as a mere chore to be performed. Though given access to state archives, he did not use them. The result was a poor work, merely glorifying the rulers of Venice, yet he wrote shortly after Machiavelli and contemporaneously with Guicciardini in Florence (Bouwsma 1968). Bouwsma's summary is pertinent:

> the weakness in Bembo's historical understanding was not merely personal. It was symptomatic of the general political climate of the Republic. . . . [H]owever instructive the truth might be, . . . the Council of Ten had no compunction about deleting from or adding to Bembo's work in any case where interests of "the state and the quiet of the Republic" might be affected. . . . Venice still regarded history only as a means to glorify and shore up the state, not as a way to understand the political and social world. (1968:139)

Although Bembo's patrons were generally pleased with his efforts (the results of which were turned over to them after his death), they were not pleased with his unkind statements about some of their ancestors. The offending passages were deleted from the earliest Latin and vernacular printings (Cochrane 1981).

In addition to having access to the Venetian archives, Bembo also succeeded in having the government force Marin Sanudo (1466–1535) to make available his remarkable diaries. Sanudo was a member of a very old, distinguished, active, and influential Venetian family. With the idea in mind of writing a "true" political history of Venice, he amassed an enor-

mous amount of material relevant to the internal and external affairs of
the state. But he either lost faith in his ability as a historian or could never
decide when to stop adding to his diaries and start writing his history. It
was a great blow to Sanudo when Bembo, rather than he, was appointed
"public historiographer" and then forcibly given access to Sanudo's life's
work. Sanudo had been actuated by the highest historical standards, but
his project was aborted. Sanudo's diaries were not published until 1879
and later (Cochrane 1981; Gilbert 1965; Logan 1972).

Daniele Barbaro (1513–1570) succeeded Bembo in 1547. In his youth he
had been a friend of a Florentine historian, Benedetto Varchi (1503–1565).
On returning from an ambassadorship in England he wrote a particularly
good account of life and customs there (Logan 1972). Barbaro wrote in a
spirit very different from that of Bembo. What he did, he did well. But
after three years he abandoned his task. Moreover, "what is particularly
striking is that the Venetian government failed to appreciate or preserve
what he had written" (Bouwsma 1968:142). Within a generation Barbaro
and his work were largely forgotten, and his manuscript was lost until the
nineteenth century. Indeed, for the next thirty years no official history of
Venice was written even though a series of nobles continued to be appointed to the post of state historian (Bouwsma 1968; Logan 1972).

In the mid-1500s the government ordered that an official diary be kept
and summarized as a chronicle, but nothing was made public. Historical
understanding, briefly flirted with, was no longer deemed necessary. It
was, in fact, an affront to the Venetian notion of changelessness.

As for unofficial history, the only substantial contribution in this period,
Nicolò Zeno's *Origine de' Barbari* confined itself to the relatively safe topic
of the republic's origins. While it showed occasional signs of a critical
sense, its description of early Venetian society "was not history but the
projection of a static and utterly abstract ideal," and it persisted in repudiating, "with considerable indignation, the notion that the early settlers
of Venice might have had any but the highest social origins" (Bouwsma
1968:143; see also Cochrane 1981).

Two views of Venice written in the 1520s provide an interesting contrast.
One was written by a Venetian, the other by a Florentine visiting Venice
and Padua. Both authors were concerned to analyze Venetian institutions,
yet Donato Giannotti presented a "realistic awareness of historical development" (Bouwsma 1968:154), while Gasparo Contarini, the Venetian,
presented an image of "static perfection" and showed no historical sense
(Bouwsma 1968:145). For Contarini, Venice "seems to have been born

already mature out of the almost supernatural wisdom of her founding fathers" (Bouwsma 1968:152; see also Gilbert 1968, Cochrane 1981, and Logan 1972 for more sympathetic evaluations of Contarini).

In spite of their shortcomings as public historians, it bears remembering that the Venetians were in many ways practical men. They developed statistical science to the same level as, and perhaps earlier than, the Florentines (Burckhardt [1860] 1954), and they kept very good records, enormous archives (Plumb 1961). After the mid-1500s, ambassadorial reports, especially those from Rome, began to display both political and historical analysis. Record keeping probably widened the perceived gap between myth and reality for those Venetians privy to the latter (Bouwsma 1968). The first important product of the improving ambassadorial accounts were the *Relazioni* (1558) of Bernardo Navagero, who took an objective view of the development of ecclesiastical institutions. This line of development was to culminate in the writings of Paulo Sarpi, of whom more later (Bouwsma 1968).

At about this time, in 1560, Francesco Patrizi produced a theoretical work in dialogue form on the writing of history. It stressed the value of history, especially for republics, and discussed such interesting points as the fact that although every history is written from a particular point of view, and hence is inherently subjective, histories nevertheless exhibit degrees of reliability: they are not equally subjective. Generally the work showed skepticism toward the possibility of generalizations, much as in Guicciardini's writings (Bouwsma 1968; Logan 1972; Reynolds 1953). Bouwsma evaluation makes an important point:

Patrizi's work suggests a growing disposition among Venetians to view the world realistically and historically rather than ideally and systematically. But they were not quite ready (nor were they ever entirely pleased) to apply this new insight directly to their own republic. They preferred to direct it first to the understanding of neighboring societies, notably those against which they felt some animus. (1968:167–68)

In other words, they clearly perceived the value of history, but they also recognized the danger it posed for a regime such as Venice's. Thus Venice was to become historically minded, with the proviso that the history of Venice itself was exempt from critical scrutiny. History was a weapon to turn upon others.

The events that began to yank Venice out of her complacent view of an unchanging past and present were the combined threats of Spain and

Rome, on the one hand, and on the other the stimulation of the defeat of the Turks at Lepanto in 1571 (Bouwsma 1968). Agostino Valier, for example, composed a history shortly after Lepanto. The work covers the period to 1580 and contains interesting comments on the value of history. Although he objected, on religious grounds, to the humanist notion that the study of the classics should be the principal mark of a scholar, Valier thought that history could be a science of life. However, he no longer considered himself a Venetian, having moved into and identified with the Church's hierarchy. He wanted Venetian history to be put in the "mundane world" and was disturbed by the lack of historical writing in Venice. He was largely responsible for the appointment there in 1577 of an official historian, Alvise Contarini, nephew of Gasparo. Unfortunately, Alvise died two years later. But history was revived in Venice by Alvise's successor, Paolo Paruta (Bouwsma 1968; Logan 1972).

Paruta (1540–1598) was one of the lesser nobles still engaged in trade. His historical writings per se are of less interest here than the views he expressed in typical humanist dialogue form in his *Della Perfezione della Vita Politica* and *Vita Civile*. Paruta saw man as flesh and blood, complex in personality. In one of the dialogues, Paruta's master defends wealth as an essential component in true nobility, which shows a certain wavering on the role of descent in nobility. But in other ways he argued for traditional inequality. He used historical data to defend his arguments (Bouwsma 1968).

Paruta put in the mouth of Daniele Barbaro a defense of history as the handmaiden of politics and as an essential element in the education of a patrician. He leaned toward Guicciardini, however, in seeing no regularities in history, and hence seeing only a limited value in the "lessons of history." While much of this was long since commonplace in Florence, in Venice Paruta's views heralded "a major shift in perspective," a new willingness to discuss politics and history (Bouwsma 1968:223). Paruta seems to have stimulated a few decades of historical writing, but of a "severely factual" type (Logan 1972:58).

Paruta's *Historia Vinetiana*, for the most part a "competent and conventional narrative," also hinted at a new view: it recognized change in Venice and the dangers to Venice in his time (Bouwsma 1968:279). A faction that came to power in Venice in the final decades of the 1500s, the *giovani*, was no less aware of "the vulnerability of the Republic to historical change and the particular precariousness of its own time" (Bouwsma 1968:232). The leader of the *giovani* was Leonardo Donà (1536–1612), who had received an extensive education in the classics and history, and who retained his interest in history, being specially partial to Guicciardini. Service overseas had given him a peculiar sensitivity to Venice's problems. Although he does not elaborate, Bouwsma says that the intellectual-political leadership provided by the *giovani* combined men of differing social background and that this was unusual "in a period when distinctions of class were generally more pronounced" (Bouwsma 1968:236). Logan (1972:64) describes the *giovani* as "young activists, often political 'outsiders' who were breaking into the bastions of power, [and who] tended to move in circles . . . where scientific and historical studies, together with political observation, were probably the main topic of discussion."

An interest in history had become too general in Italy to be ignored. As the Catholic Reformation got underway it was forced to use history itself to attack Renaissance historicism. Giovanni Botero (1544–1611), for example, defended hagiography as the highest form of history (Bouwsma 1968).

The stage was now set for a great competition of historical writing, in which the Venetians tended to use history not so much as a tool but as a weapon. "Each side was more effective in attacking the historical myths of its opponents than in presenting its own history" (Bouwsma 1968:476). An anonymous and devastating attack on Venetian myths and social stratification was published in Mirandola in 1612, but it received no Venetian reply. As Bouwsma notes, "Perhaps it came too close to the truth" (1968:504).

The most popular secular history in Venice in this period was Enrico Davila's *Istorica delle Guerre Civili de Francia*, published in Venice in 1630 (Bouwsma 1968). A Paduan, and hence presumably not a Venetian noble, Davila was brought up in France, and in Venice he was associated with the *giovani*. Davila was to become a very good historian, often compared favorably to Guicciardini. Both Hume and Gibbon ranked Davila among the few great modern historians (Bouwsma 1968; see also Nadel 1964). Davila had a great "distrust of aristocratic factions," that is, the French nobility. He was keenly interested in causation, seeing human egotism as the main motive force in political history, and he was no less keenly interested in revealing the disparity between people's professed and actual motives. He felt that in order to understand human nature, one needed to study a people's early institutions (Bouwsma 1968). In short, he possessed the finest of Renaissance historiographical skills, but he applied them to France, not to Venice.

Fra Paolo Sarpi (1552–1623) was to become no less a master historian. Renaissance historians had discovered that the world changes and that the past was therefore different from the present. Sarpi was one of the first to examine the process of change over several centuries. In a work on ecclesiastical benefices he tried to show how the Church had abandoned its "original poverty and democratic structure and had become a hierarchical, property-owning body" (Logan 1972:122). Bouwsma calls Sarpi's *History of the Council of Trent* "one of the great masterpieces of European historiography" (1968:556; see also Cochrane 1981 and Thompson 1942:I). It drew fully on the advances both of the Florentines and the Venetian *giovani* historians. It too applied the new historiography to the history of the Church—and of course met stiff resistance.

Sarpi saw history as an empirical study designed to seek the truth about the past. He saw historical truth as autonomous and as illuminated only by the historian's general understanding of human nature and human affairs. Truth took precedence over form. He felt that historical writing was useful, sometimes urgent; hence, a historical work was to be judged above all by its utility. He saw the historian's task as the laborious accumulation of detail, especially from contemporary sources. He saw that great changes often resulted from numerous small causes. While Sarpi was necessarily selective in piecing together his history, he was utterly naturalistic. He emphasized the role of individuals in history. Sarpi applied functional and comparative analytic schemes by, for example, stressing the relationship between education and the form of government. Sarpi's history of the Council of Trent was "no mere narrative but an extended and complex essay in historical explanation" (Bouwsma 1968:597; see also Cochrane 1981 and Logan 1972).

It was reported that Sarpi first developed an interest in history not in Venice but at the court of Mantua, where he saw its practical utility for understanding politics. His purpose in writing the *History of the Council of Trent* was no less practical; it was to defend the interests of Christendom (Bouwsma 1968). He also thought the truth would defend Venice against the threat of Rome. The work quickly went into several translations and just as quickly went on the papal Index of proscribed writings. Bouwsma described it as a "historiographical masterpiece on a subject of general interest" and said that it has some claim to be considered "the last major literary achievement of the Italian Renaissance" (1968:623). Cochrane called it "one of the most famous works of history of all time" (1981:475). For

Gibbon and Hume, Sarpi fell among the few great modern historians (Bouwsma 1968).

Yet Sarpi's history is not a history of Venice, and his views, so common in Florence, were shared by only "some elements in the Venetian patriciate" (Bouwsma 1968:572). Sarpi's writings, Bouwsma concluded, "suggest a middle-class revulsion against the decadence of an aristocratic and ecclesiastical formalism which still sought to translate into political relations a pattern of order that no longer carried conviction. In so chaotic a social world such deference to hierarchical obligation seemed ridiculous" (1968:578). Sarpi would have been suspicious of "all universal, hierarchically articulated, authoritative systems" (1968:578). Sarpi was not a noble (Wootton 1983:8).

Neither Davila nor Sarpi was an official historian of Venice, but under the *giovani* the post had been reanimated, beginning, as mentioned above, with Paruta. When the latter died in 1598 he was succeeded by Andrea Morosini (1558–1618), who in turn was succeeded in 1620 by his cousin, Nicolò Contarini (doge in 1630); all were *giovani* associates. While not on a par with Davila and Sarpi, the official historians showed various signs of improving historical sense. Morosini's *Historia Veneta*, for example, showed more careful research and gave some attention to Venice's internal developments (Bouwsma 1968; Cochrane 1981). Nicolò Contarini's *Historie Vinitiane*, written in the 1620s, was perhaps the best example of official Venetian historiography. It gave considerable attention to economic matters and was outstanding in its organization of material and its causal analysis. Contarini was a good literary portraitist too (Logan 1972). Unfortunately, his history was not published until 1958 (Cochrane 1981).

Before closing this description of Venetian historiography, a few further points should be noted. Venetian historiography was primarily in the vernacular, it tended to a severe factualism, it tended to collapse the distinction between antiquarianism and "true" history but to strongly emphasize the former, and it was mostly produced by nobles, although those connected with the *giovani* were probably to some degree tinged with the mentality of the upwardly mobile (Logan 1972). In addition, James Davis observed that political analysis also eventually came to Venice:

Some Venetians . . . did write essays and books about their government during the last two centuries of the Republic. . . . Most of them were written by noblemen who were not important members of the government. None of them attack the aristocratic constitution itself, but in general they are marked by resentment against the *grandi* and it is significant that none of them were published before the fall of the Republic. (Davis 1962:139)

It is no less significant that three of the six examples of such writings that Davis 1962 gives were anonymous. Logan (1972:63) traces a "passionate interest in politics" among Venetian intellectuals to international crises of the early sixteenth century but notes that they pursued this interest less "to draw lessons from the past" than "to understand the world in which Venice [then] found herself." When the Venetians did show a greater interest in political analysis (Bouwsma 1968), it was apparently not creative. The Venetian interest in politics generally did not include Venice's own internal affairs. As Logan points out, "The ruling oligarchy was undoubtedly resistant to questionings of the Venetian political system" (1972:275).

Venice's problems were not solved by her historians, nor by a turn to political science. By the mid-1600s the republic was in sharp decline. In spite of the admission of new members to the nobility at this time (Logan 1972), oligarchy intensified, and Renaissance thought took root in other parts of Europe (Bouwsma 1968).

Concomitants

Before drawing conclusions from the Venetian case, a review of the concomitants is in order. The relative absence of individualism, biography, and realistic portraiture, as well as the tardiness with which Venetians adopted humanistic studies and political science, have already been noted. Burckhardt remarked on the lesser secularity of Venice:

This government, which had the clergy so thoroughly in control, . . . displayed an official piety of a most singular kind. The bodies of saints and other relics . . . were bought at the greatest sacrifices and received by the Doge in solemn procession. . . . These measures were not the fruit of any popular excitement, but of the tranquil resolutions of the heads of the Government, and might have been omitted without attracting any comment, and at Florence, under similar circumstances, would certainly have been omitted. (1954:60)

For the Venetians, "religious conformity was a civic virtue" (Rose 1969:193).

Contributions to the social sciences are rarely mentioned in connection with the Venetians, but the great ethnographic and geographic contribution of Marco Polo cannot be forgotten. Gianotti noted a contradiction in the Venetians' thought in that they showed an undue veneration for their ancient practices and yet were "curious investigators of all the customs that could be observed in their own times" (Bouwsma 1968:154). Logan 1972 mentions linguistic and archaeological studies by Venetians.

In the natural sciences, Venetian activities were apparently substantial, though it may be recalled that Berenson (1967) found the scientific attitude in some ways stronger in Florence than in Venice. Daniele Barbaro devoted himself to the study of mathematics and science, and was commissioned by the Venetian senate to found the world's first botanical garden, at Padua (Logan 1972). Pietro Bembo's first work, on Mt. Etna, was on geography and natural history (Logan 1972). Sarpi was a great natural scientist, almost on a par with Leonardo da Vinci, and may even have been an atheist (Cochrane 1981; Thompson 1942:I; Wootton 1983). An array of outstanding scientists—Copernicus, Vesalius, Galileo, and Harvey—had some connection with Venetian thinkers in that, although they were not Venetians, at one time or another they were at Padua, which in turn was closely tied to Venice (Logan 1972). Whether Venice differed from other Renaissance Italian cities with respect to divination, I have not been able to ascertain.

The conservative and somewhat rigid control of education in Venice suggests that theories of education did not flourish there, and catering to the special needs of the chancellery does not necessarily imply an education open to all. But these are weak indications either way. Venetian conceptions of human nature are also only weakly indicated. At least one Venetian wrote a defense of hereditary nobility (Kristeller 1965), and Paolo Paruta reported a debate, presumably wholly or partly fictitious, in which an argument that "nobility is essentially a matter of birth" was presented with some sympathy (Bouwsma 1968:216). A book published in Venice in 1544 argued that some men are born to rule, and some to be ruled, with the two distinguishable even by bodily appearance (Martines 1979). But the main defense of hereditary stratification was not so much a philosophical one as the constant reiteration of the theme that Venice had always been ruled by nobles (Bouwsma 1968).

Insofar as Renaissance Venetians attempted to defend their social system philosophically, they focused more on the government than on the system of stratification. Venetians, and other Renaissance thinkers, likened Venice to Sparta—not because they both possessed hereditary nobilities but because they both possessed that balanced constitution that Polybius had argued was the basis of stable government in Sparta and Rome. In the Venetian argument, the doge represented the monarchy, the Council of Ten stood for the aristocracy, and the Great Council represented the people, the many. The Venetians were not alone in defining the "people" in this rather narrow sense, and the Great Council was in fact a large body (Bouwsma 1968; Lane 1966). On the basis of its size, it was possible to defend the Great Council as a democratic institution. Moreover, at least some Venetian historians did not attempt to efface the memory of the time when a genuinely popular assembly had played an important role in Venice (Lane 1966; Bouwsma 1968). But if the Venetians did not provide a direct philosophical defense of hereditary rank in Venice, they did not defend equality either—and certainly not the ideal of social mobility. The Venetians were fully aware that they were not as democratic as the Florentines (Bouwsma 1968).

Although clearly more castelike than Florence, Venice did not show the full complex of expected concomitants. And in the long run Venice came to share many traits with Florence, without any important change in social stratification. Is this an exception? If we look at the pattern of resistances—those developments that came only slowly or imperfectly to Venice—they are on the whole quite consistent with the predictions I would make. When Venice did become historically minded, it was with an unusual twist: its sound history was of other states, or of interstate relations; it did not much turn its sound historical analysis upon itself. For the Venetians, to repeat, history was more a weapon of interstate conflict than a tool for understanding human affairs for application at home. Until examining Venetian historiography I had assumed, perhaps not very consciously, that most history would have an intrasocietal reference. Logan (1972) makes the pertinent observation that most of the ancient historians—Thucydides was an exception—wrote the history of their own peoples and hence were not suitable as models for the Venetians, who wanted to analyze interstate relations. The Venetians force a distinction between what might be called endohistory and exohistory. As exohistorians the Venetians ultimately joined and rivaled their Italian Renaissance fellows. But in the field of endohistory, where my hypothesis mainly applies and where, I suppose, most peoples put their principal efforts (as suggested by Huizinga's 1963 definition of history), the Venetians did not much improve upon medieval standards. In this sense, the Venetians pose no exception. Moreover, it should be recalled that much of Venetian historical writing tended to be secret, to be ignored, or to be quashed—all consistent with this book's hypothesis. Finally, Venice's finest historians were not noble.

CONCLUSION

Looking back now to the section on medieval Europe in the previous chapter, it can be seen that the Renaissance, at least as illustrated in Florence, brought about de facto, de jure, and ideologically defended open stratification, in contrast to what went before. Simultaneously, sound history developed along with the other concomitants of openness, again in contrast to medieval patterns. The Renaissance sense of history, and many of the concomitants too, are often explained as borrowings from classical standards. There is some truth to this, and no doubt the extent to which the Renaissance borrowed from the Muslims and the Chinese is understated at present. But it was not *mere* borrowing. It was borrowing engendered by social conditions. Where these social conditions did not prevail—as in Venice, which was no less prosperous, urban, populous, and bourgeois than Florence, but whose rulers made the culturally fateful choice of closing its system of stratification—medieval or medieval-like patterns persisted until interstate politics forced the Venetians to use every tool available to oppose their enemies. In this context they became very good historians but essentially exohistorians.

Although my analysis does not proceed closer to the present, it should be kept in mind that the progressive features of the Renaissance described in this chapter later spread to other parts of Europe. Exploration, colonization, and the ramified consequences of the industrial revolution gave great scope to patterns of upward mobility. In time, political revolutions and reforms swept away most of the privileges of hereditary rank. Modern European societies—including such of its offshoots as Australia, Canada, and the United States—are fundamentally open, even though descent confers disabilities on various minority groups within them. Modern Western historiography reflects these conditions.

CHAPTER 7

Conclusion

The preceding chapters have ranged widely from my initial disappointed realization of the meagerness of the written historical materials provided by a Malay state in northwest Borneo. A series of comparisons has shown that this state, Brunei, was not anomalous: its ahistoricity is typical of literate caste-organized societies. Comparison shows the obverse too: that a relatively sound and extensive production of written historical materials is commonly associated with open patterns of social stratification. Also, the view of the past proved to be but one of several concomitants of the mode of social stratification. A syndrome of traits tends to develop in societies characterized by open patterns of social mobility, while an opposed syndrome tends to develop in caste-organized societies. These findings can be put in perspective by answering the following questions: Are there exceptions to be explained? Are there alternative explanations for historiographic quality? If the basic argument of the book is correct, why is it correct? What produces the correlation between the mode of social stratification and the quality of historiography? What logic connects them, and how do they fit into the overall organization of society and culture?

EXCEPTIONS

Few generalizations about human affairs are without exceptions. In the course of my studies I found three kinds of exceptions to my hypothesis.

First, I found some that turned out to be only apparent, not actual, exceptions, as with Kashmir, Sparta, and early Renaissance Venice. In each case they were exceptional—within their contexts—both in their historiography *and* in their mode of social stratification, and hence turned out not to be exceptions at all. Another apparent exception, but found outside the range of societies I studied, will be discussed below. Second, there were exceptions that forced me to modify my definitions or hypothesis. One case was provided by medieval China: its actual rates of social mobility declined, but the quality of its historiography did not. This and other considerations suggest that it is the ideal or perceived pattern of social stratification more than the actual rate of social mobility that shapes historiography. Another case was late Renaissance Venetian historiography, which was characterized by sound history of other peoples and international affairs but persistent adherence to myth in presenting the Venetian past. This suggests a distinction between endo- and exohistory, and further suggests that the principal hypothesis applies essentially to endohistory, which is probably the core of most peoples' historical writings.

The third type of exception occurs precisely where I had originally predicted it. That is, in my earliest attempt to test the hypothesis that caste was peculiarly associated with ahistoricity, I expected some cases of ahistoricity to result from other causes. I expected caste always to be accompanied by ahistoricity, but I expected open societies sometimes to be accompanied by sound historiography and sometimes not. Initially, however, I found openness to be invariably accompanied by sounder historiography, and I therefore modified my hypothesis to fit this empirical tendency. But in the long run I noted at least one case of ahistoricity in the absence of caste: the dark age in Byzantine history, mentioned in chapter 5. I do not know how to explain this case. It is entirely likely that a closer analysis than I have provided would unearth numerous small-scale rises and declines in the quality of historiography quite unconnected with the pattern of social stratification. I do not believe that this exception, nor others that remain small in scale, seriously detracts from the otherwise strong validation presented for the main hypothesis of this book.

To return now to apparent exceptions, the following case was referred to me by M. G. Smith (personal communication). He noted that ethnohistorical research among the Rwanda, a caste-organized people of East Africa, shows them to be reasonably good historians. Traditionally the Rwanda were not literate, so properly they fall outside the scope of my research. My initial decision to sample only literate societies was, however, largely methodological; I had no reason to think that the hypothesis would not apply to the oral accounts of the past of preliterate peoples. The Rwanda case led me to ask if a society possessing only oral history might in some way avoid the connection between caste and ahistoricity that is found in literate societies. Perhaps if one had interviewed well-informed early Renaissance Venetians, for example, they would have been able to provide good oral history, at least for the recent past. Recall that the Venetian government kept extensive archival materials. It follows that at least some Venetians even early in the Renaissance probably realized certain of the values of history. But they had no good reason to see that their historical materials went into the public domain. Hence the ahistorical tradition that is associated with caste does not preclude the possibility that historical materials and a sound sense of history may be the exclusive property of certain members of the elite. Following this line of reasoning, a closed society might keep track of and account for its past in two ways: one consisting of unsound accounts for public consumption, and the other, sound accounts comprising the confidential knowledge of the past kept by the ruling strata. If the ethnohistorian can tap the latter source, he may thus find sound history in a closed society. It may be relevant that since the Rwanda kingdom no longer exists as such, any need for secrecy that once existed perhaps no longer does.

This line of speculation is confirmed by an early ethnographic report on the Rwanda. In a report of an expedition conducted in the first decade of this century, the Hutu, the hereditary subordinate mass, were said to know little about Rwandan history. The Tutsi, hereditary overlords, did know their history, but they were loathe to reveal it, considering it a secret of their caste. One man who revealed part of the history feared for his life, though he may have had additional reasons for his fear (Czekanowski 1917). A report based on a further visit to Rwanda in about 1925 indicates that the Rwanda had specialists whose duty was to memorize the deeds and actions of the rulers. Their accounts mixed myth, legend, and at least an outline of history (Pagès 1933). It is entirely possible that these specialists knew considerable sound history. But if Czekanowski's account is correct, the secret nature of Rwandan history makes it yet another exception that supports the rule.

The Rwanda case helps to close the gap between the ahistorical and the historically minded peoples. It is not so much that they differ in mentality—a point that Indians make when they say they *could* have written histories but just chose not to—as that they differ in how they employ the advantages conferred by the study of history. In the open society, history goes into the public domain, where competition pushes it to high levels of development. In the closed society, if history exists at all it is the guarded information of the members of the dominant caste, whose reticence to air their affairs and whose restricted numbers and limited free time prevent them from going much beyond the keeping of archives for consultation as needed. It is thus entirely possible that a study of the relationship between caste and historiography among nonliterate peoples might not turn up the strong correlation that I have found, because anthropologists are often able to penetrate beyond the history available for public consumption, especially when changed conditions make representatives of declining nobilities less reticent to discuss their former affairs. The consequences of caste for views of the past in preliterate societies deserve further study.

In sum, most exceptional cases have either turned out not to be exceptions or have been accommodated by refined definitions or hypotheses. The only real exceptions are few in number, are of relatively small scale, and are in a form that does little to detract from the numerous confirmatory cases.

ALTERNATIVE EXPLANATIONS

The connection between social stratification and historiography becomes more convincing when it is compared with alternative explanations of variation in historiographic quality. The following have been suggested as determinants of ahistoricity (the list is probably far from complete): an agricultural emphasis, defective means of measuring time, foreshortened time scales, cyclic concepts of time, otherworldly religions, civilizational decline, poor economic conditions, illiteracy, lack of urbanization, war, peace, political decentralization, borrowing, "dark" ages, and "holism." The principal defect of most of these explanations is that although they may explain *some* variation, they explain relatively little of it. Thus, while it may be true that some societies are agricultural in emphasis and are also ahistorical, a casual glance around the world shows societies heavily dependent on agriculture yet having a good sense of history. How, for example, could the distinction between China and India in any way be linked to the degree of dependence on agriculture? In a like manner, simple, accurate, and rational modes of reckoning time may indeed facilitate the writing of history, but they do not motivate it. The cumbersome Chinese method, based on dynasties and reigns, coexisted with a very sound historiography.

It may be true that Western historiography has been improved by the vast time scale opened behind us by modern science, but it is notorious that the Greeks initially attempted to explain their history within the span of relatively few generations of descent from the gods, while the Egyptians casually produced the concrete evidence of a much larger number of generations here on earth yet wrote no histories. Indian notions of time were, to say the least, grandiose (Zimmer 1962), though it must be pointed out that their present age has lasted only some five thousand years (Pocock 1964). However, five thousand years sufficed for most sound Western historiographies until recent times.

The very fact that Indians believed in the infinite repetition of ages, it has been argued, radically devalued history for them (Dumont 1970b): If events are preordained and repetitious, why bother with them? But many peoples who objectively study history draw opposite conclusions from similar premises: precisely because events may repeat themselves, it is of practical value to know the details (Trompf 1979). Ibn Khaldun provides the most notable example of this. The expectation of cyclic repetition is the basis not only of historical studies but also of astronomy/astrology and other ancient sciences.

Assuming that no very peculiar definition is attached to the term *otherworldly*, it is apparent that the otherworldliness of Judaism, Buddhism, Islam, and Christianity in some periods has not prevented the development of relatively sound historiography even though among some peoples otherworldliness and unsound historiography may coincide. Max Weber ([1922] 1963:266, 268), for example, considered "authentic ancient Buddhism" to be "the ultimate ethic of world-rejection." Initially it rejected not only this world but the other world too; however, as soon as it became popular it "transformed itself into a savior religion . . . with hopes for the world beyond." How can Sri Lanka's relatively sound historiography be explained in this context? In what respect is Buddhism less otherworldly than Hinduism? True, it cannot be said that otherworldliness *favors* the development of sound historiography, but the mode of social stratification is a more reliable indicator of the quality of historiography.

Civilizational rise and decline may account for some fluctuations in historiography. That it was a factor in the rise of rational thought and historical writing among the classical Ionian Greeks and in the decline of literature, including history, among early medieval Europeans, is quite plausible. But the striking cases of ahistoricity in India and Renaissance Venice, for example, are incomprehensible in terms of civilizational decline. "The owl of Minerva takes flight at twilight," Hegel said, and many fine historians did write in the twilight of a civilization: Manetho in Egypt, Tacitus in Rome, Machiavelli and Guicciardini in Florence, and so on. But Ssu-ma Ch'ien wrote at the height of the Han dynasty, and Herodotus wrote before Athenian civilization was in decline. If there are tendencies here, they are less sharply marked than those associated with open and closed societies.

Civilizational decline and poor economic conditions are often one and the same, as in Europe's Dark Ages. Yet one could hardly claim that the poverty of the rajas of India allowed them to patronize mythographers but prevented them from patronizing historians. Was Athens that much more prosperous than Sparta? Economic conditions may be a factor, but a factor of uncertain consequence.

Since all the societies discussed in the preceding chapters were literate, the effects of literacy have not been fully explored here. But two points may be made. First, however effective literacy may be in facilitating historical writing (Bohannan 1952; Goody and Watt 1963), it does not motivate it. The lesson of fully literate but ahistorical societies is conclusive on that point. Second, *relative* literacy could be a factor—as, for example, in medieval Europe—but it would require further research to quantify its effects and to determine causal direction; it is entirely possible that a high rate of illiteracy is a *result* of hereditary stratification.

Urbanization is said to be a requisite of a sound sense of history, in the sense that until a civilization has urban centers, no part of it—rural or urban—will produce histories. But while urbanization may be a necessary cause, as with literacy, it is far from a sufficient cause. The Indians, most notably, were not spurred to historical writing though they were as literate and urbanized as their contemporaries who were historically minded. Urbanization may facilitate historical writing, but it does not necessarily motivate it.

Claims that war or peace promote historiography have little merit as general rules. Much history is concerned with warfare, which disposes of the argument for peace, but many societies thoroughly familiar with warfare wrote little or no history. Herodotus and Thucydides illustrate the former case and the Spartans the latter.

Centralization among some peoples may indeed have spurred historical writing, but the difference between the Hebrews and the ancient Egyptians could not be explained in these terms, nor could the efflorescence of historiography among the classical Greek city-states. In China the quality of historiography was affected but little during periods of decentralization.

Borrowing does play a part in the history of history, but its explanatory limitations are evident. Taking, for example, the five cases that present the fullest manifestation of the open-society syndrome of traits—Renaissance Florence, late republican and early imperial Rome, Ionian Greece, China, and classical Islam—all but one is definitely connected by borrowing, and that one case, China, probably deserves much more attention as a source for cultural borrowing by the Muslims and Renaissance Europeans than is often recognized. But it would be very difficult to show that the Greeks borrowed from the Chinese, or vice versa, and the similarity of complex developments in places so distant from each other at almost the same early periods of time is too striking to be a coincidence. At the other end of the scale, those societies that showed the closed-society syndrome most fully—medieval Europe, India, Sparta, and the Malay states—have only two cases linked by borrowing (the Malay states and Indians). The medieval Europeans and the Spartans have no obvious links to each other or to India and the Malays. Again, the complex similarities of these cases are too great to be a coincidence. Borrowing accounts for many peculiarities of historiography in Southeast Asia. It is not unreasonable to suggest that Southeast Asian ahistoricity resulted from the influence of Hindu India, but from whom did India borrow its ahistoricity? From whom did medieval Europe borrow it? The most important limitation of borrowing as a general determinant of historiographic quality is evident in the failure of various ahistorical peoples to borrow historiography from neighbors possessing its sound varieties. Medieval Europe borrowed only very belatedly—if at all—from the historiography of the Muslims (Rosenthal 1968), although it did borrow many other features of Islamic thought. The Indians were in loose contact for centuries with historically minded peoples, and they borrowed much from them. But they did not adopt historical writing until conquered by Muslims. On the other hand, the Romans did borrow from the Greeks, the Vietnamese borrowed from the Chinese, and the Florentines borrowed from the Byzantines and earlier sources. Under the right conditions—when the motivation to write history is present—borrowing may take place. But the opportunity to borrow does not create these conditions; open stratification does.

One or another variant of the idea found in Collingwood 1946 about the illusory nature of dark ages—variants that are at times only implicit in the writings of some present-day anthropologists and historians—will, I believe, provide the most frequent arguments against my conclusions (and the assumptions and methods upon which they rest). Collingwood argued that what appear to be dark ages from the viewpoint of modern Western historiography may merely be periods in which history was written on the basis of principles we are poorly equipped to grasp. If so, there is, paradoxically, challenging historical research to do among peoples who only appear to have no history. For example, some modern historians examine a document not so much to discover what actual events it describes as to ascertain what it meant to those who wrote it, and perhaps to those for whom it was written. The document's accuracy, as I understand it, is less interesting or significant than its purpose or meaning and its author's intentions and point of view. Discovering the purpose or meaning of documents produced by persons outside the Western world is a task for which anthropologists are, as many historians acknowledge, appropriately trained. Broadening the scope of what anthropologists call ethnohistory (which is at present largely confined to discovering "what actually happened") to include not only comparative historiography in the narrow sense but also the comparison of the views of the past of peoples generally considered to lack history could effect a useful synthesis of the fields of the historian, the ethnohistorian, the folklorist, and the mythologist (e.g., Dirks 1982 and Reid and Marr 1979).

A variation of Collingwood's position holds that modern Western historiography, perhaps conceived of as decisively shaped by world capitalist interests, imposes ahistoricity upon the rest of the world. In this variant, modern Western historians look at the sense of the past of other peoples through glasses so distorted that they see no meaningful past there. (This variant, as applied to eighteenth- and nineteenth-century Western historians, may be found in Cohn 1981.) But if this is so, how do we account for Western historians' admiration for some non-Western historiographic traditions? For example, Cohn 1981 quotes the colonial historian James Mill's stern condemnation of Indian historiography as though it were a general condemnation of the historiography of non-Western peoples (the "external others" in Cohn's terms) (Mill:1826, I). There is, to be sure, no doubt that Mill had a low opinion of Asian historians. But he expressed a higher opinion of Muslim historiography: "the grand article in which the superiority of the Mahomedans appears is history. . . . Among the Mahomedans of India the art of composing history has been carried to a greater perfection than in any other part of Asia" (1826:II, 460). Ignoring the discriminations Western historians make in their assessments of non-Western historical writing imposes more unsoundness on the Western historian than facts allow.

Now, nothing in this book denies that Western historiography has hidden (or public) agendas that reflect the concerns of dominant elements in Western societies, nor that the discovery of these agendas would not be beneficial. But the evidence does not support the notion that these agendas prevent any positive assessment of non-Western traditions of historical writing.

Another, and more persuasive, variant holds that when Western historians observe other peoples' accounts of the past that resemble our own, they label these as sound, but they have not measured soundness, only similarity. This variant acknowledges that Western thinkers see differences among other peoples, yet it alleges that these differences are not objective. But how does this variant account for the correlation between judgments of the quality of historical writing and the patterns of stratification? This variant can only make sense if it posits that Western historians—or whatever scholars make the judgments—have a built-in predisposition to make linked judgments: when they see sound history they must also see open stratification; when they see unsound history in a given society they must impose caste upon it. Or, if they see caste, they must then imagine that the people in question have no history, and so on. Two considerations bolster this critique. One is that judgments, rather than explicit measurements, have often been involved in the materials I cite, and even more so in the sense I make of them. The other is that Western historians in many periods were aware of the model provided by Athens and Sparta (or by the images of Athens and Sparta in Western thought). The Florentine historians, for example, might very well have imposed the image of Sparta on the Middle Ages. Should this variant prove to be correct, I will be pleased to take credit for discovering and documenting it. But certain considerations militate against it.

First, Westerners have not been the only ones to judge. In chapter 2, I noted that, centuries ago, a Muslim scholar judged the Indians to be relatively uninterested in history and to be caste organized. It could be countered that classical Muslims were influenced in the same way as Westerners by the image of Athens and Sparta generated mostly by Athenians or their sympathizers. But as noted in chapter 5, there is no strong evidence that the classical Muslims read Greek historical literature, so this counterargument must at present be judged to carry little weight.

Second, this variant posits a very widespread but essentially unconscious set of assumptions (derived from the Athens-Sparta model or something even earlier) in the minds of Western historians and social scientists (both defined in the widest sense), even though these assumptions lie very close to matters that have received considerable conscious scrutiny: the roots of historical consciousness and the nature of social stratification. This is improbable.

Third, this variant presumes that some (or all) of the analysis of Chinese and Indian historiography and social stratification—to take only the most striking cases—is in effect a hoax. For some critics (for example, Michel Foucault) it would simply be part of a massive hoax in which all history (and science) is a myth composed in the present to suit present assumptions (Megill 1979). Most, however, would see the hoax on a smaller scale. They might say, for example, that Hindu Indian and Chinese stratification are not really all that different. Because actual rates of social mobility, as I have conceded, are largely unknown for Hindu India, it is hard to counter this argument in these terms. But would the critics also argue that even the images of stratification in the minds of Hindu Indians and Chinese are not all that different? Or that these images are irrelevant to the comprehension and presentation of the past? If so, there is nothing I can say here that has not already been said in earlier chapters. Most critics, I expect, would simply say that Indian, or medieval European, historiography has not been adequately assessed, which returns us to Collingwood's view.

The evidence does not support the idea that dark ages are illusory, even if their label misleads. True, the darkness is perceived from particular perspectives, while from other perspectives dark ages and places may appear brilliant. Many Westerners now find Indian spiritualism dazzling, and many Indians perceive the West to be spiritually dark. Many medieval Europeans would no doubt agree with those Indians and see our age as dark. These perceptions are not wholly illusory: real differences are perceived and judged. The Dark Ages of Europe had their real counterpart in Hindu India and elsewhere. In ages and places termed dark because of their historiographic tradition, fictitious accounts of the past flourish or predominate. However artistic or intellectual these accounts may be, and however properly we must rely on them in order to understand those periods, what passes for history in them differs systematically from what passes for history in times and places where literate societies have open systems of stratification. The dark ages are not simply different, they are different in uniform ways. When we study accounts of the past written in the dark ages that accompany closed social stratification, we must be students of ideology more than of what really happened, except in a roundabout way. That is, insofar as we can divine the roots, the purposes, and the consequences of the ideology imbedded in the accounts of the past, we discover something of what really happened—that is, that the authors really thought and wrote about the (alleged) past in a certain way and that they did so for reasons and with consequences that warrant analysis (see especially Southern 1970 or virtually any of the modern historians working with the texts from ahistorical peoples). I will return to this topic below.

The definitive refutation of the idea that dark ages are wholly illusory rests on an assessment of probability. How probable is it that when a society is judged ahistorical (dark) that all or most of the other concomitants will fall into place by accident? When one is simply imposing imaginary situations upon others, why not impose them willy-nilly? Why not, for example, say that the Chinese were surprisingly sound historians but were as spiritually oriented as Hindu Indians, or did not believe that human nature was essentially uniform? If the elements of the syndromes were attributed capriciously to other peoples, they could emerge as syndromes only by an astonishingly improbable accident. Alternatively, the hoax we play upon ourselves is even grander—and all the more improbable—than was discussed above.

Dumont (1970b) holds that individualism has some intrinsic connection with historical writing, and he argues that a view of India's past that is true to Indian conceptions would not be individualistic. But Dumont (1970a) in turn traces the absence of the individual as a cultural category in India not to hereditary stratification but to its "holism," that is, its organicism in the sense understood in Plato's *Republic*. If society and the individual are opposed conceptions, then in India the social whole is the dominant conception. In this conception individuals only fulfill roles or functions whose meaningfulness derives from the part they or their functions play in the social whole. But Chinese conceptions of society were no less fundamentally holistic than India's. As Needham points out, "the organicist view in which every phenomenon was connected with every other according to hierarchical order was universal among Chinese thinkers" (1963:121). Yet individualism played a larger role in China than in

India, and the historical-mindedness of the Chinese is an even more striking contrast. The difference between China and India was not that one was holistic and the other not, but rather that in Hindu conceptions a person was born to his status or role, while for the Chinese he could achieve it. The latter situation liberates the individual; the former does not. Dumont's decision to avoid directly confronting the specifically hereditary nature of Indian society is the most puzzling and unfortunate aspect of his stimulating analysis of caste (1970a:46). He was correct to associate weakened individualism with a sense of the past that is hard to describe as historical, but these in turn should have been associated with hereditary hierarchy rather than holism.

In conclusion, open social stratification as a spur to historical writing and closed stratification as a barrier to it appear to be more potent determinants than any others reviewed here.

CONCOMITANTS

Although the main concern of this book is the relationship between modes of social stratification and the quality of historiography, it is apparent that the quality of historiography was often only part of a larger pattern. Understanding this larger pattern, the two contrasting syndromes of traits associated with open and with closed stratification, helps to understand variations in the quality of historiography. The functional interrelatedness of the various parts of the syndromes and the extreme unlikelihood of their developing by chance provide another sort of evidence on behalf of this book's main argument. The traits tending to accompany sound historiography and open stratification are individualism; a uniform conception of human nature; biographical writing; realistic portraiture; uniform education, or educational theory as a major literary genre; a humanistic-secular orientation; an interest in social science (especially political science) and in natural science; and elaborate divination. The absence of these traits, and in some cases the presence of their opposites, tends to accompany closed stratification and unsound historiography.

The possibility that variations in the concept of the individual might explain variations in historiographic quality was one of the first hypotheses I entertained. As I noted earlier, I was temporarily sidetracked by the observation that modern Malays did not seem to repress individualism to any notable degree. Later, however, when I read Ullmann's description

(1966a) of the medieval European tendency to be less concerned with the individual and more with the office, and to be meticulous in the description of the symbolic attributes of office—which was virtually identical to what I found when comparing Brunei and British accounts of a single historical event (Brown 1971a)—it was clear that individualism and its absence deserved renewed attention. Concerning the Malay case, it turned out that traditional Malays did repress individuality, even if this is less obvious among modern Malays. In addition, since literary works are more likely to express ideology than is everyday behavior, Malay histories exhibited repression of individualism even more fully than did everyday life.

Among the meanings of individualism is the ability to pursue one's goals with minimal social regulation, propriety in the emphasis on one's own views and uniqueness, and the identification of persons not in terms of the groups or categories to which they belong but in terms of their unique, intrinsic character. Individualism also refers to the ability to seek out the social status appropriate to one's intrinsic character and to be free to move from one status to another in accordance with autonomous desires and abilities. In this latter sense, individualism is a direct logical derivative of the mode of stratification: caste societies by definition prevent or discourage this important aspect of individual expression.

Significant expressions of individualism in the above senses occurred among the Ionian Greeks, the republican and early imperial Romans, the Chinese, the Muslims, and the Renaissance Florentines. The ancient Hebrews, Assyrians, and Babylonians also showed some indications of individualism. Clear signs of repressing individualism were found not only among the Malays but also among Hindu Indians, Spartans, medieval Europeans, Renaissance Venetians, and Balinese. The only contradictory finding was presented by at least a certain degree of individualism in the Homeric epics. Thus in what appear to be the more extreme or consistent open and closed societies, individualism and its opposite vary with the mode of stratification.

A uniform conception of human nature that denies, at least within a given society, the existence or relevance of racial or specieslike distinctions and, on the contrary, asserts that people (disregarding sex and age) are basically alike except for differences induced by their differing environments, is perhaps the most fundamental of all the concomitants of the open society, for it underlies or implies, directly or indirectly, all the other concomitants and the writing of history. For example, a paradoxical result of the conception of an essentially uniform human nature—which posits that people are all basically alike—is an emphasis on individualism—that is, a belief that each individual is distinct or unique, or at least potentially so. Individualism, in turn, manifests itself in a flourishing biographical literature and a realistic portraiture that, instead of presenting stereotypes, strive to present the concrete physical (and psychological) characteristics of each individual portrayed.

I first considered the linkage between the conception of human nature and the mode of stratification in the analysis of caste societies, for the hereditary transmission of rank, when defended by an ideology, rests on the assumption that men are *substantially* different and unequal, that their substance and inequality are inherited, and that individual variation not based on descent is of secondary importance. In this view, the differences between kinds of people—nobles and commoners, say—are like the differences between eagles and chickens: the differences between their species overshadow and render insignificant any comparison of the individual character of any particular eagle with any particular chicken. Although he dealt with the preliterate Rwanda of Africa (mentioned above because of their sound but secret history), Jacques Maquet's analysis of "the premise of inequality" is applicable generally. He states that "the more obvious rationalization of a caste structure is the belief that there are inborn and fundamental differences between the members of different castes" (1961:170). Maquet concluded that "a 'racial' theory seems the only ideology perfectly consistent with a caste structure," and thus "such a theory is a necessary 'superstructure' (in the Marxist sense) of a caste system" (1961:171). In my reading of the literature on the Homeric Greeks, Spartans, Hindu Indians, medieval Europeans, and Balinese, I find that Maquet's analysis fits them nicely. The basic idea was also found among the Egyptians and the Malays, but it is not certain that it did more than distinguish royalty from all others (the idea of the divinity of royalty, of course, occurs in open societies too). Only in the case of the late western imperial Romans and the Venetians can we say or suspect that the idea was absent in a closed society. Thus Maquet's argument stands up very well.

The open societies, on the other hand, present a rather strong case for correlation between openness and a uniform view of human nature (excluding, of course, differences of age and sex and the influence of the environment). Its attendant individualism has already been noted: individual differences that are of secondary importance when caste classifies people into species come into sharper focus when intrahuman or intrasocietal speciation is absent.

A uniform conception of human nature was apparent among the Chinese, Ionian Greeks, Romans, Byzantines, Renaissance Florentines, Muslims, Burmese, and Hebrews (with certain qualifications). The ancient Hebrews present a case that allows or requires a modified interpretation. The Hebrews considered themselves in some sense a people apart, but for most periods that we know them they recognized no significant hereditary distinctions among themselves. This calls for a distinction between endoracism and exoracism. In this view the caste-organized societies are endoracist, allowing for fundamental distinctions of humanity among themselves. The open societies may be either exoracist or simply nonracist, the former allowing only for fundamental distinctions that primarily distinguish the members of their society from others.

Even in the modern world—with its ease of international movement and communication—distinctions within one's society are of obvious importance. They were more important in the past, when outside contacts were less significant. It is probably also the case, as discussed with respect to Venice in the last chapter, that most historical writing is endosocietal in reference rather than exosocietal. If we confine the analysis of conceptions of human nature to intrasocietal conceptions, then we can perhaps add the Hebrews to the list of those societies with a uniform conception of human nature. And although the Sri Lankans may have been endoracists, there is still the consideration that one race, the dominant one, was the majority of the populace. Thus for most Sri Lankans, to the extent that they did posit fundamental differences among themselves, the differences were of marginal significance. Moreover, the Sri Lankans attached less significance to interrace (i.e., intercaste) differences than did the Hindus. By either way of looking at conceptions of human nature—whether the distinction is simply between racists and uniformitarians, or between endoracists on the one hand and exoracists and uniformitarians on the other— the conception of human nature does vary in accord with the stratification system.

The next concomitants to be discussed are biography and realistic portraiture. Biography was a major literary genre among the Chinese, Ionian Greeks, Romans, Renaissance Florentines, Byzantines, Muslims, and Vietnamese. Among the closed societies, only the Egyptians showed an interest in rudimentary biography. The counterpart of biography in the visual arts is realistic portraiture, which requires a high level of technical development in addition to the motivation to produce it. Realistic portraiture appeared among the Chinese, Ionian Greeks, Romans up to late imperial times,

Renaissance Florentines, and, with important qualifications, the Renaissance Venetians. Chinese portraiture was not as realistic as the others, though the intention of creating an individualistic representation was there. Byzantine portraiture was usually stereotyped, but at times it could be reasonably realistic. Muslims in most places have had a strict religious prohibition of portraiture, but Muslims in India, where stereotyped portraiture was normal, produced or commissioned portraits of marked realism. For a brief period, ancient Egyptians succeeded in producing realistic portraiture. Some occurred in Venice too, though with less individualization than in Florence. Biography and realistic portraiture, both derivatives or indicators of individualism, generally correlate with open stratification. The opposed pattern—production of stereotyped biography and portraits (e.g., hagiography and iconography)—flourished not only in societies that possibly lacked the technical ability to produce realistic portraiture but also in such societies as India and medieval Europe, which were hereditarily closed and hence provided infertile soil for these offshoots of individualism.

All peoples have an educational system of some sort, but in open societies the literature of education becomes more highly developed. The reason for this, I suggest, is that in an open society the influence of environment is considered to be vital in shaping human behavior. Since people are believed to be inherently alike but to act differently, the environment must determine these differences, hence manipulation of the environment becomes important. In the caste society, on the other hand, heredity is considered to be fundamentally important and not subject to much modification. Moreover, each person is born to a known role, and such education as he or she receives is not general education but education specific to his or her caste. Quite as many essays on education might be written in a caste society, but each essay would be irrelevant to most members of the society. In the open society there is a larger potential audience for each text on education and a larger number of potential authors of generally useful texts. Hence, in open societies the literature on education is more sophisticated.

No less a concomitant of openness is an egalitarian system of education. Educational materials as a major genre, and/or egalitarian education, are most clearly found among the Ionian Greeks, republican and early imperial Romans, Byzantines, Chinese, Muslims, and Renaissance Florentines. The relative absence of such literature, or of egalitarian education, seems clear among the Hindu Indians, medieval Europeans, and Malays, but it is suggested among the Venetians too. The findings are consistent, but this concomitant needs further study.

The humanistic-secular attitude ascribes significance to the mundane behavior of people and places less stress on divinity. Such an attitude in open societies allows the production of literature that makes relatively little reference to the supernatural. In closed societies, by contrast, the dominant elements are alleged to partake of the divine as an inherent part of their nature (or to partake of it to a greater degree than their inferiors), which removes them and their actions from the realm of humanistic-secular scrutiny (and probably also inspires them, through divine self-interest, to be unusually productive religious ideologues). Among the Indians, Homeric Greeks, and Balinese, the ruling strata's claims to divine descent are well documented. Similar notions are equally well documented among the Malays and Egyptians, but whether they applied to nobility as a whole or only to royalty is an obscure point. The medieval Europeans, and perhaps the late western Romans, attempted to align their pedigrees with those of the saints or gods. The humanistic-secular attitude, on the other hand, was well-attested among the Ionian Greeks, republican and early imperial Romans, Chinese, Muslims, Vietnamese, Renaissance Florentines, and, to a lesser degree, the Byzantines.

The humanistic-secular attitude (or this-worldliness) is often considered the most fundamental of all traits underlying the distinctive features of classical and modern Western civilization. Certainly the existence of biography and realistic portraiture, as opposed to hagiography and iconography, to a large degree presumes this attitude. Similarly, the nature of education is shaped by, and the various human sciences depend on, the presence of a humanistic-secular attitude. It may be, therefore, that humanistic secularism should be considered to be logically on a par with the uniform conception of human nature, with each entailing the other. However, I do not believe it is possible to derive individualism directly, or the efflorescence of educational theory exclusively, from the humanistic-secular attitude. So the uniform conception of human nature in some sense remains a more fundamental consideration.

The sciences, divination partly excluded, all result from pragmatic attempts of individuals and collectivities to assert some control over their future through the thoughtful analysis of cause-and-effect relationships. History, political science, and the rest of the social sciences all rest simultaneously on the problematic nature of human behavior when descent does not "explain" why people behave the way they do, and on the humanistic-secular attitude, which allows human behavior to be of interest in its own right. The natural sciences are not directly caught up in this nexus, but because the same grand ritual or religious schemes that "explain" human nature in caste societies often also "explain" the nature of nature (i.e., cosmology), the subject matter of the natural sciences tends to be outside the realm of objective analysis (astronomy, as in India, is a notable exception). Divination is more directly caught up in the relationships entailed by the uniform conception of human nature, because when this conception does not prevail, the ruling strata are composed of deities, who ipso facto have little or no need of divination. But when the divine do not walk among us, or when we cannot be so sure who they are even if some do, then divination may flourish as an adjunct to the sciences used to conduct human affairs. The anxieties associated with social placement in the open society provide strong incentives to divination. Thus although divination is probably found in all societies, it appears to be more widely and avidly pursued in the open ones.

HUMAN NATURE AND HISTORIOGRAPHY

In this and the next two sections I present various perspectives on the question of why historiography is shaped by social stratification. My first approach to this question was to ask if historiographical quality might not be a structural implication of caste. Specifically, I wondered if some logically or empirically necessary condition underlying caste might not clash with or contradict some equally necessary condition underlying sound historical writing. If so, then the two would be logically incompatible. In short, I attempted to explore the *logic* connecting historiography and social stratification. Simultaneous exploration of the other concomitants of openness and closure showed the importance of the conception of human nature in the nexus between hierarchy and history. This section focuses on that nexus.

The belief in multiple human natures and the belief in a totally uniform human nature are both erroneous. By the former I mean those racialist beliefs, characteristic of caste societies, that posit the hereditary transmission of complex and gross behavioral, mental, and spiritual characteristics within allegedly discrete human stocks. Since the pioneering studies of Franz Boas (1911), such beliefs have consistently been shown to lack validity. By a "belief in a totally uniform human nature" I mean the belief found in Taoism, in some forms of socialist thought, and perhaps even among extreme cultural relativists and psychological behaviorists that all persons are inherently alike and vary only as a result of their differing environments. Our present knowledge of human genetics provides a theoretical basis for understanding how complex and gross physical and mental characteristics can be inherited but in a way that systematically provides for much randomness. As a result of this randomness, brought about during reproduction by the halving of each parent's genetic material, each offspring (barring multiple births) is a unique assemblage of genetic material. Each has most features in common with the rest of humanity, but each has a mix of genetic material that makes the individual unlike his or her parents, often in quite significant ways. Of the two beliefs, the belief in a multiplicity of human natures appears to be by far the more detrimental to the development of sound historiography and the study of humanity, because it provides the least insight into the actions of real people; interaction with the environment is far more important than the racialist theory allows.

The racialist ideological assumptions of caste, and the social situation they underpin, affect the development of historiography in a number of other ways too. First, they drastically shift the focus of historical problems. The racialist ideology that underpins caste implies that the essential parts of the "historical" record are certain real or alleged genealogical considerations, not those subtleties of individual variation that in the long run almost always run counter to what the genealogical "facts" should determine. For if people's behavior is basically determined by genealogy, to know their genealogy is to know the main parts of the historical record. But since human behavior is not in fact so thoroughly determined by descent, the historian in the closed society is squarely faced with the task of reconciling assumptions with facts. As many historians and anthropologists can attest, the historian in the closed society frequently resolves this problem by juggling the genealogies to fit the behavior. The Indian and the medieval European materials provide well-known illustrations. When upward mobility did occur in Hindu India, it was explained, not by straightforward accounts of the results of human effort, diligence, luck, and the like, but rather by the fabrication of genealogies that made the high status a function of descent.

Second, the idea of a multiplicity of human types makes allegations of extraordinary, superhuman, and even supernatural actions plausible; the fact that one cannot oneself perform superhuman feats does not imply that others cannot. A person cannot use introspection or personal experience to judge others unless they belong to his race, his species—his caste. (Monstrous races, as well as divinities that combine animal, human, and imaginary forms, may well be extrapolations from the idea of a multiplicity of human species.)

A third effect comes into play when or if a historian actually does observe human behavior, or the record of it, in a detached or scientific way. If the historian observes that any number of important dimensions of the human personality cut directly across the hereditary rank categories, or if investigations show that certain individuals or groups underwent a change of rank contrary to what is deemed proper or possible, he or she would certainly think twice before making these observations part of the history. To do so would invite doubt about the validity of the very assumptions on which authority is allocated in his or her social system. If the historian's own position would not thereby be undermined, the position of his or her most likely patrons—the rulers—surely would be. Maquet, though still referring to a preliterate closed society, has formulated the idea neatly: "verbal behavior toward a superior must express dependence rather than 'truth.' " "Indeed one is supposed to use language not to say what is thought to conform to reality but what is thought to conform to the ruler's opinion" (1961:169; for an analogous situation in India, see Tyler 1973).

Patronage—the matter of who commissions or supports the historian— is clearly one of the decisive factors in the development of historiography. The peculiar feature of the caste-organized society is the idealized continuity and exclusiveness of the patrons. As both the principal subject matter of accounts of the past and the ultimate arbiters of those accounts, they operate in a system without external checks. Moreover, once supernatural claims are made—on behalf of the dominant caste—there are no objective limits to the claims.

It is important to note that the caste-organized society differs in a very significant way from ordinary despotisms or totalitarian societies. The latter also pose problems for the historian, but more in the realm of contemporary history. Candid commentaries on the present rulers invite loss of patronage, or worse fates. But candid comments on past rulers can often be tolerated, for the current rulers do not see themselves as part of a "race" of rulers for whom comments on earlier members have decisive implications for themselves.

Fourth, and closely related to the first, is that problems central to modern historiography—the cause-and-effect relationships between individual motivations and capacities and the course of human events—cannot be problems in the closed society. The problems are "solved" by knowing genealogies. A particular group rules, for example, not because its members or their ancestors exerted themselves, crushed their enemies, and perhaps were lucky too, or because they monopolize physical resources, manipulate people, and propagandize, but because they are a ruling stock, composed of persons who uniquely inherit the right, the duty, and the ability to rule. To search for alternative explanations subverts the foundations of the closed society by showing that the hereditarian explanation is either superfluous or wrong.

In the open society, things are quite different. While logic does not require that an open society necessarily possesses a sound historiography, its conception of human nature is at least compatible with one. And since the placement of individuals in the open system is problematic, individuals have good reason to be concerned to discover the causes and consequences of placement. Their concern may give rise to theories of luck, fate, and the like, but it may also give rise to accurate records of human activity and its consequences.

While open societies come in a variety of forms—including such polar extremes as despotisms and democracies—and hence rest on a variety of assumptions about human nature, apparently none rests on an assumption so crippling to historical truth as the racialist assumption that underpins caste. Hence open societies as a whole contrast with closed societies in the quality of their historiography. The view of the past in the closed society regularly slants toward the *ideological*; in the open society the scope for accurate *knowledge* of the past is regularly greater. The distinction between ideology and knowledge is discussed below, but first it remains to explore various residual factors in the logic that connects social stratification with the quality of historiography.

STRATIFICATION AND HISTORIOGRAPHY

Both the caste and open societies discussed herein were stratified. In most or all of the caste societies, this ranking was considered normal or proper, at least by the societies' dominant ideologues, a point well illustrated in Dumont's *Homo Hierarchicus* (1970a). In the open societies, it may or may not have been considered right and proper for people to be ranked. Thus in China the Confucianists considered rank to be natural and proper, but the Taoists did not. In the caste-organized societies, rank was essentially inherited. In the open societies, insofar as rank was considered proper it was not in essence or necessarily based on birth. It follows that in the caste society the rulers were fixed in place, or were presumed to be properly fixed in place, while in the open society there was a flow of persons into and out of the ruling stratum or strata. In both kinds of societies, indigenous attempts were made to understand, explain, or justify the mode of stratification. In each kind of society, conceptions of people and their interrelationships were elaborated.

These conditions are linked to historical writing by the problem of patronage, for in each kind of society the historian or mythographer needs patrons (even if it be self-patronage). In the caste society the patrons, as hereditary monopolists of power and authority, have no competition in developing ideology. They can say anything about themselves without fear of contradiction, except from their peers, who, of course, benefit equally from any claim to exalted status for themselves. The truth is often a casualty. And this affects members of lower strata too, for in the caste-organized society it is wiser to agree with one's superior than to point out their errors. Under these conditions, a sort of involution occurs, in which only the effectiveness of the ideology is relevant, pushing it to ever greater heights of logical closure and aesthetic refinement. India especially illustrates these points.

In the open society, on the other hand, the patrons can be comprehended as a category or group that may indeed have great continuity in the cultural and some social senses, but its members—seen as individuals or representatives of particular families or lineages—are not constant. Old members, families, or lines drop out, and new ones enter. It is logically necessary in such conditions that there be persons not in the ruling strata who have considerable insight into its personnel, activities, and characteristics: the ex-members remember, and the soon-to-be members are learning what these characteristics are. (Both the requirements and the possibilities of this movement into responsible and rewarding positions, by the way, are incentives to educational development.) It follows from this that the patrons of intellectual activity are not nearly as exclusive a group as in the caste society. Above all, no current member of the ruling stratum could set forth a hereditary claim for the stratum's position without informed objections from outside the stratum. This means that the hereditary argument, though often set forth, cannot prevail, and hence the description, analysis, or understanding of the system must take some other form.

One of the forms that it can and does take is the practice of explaining things by fate or fortune. Such explanations have the advantage of simplicity—and elegance, since they can explain everything. But perhaps because they explain everything and because they provide no pragmatic or even ideological guide to choice (barring techniques of divination), fate and fortune never prove to be fully acceptable and exclusive ideologies. As for divination, it founders on the problem of inconsistency: unless the diviner manipulates the results, no method of divination ever produces the consistency and accuracy that would make it useful in the everyday conduct of affairs. It is not therefore discarded, but it is used as only one of several modes of arriving at decisions, or it is used where no other mode of decision making is more effective. Among the important alternative modes of decision making is the application, by analogy, of knowledge of the past to present and future situations. All, or virtually all, of the historically minded peoples defend historical writing in this framework of pragmatic usefulness.

The key element in knowledge of the past is developed through the observation of human behavior and of other forms of behavior that can be related to human behavior. (In some cases it is divination itself that leads to the observation of human behavior, as was the case in China and Mesopotamia.) One of the simplest effective means of studying human behavior is provided by the historical record. It is particularly effective where the kind of behavior that is of interest cannot be observed in multiple cases at one time, as, for example, in the case of the behavior of kings. If kings are common, then of course one can generalize about them synchronously, but kings have often been sufficiently rare that no one person could observe many at one time. Moreover, the most important things that kings do are not done every day, which further enhances the utility of a record.

Objective records of human behavior are always subject to divergent interpretations and to the perception of different patterns within them. What we know about open systems of social stratification is that they do not lead to such unanimity of opinion about human nature as that characteristic of caste societies. Hence the diversity of opinion so well illustrated in the Hundred Philosophers period of Chinese history and its parallel among the classical Greeks is a consistent if not necessary consequence of their patterns of social stratification. But once the practice of observing human behavior to find useful generalizations emerges, two further developments follow. One is the progressive elimination of certain modes of interpretation as they lose out in competition with increasingly refined, sounder ones. The second is the elaboration of distinct genres of historical and social-scientific thought. Under these conditions—the unchecked elaboration of a hereditary elite's ideology in the closed society and the growth, however faltering, of rudimentary empiricism in the open society—the relative development of ideology and knowledge is sharply affected.

TRANSITIONS AND CAUSATION

However much they may suggest that social stratification and a society's view of the past are not linked accidentally, correlation and logical connection imply nothing about causal direction. Some sense of direction, however, emerges from a consideration of cases involving change. Of those cases in which change consisted of transitions from caste to open stratification, the best documented is the transition that took place in Florence, followed by the transitions taking place among the Ionian Greeks, early republican Romans, Chou Chinese, and perhaps the classical Muslims. Although the Sri Lankan case itself has little to tell us, it rests upon the previous transition from caste to open society advocated by the Buddha. The transitions that apparently took place among the Hebrews, Assyrians, and Babylonians are too obscure to tell us much.

Changes in the opposite direction appear to be rare. The only clear-cut case is the transition that took place in the late western Roman Empire. The *serrata*—the closing of the Great Council in Venice—can be seen as a step to maintain closure (although after some change of personnel at the top) just as well as it can be considered a step to effect it in a previously open society.

The opening of Greek stratification among the Ionians seems to have been gradual, or at any rate to have been largely accomplished by the time historical writing emerged. Hence any direct causal link must run from stratification to the society's view of the past. In early republican Rome the long struggle of the plebs was almost complete before the development of historical writing (some minor forms perhaps excluded). Rome's wars with Carthage, which gave greater scope to social mobility, were also underway before Roman historiography really took off. Again, social developments preceded the development of historiography. Among the classical Muslims, the opening of society under the Abbasids and the development of historiography were either simultaneous developments or the former preceded. The transition was gradual among the Florentines

and probably most other Renaissance Italians. In Florence the fullest flowering of historiography and of the ideology of social mobility probably
took place after the period of the highest rates of social mobility. Whether
gradually or abruptly, in China the sense of history was pushed to sound
levels in conjunction with a conscious attack on the idea of hereditary
stratification, much as occurred in Florence. But the Chinese were more
clearly attacking past practices than existing ones, which again makes a
case for the change in stratification having preceded the development of
sound historiography, thus precluding any causal chain running from the
latter to the former. On the other hand, it could be argued that if the
historian-ideologues of China and Florence (and perhaps Ionia and republican Rome as well) had not attacked caste, it might have been reestablished. Following this line of reasoning, the ideas generated in conjunction
with the writing of history may have helped to maintain the open society
and prevent a return to caste.

Similarities of the Chinese, Ionian Greek, Muslim, and Renaissance
Florentine cases (and possibly the Roman) deserve a digression. Each case
was marked by exuberant cultural development that may have resulted
from the energies unleashed and the motivations fired by conditions peculiar to the transition from a closed to an open society. In these conditions,
faith in the rewards of merit or effort may be greater than at any other
time: people really are able to climb the ladder of success. And this effort
may have produced so much, may have so strongly validated the ideology
of openness, that the ideology could remain vigorous even when reality
was something quite different, as in medieval China and perhaps in fifteenth-century Florence.

The conditions in which the Buddha rejected caste—the pretensions of
the Brahmans in particular—are not well documented. There is some
evidence, however, that it was a period of increasing population, trade,
and urbanization. There is no evidence that a sense of history led the
Buddha to advocate an open society. On the contrary, Buddhism's historical sense is usually seen as a result of the Buddha's life and teaching.

In late antiquity, the simultaneous closing of society and the decline of
historiography, at least in the western empire, were accompanied by substantial economic and military problems. Simple causal arguments for the
decline reflect preconceptions as much as reality. However, it is difficult
to imagine how the decline of historiographic quality could have brought
about caste organization. Hence, either they both reflect some other un-

derlying cause or causes, or changing stratification brought about the decline in historiography.

Although the cases of transition that are sufficiently well documented to tell us something about causation are few, they nonetheless suggest that stratificational conditions preceded and perhaps caused the changing view of the past; or that the two were simultaneous developments, possibly from common causes. In no case is there evidence for sound history preceding and perhaps causing the opening of social stratification.

What other considerations bear on this matter? One is the commonsense observation that if literate peoples do not write history, there is nothing in this fact alone that logically compels them to be caste-organized. It was this line of reasoning that I originally followed in predicting that while caste would always be accompanied by an ahistorical sense, the latter might sometimes occur in the absence of caste. Caste would determine an ahistorical sense, but an ahistorical sense would not necessarily indicate caste. However, the ahistorical sense is regularly associated with caste and rarely with open stratification. This suggests not only that a causal link exists but, since we cannot see why an ahistorical sense could determine caste, that caste must determine an ahistorical sense.

A final consideration stemming from cases of transition between caste and open societies concerns the following question: If, in a caste-organized society when actual social mobility occurs the new men at the top typically fabricate hereditary claims to their positions, why did the new men among the Greeks, the Chinese, or the Florentines, for example, give up this strategy and claim individual merit as the basis of and justification for their rise? One of the answers to this question is provided by the Chinese. The Western Chou dynasty (1111–771 B.C.), when it displaced the Shang, was apparently more concerned to undermine Shang hereditary claims than to ensure its own, and hence rejected a general hereditary right to rule in favor of the concept of the Mandate of Heaven, which mandate would go to those whose behavior merited it (Munro 1969).

Another answer to this question concerns changing rates of social mobility. New men might abandon the ploy of claiming high descent when too many men could make the claim, because what can be believed when relatively small numbers rise to the top may strain credulity when relatively large numbers make their way up. Thus the decision to abandon hereditary claims may actually point to increasing rates of social mobility. In the relevant cases—China, Ionian Greece, republican Rome, classical Islam, and Renaissance Florence—historians are of the opinion that rates of social mobility were on the increase. Perhaps this is the crucial fact in the Chinese case, since it makes reasonable a change that otherwise looks like a blunder: if changes in the structure of society did not create greater scope for social mobility—through, for example, the development of trade (Munro 1969)—then the Chou had little reason not to assert some sort of hereditary claim to rule.

On the other hand, there is little or no evidence that the Chinese ever considered their kings (and nobles) to be divine. If they did not, then they may not have developed the ideology that Maquet, as discussed above, suggests to be the most natural for a hereditarily closed society, and the Chinese ideology—whatever it was—may thus have been inadequate for the defense of hereditary rank. The abandonment of the ideology, or its transmutation, might then have reflected merely an ideological shift rather than a new social reality.

The Chinese case in particular, and all the transitional cases in general, deserve further attention, but the evidence currently available tends to support the view that high rates of social mobility promote both anticaste ideology and sound historical writing. However, once the anticaste ideology is established, it may persist, and so too may sound history, in periods of low actual rates of social mobility.

IDEOLOGY AND KNOWLEDGE

In the social sciences the word *ideology* is used in two distinct ways. In the generic sense it contrasts with such terms as *society*, *economy*, and *technology*. In this sense, ideology may include knowledge. But social scientists also use ideology more specifically, as a term contrasting with *knowledge*. In this sense, knowledge is fact and ideology is something else. In this latter sense, unsound accounts of the past are a part of ideology, while real history is knowledge. Hence, the relevance of a recent discussion of the roots of ideology and knowledge.

Maurice Bloch argues that human discourse comprises two kinds of human cognition: knowledge and ideology. Knowledge results from the "requirements of human action on nature," that is, practical activities such as production and reproduction. Ideology (including ritual) is a product or manifestation of social structure, especially of "instituted hierarchy" (1977:278). Knowledge rests on such concepts of universal validity as linear time, which the comparative study of semantics suggests to be a universal. Knowledge may be used to criticize, and hence to effect change in, the nexus of social structure and ideology. With this formulation, Bloch provides a solution to the problem created by Émile Durkheim's idea that "cognition is [primarily or only] socially determined" (1977:278). For if Durkheim's formulation were correct and a people's cognitive framework were merely and solely a reflection of their social system, they would be unable to formulate concepts to criticize and change their social system.

Bloch also observes that the amount of social structure and ideology in a society is variable. Some societies—he gives, among others, the examples of India and Bali—have a lot, some little. Nonhierarchical peoples going about their productive and reproductive activities in a straightforward manner need not have much in the way of social structure and ideology. Not only are they a variable in quantity, but social structure and ideology, not being anchored in the world of nature, often exhibit qualitative variants that make specific societies or cultures difficult to compare.

It is imperative that anthropologists distinguish knowledge from ideology. Moreover, Bloch's argument that instituted hierarchy is a fertile source of ideology is essentially correct and is a powerful synthesis of disparate case material. To treat each people's cognitive system (or elements thereof) as just one of many ideologies, no one of which, and no parts of which, can be objectively compared cross-culturally, collapses the specific into the general meaning of the word ideology and entails an excessively relativistic view that poses for anthropology the same problems posed by the excesses of historicism in history (to be discussed below). Bloch is correct in pointing out that semantic universals found in the language of practical affairs are good evidence for knowledge.

But the danger of ethnocentrism is as real as that of excessive relativity. The task of separating knowledge from ideology is not easy. Part of the problem is that ideology and knowledge do not always come in the neatly separate packages that Bloch's argument seems to imply. Much human discourse interweaves the two almost inextricably. Moreover, knowledge accumulates slowly, and a great deal of honest error masquerades as knowledge at any given time. The boundary between honest error and ideology is frequently uncertain. When human knowledge cannot bring about practical results of great urgency—such as regular and adequate food crops—magic often appears, to assuage anxiety over the outcome. It is difficult to label magic of this sort as a form of knowledge, but hierarchy has no obvious role in its development.

Bloch's notion of ideology and its genesis must therefore be modified in two ways. First, it must be understood that ideology and knowledge form a continuum and are often mixed together. Second, it must be understood that either ideology is by definition that form of cognition that is connected with hierarchy, or that ideology can spring from sources other than social hierarchy. These modifications do not imperil Bloch's basic argument; they merely refine it.

Equally capable of refinement is Bloch's notion of "instituted hierarchy." All of Bloch's examples are ascriptive, hereditarily determined hierarchies, based either on descent or on sex. A hierarchy based on achievement is not necessarily any less instituted, and may be associated with essentially practical matters, as in modern industry. In the preceding chapters we have seen a striking correlation between hereditary hierarchies with mythical views of the past, on the one hand, and on the other hand, hierarchies based on achievement correlated with sounder historical views. In addition, we found a set of correlates of hereditary versus open stratification, many of which are meaningfully subsumed under the contrast between ideology and knowledge. It follows, then, that "instituted hierarchy" should be limited to hereditary hierarchies, or—and this seems more likely—that among instituted hierarchies the hereditary ones are particularly efficacious producers of ideology.

There remains one final consideration. Does an increase in ideology imply a decrease in knowledge, or can a people develop hierarchy, ritual, and ideology to a high level without any impairment in the development of knowledge? Whatever Bloch's views, my own findings suggest that ritual and ideology seem often to have absorbed the intellectual and physical resources that might have been put to use in more mundane affairs and hence to have stultified the acquisition of knowledge. Certainly this study shows that the social and historical sciences suffered at the expense of hierarchy and ideology.

CULTURAL RELATIVITY

No comparative study can fail to have implications for debates on cultural relativity, always a major issue in anthropology and related disciplines. In its extreme form, cultural relativism posits that each society or civilization has its own distinctive culture, which can only be understood or judged in its own terms. Western social science is therefore powerless to judge or analyze foreign cultures, because Western social science, being a product of Western culture, can only judge or analyze in Western, and hence culture-bound, concepts. Appropriate illustrations of misunderstandings due to ethnocentric preconceptions are readily cited. However, extreme cultural relativism—the notion that one ideology or culture is as valid as the next—puts us in a situation analogous to a court trial in which each witness can be judged only in his own frame of reference. It is a room with no exit.

There are a number of problems with extreme forms of cultural relativism, not the least of which is the fact that its advocates are often Western social scientists who use it to argue against positions or parties they disfavor but who also wish to hold that their own argument or method surmounts the problem and does present a meaningful understanding of other cultures. A second, and far more important, problem with extreme cultural relativism is that, except for cultural borrowing, it offers no explanation of cross-cultural regularities, which its advocates often insist do not exist, are not important, are uninteresting, or cannot be explained by anyone else either. A third problem is the one of moral judgment. This problem in anthropology has its exact parallel in history. Just as, according to cultural relativism, other cultures must be judged on their own terms, so too, according to historicism, each period in time (and place) must be judged on its terms. It has been a lively and generally productive orientation, but it has its limitations: few modern Western historians could bring themselves to judge Nazism on its own terms. Geoffrey Barraclough's 1979 discussion of this problem in history is fully applicable to anthropology.

I intend to focus on the second problem. Every cross-cultural regularity is a challenge to the idea of extreme cultural relativity and demands some sort of explanation. Of specific interest here is the widespread popular interest, documented in previous chapters, in hierarchy and descent. In the caste-organized societies, descent and hierarchy are conjoined. So far as the data allow us to determine, the conjunction is no accident; it is normally buttressed by explicit ideology, which may or may not, however, be accepted by all. Generally we know the ideology of the dominant strata but less commonly that of their underlings. When we do know the views of the inferiors, they do not always conform to the dominant ideology, though sometimes they do.

In the open societies, by contrast, ideology disjoins hierarchy and kinship. Again this is no accident but is explicitly formulated. What is curious is that the ideology is often, if not always, formulated in explicit contraposition to the hereditary transmission of rank (in caste societies, by contrast, the alternative ideology receives little attention). Equally curious is that even within the bosom of the open society, in spite of the prevailing ideology, we find men boasting of their own lineage and taking pride in stepping into the (high) positions of their fathers. Sometimes it is the very ideologues of meritocracy who point with pride to their lineage.

Thus when it comes to hierarchy—among literate peoples anyway—human minds seem to think very much alike, in spite of wide separation in space and time. In caste-organized societies, people in high positions take pride in their lineage and offer preferments to their descendants or other kin as a matter of right and propriety. In open societies, where right and propriety are quite different, people in high places still often take pride in their lineage and attempt to favor their kin. Moreover, insofar as people succeed in establishing themselves as a hereditarily superior caste, there are even further limits to the way they think, for almost everyone hits upon the notion of deification of superiors: what is said to separate one caste from another is simply distance from the supernatural. Thus we find here a severely limited set of ideas, not the variability that cultural relativism leads us to expect. If the human mind were a tabula rasa, passively accepting the writ of culture, such limitations would be intelligible only as extraordinary coincidences or as the product of systematic borrowing. The unlikelihood of either of these explanations was addressed earlier, and it follows that the human mind is not a tabula rasa (see Symons 1979). Some specific universals of the human psyche must underlie the tendency of individuals to claim hereditary distinction even when meritocracy is the societal norm.

Equally suggestive of a universal psyche are the two syndromes of other cultural traits that accompany meritocracy and caste. It is true, of course, as discussed earlier, that Europe, India, and China have long responded to the pulses of each others' cultural life, but it strains belief to argue, for example, that China and the Mediterranean would develop in tandem for several centuries—through processes of cultural diffusion—while bypassing India, and that Europe and India then interchanged cultural orientations for several more centuries while cutting themselves off from China. It is very much more likely that some sorts of constraint operate on human thought so that certain conditions make particular cultural developments more expectable or "natural" than others. I see no reason to preclude the possibility that certain features of human nature are among the conditions that limit or channel cultural development in general, and, in this particular case, lead to the two syndromes connected with caste and meritocracy.

True, these syndromes may be governed more by consistency than by necessity, but the discovery of what constitutes consistency leads us no less to human nature and to the view that extreme cultural relativism cannot explain that nature.

THE USES OF HISTORY

The regularity with which historical writing emerges as a genre when hereditary stratification poses no barrier to it implies that history serves some widespread purpose or has its roots in some facet of human nature or widespread feature of the human predicament. But to grasp any widespread purpose of history, we must realize at the outset that the recent conception of writing history for history's sake, as an end in itself that needs no further justification, is far from being a universal conception even now and has virtually no counterpart in the history of historical writing. With monotonous regularity, the historians of diverse civilizations justify history as a guide to life, using the past to understand and make decisions for the present and future. This conception of history's usefulness was as clearly enunciated in China as in the West.

History's usefulness, however, could take two analytically separable forms, though the distinction has rarely been made by historians themselves. History could tell us how we ought to behave in terms of some moral system that had its own justification, or history could tell us how we ought to behave in terms of what has empirically been shown to work or not to work. The former leads to relatively unsound history, as when neo-Confucianists compiled historical materials to support preconceived moral standards; the latter leads to the relatively sound, as when Chinese historians sought objectively for patterns in history that could be used to assist decision making. The two are often intertwined (Hartwell 1971). In either case, the historian's audience or patrons have the same motives. They read (or listen to) a history in part because they believe it will offer them a guide to life. The historian must either respond to the desires of his audience or risk losing it.

The second most frequently cited reason for writing history is, I believe, its entertainment value. Sound and unsound presentations of the past share an entertainment function, although it is generally recognized that too much emphasis on entertainment can lead to the sacrifice of sound standards. Sigismondo de' Conti (c. 1440–1512), who hit upon the idea of man possessing a "natural" interest in his past, overstated the case when he said that man "will probably read history no matter how clumsily it is written" (Cochrane 1981:158). Historians generally have been mindful of those topical and stylistic matters that will make their works, if not positively entertaining, at least not unduly painful to read. There is good evidence that the average modern purchaser of a history book has very definite entertainment standards. Historians who veer from those standards do not sell well.

Using history as a guide to life and reading history for entertainment are not incompatible. While not all forms of learning are pleasant, some are. Most forms of play, for example, are entertaining, and yet we learn physical and mental skills from them. A well-told story is not only entertaining but also may teach us something about human behavior, which may in turn prove useful in the conduct of our lives. Further evidence for the analogy with play is the content of popular history. Among the historically minded peoples, popular history must be linked to identifiable, distinctive individuals. It is markedly biographical. Without ever using the term "social mobility," that is precisely what it is often about: ups and downs, rises and falls, triumphs and defeats. The ubiquity of histories of wars and battles, with all their potential for social mobility, is notable in this context, as is the common preoccupation of historians with politics in general.

Despite the fact that students in history classes may find history tedious and that books by professional historians do not dominate the best-seller lists, the popular press carries a heavy cargo of contemporary history and a considerable amount of more distant history, often biographical. Historical novels often sell well, and their specifically historical content is certainly part of what makes them interesting. Tale-telling (often presenting maxims for behavior), if not a cross-cultural universal, must be very nearly so. To be sure, a history need not be quite like an oral tale. But the similarity is often obvious, and is often noted.

Listening to tales about the past and reading histories are, to be sure, not the only ways to learn how to behave effectively. Trial-and-error experience is an effective teacher too. But a surprising number of extraordinarily successful individuals managed to combine learning from history with learning from experience. The ethnographic record is replete with examples, and few modern statesmen are exceptions.

At any rate, an argument can be made not only that history is a means for the discovery of regularities in human interaction but also that by the very set of topics it typically treats it unintentionally tells us something more: that human life everywhere is decisively shaped by the possibilities and realities of social mobility, that humans are obsessed with rank and mobility, and perhaps that human beings find thinking and learning about the manifold forms of social mobility intrinsically interesting. That the historian and social scientist have centered so many of their labors on this topic tells us something important about human nature.

References Cited

Abdul Latif bin Haji Ibrahim and P. M. Dato Shariffuddin

    1979   The Discovery of an Ancient Muslim Tombstone in Brunei. *Brunei Museum Journal* 4 (3): 31–37.

Ahmed, Akbar S.

    1984   Al-Beruni: The First Anthropologist. *Rain* 60:9–10

Ahmed, Munir-ud-din

    1968   *Muslim Education and the Scholar's Social Status up to the 5th Century Muslim Era (11th Century Christian Era) in the Light of the Ta'rikh Baghdad.* Zurich: Verlag 'Der Islam.'

Akin Rabibhadana

    1969   *The Organization of Thai Society in the Early Bangkok Period, 1782–1873.* Data Paper No. 74. Southeast Asia Program, Cornell University, Ithaca, N.Y.

Alföldi, Andrew

    1952   *A Conflict of Ideas in the Late Roman Empire: The Clash between the Senate and Valentinian I.* Oxford: Clarendon Press.

Andaya, Barbara Watson, and Virginia Matheson

    1979   Islamic Thought and Malay Tradition: The Writings of Raja Ali Haji of Riau. In Reid and Marr, pp. 108–28.

Andaya, Leonard Y.

    1979   A Village Perception of Arung Palakka and the Makassar War of 1666–69. In Reid and Marr, pp. 360–78.

Anderson, Benedict O'Gorman

    1979   A Time of Darkness and a Time of Light: Transposition in Early Indonesian Nationalist Thought. In Reid and Marr, pp. 219–48.

339

Antal, Frederick
1947 *Florentine Painting and Its Social Background: The Bourgeois Republic before Cosimo de' Medici's Advent to Power, XIV and Early XV Centuries.* London: Kegan Paul.

Arnakis, G. Georgiades
1954 The Eastern Imperial Tradition. In Fitzsimons et al., pp. 67–89.

Arnheim, M.T.W.
1972 *The Senatorial Aristocracy in the Later Roman Empire.* Oxford: Clarendon Press.

Ashmole, Bernard
1964 *The Classical Ideal in Greek Sculpture.* Cincinnati: University of Cincinnati.

Aymonier, Étienne
1900 *Le Cambodge.* Vol. 1: *Le Royaume Actuel.* Paris: Ernest Leroux.

Backus, Charles
1981 *The Nan-chao Kingdom and T'ang China's Southwestern Frontier.* Cambridge: Cambridge University Press.

Badian, E.
1966 The Early Historians. In Dorey, ed., pp. 1–38.

Bailey, F. G.
1963 Closed Social Stratification in India. *Archives Européens de Sociologie* 4:107–24.

Balazs, E.
1964 *Chinese Civilization and Bureaucracy: Variations on a Theme.* Trans. H. M. Wright, ed. Arthur F. Wright. New Haven: Yale University Press.

Baldry, H. C.
1965 *The Unity of Mankind in Greek Thought.* Cambridge: Cambridge University Press.

Barber, Bernard
1968 Social Mobility in Hindu India. In Silverberg, pp. 18–35.

Barker, Ernest
1957 *Social and Political Thought in Byzantium: from Justinian I to the Last Palaeologus.* Oxford: Clarendon Press.

Barnes, Harry Elmer
1922 History, Its Rise and Development: A Survey of the Progress of Historical Writing from Its Origins to the Present Day. Reprinted from the 1922 edition of the *Encyclopedia Americana* [New York, Chicago: The Encyclopedia Americana Corp.].
1937 *A History of Historical Writing.* Norman: University of Oklahoma Press.

Baron, Hans
1960 The Social Background of Political Liberty in the Early Italian Renaissance. *Comparative Studies in Society and History* 2:440–51.
1966 *The Crisis of the Early Italian Renaissance: Civic Humanism and Republican Liberty in an Age of Classicism and Tyranny.* Princeton, N.J.: Princeton University Press.

1968a   Cicero and the Roman Civic Spirit in the Middle Ages and the Early
         Renaissance. In Cheyette, pp. 291–314. Revision of a 1938 paper.
1968b   *From Petrarch to Leonardo Bruni: Studies in Humanistic and Political
         Literature.* Chicago: University of Chicago Press.
Baron, Salo Wittmayer
1952   *A Social and Religious History of the Jews.* Vols. 1 and 2. 2d ed. New
         York: Columbia University Press.
Barraclough, Geoffrey
1979   *Main Trends in History.* New York: Holmes and Meier, Publishers.
Basham, A. L.
1959   *The Wonder That Was India: A Survey of the Culture of the Indian Sub-
         continent before the Coming of the Muslims.* New York: Grove Press.
1961   The Kashmir Chronicle. In Philips, pp. 57–65.
Bastin, John
1964   Problems of Personality in the Reinterpretation of Modern Malayan
         History. In *Malayan and Indonesian Studies: Essays Presented to Sir
         Richard Winstedt on His Eighty-fifth Birthday*, ed. John Bastin and R.
         Roolvink, pp. 141–55. Oxford: Clarendon Press.
Bayley, C. C.
1961   *War and Society in Renaissance Florence: The* De Militia *of Leonardo
         Bruni.* University of Toronto Press.
Beasley, W. G., and E. G. Pulleyblank, eds.
1961   *Historians of China and Japan.* London: Oxford University Press.
Bechert, Heinz
1978   The Beginnings of Buddhist Historiography: *Mahavamsa* and Political
         Thinking. In *Religion and Legitimation of Power in Sri Lanka*, ed.
         Bardwell L. Smith, pp. 1–12. Chambersburg, Pa.: ANIMA Books.
Becker, Howard, and Harry Elmer Barnes
1961   *Social Thought from Lore to Science.* Vol. 1. 3d ed. New York: Dover
         Publications.
Becker, Marvin B.
1960a   Some Aspects of Oligarchical, Dictatorial and Popular *Signorie* in
         Florence, 1282–1382. *Comparative Studies in Society and History* 2:421–
         39.
1960b   The Republican City State in Florence: An Inquiry into its Origin
         and Survival (1280–1434). *Speculum* 35:39–50.
1967   *Florence in Transition.* Vol. 1: *The Decline of the Commune.* Baltimore:
         Johns Hopkins University Press.
1968a   *Florence in Transition.* Vol. 2: *Studies in the Rise of the Territorial State.*
         Baltimore: Johns Hopkins University Press.
1968b   The Florentine Territorial State and Civic Humanism in the Early
         Renaissance. In Rubinstein, ed., pp. 109–39.
1971   Towards a Renaissance Historiography in Florence. In Molho and
         Tedeschi, pp. 141–71.
Becker, Marvin B., and Gene A. Brucker
1956   The *Arti Minori* in Florentine Politics, 1342–1378. *Mediaeval Studies*
         18:93–104.

Berenson, Bernard
    1954   The Arch of Constantine: Or the Decline of Form. New York: Macmillan Co.
    1967   *The Italian Painters of the Renaissance.* London: Phaidon Press.
Berg, C. C.
    1961   Javanese Historiography—A Synopsis of its Evolution. In D.G.E. Hall, pp. 13–23.
    1965   The Javanese Picture of the Past. In Soedjatmoko et al., pp. 87–117.
Beruni, al
    1879   *The Chronology of Ancient Nations: An English Version of the Arabic Text of the Atharul-Bakiya of AlBiruni; or, "Vestiges of the Past," Collected and Reduced to Writing by the Author in A.H. 390–1, A.D. 1000.* Trans. Edward C. Sachau. London: William H. Allen and Co. Written in 1000.
    1910   *AlBeruni's India: An Account of the Religion, Philosophy, Literature, Geography, Chronology, Astronomy, Customs, Laws and Astrology of India about A.D. 1030.* Trans. Edward C. Sachau. 2 vols. London: Kegan Paul, Trench, Trübner and Co. Written c. 1030.
Beteille, André
    1967   Race and Descent as Social Categories in India. *Daedulus* 96:444–63.
Bitton, Davis
    1969   *The French Nobility in Crisis 1560–1640.* Stanford: Stanford University Press.
Blackmore, M.
    1960   The Rise of Nan-chao in Yunan. *Journal of Southeast Asian History* 1:47–61.
Blair, Emma Helen, and James Alexander Robertson, eds.
    1903–9   *The Philippine Islands, 1493–1803.* 55 vols. Cleveland, O.: A. H. Clark Co.
Bloch, Marc
    1961   *Feudal Society.* Trans. L. A. Manyon. 2 vols. Chicago: University of Chicago Press.
Bloch, Maurice
    1977   The Past and the Present in the Present. *Man* 12 (2): 278–92.
Boas, Franz
    1911   *The Mind of Primitive Man.* New York: Macmillan Co.
Bodde, Derk
    1946   Dominant Ideas. In *China*, ed. Harley Farnsworth MacNair, pp. 18–28. Berkeley: University of California Press.
    1961   Myths of Ancient China. In *Mythologies of the Ancient World*, ed. Samuel Noah Kramer, pp. 367–408. New York: Anchor Books.
    1967   *China's First Unifier: A Study of the Ch'in Dynasty as Seen in the Life of Li Ssŭ 280?–208 B.C.* Hong Kong: Hong Kong University Press. Originally published 1938.
Bodde, Derk, and Clarence Morris
    1967   *Law in Imperial China: Exemplified by 190 Ch'ing Dynasty Cases.* Cambridge, Mass.: Harvard University Press.

Bohannan, Laura
   1952   A Genealogical Charter. *Africa* 22: 301–15.
Boissier, Gaston
   n.d.   *Cicero and His Friends: A Study of Roman Society in the Time of Caesar.* Trans. Adnah David Jones. 6th ed. London: Ward, Lock and Co.
Bondanella, Peter E.
   1973   *Machiavelli and the Art of Renaissance History.* Detroit: Wayne State University Press.
Bosl, Karl
   1968   Ruler and Ruled in the German Empire from the Tenth to the Twelfth Century. In Cheyette, pp. 357–75.
   1978   "Noble Unfreedom": The Rise of the Ministeriales in Germany. In Reuter, pp. 291–311.
Bottoms, J. C.
   1965   Some Malay Historical Sources: A Bibiographical Note. In Soedjatmoko et al., pp. 156–93.
Bouwsma, William J.
   1968   *Venice and the Defense of Republican Liberty: Renaissance Values in the Age of the Counter Reformation.* Berkeley and Los Angeles: University of California Press.
   1973   *The Culture of Renaissance Humanism.* Washington, D.C.: American Historical Association.
Bracciolini, Poggio
   1978   On Nobility. In *Humanism and Liberty: Writings on Freedom from Fifteenth-Century Florence*, trans. and ed. Renée Neu Watkins, pp. 121–48. Columbia: University of South Carolina Press. Written in 1440.
Breckenridge, James D.
   1968   *Likeness: A Conceptual History of Ancient Portraiture.* Evanston, Ill.: Northwestern University Press.
Briggs, Lawrence Palmer
   1951   The Ancient Khmer Empire. *Transactions of the American Philosophical Society*, vol. 41, pt. 1.
Brown, Alison
   1979   *Bartolomeo Scala, 1430–1497, Chancellor of Florence: The Humanist as Bureaucrat.* Princeton, N.J.: Princeton University Press.
Brown, D. E.
   1970a   Social Stratification in Brunei. *South-East Asian Journal of Sociology* 3:27–38.
   1970b   *Brunei: The Structure and History of a Bornean Malay Sultanate.* Monograph of the *Brunei Museum Journal.* Brunei: Brunei Museum.
   1971a   The Coronation of Sultan Muhammad Jamalul Alam, 1918. *Brunei Museum Journal* 2 (3): 74–80.
   1971b   Four Brief Notes on the History of Brunei. *Brunei Museum Journal* 2 (3): 173–76.
   1973   Hereditary Rank and Ethnic History: An Analysis of Brunei Historiography. *Journal of Anthropological Research* 29:113–22.

1980   Hiranyagarbha—the Hindu Cosmic Egg—and Brunei's Royal Line. *Brunei Museum Journal* 4 (4): 30–37.

Brown, Horatio F.
1907   *Studies in the History of Venice.* Vol. 1. New York: E. P. Dutton and Co.

Brown, Percy
1975   *Indian Painting under the Mughals, A.D. 1550 to A.D. 1750.* New York: Hacker Art Books. Originally published 1924.

Brown, Peter
1971   *The World of Late Antiquity, AD 150–750.* London: Harcourt Brace Jovanovich.

Brown, W. Norman
1961   Mythology of India. In *Mythologies of the Ancient World*, ed. Samuel Noah Kramer, pp. 277–328. New York: Anchor Books.

Brucker, Gene A.
1962   *Florentine Politics and Society, 1343–1378.* Princeton, N.J.: Princeton University Press.

1964   The Structure of Patrician Society in Renaissance History. *Colloquium* 1:2–11.

1967   Introduction: Florentine Diaries and Diarists. In *Two Memoirs of Renaissance Florence: The Diaries of Buonaccorso Pitti and Gregorio Dati*, trans. Julia Martines, ed. Gene Brucker. New York: Harper and Row.

Buchari
1965   Epigraphy and Indonesian Historiography. In Soedjatmoko et al., pp. 47–73.

Buckler, Georgina
1948   Byzantine Education. In *Byzantium: An Introduction to East Roman Civilization*, ed. Norman H. Baynes and H. St. L. B. Moss, pp. 200–220. Oxford: Clarendon Press.

Bull, Ludlow
1955   Ancient Egypt. In Dentan, pp. 1–34.

Burckhardt, Jacob
1954   *The Civilization of the Renaissance in Italy.* New York: Random House. Originally published 1860.

Burke, Peter
1969   *The Renaissance Sense of the Past.* New York: St. Martin's Press.

Burrows, Millar
1955   Ancient Israel. In Dentan, pp. 99–131.

Bury, J. B.
1909   *The Ancient Greek Historians.* London: Macmillan and Co.

n.d.   *The Imperial Administrative System in the Ninth Century: With a Revised Text of the Kletorologion of Philotheos.* New York: Burt Franklin. Originally published 1911.

n.d.   *A History of Greece to the Death of Alexander the Great.* New York: Random House. Originally published 1937.

Butterfield, H.
1951   *The Whig Interpretation of History.* New York: Charles Scribner's Sons.

Cady, John F.
    1964   *Southeast Asia: Its Historical Development.* New York: McGraw-Hill
           Book Co.
Campbell, J.
    1966   Bede. In Dorey, ed., pp. 159–90.
Carroll, John
    1982   Berunai in the Boxer Codex. *Journal of the Malaysian Branch of the
           Royal Asiatic Society* 55 (2): 1–25.
Chabot, H. Th.
    1950   *Verwantschaap, Stand en Sexe in Zuid-celebes.* Groningen and Jakarta:
           Wolters.
Chambers, Mortimer
    1966   The Crisis of the Third Century. In Lynn White, Jr., pp. 30–58.
Chandler, David
    1979   Cambodian Palace Chronicles (*rajabangsavatar*), 1927–1949: Kingship
           and Historiography at the End of the Colonial Era. In Reid and Marr,
           pp. 207–17.
Chang, Kwang-chih
    1977   *The Archaeology of Ancient China.* 3d ed. New Haven: Yale University
           Press.
Charanis, Peter
    1944–45 On the Social Structure of the Later Roman Empire. *Byzantion* 17:39–
           57.
    1951   On the Social Structure and Economic Organization of the Byzantine
           Empire in the Thirteenth Century and Later. *Byzantinoslavia* 12:94–
           153.
Charnvit Kasetsiri
    1979   Thai Historiography from Ancient Times to the Modern Period. In
           Reid and Marr, pp. 156–70.
Ch'en, Ch'i-yün
    1975   *Hsün Yüeh (A.D. 148–209): The Life and Reflections of an Early Medieval
           Confucian.* Cambridge: Cambridge University Press.
    1980   *Hsün Yüeh and the Mind of Late Han China: A Translation of the* Shen-
           Chien *with Introduction and Annotations.* Princeton, N.J.: Princeton
           University Press.
Cheyette, Fredric L., ed.
    1968   *Lordship and Community in Medieval Europe.* New York: Holt, Rine-
           hart, and Winston.
Chrimes, K.M.T.
    1942   *Ancient Sparta: A Re-examination of the Evidence.* Manchester: Man-
           chester University Press.
Ch'ü, T'ung-tsu
    1972   *Han Social Structure.* Ed. Jack L. Dull. Seattle: University of Wash-
           ington Press.
Cicero, Marcus Tullius
    1950   *Brutus, On the Nature of the Gods, On Divination, On Duties.* Trans.

Hubert M. Poteat. Introduction by Richard McKeon. Chicago: University of Chicago Press.

Cochrane, Charles Norris
  1929   *Thucydides and the Science of History*. London: Oxford University Press.

Cochrane, Eric
  1981   *Historians and Historiography in the Italian Renaissance*. Chicago: University of Chicago Press.

Coedès, G.
  1966   *The Making of South East Asia*. Trans. H. M. Wright. Berkeley: University of California Press.
  1968   *The Indianized States of Southeast Asia*. Ed. Walter F. Vella. Trans. Susan Brown Cowing. Honolulu: East-West Center Press.

Cohn, Bernard S.
  1961   The Pasts of an Indian Village. *Comparative Studies in Society and History* 3:241–49.
  1971   *India: The Social Anthropology of a Civilization*. Englewood Cliffs, N.J.: Prentice-Hall.
  1981   Anthropology and History in the 1980s: Toward a Rapprochement. *Journal of Interdisciplinary History* 12:227–52.

Colgrave, Bertram
  1969   Historical introduction to *Bede's Ecclesiastical History of the English People*, ed. Bertram Colgrave and R.A.B. Mynors. Oxford: Clarendon Press.

Collingwood, R. G.
  1946   *The Idea of History*. Oxford: Clarendon Press.

Contenau, Georges
  1954   *Everyday Life in Babylon and Assyria*. Trans. K. R. Maxwell-Hyslop and A. R. Maxwell-Hyslop. London: Edward Arnold.

Coomaraswamy, Ananda K.
  1931   Foreword to *Portrait Sculpture in South India*, by T. G. Aravamuthan. London: India Society.
  1975   *Rajput Painting: Being an Account of the Hindu Paintings of Rajasthan and the Panjab Himalayas from the Sixteenth to the Nineteenth Century. Described in their Relation to Contemporary Thought*. New York: Hacker Art Books. Originally published 1916.

Cosenza, Mario Emilio
  1962   *Biographical and Bibliographical Dictionary of the Italian Humanists and of the World of Classical Scholarship in Italy, 1300–1800*. Vol. 5. Boston: G. K. Hall and Co.

Covarrubias, Miguel
  1937   *Island of Bali*. New York: Alfred A. Knopf.

Cowan, C. D., and O. W. Wolters, eds.
  1976   *Southeast Asian History and Historiography: Essays Presented to D.G.E. Hall*. Ithaca, N.Y.: Cornell University Press.

Creel, Herrlee Glessner
  1937   *The Birth of China: A Study of the Formative Period of Chinese Civilization*. New York: Frederick Ungar Publishing Co.

Crombie, A. C., ed.

1963   *Scientific Change: Historical Studies in the Intellectual, Social and Technical Conditions for Scientific Discovery and Technical Invention, from Antiquity to the Present.* London: Heinemann.

Czekanowski, Jan, ed.

1917   *Forschungen im Nil-Kongo-Zwischengebiet.* Vol. 1. Leipzig: Klinkhard und Biermann.

Dalton, O. M.

1927   Introduction. Vol. 1 of *The History of the Franks*, by Gregory of Tours. Trans. O. M. Dalton. Oxford: Clarendon Press.

Dannenfeldt, Matthew A.

1954a   The Heritage of Antiquity. In Fitzsimons et al., pp. 1–14.

1954b   The Italian Renaissance. In Fitzsimons et al., pp. 91–103.

Dasgupta, Surama

1968   The Individual in Indian Ethics. In Moore, pp. 285–97.

Davis, James Cushman

1962   *The Decline of the Venetian Nobility as a Ruling Class.* Baltimore: Johns Hopkins University Press.

Davis, Natalie Z.

1981   Anthropology and History in the 1980s: The Possibilities of the Past. *Journal of Interdisciplinary History* 12:267–75.

de Bary, Wm. Theodore

1959   Some Common Tendencies in Neo-Confucianism. In *Confucianism in Action*, ed. David S. Nivison and Arthur F. Wright, pp. 25–49. Stanford: Stanford University Press.

Demiéville, P.

1961   Chang Hsueh-Ch'eng and His Historiography. In Beasley and Pulleyblank, pp. 167–85.

Dentan, Robert C., ed.

1955   *The Idea of History in the Ancient Near East.* New Haven: Yale University Press.

de Silva, K. M.

1981   *A History of Sri Lanka.* London: C. Hurst and Co.

Dhalla, Manecki Nusservanji

1922   *Zoroastrian Civilization: From the Earliest Times to the Downfall of the Last Zoroastrian Empire, 651 A.D.* New York: Oxford University Press.

Diehl, Charles

1948   Byzantine Art. In *Byzantium: An Introduction to East Roman Civilization*, ed. Norman H. Baynes and H. St. L. B. Moss, pp. 166–99. Oxford: Clarendon Press.

1957   *Byzantium: Greatness and Decline.* Trans. Naomi Walford. New Brunswick, N.J.: Rutgers University Press.

Dirks, Nicholas

1982   The Pasts of a Pālaiyakārar: The Ethnohistory of a South Indian Little King. *Journal of Asian Studies* 41:655–83.

Djajadiningrat, Hoesein
    1965   Local Trade and the Study of Indonesian History. In Soedjatmoko
             et al., pp. 74–85.
Dorey, T. A.
    1966   Caesar: The "Gallic War." In Dorey, ed., pp. 65–84.
Dorey, T. A., ed.
    1966   *Latin Historians*. London: Routledge and Kegan Paul.
Douglas, David C.
    1964   *William the Conqueror: The Norman Impact upon England*. Berkeley:
             University of California Press.
Duby, Georges
    1968   The Nobility in Eleventh- and Twelfth-Century Mâconnais. In Chey-
             ette, pp. 137–55.
Dumézil, Georges
    1970   *Archaic Roman Religion*. Trans. Philip Krapp. Vol. 1. Chicago: Uni-
             versity of Chicago Press.
Dumont, Louis
    1965   The Modern Conception of the Individual: Notes on Its Genesis and
             That of Concomitant Institutions. *Contributions to Indian Sociology*
             8:13–61.
    1970a   *Homo Hierarchicus: An Essay on the Caste System*. Trans. Mark Sains-
             bury. Chicago: University of Chicago Press.
    1970b   The Individual as an Impediment to Sociological Comparison and
             Indian History. In *Religion/Politics and History in India: Collected Papers
             in Indian Sociology*, pp. 133–150. Paris and The Hague: Mouton Pub-
             lishers.
    1977   *From Mandeville to Marx: The Genesis and Triumph of Economic Ideology*.
             Chicago: University of Chicago Press.
Duri, A. A.
    1962   The Iraq School of History to the Ninth Century—A Sketch. In Lewis
             and Holt, pp. 46–53.
Eberhard, Wolfram
    1962   *Social Mobility in Traditional China*. Leiden: E. J. Brill.
Ebrey, Patricia Buckley
    1978   *The Aristocratic Families of Early Imperial China: A Case Study of the
             Po-Ling Ts'ui Family*. Cambridge: Cambridge University Press.
Edelstein, Ludwig
    1963   Motives and Incentives for Science in Antiquity. In Crombie, pp. 15–
             41.
Elvin, Mark
    1973   *The Pattern of the Chinese Past*. Stanford: Stanford University Press.
Encyclopaedia Judaica.
    1971   16 vols. New York: Macmillan Co.
Errington, Shelly
    1979   Some Comments on Style in the Meaning of the Past. In Reid and
             Marr, pp. 26–42.

Esnoul, A. M.
    1968   La divination dans l'Inde. In *La Divination*, ed. André Caquot and Marcel Leibovici, pp. 115–39. Paris: Presses Universitaires de France.

Fehl, Noah Edward
    1964   *History and Society*. Hong Kong: Chung Chi Publications.

Ferguson, Wallace K.
    1948   *The Renaissance in Historical Thought: Five Centuries of Interpretation*. Houghton Mifflin Co.

Finkelstein, J. J.
    1963   Mesopotamian Historiography. *Proceedings of the American Philosophical Society* 107:461–72.

Finley, M. I.
    1959   Was Greek Civilization Based on Slave Labour? *Historia* 8:145–64.
    1962   *The World of Odysseus*. Rev. ed. Harmondsworth, Eng.: Penguin Books.
    1973   *Democracy: Ancient and Modern*. New Brunswick, N.J.: Rutgers University Press.

Finley, M. I., ed.
    1974   *Studies in Ancient Society*. London: Routledge and Kegan Paul.

Fitzsimons, Matthew A., Alfred G. Pundt, and Charles E. Nowell, eds.
    1954   *The Development of Historiography*. Harrisburg, Pa.: Stackpole Co.

Forrest, W. G.
    1968   *A History of Sparta, 950–192 B.C.* London: Hutchinson University Library.

Fox, Richard G.
    1969   *Varna* Schemes and Ideological Integration in Indian Society. *Comparative Studies in Society and History* 11:27–45.

Frank, Tenney
    1916   Race Mixture in the Roman Empire. *American Historical Review* 21:689–708.

Franke, Herbert
    1961   Some Aspects of Chinese Private Historiography in the Thirteenth and Fourteenth Centuries. In Beasley and Pulleyblank, pp. 115–34.
    1974   Chinese Historiography under Mongol Rule: The Role of History in Acculturation. *Mongolian Studies* 1:15–26.

Franke, Wolfgang
    1961   The Veritable Records of the Ming Dynasty (1368–1644). In Beasley and Pulleyblank, pp. 60–77.
    1968   *An Introduction to the Sources of Ming History*. Kuala Lumpur: University of Malaya Press.

Frankfort, Henri
    1951   *The Birth of Civilization in the Near East*. Bloomington: Indiana University Press.
    1961   *Ancient Egyptian Religion: An Interpretation*. New York: Harper and Brothers. Originally published 1948.

Friederich, R.
    1959   *The Civilization and Culture of Bali*. Ed. Ernst R. Rost. Calcutta: Susil Gupta. Originally published 1877.

Friedman, John Block

1981   *The Monstrous Races in Medieval Art and Thought*. Cambridge, Mass.: Harvard University Press.

Frost, Frank J.

1987   *Greek Society*. 3d ed. Lexington, Mass.: D. C. Heath and Co.

Fung, Yu-lan

1952   *A History of Chinese Philosophy*. Vol. 1: *The Period of the Philosophers (From the Beginnings to Circa 100 B.C.)*. Trans. Derk Bodde. Princeton, N.J.: Princeton University Press.

1964   *Chung-kuo che hsüeh shih hsin pien*. Rev. ed. Vol. 1. Peking: Jen-min.

Fürer-Haimendorf, C. von

1961   The Historical Value of Indian Bardic Literature. In Philips, pp. 87–93.

Gardner, Charles S.

1961   *Chinese Traditional Historiography*. Cambridge, Mass.: Harvard University Press. Originally published 1938.

Garin, Eugenio

1965   *Italian Humanism: Philosophy and Civic Life in the Renaissance*. Trans. Peter Munz. Oxford: Basil Blackwell. Originally published 1947.

Garnsey, Peter

1970   *Social Status and Legal Privilege in the Roman Empire*. Oxford: Clarendon Press.

Geertz, Clifford

1959   Form and Variation in Balinese Village Structure. *American Anthropologist* 61:991–1012.

1966   *Person, Time and Conduct in Bali: An Essay in Cultural Analysis*. Cultural Report Series No. 14. Southeast Asia Studies, Yale University.

1980   *Negara: The Theatre State in Nineteenth-Century Bali*. Princeton, N.J.: Princeton University Press.

Gelzer, Matthias

1969   *The Roman Nobility*. Trans. Robin Seager. Oxford: Basil Blackwell. Originally published 1912.

Genicot, Léopold

1968   The Nobility in Medieval *Francia*: Continuity, Break, or Evolution? In Cheyette, pp. 128–36.

1978   Recent Research on the Medieval Nobility. In Reuter, pp. 17–35.

Ghoshal, U. N.

1961   Presidential Address. In *Indian History Congress, Proceedings of the Twenty-third Session, Aligarh, 1960*. Part 1, pp. 1–20.

Gibb, H.A.R.

1933   The Islamic Background of Ibn Khaldun's Political Theory. *Bulletin of the School of Oriental Studies* 7:23–31.

Gibb, Hamilton

1962   Islamic Biographical Literature. In Lewis and Holt, pp. 54–58.

Gilbert, Felix

1965   *Machiavelli and Guicciardini: Politics and History in Sixteenth-Century Florence*. Princeton, N.J.: Princeton University Press.

1967   The Renaissance Interest in History. In *Art, Science, and History in the Renaissance*, ed. Charles Singleton, pp. 373–87. Baltimore: Johns Hopkins University Press.

1968   The Venetian Constitution in Florentine Political Thought. In Rubinstein, ed., pp. 463–500.

Gilmore, Myron P.

1952   *The World of Humanism, 1453–1517*. New York: Harper and Row.

Godakumbura, C. E.

1961   Historical Writing in Sinhalese. In Philips, pp. 72–86.

Godolphin, Francis R. B., ed.

1942   *The Greek Historians*. 2 vols. New York: Random House.

Goody, Jack, and Ian Watt

1963   The Consequences of Literacy. *Comparative Studies in Society and History* 5 (3): 304–45.

Gordon, Edmund I.

1960   A New Look at the Wisdom Literature of Sumer and Akkad. *Bibliotheca Orientalis* 17:122–52.

Gordon, Mary L.

1924   The Nationality of Slaves under the Early Roman Empire. *Journal of Roman Studies* 14:93–111.

Goris, R.

1960   The Position of the Blacksmiths. In *Bali: Studies in Life, Thought, and Ritual. Selected Studies on Indonesia by Dutch Scholars*, vol. 5, pp. 291–99. The Hague: W. van Hoeve. Originally published 1929.

n.d.   *The Island of Bali: Its Religion and Ceremonies*. Batavia: G. Kolff and Co.

Graaf, H. J. de

1965   Later Javanese Sources and Historiography. In Soedjatmoko et al., pp. 119–36.

Grabar, A.

1967   Byzantine Architecture and Art. In Hussey, pp. 307–53.

Green, Louis

1972   *Chronicle into History: An Essay on the Interpretation of History in Florentine Fourteenth-Century Chronicles*. Cambridge: Cambridge University Press.

Grendler, Paul F.

1971   The Concept of Humanist in Cinquecento Italy. In Molho and Tedeschi, pp. 445–63.

Grunebaum, Gustave E. von

1961   *Medieval Islam: A Study in Cultural Orientation*. 2d ed. Chicago: University of Chicago Press.

1962   Self-Image and Approach to History. In Lewis and Holt, pp. 457–83.

1964   *Modern Islam: The Search for Cultural Identity*. New York: Vintage Books.

1970   *Classical Islam: A History, 660–1258*. Trans. Katherine Watson. Chicago: Aldine Publishing Co.

Gullick, J. M.

1958   *Indigenous Political Systems of Western Malaya*. London School of Economics Monographs on Social Anthropology, No. 17. London: Athlone Press.

Gwynn, Aubrey

1926   *Roman Education from Cicero to Quintilian*. Oxford: Clarendon Press.

Hall, D.G.E.

1950   *Burma*. London: Hutchinson's University Library.

1961a   Introduction to *Historians of South East Asia*, ed. D.G.E. Hall. London: Oxford University Press.

1961b   British Writers of Burmese History from Dalrymple to Bayfield. In Hall, ed., pp. 255–66.

1964   *A History of South-East Asia*. 2d ed. London: Macmillan and Co.

Hall, D.G.E., ed.

1961   *Historians of South East Asia*. London: Oxford University Press.

Hall, Kenneth R.

1980   *Trade and Statecraft in the Age of the Cōlas*. New Delhi: Abhinar Publications.

Hammond, Lincoln Davis

1963   *Travelers in Disguise: Narratives of Eastern Travel by Poggio Bracciolini and Ludovico de Varthema*. Trans. John Winter Jones. Revised, with an introduction by L. D. Hammond.

Hammond, N.G.L., and H. H. Scullard, eds.

1970   *The Oxford Classical Dictionary*. 2d ed. Oxford: Clarendon Press.

Han, Fei

1959   *The Complete Works of Han Fei Tzŭ: A Classic of Chinese Political Science*. Vol. 1. Trans. W. K. Liao. London: Arthur Probsthain.

Han, Yu-shan

1955   *Elements of Chinese Historiography*. Hollywood, Calif.: W. M. Hawley.

Hanks, Lucien M., Jr., and Jane R. Hanks

1964   Siamese Tai. In LeBar et al., pp. 197–205.

Hardy, P.

1961   Some Studies in Pre-Mughal Muslim Historiography. In Philips, pp. 115–27.

Harper, Edward B.

1968   A Comparative Analysis of Caste: The United States and India. In Singer and Cohn, pp. 51–77.

Hartwell, Robert M.

1971   Historical Analogism, Public Policy, and Social Science in Eleventh- and Twelfth-Century China. *American Historical Review* 76:690–727.

Haskins, Charles Homer

1915   *The Normans in European History*. Boston: Houghton Mifflin Co.

1966   *The Renaissance of the Twelfth Century*. Cleveland: World Publishing Co. Originally published 1927.

Hastings, James, ed.

1928   *Encyclopaedia of Religion and Ethics*. 13 vols. New York: Charles Scribner's Sons.

Hauck, Karl
1978   The Literature of House and Kindred Associated with Medieval Noble
        Families. Illustrated from Eleventh- and Twelfth-Century Satires on
        the Nobility. In Reuter, pp. 61–85.
Headly, D.
1950   Some Bisaya Folklore. *Sarawak Museum Journal* 5 (2): 187–92.
Hearn, Maxwell K.
1979   An Ancient Chinese Army Rises from Underground Sentinel Duty.
        Smithsonian 10 (8): 39–51.
Henderson, M. I.
1963   The Establishment of the *Equester Ordo. Journal of Roman Studies* 53:61–
        72.
Herodotus
1942   *The Persian Wars*. Trans. George Rawlinson. In *The Greek Historians:
        The Complete and Unabridged Works of Herodotus, Thucydides, Xenophon,
        Arrian*. Ed. Francis R. B. Godolphin. Vol. 1. New York: Random
        House. Written in fifth century B.C.
Hexter, J. H.
1968   The Rhetoric of History. In *International Encyclopedia of the Social
        Sciences*, vol. 6., pp. 368–94.
Hill, H.
1952   *The Roman Middle Class in the Republican Period*. Oxford: Basil Black-
        well.
1969   Nobilitas in the Imperial Period. *Historia* 18:230–50.
Hitti, Philip K.
1960   *History of the Arabs from the Earliest Times to the Present*. 7th ed. London:
        Macmillan and Co.
1968   *The Arabs: A Short History*. 5th ed. New York: St. Martin's Press.
Ho, Ping-ti
1964   *The Ladder of Success in Imperial China: Aspects of Social Mobility, 1368–
        1911*. New York: John Wiley and Sons.
Hollister, C. Warren
1966   Twilight in the West. In Lynn White, Jr., pp. 179–205.
Holmes, George
1969   *The Florentine Enlightenment, 1400–50*. New York: Pegasus.
1975   *Europe: Hierarchy and Revolt, 1320–1450*. Sussex, Eng.: Harvester Press.
Honey, P. J.
1961   Modern Vietnamese Historiography. In D.G.E. Hall, ed., pp. 94–
        104.
Hooykaas, C.
1961   A Critical Stage in the Study of Indonesia's Past. In D.G.E. Hall, ed.,
        pp. 313–25.
Hopkins, Keith
1961   Social Mobility in the Later Roman Empire: The Evidence of Au-
        sonius. *Classical Quarterly* 11:239–49.
1974   Elite Mobility in the Roman Empire. In Finley, ed., pp. 103–20.
1978   *Conquerors and Slaves*. Cambridge: Cambridge University Press.

Hoxie, Albert
  1966   Mutations in Art. In Lynn White, Jr., pp. 266–90.
Hsieh, Yu-Wei
  1968   The Status of the Individual in Chinese Ethics. In Moore, pp. 271–
            84.
Hsu, Cho-yun
  1965   *Ancient China in Transition: An Analysis of Social Mobility, 722–222 B.C.*
            Stanford: Stanford University Press.
Huart, Clement
  1927   *Ancient Persia and Iranian Civilization.* Trans. M. R. Dobie. New
            York: Alfred A. Knopf.
Huizinga, Johan
  1950   *The Waning of the Middle Ages: A Study of the Forms of Life, Thought
            and Art in France and the Netherlands in the XIVth and XVth Centuries.*
            London: Edward Arnold and Co. Originally published 1924.
  1963   A Definition of the Concept of History. Trans. D. R. Cousin. In
            Philosophy and History: Essays presented to Ernst Cassirer, ed. Raymond
            Klibansky and H. J. Paton, pp. 1–10. New York: Harper and Row.
Hulsewé, A.F.P.
  1961   Notes on the Historiography of the Han Period. In Beasley and
            Pulleyblank, pp. 31–43.
Hussey, J. M., ed.
  1967   *The Cambridge Medieval History.* Vol. 4: *The Byzantine Empire,* Part
            2: Government, Church and Civilization. Cambridge: Cambridge Uni-
            versity Press.
Huxley, G. L.
  1962   *Early Sparta.* Cambridge, Mass.: Harvard University Press.
Ibn Khaldûn
  1958   *The Muqaddimah: An Introduction to History.* Trans. Franz Rosenthal.
            3 vols. Princeton, N.J.: Princeton University Press.
  1967   *The Muqaddimah: An Introduction to History.* Trans. Franz Rosenthal,
            ed. N. J. Dawood. Princeton, N.J.: Princeton University Press.
Inden, Ronald B.
  1976   *Marriage and Rank in Bengali Culture: A History of Caste and Clan
            in Middle Period Bengal.* Berkeley: University of California Press.
Irsigler, Franz
  1978   On the Aristocratic Character of Early Frankish Society. In Reuter,
            pp. 105–36.
Jacobsen, Thorkild
  1943   Primitive Democracy in Ancient Mesopotamia. *Journal of Near Eastern
            Studies* 2:159–72.
Jenkins, R.J.H.
  1967   Social Life in the Byzantine Empire. In Hussey, pp. 79–103.
Johns, A. H.
  1976   Islam in Southeast Asia: Problems of Perspective. In Cowan and
            Wolters, pp. 304–20.

1979 The Turning Image: Myth and Reality in Malay Perceptions of the Past. In Reid and Marr, pp. 43–67.

Johnson, David G.

1977 *The Medieval Chinese Oligarchy*. Boulder, Colo.: Westview Press.

Jones, A.H.M.

1956 Slavery in the Ancient World. *Economic History Review* 9:185–99.

1963 The Social Background of the Struggle Between Paganism and Christianity. In *The Conflict between Paganism and Christianity in the Fourth Century*, ed. Arnaldo Momigliano, pp. 17–37. Oxford: Clarendon Press.

1964 *The Later Roman Empire, 284–602: A Social, Economic and Administrative Survey*. 2 vols. Norman: University of Oklahoma Press.

1967 *Sparta*. Cambridge, Mass.: Harvard University Press.

1974 The Roman Colonate. In Finley, ed., pp. 288–303.

Kalhana

1961 *Kalhana's Rajatarangini: A Chronicle of the Kings of Kasmir*. Trans. M. A. Stein. 2 vols. Delhi: Motilal Banarsidass. Translation originally published 1900.

Kaul, Gwasha Lal

1967 *Kashmir Throughout the Ages (5000 B.C. to 1967 A.D.)*. Srinagar, Kashmir: Chronicle Publishing House.

Kautalya

1963 *The Kautilīya Arthásāstra*. Part 2. Trans. R. P. Kangle. Bombay: University of Bombay. Written in third century B.C.

Keightley, David N.

1978 *Sources of Shang History: The Oracle Bone Inscriptions of Bronze-Age China*. Berkeley: University of California Press.

Kelley, Donald R.

1970 *Foundations of Modern Historical Scholarship: Language, Law, and History in the French Renaissance*. New York and London: Columbia University Press.

Kent, Dale

1978 *The Rise of the Medici: Faction in Florence, 1426–1434*. Oxford: Oxford University Press.

Khoo, Kay Kim

1979 Local Historians and the Writing of Malaysian History in the Twentieth Century. In Reid and Marr, pp. 299–311.

Kierman, Frank Algerton, Jr.

1962 *Ssu-ma Ch'ien's Historiographical Attitude as Reflected in Four Late Warring States Biographies*. Wiesbaden: Otto Harrassowitz.

King, Florence

1976 *Southern Ladies and Gentlemen*. New York: Bantam Books.

Kirshner, Julius

1971 Paolo di Castro on *cives ex privilegio*: A Controversy over the Legal Qualifications for Public Office in Early Fifteenth Century Florence. In Molho and Tedeschi, pp. 227–64.

Kosambi, D. D.

1952   Ancient Kosala and Magadha. *Journal of the Bombay Branch, Royal Asiatic Society* 27:180–213.

1955   The Basis of Ancient Indian History. *Journal of the American Oriental Society* 75:35–45, 226–37.

Krader, Lawrence

1968   Person, Ego, Human Spirit in Marcel Mauss: Comments. *Psychoanalytic Review* 55:482–90.

Kristeller, Paul Oskar

1961   *Renaissance Thought: The Classic, Scholastic, and Humanistic Strains.* New York: Harper and Brothers.

1965   *Renaissance Thought II: Papers on Humanism and the Arts.* New York: Harper and Row.

Kroeber, A. L.

1952   History and Science in Anthropology. In *The Nature of Culture*, pp. 63–65. Chicago: University of Chicago Press. Originally published 1935.

Kumar, Ann

1979   Javanese Historiography in and of the "Colonial Period": A Case Study. In Reid and Marr, pp. 187–206.

Kumar, Sudarshan

1969   Social Conditions in Ancient Kashmir (c. A.D. 855–1150). Ph.D. thesis, University of London.

Labalme, Patricia H.

1969   *Bernardo Giustiniani: A Venetian of the Quattrocento.* Rome: Edizioni di Storia et Letteratura.

Lacroix, Benoit

1954a   Carolingian Humanism and Its Historiography. In Fitzsimons et al., pp. 27–35.

1954b   Early Medieval Historiography. In Fitzsimons et al., pp. 15–25.

Lambert, W. G.

1960   *Babylonian Wisdom Literature.* Oxford: Clarendon Press.

Lambton, Ann K. S.

1962   Persian Biographical Literature. In Lewis and Holt, pp. 141–51.

Lancman, Eli

1966   *Chinese Portraiture.* Rutland, Vt.: Charles E. Tuttle Co.

Lane, Frederic C.

1966   *Venice and History: The Collected Papers of Frederic C. Lane.* Baltimore: Johns Hopkins University Press.

Lawrence, A. E.

1911   Stories of the First Brunei Conquests on the Sarawak Coast. *Sarawak Museum Journal* 1 (1): 120–24.

Leach, E. R.

1960   What Should We Mean by Caste? In Leach, ed., pp. 1–10.

Leach, E. R., ed.
 1960 *Aspects of Caste in South India, Ceylon and North-West Pakistan.* Cambridge: Cambridge University Press.
LeBar, Frank M., Gerald C. Hickey, and John K. Musgrave
 1964 *Ethnic Groups of Mainland Southeast Asia.* New Haven: Human Relations Area Files Press.
Leclant, Jean
 1968 Éléments pour une Étude de la Divination dans l'Égypte Pharaonique. In *La Divination,* ed. André Caquot and Marcel Leibovici, pp. 1–23. Paris: Presses Universitaires de France.
Legge, James
 1960 *The Chinese Classics.* 5 vols. Hong Kong: Hong Kong University Press.
Lessa, William A.
 1968 *Chinese Body Divination: Its Forms, Affinities, and Functions.* Los Angeles: United World.
Levine, Philip
 1966 The Continuity and Preservation of the Latin Tradition. In Lynn White, Jr., pp. 206–31.
Lévi-Strauss, Claude
 1979 *Myth and Meaning.* New York: Schocken Books.
Levy, Reuben
 1957 *The Social Structure of Islam.* Cambridge: Cambridge University Press.
Lewis, Bernard
 1962 The Use by Muslim Historians of Non-Muslim Sources. In Lewis and Holt, pp. 180–91.
Lewis, Bernard, and P. M. Holt, eds.
 1962 *Historians of the Middle East.* London: Oxford University Press.
Lichtheim, Miriam
 1966 Autonomy versus Unity in the Christian East. In Lynn White, Jr., pp. 119–46.
Litchfield, R. Burr
 1971 Office-Holding in Florence after the Republic. In Molho and Tedeschi, pp. 531–55.
Logan, Oliver
 1972 *Culture and Society in Venice, 1470–1790.* New York: Charles Scribner's Sons.
Lohuizen-de Leeuw, J. E. van
 1970 India and its Cultural Empire. In *Orientalism and History,* 2d ed., ed. Denis Sinor. Bloomington: Indiana University Press.
Loon, P. van der
 1961 The Ancient Chinese Chronicles and the Growth of Historical Ideas. In Beasley and Pulleyblank, pp. 24–30.
Lot, Ferdinand
 1961 *The End of the Ancient World and the Beginnings of the Middle Ages.* New York: Harper and Row. Originally published 1937.

Lovejoy, Arthur O.
  1942   *The Great Chain of Being: A Study of the History of an Idea*. Cambridge,
          Mass.: Harvard University Press.
Low, Hugh
  1880   Sĕlĕsîlah (Book of the Descent) of the Rajas of Bruni. *Journal of the
          Straits Branch of the Royal Asiatic Society* 5:1–35.
Luce, G. H.
  1976   Sources of Early Burma History. In Cowan and Wolters, pp. 31–42.
Lucretius
  1962   *On the Nature of the Universe*. Trans. Ronald Latham. Baltimore:
          Penguin Books.
M. Hilmy M. Ahmad
  1962   Some Notes on Arabic Historiography during the Zengid and Ayyu-
          bid Periods (521/1127–648/1250). In Lewis and Holt, pp. 79–97.
Ma, Ch'ang-shou
  1962   *Nan-chao Kuo-nei ti Pu-tsu-tsu-ch'eng ho Nu-ti-chih-tu* (The tribal com-
          position of Nanchau and its slavery system). Shanghai.
McAlister, John T., and Paul Mus
  1970   *The Vietnamese and Their Revolution*. New York: Harper and Row.
McDonald, A. H.
  1954   The Roman Historians. In *Fifty Years of Classical Scholarship*, ed. Maur-
          ice Platnauer, pp. 384–412. Oxford: Basil Blackwell.
Macdonell, Arthur A.
  1929   *History of Sanskrit Literature*. New York: Appleton.
Macfarlane, Alan
  1978   *The Origins of English Individualism: The Family, Property and Social
          Transition*. New York: Cambridge University Press.
McKeon, Richard
  1950   Introduction to Cicero 1950.
MacMullen, Ramsay
  1964   Social Mobility and the Theodosian Code. *Journal of Roman Studies*
          54:49–53.
  1974   *Roman Social Relations, 50 B.C. to A.D. 284*. New Haven: Yale University
          Press.
Majumdar, R. C.
  1961   Ideas of History in Sanskrit Literature. In Philips, pp. 12–28.
Malinowski, Bronislaw
  1948   *Magic, Science and Religion, and Other Essays*. Garden City, N.Y.:
          Doubleday and Co.
Malleret, L.
  1961   The Position of Historical Studies in the Countries of Former French
          Indo-China in 1956. In D.G.E. Hall, ed., pp. 301–12.
Mandelbaum, David G.
  1970   *Society in India*. 2 vols. Berkeley: University of California Press.
Maquet, Jacques J.
  1961   *The Premise of Inequality in Ruanda*. London: Oxford University Press.

Marr, David
  1979   Vietnamese Historical Reassessment, 1900–1944. In Reid and Marr, pp. 313–39.

Marriott, McKim, ed.
  1955   *Village India: Studies in the Little Community*. Chicago: University of Chicago Press.

Marriott, McKim, and Ronald B. Inden
  1977   Toward an Ethnosociology of South Asian Caste Systems. In *The New Wind: Changing Identities in South Asia*, ed. Kenneth David, pp. 227–38. The Hague: Mouton Publishers.
  1981   Caste Systems. In *The New Encyclopedia Britannica*. 3:982–91.

Martin, Ronald
  1981   *Tacitus*. London: Batsford Academic and Educational.

Martines, Lauro
  1963   *The Social World of the Florentine Humanists, 1390–1460*. Princeton, N.J.: Princeton University Press.
  1979   *Power and Imagination: City-States in Renaissance Italy*. New York: Alfred A. Knopf.

Maspero, Gaston
  1968   *The Dawn of Civilization*. Trans. M. L. McClure. Vol. 1. New York: Frederick Ungar Publishing Co. Reprinted from edition of 1894.

Masui, Tsuneo
  1966   *Ajia no rekishi to rekishika* (History and historians of Asia). Tokyo: Yoshikawa-Kobunkan.

Mayer, Adrian C.
  1958   The Dominant Caste in a Region of Central India. *Southwestern Journal of Anthropology* 14:407–27.

Megill, Alan
  1979   Foucault, Structuralism, and the Ends of History. *Journal of Modern History* 51:451–503.

Mei, Y. P.
  1968   The Individual in Chinese Social Thought. In Moore, pp. 333–46.

Menzel, Johanna M., ed.
  1963   *The Chinese Civil Service: Career Open to Talent?* Boston: D. C. Heath and Co.

Michell, H.
  1952   *Sparta*. Cambridge: Cambridge University Press.

Mierow, Charles Christopher
  1928   Introduction: Otto of Freising and the Philosophy of History. In *The Two Cities: A Chronicle of Universal History to the Year 1146 A.D.* Trans. Charles Christopher Mierow, pp. 1–84. New York: Columbia University Press.

Mill, James
  1826   *The History of British India*. 3d ed. 6 vols. London: Baldwin, Craddock, and Joy.

Millar, Susan Bolyard
  1983   On Interpreting Gender in Bugis Society. *American Ethnologist* 10:477–
              93.
Miller, Eric J.
  1954   Caste and Territory in Malabar. *American Anthropologist* 56:410–20.
Miller, Philip S.
  1954   Introduction to *The Development of Historiography*, ed. Fitzsimons et
              al.
Misch, Georg
  1950   *History of Autobiography in Antiquity*. 3d ed. Trans. E. W. Dickes. Vol.
              1. London: Routledge and Kegan Paul.
Miyazaki, Ichisada
  1976   *China's Examination Hell: The Civil Service Examinations of Imperial
              China*. Trans. Conrad Schirokauer. New York: Weatherhill.
Mo Tzu
  1963   *Mo Tzu: Basic Writings*. Trans. Burton Watson. New York: Columbia
              University Press.
Mohammad Ali
  1965   Historiographical Problems. In Soedjatmoko et al., pp. 1–23.
Molho, Anthony, and John A. Tedeschi, eds.
  1971   *Renaissance Studies in Honor of Hans Baron*. De Kalb: Northern Illinois
              University Press.
Momigliano, Arnaldo
  1966   *Studies in Historiography*. London: Weidenfeld and Nicolson.
  1977   *Essays in Ancient and Modern Historiography*. Middletown, Conn.: Wes-
              leyan University Press.
  1978a   The Historians of the Classical World and Their Audiences. *American
              Scholar* 47:193–204.
  1978b   Greek Historiography. *History and Theory* 17:1–28.
  1982   History in an Age of Ideologies. *American Scholar* 51:495–507.
Moore, Charles A., ed.
  1968   *The Status of the Individual in East and West*. Honolulu: University
              of Hawaii Press.
Morris, Brian
  1978   Are There Any Individuals in India? A Critique of Dumont's Theory
              of the Individual. *Eastern Anthropologist* 31:365–77.
Mote, F. W.
  1964   Problems of Thai Prehistory. *Sangkhomsat Parithat* (Social science
              review) 2 (2): 100–109.
Mundy, Rodney
  1848   Captain Mundy's Journal. In *Narrative of Events in Borneo and Celebes,
              down to the Occupation of Labuan: From the Journals of James Brooke,
              Esq., Rajah of Sarawak, and Governor of Labuan. Together with a Nar-
              rative of the Operations of H.M.S. Iris*. Ed. Rodney Mundy. Vol. 2, pp.
              96–395. London: John Murray.

Munro, Donald J.
    1969   *The Concept of Man in Early China*. Stanford: Stanford University Press.

Munson, Frederick P., et al.
    1963   *Area Handbook for Cambodia*. Washington: U.S. Government Printing Office.

Murray, Alexander
    1978   *Reason and Society in the Middle Ages*. Oxford: Clarendon Press.

Nadel, George H.
    1964   Philosophy of History before Historicism. *History and Theory* 3:291–315.

Needham, Joseph
    1963   Poverties and Triumphs of the Chinese Scientific Tradition. In Crombie, pp. 117–53.
    1965   *Time and Eastern Man*. Occasional Paper No. 21, Royal Anthropological Institute of Great Britain and Ireland.

Needham, Joseph, et al.
    1954–   *Science and Civilization in China*. 6 vols. to date. Cambridge: Cambridge University Press.

Nicholas, Ralph W.
    1968   Structures of Politics in the Villages of Southern Asia. In Singer and Cohn, pp. 243–84.

Nicholl, Robert, ed.
    1975   *European Sources for the History of the Sultanate of Brunei in the Sixteenth Century*. Brunei Museum, Special Issue No. 9.

Nilakantra Sastri, K. A.
    1953   *History of India*. Part 1: *Ancient India*. Madras: S. Viswanathan.
    1955   *The Cōḷas*. 2d ed. Madras: University of Madras.

Noorduyn, J.
    1961   Some Aspects of Macassar-Buginese Historiography. In D.G.E. Hall, ed., pp. 29–46.
    1965   Origins of South Celebes Historical Writing. In Soedjatmoko et al., pp. 137–55.

Obermann, Julian
    1955   Early Islam. In Dentan, pp. 237–310.

Olmstead, A. T.
    1916   *Assyrian Historiography: A Source Study*. University of Missouri Studies in Social Science, ser. 3, vol. 1.

Oppenheim, Leo
    1964   *Ancient Mesopotamia: Portrait of a Dead Civilization*. Chicago: University of Chicago Press.

Origo, Iris
    1957   *The Merchant of Prato: Francesco DiMarco Datini*. New York: Alfred A. Knopf.

Ostrogorsky, George
  1957   *History of the Byzantine State.* Trans. Joan Hussey. New Brunswick, N.J.: Rutgers University Press.

Pagès, G.
  1933   *Un Royaume Hamite au Centre de l'Afrique: Au Ruanda sur le Bords du Lak Kivu.* Brussels: Libraire Falk fils, Georges van Campenhaut, Successeur.

Painter, Sidney
  1960   Foreword to *The Life of Charlemagne,* by Einhard. Ann Arbor: University of Michigan Press.

Palmier, L. H.
  1960   *Social Status and Power in Java.* London School of Economics Monographs on Social Anthropology, no. 20. London: Athlone Press.

Pan Ku
  1938   *The History of the Former Han Dynasty.* Trans. Homer H. Dubs. Baltimore: Waverly Press. Written in first century A.D.

Pan Ku [et al.]
  1974   *Food and Money in Ancient China: The Earliest Economic History of Ancient China to A.D. 25.* Trans. Nancy Lee Swann. New York: Octagon Books. Written in first century A.D.

Pargiter, F. E.
  1972   *Ancient Indian Historical Tradition.* Delhi: Motilal Banarsidass. Originally published 1922.

Pathak, Vishwambhar Sharan
  1966   *Ancient Historians of India: A Study in Historical Biographies.* New York: Asia Publishing House.

Paul, G. M.
  1966   Sallust. In Dorey, ed., pp. 85–113.

Pearson, Lionel
  1939   *Early Ionian Historians.* Oxford: Clarendon Press.

Pellat, Charles
  1962   The Origin and Development of Historiography in Muslim Spain. In Lewis and Holt, pp. 118–25.

Perera, L. A.
  1961   The Pali Chronicle of Ceylon. In Philips, pp. 29–43.

Pharr, Clyde
  1952   *The Theodosian Code and Novels and the Sirmondian Constitutions: A Translation with Commentary, Glossary, and Bibliography.* Princeton, N.J.: Princeton University Press.

Philips, C. H., ed.
  1961   *Historians of India, Pakistan, and Ceylon.* London: Oxford University Press.

Pieris, Ralph
  1956   *Sinhalese Social Organization: The Kandyan Period.* Colombo: Ceylon University Press.

Pigeaud, Theodore G. Th.

1960–63   *Java in the 14th Century: A Study in Cultural History.* 5 vols. 3d ed.,
          rev. The Hague: M. Nijhoff.

1977   Javanese Divination and Classification. In *Structural Anthropology in
          the Netherlands: A Reader,* ed. P. E. de Josselin de Jong, pp. 64–82.
          The Hague: Martinus Nijhoff. Originally published 1928.

Pitti, Buonaccorso, and Gregorio Dati

1967   *Two Memoirs of Renaissance Florence: The Diaries of Buonaccorso Pitti
          and Gregorio Dati.* Trans. Julia Martines, ed. Gene Brucker. New York:
          Harper and Row. Written in fifteenth century.

Plumb, J. H.

1961   *The Italian Renaissance: A Concise Survey of Its History and Culture.*
          New York: Harper and Row.

Pocock, David F.

1964   The Anthropology of Time Reckoning. *Contributions to Indian Soci-
          ology* 7:18–29.

Prinz, Friedrich

1965   *Frühes Mönchtum im Frankenreich: Kultur und Gesellschaft in Galien,
          den Rheinlanden und Bayern am Beispiel der monastischen Entwicklung
          4.–8. Jh.* Munich and Vienna: Oldenbourg.

Pulleyblank, E. G.

1961   Chinese Historical Criticism: Liu Chih-chi and Ssu-ma Kuang. In
          Beasley and Pulleyblank, pp. 135–66.

Pulleyblank, E. G., and W. G. Beasley

1961   Introduction to *Historians of China and Japan,* ed. Beasley and Pul-
          leyblank.

Radcliffe-Brown, A. R.

1952   Religion and Society. In *Structure and Function in Primitive Society:
          Essays and Addresses,* pp. 153–177. Glencoe: Free Press. Originally pub-
          lished 1945.

Rawson, Elizabeth

1975   *Cicero: A Portrait.* London: Penguin Books.

Ray, H. C.

1973   *The Dynastic History of Northern India (Early Medieval Period).* New
          Delhi: Manshiram Manoharlal Publishers.

Reid, Anthony, and David Marr, eds.

1979   *Perceptions of the Past in Southeast Asia.* Singapore: Heinemann Ed-
          ucational Books (Asia).

Reuter, Timothy, ed.

1978   *The Medieval Nobility: Studies on the Ruling Classes of France and Ger-
          many from the Sixth to the Twelfth Century.* Amsterdam: North Holland
          Publishing Co. Introduction by Reuter.

Reynolds, Beatrice

1953   Shifting Currents in Historical Criticism. *Journal of the History of Ideas*
          4:471–92.

Reynolds, Craig J.
    1979   Religious Historical Writing and the Legitimation of the First Bang-
              kok Reign. In Reid and Marr, pp. 90–107.
Ricklefs, M. C.
    1976   Javanese Sources in the Writing of Modern Javanese History. In Cowan
              and Wolters, pp. 332–44.
Rifkin, Lester H.
    1953   Aristotle on Equality: A Criticism of A. J. Carlyle's Theory. *Journal
              of the History of Ideas* 14:276–83.
Rose, Paul Lawrence
    1969   The Accademia Venetiana: Science and Culture in Renaissance Venice.
              Studi Veneziani 11:191–242.
Rosenthal, Franz
    1958   Translator's introduction to *The Muqaddimah: An Introduction to His-
              tory*, by Ibn Khaldun. Vol. 1. Princeton, N.J.: Princeton University
              Press.
    1962   The Influence of Biblical Tradition on Muslim Historiography. In
              Lewis and Holt, pp. 35–45.
    1968   *A History of Muslim Historiography*. 2d. rev. ed. Leiden: E. J. Brill.
Rowe, William L.
    1968   The New Cauhans: A Caste Mobility Movement in North India. In
              Silverberg, pp. 66–77.
Rowland, Benjamin
    1953   *The Art and Architecture of India*. Baltimore: Penguin Books.
Rubinstein, Nicolai
    1965   The Beginnings of Political Thought in Florence: A Study in Me-
              diaeval Historiography. *Journal of the Warburg and Courtauld Institutes*
              5:198–227. Vaduz: Kraus Reprint, Ltd. Originally published 1942.
    1968   Florentine Constitutionalism and Medici Ascendency in the Fifteenth
              Century. In Rubinstein, ed., pp. 442–62.
Rubinstein, Nicolai, ed.
    1968   *Florentine Studies: Politics and Society in Renaissance Florence*. Evanston,
              Ill.: Northwestern University Press.
Runciman, Steven
    1948   *Byzantine Civilization*. London: Edward Arnold and Co.
Russell, J. G.
    1954a   Renaissance of the Twelfth Century. In Fitzsimons et al., pp. 37–50.
    1954b   The Thirteenth Century. In Fitzsimons et al., pp. 51–65.
Ryan, Bryce
    1953   *Caste in Modern Ceylon*. New Brunswick, N.J.: Rutgers University
              Press.
Saggs, H.W.F.
    1962   *The Greatness That Was Babylon: A Sketch of the Ancient Civilization
              of the Tigris-Euphrates Valley*. New York: Hawthorn Books.

Saksena, S. K.
1968   The Individual in Social Thought and Practice in India. In Moore, pp. 347–57.

Sanford, Eva Matthews
1944   The Study of Ancient History in the Middle Ages. *Journal of the History of Ideas* 5:21–43.

Sangermano, Father
1969   *A Description of the Burmese Empire.* Trans. William Tandy. New York: Augustus M. Kelley. Originally published 1833.

Saxena, K. S.
1974   *Political History of Kashmir (B.C. 300–A.D. 1200).* Aminabad: Upper India Publishing House.

Sayce, A. H.
1900   *Babylonians and Assyrians: Life and Customs.* London: John C. Nimmo.

Schevill, Ferdinand
1936   *History of Florence from the Founding of the City through the Renaissance.* New York: Harcourt, Brace and Co.

Schlesinger, Walter
1968   Lord and Follower in Germanic Institutional History. In Cheyette, pp. 664–99.

Schmid, Karl
1978   The Structure of the Nobility in the Earlier Middle Ages. In Reuter, pp. 37–59. Originally published 1959.

Schrieke, B.
1955   *Indonesian Sociological Studies: Selected Writings of B. Schrieke.* Part 1. The Hague: W. van Hoeve.
1957   *Ruler and Realm in Early Java.* Part 2 of *Selected Writings of B. Schrieke.* Indonesian Sociological Studies. The Hague: W. van Hoeve.

Schwartzberg, Joseph E.
1968   Caste Regions of the North Indian Plain. In Singer and Cohn, pp. 81–113.

Seigel, Jerrold E.
1968   *Rhetoric and Philosophy in Renaissance Humanism: The Union of Eloquence and Wisdom, Petrarch to Valla.* Princeton, N.J.: Princeton University Press.

Seneviratne, H. L.
1978   *Rituals of the Kandyan State.* Cambridge: Cambridge University Press.

Shah, A. M., and R. G. Shroff
1959   The Vahivanca Barots of Gujarat: A Caste of Genealogists and Mythographers (with a foreword by M. N. Srinivas). In *Traditional India: Structure and Change,* ed. Milton Singer, pp. 40–70. Philadelphia: American Folklore Society.

Shalaby, Ahmad
1954   *History of Muslim Education.* Beirut: Dar al-Kashshaf.

Shariffuddin, P. M., and Abdul Latif Hj. Ibrahim
    1974   The Genealogical Tablet (*Batu Tarsilah*) of the Sultans of Brunei. *Brunei Museum Journal* 3 (2): 253–64.
Sherley-Price, Leo
    1977   Introduction to *A History of the English Church and People*, by Bede. Trans. Leo Sherley-Price. Rev. ed. Harmondsworth, Eng.: Penguin Books. Originally published 1955.
Shotwell, James T.
    1923   *An Introduction to the History of History*. New York: Columbia University Press.
Siegel, James
    1969   *The Rope of God*. Berkeley: University of California Press.
    1976   Awareness of the Past in the Hikayat Potjoet Moehamat. In Cowan and Wolters, pp. 321–31.
    1979   *Shadow and Sound: The Historical Thought of a Sumatran People*. Chicago: University of Chicago Press.
Silverberg, James, ed.
    1968   *Social Mobility in the Caste System in India: An Interdisciplinary Symposium*. The Hague: Mouton.
Singer, Milton, and Bernard Cohn, eds.
    1968   *Structure and Change in Indian Society*. Chicago: Aldine Publishing Co.
Singh, Saran
    1980   The Coinage of the Sultanate of Brunei, 1400–1980. *Brunei Museum Journal* 4 (4): 38–103.
Sircar, D. C.
    1965   *Indian Epigraphy*. Delhi: Motilal Banarsidass.
Skeat, Walter William
    1967   *Malay Magic: Being an Introduction to the Folklore and Popular Religion of the Malay Peninsula*. New York: Dover Publications. Originally published 1900.
Skinner, G. William
    1960   Change and Persistence in Chinese Culture Overseas: A Comparison of Thailand and Java. *South Seas Society Journal* 16:86–100.
Smith, R. B.
    1976   England and Vietnam in the Fifteenth and Sixteenth Centuries: An Essay in Historical Comparison. In Cowan and Wolters, pp. 227–45.
Snouck Hurgronje, C.
    1906   *The Achehnese*. Trans. A.W.S. O'Sullivan. Vol. 1. Leiden: E. J. Brill.
Soedjatmoko
    1965a   Introduction to *An Introduction to Indonesian Historiography*, ed. Soedjatmoko et al.
    1965b   The Indonesian Historian and His Time. In Soedjatmoko et al., pp. 404–15.

Soedjatmoko et al., eds.
1965   *An Introduction to Indonesian Historiography*. Ithaca, N.Y.: Cornell University Press.

Soemarsaid Moertono
1968   *State and Statecraft in Old Java: A Study of the Later Mataram Period, 16th to 19th Century*. Monograph Series, Modern Indonesia Project, Southeast Asia Program, Cornell University.

Southern, R. W.
1970   Aspects of the European Tradition of Historical Writing: 1. The Classical Tradition from Einhard to Geoffrey of Monmouth. *Transactions of the Royal Historical Society* 20:173–96.

Speiser, E. A.
1955   Ancient Mesopotamia. In Dentan, pp. 35–76.

Spiegel, Gabrielle M.
1983   Genealogy: Form and Function in Medieval Historical Narrative. *History and Theory* 22:43–53.

Spitz, Lewis W.
1971   Humanism in the Reformation. In Molho and Tedeschi, pp. 641–62.

Sprenkel, Otto Berkelbach van der
1973   Genealogical Registers. In *Essays on the Sources for Chinese History*, ed. Donald D. Leslie, Colin Mackerras, and Wang Gungwu, pp. 83–99. Columbia: University of South Carolina Press.

Spuler, Bertold
1962   The Evolution of Persian Historiography. In Lewis and Holt, pp. 126–32.

Srinivas, M. N.
1955   The Social System of a Mysore Village. In Marriott, ed., pp. 1–35.
1968   Mobility in the Caste System. In Singer and Cohn, pp. 189–207.

Ssu-ma, Ch'ien
1961   *Records of the Grand Historian of China*. Translated from the *Shih chi* of Ssu-ma Ch'ien. Trans. Burton Watson. 2 vols. New York: Columbia University Press.
1969   *Records of the Historian: Chapters from the* Shih Chi *of Ssu-ma Ch'ien*. Trans. Burton Watson. New York: Columbia University Press.

Starn, Randolph
1971   Francesco Guicciardini and His Brothers. In Molho and Tedeschi, pp. 409–44.

Starr, Chester G.
1958   An Overdose of Slavery. *Journal of Economic History* 18:17–32.
1968   *The Awakening of the Greek Historical Spirit*. New York: Alfred A. Knopf.

Stein, Burton
1968   Social Mobility and South Indian Hindu Sects. In Silverberg, pp. 78–94.

1980 *Peasant State and Society in Medieval South India*. Delhi: Oxford University Press.

Stein, M. A.

1961 Introduction to *Kalhaṇa's Rājataraṅgiṇī*. Trans. M. A. Stein. Vol. 1. Delhi: Motilal Banarsidass.

Stenton, F. M.

1971 *Anglo-Saxon England*. 3d ed. Oxford: Clarendon Press.

Stock, Brian

1978 Science, Technology, and Economic Progress in the Early Middle Ages. In *Science and the Middle Ages*, ed. David C. Lindberg, pp. 1–51. Chicago: University of Chicago Press.

Stockton, David

1971 *Cicero: A Political Biography*. London: Oxford University Press.

Stott, Wilfrid

1963 The Expansion of the Nan-Chao Kingdom Between the Years 750–860. *T'oung Pao* 50:190–220.

Struever, Nancy S.

1970 *The Language of History in the Renaissance: Rhetoric and Historical Consciousness in Florentine Humanism*. Princeton, N.J.: Princeton University Press.

Supomo, S.

1979 The Image of Majapahit in Later Javanese and Indonesian Writing. In Reid and Marr, pp. 171–85.

Sweeney, Amin

1968 Silsilah Raja-Raja Berunai. *Journal of the Malaysian Branch, Royal Asiatic Society* 41 (2): 1–82.

1980 *Reputations Live On: An Early Malay Autobiography*. Berkeley: University of California Press.

Swellengrebel, J. L.

1969 Nonconformity in the Balinese Family. In *Bali: Further Studies in Life, Thought, and Ritual*. Selected Studies on Indonesia, vol. 8, pp. 201–12. The Hague: W. van Hoeve.

Syme, Ronald

1958 *Tacitus*. 2 vols. Oxford: Clarendon Press.

1979 *The Roman Revolution*. Oxford: Oxford University Press. Originally published 1939.

Symons, Donald

1979 *The Evolution of Human Sexuality*. New York: Oxford University Press.

Taylor, Lily Ross

1966 *Roman Voting Assemblies from the Hannibalic War to the Dictatorship of Caesar*. Ann Arbor: University of Michigan Press.

Tellenbach, Gerd

1978 From the Carolingian Imperial Nobility to the German Estate of Imperial Princes. In Reuter, pp. 203–42.

Tet Htoot, U
 1961   The Nature of the Burmese Chronicles. In D.G.E. Hall, ed., pp. 50–
          62.
Thapar, Romila
 1978   *Ancient Indian Social History: Some Interpretations*. New Delhi: Orient
          Longman.
Thompson, E. A.
 1966   Ammianus Marcellinus. In Dorey, ed., pp. 143–57.
Thompson, James Westfall
 1942   *A History of Historical Writing*. 2 vols. New York: Macmillan Co.
Thorpe, Lewis
 1969   Introduction to *Two Lives of Charlemagne*, by Einhard and Notker the
          Stammerer. Trans. Lewis Thorpe. Harmondsworth, Eng.: Penguin
          Books.
Tin Ohn
 1961   Modern Historical Writing in Burmese, 1724–1942. In D.G.E. Hall,
          pp. 85–93.
Tjan Tjoe Som
 1965   Chinese Historical Sources and Historiography. In Soedjatmoko et.
          al., pp. 194–205.
Tocqueville, Alexis de
 1955   *The Old Regime and the French Revolution*. Trans. Stuart Gilbert. Gar-
          den City, N.J.: Doubleday, Anchor Books. Originally published 1856.
Totah, Khalil A.
 1926   *The Contribution of the Arabs to Education*. New York: Bureau of
          Publications, Teachers College, Columbia University.
Toynbee, Arnold
 1959   A Muslim Study of History. Review of *The Muqaddimah: An Intro-
          duction to History*. Trans. Franz Rosenthal. *The Observer*, Feb. 22, 1959,
          p. 21.
Treggiari, Susan
 1969   *Roman Freedmen during the Late Republic*. Oxford: Clarendon Press.
Trinkhaus, Charles
 1965   *Adversity's Noblemen: The Italian Humanists on Happiness*. New York:
          Octagon Books. Originally published 1940.
Trompf, G. W.
 1979   *The Idea of Historical Recurrence in Western Thought: From Antiquity
          to the Reformation*. Berkeley: University of California Press.
Tsien, Tsuen-hsuen
 1962   *Written on Bamboo and Silk: The Beginnings of Chinese Books and In-
          scriptions*. Chicago: University of Chicago Press.
Twitchett, D. C.
 1961   Chinese Biographical Writing. In Beasley and Pulleyblank, pp. 95–
          114.

Tyler, Stephen A.
  1973   *India: An Anthropological Perspective*. Pacific Palisades, Calif.: Goodyear
            Publishing Co.
Ullman, B. L.
  1946   Leonardo Bruni and Humanistic Historiography. *Medievalia et Hu-
            manistica* 4:45–61.
Ullmann, Walter
  1965   *A History of Political Thought: The Middle Ages*. Harmondsworth, Eng.:
            Penguin Books.
  1966a   *The Individual and Society in the Middle Ages*. Baltimore: Johns Hopkins
            University Press.
  1966b   *Principles of Government and Politics in the Middle Ages*. New York:
            Barnes and Noble.
Valla, Lorenzo
  1922   *The Treatise of Lorenzo Valla on the Donation of Constantine*. Trans.
            Christopher B. Coleman. New Haven: Yale University Press. Written
            in 1440.
Vasiliev, A. A.
  1952   *History of the Byzantine Empire, 324–1453*. Madison: University of Wis-
            consin Press.
Vercauteren, Fernand
  1978   A Kindred in Northern France in the Eleventh and Twelfth Centuries.
            In Reuter, pp. 87–101.
Vickery, Michael
  1979   The Composition and Transmission of the Ayudhya and Cambodian
            Chronicles. In Reid and Marr, pp. 130–54.
Vogel, K.
  1967   Byzantine Science. In Hussey, pp. 265–305.
Vryonis, Speros, Jr., ed.
  1966   Hellas Resurgent. In Lynn White, Jr., pp. 92–118.
  1968   Readings in Medieval Historiography. Boston: Houghton Mifflin Co.
Wagle, Narendra
  1966   *Society at the Time of the Buddha*. Bombay: Popular Prakashan.
Walbank, F. W.
  1966   Polybius. In Dorey, ed., pp. 39–63.
Wales, H. G. Quaritch
  1931   *Siamese State Ceremonies: Their History and Function*. London: Bernard
            Quaritch.
Walker, Benjamin
  1968   *Hindu World: An Encyclopedic Survey of Hinduism*. Vol. 1. London:
            George Allen and Unwin.
Walsh, J. R.
  1962   The Historiography of Ottoman-Safavid Relations in the Sixteenth
            and Seventeenth Centuries. In Lewis and Holt, pp. 197–211.

Walsh, P. G.
    1966   Livy. In Dorey, ed., pp. 115–42.

Wang, Gungwu
    1968   South and Southeast Asian Historiography. In *International Encyclopedia of the Social Sciences*, vol. 6, pp. 420–28.

Warder, A. K.
    1961   The Pali Canon and Its Commentaries as an Historical Record. In Philips, pp. 44–56.
    1972   *An Introduction to Indian Historiography*. Bombay: Popular Prakashan.

Watson, Burton
    1958   *Ssu-ma Chi'en: Grand Historian of China*. New York: Columbia University Press.

Watt, W. Montgomery
    1953   *Muhammad at Mecca*. Oxford: Clarendon Press.
    1968   *Islamic Political Thought: The Basic Concepts*. Edinburgh: Edinburgh University Press.

Weaver, P.R.C.
    1974   Social Mobility in the Early Roman Empire: The Evidence of the Imperial Freedmen and Slaves. In Finley, ed., pp. 121–40.

Weber, Max
    1952   *Ancient Judaism*. Trans. and ed. Hans J. Gerth and Don Martindale. Glencoe, Ill.: Free Press. Originally published as a series of essays, 1917–1919.
    1963   *The Sociology of Religion*. Trans. Ephraim Fischoff. Boston: Beacon Press. Originally published 1922.

Werner, Karl Ferdinand
    1978   Important Noble Families in the Kingdom of Charlemagne: A Prosopographical Study of the Relationship Between King and Nobility in the Early Middle Ages. In Reuter, pp. 137–202.

Westermann, William Linn
    1955   *The Slave Systems of Greek and Roman Antiquity*. Memoirs of the American Philosophical Society, vol. 40. Philadelphia.

Wheatley, Paul
    1961   *The Golden Khersonese: Studies in the Historical Geography of the Malay Peninsula Before A.D. 1500*. Kuala Lumpur: University of Malaya Press.

White, Hayden
    1973   *Metahistory: The Historical Imagination in Nineteenth-Century Europe*. Baltimore: Johns Hopkins University Press.

White, Lynn, Jr., ed.
    1966   *The Transformation of the Roman World: Gibbon's Problem after Two Centuries*. Berkeley: University of California Press.

Wiens, Harold J.
    1954   *China's March Toward the Tropics*. Hamden, Conn.: Shoe String Press.

Wilcox, Donald J.
    1969   *The Development of Florentine Humanist Historiography in the Fifteenth Century*. Cambridge, Mass.: Harvard University Press.

Wilkinson, J.V.S.
    1949   Introduction to *The Pitman Gallery of Oriental Art: Mughal Painting*,
                ed. Basil Gray. New York: Pitman Publishing Corp.
Wilson, John A.
    1951   *The Culture of Ancient Egypt*. Chicago: University of Chicago Press.
Winstedt, Richard Olaf
    1923   A Brunei Code. *Journal of the Malayan Branch, Royal Asiatic Society*
                1:251.
    1951   *The Malay Magician: Being Shaman, Saiva and Sufi*. Rev. ed. London:
                Routledge and Kegan Paul.
    1961   Malay Chronicles from Sumatra and Malaya. In D.G.E. Hall, pp. 24–
                28.
    1969   *A History of Classical Malay Literature*. Kuala Lumpur: Oxford Uni-
                versity Press.
Wiseman, T. P.
    1971   *New Men in the Roman Senate, 139 B.C.–A.D. 14*. London: Oxford Uni-
                versity Press.
Wolters, O. W.
    1976   Lê Văn Hu'u's Treatment of Lý Thân Tôn's Reign (1127–1137). In
                Cowan and Wolters, pp. 203–26.
    1979   Historians and Emperors in Vietnam and China: Comments arising
                out of Le Van Huu's History. Presented to the Tran Court in 1272.
                In Reid and Marr, pp. 60–89.
Woodside, Alexander Barton
    1971   *Vietnam and the Chinese Model: A Comparative Study of Nguyên and
                Ching Civil Government in the First Half of the Nineteenth Century*.
                Cambridge, Mass.: Harvard University Press.
Wootton, David
    1983   *Paolo Sarpi: Between Renaissance and Enlightenment*. London: Cam-
                bridge University Press.
Worsley, P. J.
    1972   *Babad Buleleng: A Balinese Dynastic Genealogy*. The Hague: Martinus
                Nijhoff.
Wyatt, David K.
    1976   Chronicle Traditions in Thai Historiography. In Cowan and Wolters,
                pp. 107–22.
Wyatt, David K., ed. and trans.
    1975   *The Crystal Sands: The Chronicles of Nagara Sri Dharrmaraja*. Data
                Paper No. 98, Southeast Asia Program, Cornell University.
Yalman, Nur
    1960   The Flexibility of Caste Principles in a Kandyan Community. In Leach,
                ed., pp. 78–112.
    1967   *Under the Bo Tree: Studies in Caste, Kinship, and Marriage in the Interior
                of Ceylon*. Berkeley: University of California Press.
Yang, Lien-sheng
    1961   The Organization of Chinese Official Historiography: Principles and

Methods of the Standard Histories from the T'ang through the Ming Dynasties. In Beasley and Pulleyblank, pp. 44–59.

Yoe, Shway [James George Scott]
1963   *The Burman: His Life and Notions*. New York: W. W. Norton and Co.

Yura Halim and M. Jamil Umar
1958   *Sejarah Berunai*. Kuala Belait: Brunei Press.

Zeydel, Edwin H.
1972   Introduction to *The Life of Charlemagne*, by Einhard. Trans. Edwin H. Zeydel. Coral Gables, Fla.: University of Miami Press.

Zimmer, Heinrich
1962   *Myths and Symbols in Indian Art and Civilization*. Ed. Joseph Campbell. New York: Harper and Row.

Index

About the Author

DONALD E. BROWN, professor of anthropology at the University of California at Santa Barbara, received his doctorate from Cornell University in 1969. He is the author of *Brunei: The Structure and History of a Bornean Malay Sultanate,* published in 1970, and of *Principles of Social Structure: Southeast Asia,* published in 1974. It was his observation that the Brunei people were less historically minded than he had expected them to be that led him to investigate the relationship between social structure and a concern for history in human societies in general. This investigation led him, in turn, to the even broader study of human universals.

DUE